THE INTERNATIONAL HUMAN RIGHT TO FREEDOM OF CONSCIENCE

The International Human Right to Freedom of Conscience

Some suggestions for its development and application

LEONARD M. HAMMER
Political Studies Department
Ramat Gan Law College
Bar Ilan University, Israel

LONDON AND NEW YORK

First published 2001 by Dartmouth Publishing Company and Ashgate Publishing

Reissued 2018 by Routledge
2 Park Square, Milton Park, Abingdon, Oxon OX14 4RN
711 Third Avenue, New York, NY 10017, USA

Routledge is an imprint of the Taylor & Francis Group, an informa business

Copyright © Leonard M. Hammer 2001

All rights reserved. No part of this book may be reprinted or reproduced or utilised in any form or by any electronic, mechanical, or other means, now known or hereafter invented, including photocopying and recording, or in any information storage or retrieval system, without permission in writing from the publishers.

Notice:
Product or corporate names may be trademarks or registered trademarks, and are used only for identification and explanation without intent to infringe.

Publisher's Note
The publisher has gone to great lengths to ensure the quality of this reprint but points out that some imperfections in the original copies may be apparent.

Disclaimer
The publisher has made every effort to trace copyright holders and welcomes correspondence from those they have been unable to contact.

A Library of Congress record exists under LC control number: 00054338

ISBN 13: 978-1-138-73429-6 (hbk)
ISBN 13: 978-1-138-73422-7 (pbk)
ISBN 13: 978-1-315-18732-7 (ebk)

Table of Contents

Acknowledgements   *viii*
Selected Abbreviations   *ix*

1 Introduction   **1**

2 A Brief History of the Development of the Right to Conscience   **9**
  Early Developments   9
  Later Developments   13
    The Emergence of Conscience as Separate from Religion   *14*
  Post World War One   23
  Conclusion   26

3 Analysis of the Treaties and Other Documents   **28**
  Introduction   28
  International Treaties   30
    UDHR, Article 18   *31*
    ICCPR, Article 18   *38*
  Regional Treaties   50
    ECHR, Article 9   *51*
    AmCHR, Article 12   *54*
    AfrCHR, Article 8   *57*
  Other Significant Documents   60
    Declaration on the Elimination of all Forms of Intolerance
      and of Discrimination Based on Religion or Belief   *61*
    Documents Referring to the Right to Conscience   *64*
  Conclusion   69

4 The *Forum Internum*   **72**
  Introduction   72
  The Notion of a 'Right' and its Implications   74
  The Internal and External Right to Conscience   79

Mill and the Forum Internum	*84*
Dimensions of the *Forum Internum*	87
Identification Problems	*87*
The Broad Scope of the Forum Internum	*92*
Analogy to Forum Externum	*95*
Freedom To	*96*
Freedom From	*98*
Significance for the Forum Internum	*100*
Forum Internum and Conscience	103
Dual Notion of Forum Internum *Beliefs*	*103*
Development and Meaning of Conscience	107
Understanding Conscience	*107*
Conscience and Moral Action	*109*
Conscience and Thought	*114*
Conclusion	118

5 The *Forum Externum* — 120

Introduction	120
Forum Internum and *Forum Externum* Compared	124
Defining 'Belief'	131
Introduction	*131*
Narrow Approach Towards Conscientious Belief	*134*
Conscience and Religion	*140*
Distinctions Between Religion and Conscience	*152*
The Negative, Freedom From, *Aspect*	*156*
Conscience and Freedom of Expression and Assembly	*160*
Distinctions Between Expression, Assembly and Conscience	*164*
Broader Approach	*172*
Limitations	182
Conclusion	184

6 Military Conscientious Objection — 186

Introduction	186
Military Conscientious Objection and Customary Law	189
Sources Within the Treaties	*190*
Recognition in International Fora	*193*
Decisions	*193*
Declarations and Resolutions	*195*
State Practice	*206*
Selective Conscientious Objection	209
Selective Objection in Resolutions and Declarations	*209*

Underlying Problems	*212*
Addressing the Problems	*213*
Current Examples of Selective Conscientious Objection	*216*
Right to Asylum for Military Conscientious Objectors	*217*
Direction for the Selective Conscientious Objector	*221*
Objection to Nuclear Weapons	*222*
Conclusion	225

7 Conscientious Objection to Taxes — 227
Introduction	227
Tax Objection	227
Church Tax	*231*
Public Support Schemes	*233*
Objection to Military Tax	*236*
Military Tax as a Unique Objection?	*239*
Conclusion	241

8 Proposing a Group-Oriented Approach to the Right to Conscience — 243
Introduction	243
Some General Points Regarding Group Beliefs	246
Introduction	*246*
Reference to the Treaties	*248*
Group Beliefs Defined	*253*
Group and Individual Conflicts	*257*
Forum Internum and New Religious Movements	*259*
Conclusion	263

9 Conclusion — 266

Bibliography	**273**
Name Index	**292**
Subject Index	**295**

Acknowledgements

I have been fortunate to have had the assistance of a number of exceptional individuals while working on this book both in thesis form and in the present book form.

In particular, Michael Anderson, Director of Studies at the British Institute of International and Comparative Law, has been an outstanding advisor. His ideas and suggestions raised intriguing questions both for my current and future academic research. His wonderful nature and disposition served as a shining example of the proper manner in which a person in academia should conduct oneself.

Peter Slinn and Matthew Craven from the Department of Law in the University of London - SOAS offered quite welcome comments while this work was still in thesis form. David Nelken of the University of Cardiff provided the impetus to have the work published following a number of extensive post-doctorate revisions and additions.

Financial assistance mainly derived from the University of London's Edmund Davis Postgraduate Fellowship Trust and the Lord Hailsham Fellowship.

On a personal note, I would not have been able to complete this book without the assistance of my spouse, Sandy, and my parents, Dr. David and Florence Hammer. My ongoing education derives from their efforts. My gratitude will always remain.

Selected Abbreviations

AfrCHR	African [Banjul] Charter on Human and People's Rights
AmCHR	American Convention on Human Rights
AmDHR	American Declaration on Human Rights
CEDAW	Convention on the Elimination of all Forms of Discrimination Against Women
CERD	Committee to Eliminate Racial Discrimination
CHR	Commission on Human Rights
CRC	Convention on the Rights of the Child
Declaration	Declaration on the Elimination of all Forms of Intolerance and Discrimination Based on Religion or Belief
ECHR	European Convention for the Protection of Human Rights and Fundamental Freedoms
ECOSOC	UN Economic and Social Council
GA	UN General Assembly
Handbook	Handbook on Procedures and Criteria for Determining Refugee Status
HRC	Human Rights Committee
ICCPR	International Covenant on Civil and Political Rights
ICESCR	International Covenant on Economic, Social and Cultural Rights
ICJ	International Court of Justice
ILO	International Labour Organisation
Minorities Declaration	Declaration on the Rights of Persons Belonging to National or Ethnic, Religious and Linguistic Minorities
Torture Convention	Convention Against Torture and Other Cruel, Inhuman or Degrading Treatment or Punishment
UDHR	Universal Declaration of Human Rights
UN	United Nations

1 Introduction

This is not a book about the human right to freedom of religion. There have been a number of recent books and articles of high quality that have addressed the right to freedom of religion in international human rights,[1] such that another book on the same topic does not seem warranted. Nonetheless, one common theme that runs through the human rights literature concerning the freedom of religion is the inescapable problems associated with the right.[2] These problems principally concern instances where the belief system either conflicts with another human right, such as the conflict between religious beliefs and the rights of women, presents an unavoidable conflict with inherent social values or the religion of the majority, or raises the universalism versus relativism debate given a limited interpretation of the right. While the literature has begun to address these issues, as have a variety of domestic and international decision making bodies, the analyses generally seem mired in these common pitfalls, partially due to epistemological approaches that simply cannot escape a pre-conceived understanding of religion and belief.

The key distinguishing factor then between this book and other works that have dealt with the right to freedom of religion is that it considers the manner in which the international human rights system addresses beliefs other than religious beliefs, or beliefs that are not necessarily of a 'religious' nature, because of their inherent differences or manner of manifestation. The contention is that after accounting for the general difficulties noted above that the human rights system associates with the right to freedom of religion, it might do well to begin to consider the right from a broader perspective. One need not root the right in a

---

[1] *See e.g.* Evans, M. (1997) (analysis of the development of the freedom of religion in international law, with a focus on the ECHR); Tahzib (1996) (summarising the international legal sources of the right and analysing a variety of international reports); Witte and Van der Vyver (1996) (two volume work focusing on general issues of comparative religion and country specific reports); Edge (1998); Edge (1996); Cullen (1996); Cumper (1995); Dickson (1995); Scheinen (1992); 1992 COE Seminar on Freedom of Conscience; Sullivan (1988); Partsch (1981); Clark (1978).

[2] The noted problems are not unique to the human right to freedom of religion.

religious framework or expressed as a conflict between the state and the religion. Upon considering the codification of the right to freedom of religion and belief in international human rights law, along with a select interpretation of the right in various international fora, it is apparent that the human right to freedom of religion incorporates a broad range of beliefs, including forms of belief that are not wholly analogous to a religious belief.

In particular, this book will consider issues like where do these alternative forms of beliefs fit in to the international human rights system, if at all? What significance does a conscientious belief for example have for a state espousing a particular religious doctrine that reflects the majority's belief system? What role should beliefs that are not part of a religious system play in society and are they entitled to the same standing as a religious belief? What are the similarities and differences that the human rights system demands in providing protection to all forms of belief? Is it at all practical even to consider beliefs external to a formalised religious belief system given the difficulties in identifying such beliefs, the dangers associated with 'objective' external bodies assessing such beliefs, and the possibility that individuals might attempt to take advantage of the right?

In a normative context, one may question whether the human rights system maintains room for other forms of beliefs that are different from the more 'familiar', doctrinal, religious systems. Do the principal international human rights treaties uphold alternative forms of religious beliefs even without any pre-determined or pre-directed mode of action deriving from the belief? What of belief systems that might be disengaged from some overarching ideals or ideas regarding the manner in which one is to conduct one's life? Alternatively, are all belief systems, religious or otherwise, entitled to the right to freedom of religion if they espouse discriminatory doctrine? What if a particular belief poses a threat to society or leads to an unfair distribution of resources due to the demands of the belief? The query is not only relevant for conflicting human rights, such as an inherently discriminatory belief system, but also applies to beliefs external to the accepted religious system that could lead to constitutive changes to the social structure.

In a sense, commentators have considered some of these questions in analyses regarding the religious rights of minorities. One can analogise between the authority's treatment of a minority religion and the individual's assertion of a belief apart from the accepted religious framework to discern the proper approach towards other forms of belief that a state might not recognise or support. Further analysis is merited however to understand how such minority belief systems can conform to the human rights framework, particularly when contrasting it with the individual right to freedom of religion and belief. For example, an individual from within the minority group might desire to manifest a particular belief that is contrary to group practices, or manifest a belief that is wholly separate from the minority group context. Factoring in the inherent tension between the right to freedom of a minority religion and the individual's right to freedom of belief would suggest that amplification of the right to conscience as an alternative belief also could assist in addressing the role of a minority group's religion or belief within the human rights framework.

The principal goal of this book is to distinguish between the more formalised, and recognised, notion of protecting religious beliefs from what this work refers to as conscientious beliefs. Given that the international human rights system, along with the majority of domestic legal systems, are hesitant to define the meaning of a religious belief for fear of unduly narrowing the right or because they recognise the essential impossibility of doing so, the freedom of religion or belief as expressed in the treaties clearly is referring to a variety of belief systems. There might not be any specific textual reference on which to base a belief or any public practice by other individuals who are manifesting a belief, yet the belief is very real for the individual making the assertion.

This book will use the term 'conscientious belief' to refer to such alternative notions of a belief external to a religious context. A conscientious belief is serving only as an example of other forms of beliefs that are not necessarily part of a formalised religious system. It is in essence a prototypical categorisation to which other belief systems could identify. Additionally, the individual might not desire to be part of a religious belief system, such that the broad understanding of an assertion of a conscientious belief is in essence not to believe at all. Focusing on the right to freedom of conscience provides the groundwork for making such assertions and for legitimating the capacity of individuals to assert what they understand to be their beliefs, in much the same manner as a religious believer would assert a religious belief.

In addressing the freedom of conscience as a human right, the goal is not to create a new form of human right. The book is not meant to expand upon the already broad and somewhat unwieldy human rights system. There are enough 'codified' human rights that lack any meaningful enforcement such that to attempt to winnow out even more from an existing human right might not prove very helpful.

Rather, in a world fraught with the emergence of extreme religious systems, and recognising the history associating religion with internal strife and much bloodshed, it is imperative to develop and understand the implications of the freedom of religion and belief. There remains a host of unresolved problems regarding the freedom of religion that raise important human rights issues. One can think of an alternative religious belief system in a religious state, that almost every state with a majority religion also has a minority belief system attempting to assert itself, and the importance of providing for the individual voice as a counter to the more pronounced assertions of entrenched religious belief systems. Even in so called secular states such as India or the US, the populace clearly is not indifferent towards religious beliefs[3] or towards conscientious beliefs external to religion.

The reality of the human right to freedom of religion, coupled with the history of religion and the consideration of current issues such as the ability to change a religious belief or uphold the right to proselytise, propels one to consider and begin to understand the significance of alternative beliefs. Judicial and scholarly interpretations of the right to freedom of conscience have thus far tended to jumble the human right to freedom of religion and belief solely within the religious belief context, thus obscuring the non-religious dimensions of the right. This book will begin to consider the right to conscience by offering an understanding of what a conscientious belief entails and proposing suggestions for the manner in which such beliefs can manifest. Expanding upon the meaning and operation of conscience assists in providing some shape and form to one's practical understanding of beliefs outside a formalised religious system, as well as enhance the opportunities for belief systems that might differ from the conscientious beliefs discussed in this book.

One's inclination might be to attempt to offer a definition for the right to freedom of religion that would address these concerns. The international human rights treaty drafters already recognised the dangers associated with such an approach in hesitating to define the meaning of

---

[3]   *See generally* Connolly (1999).

religion, particularly due to the possible limitations to the right that might result from a narrow definition. The indication is that in drafting the right to freedom of religion, the states intended to incorporate a variety of belief systems, hence the phraseology in the treaties of 'religion or belief'. The discussion in Chapter Three regarding the travaux preparatoires to the principal human rights treaties will demonstrate the intention to include a conscientious belief as meriting protection equivalent to a religious belief.

Additional indicators that suggest the necessity for considering the protection of conscientious beliefs in an analogous manner to religious beliefs are that as international and regional human rights systems emerge, a variety of claims pertaining to different beliefs will confront enforcement bodies. To provide adequate protection for all forms of belief systems, what is demanded is an understanding of belief systems that is not necessarily tied to a rather forced analogy with a religious belief. Hence the book aims to propose a jurisprudential framework to facilitate a broader application of the right to freedom of religion and belief as a means of clarifying the right and paving the way for a more even application.

As part of the attempt to understand the significance and application of a conscientious belief as exemplifying a typical assertion of a belief external to a religious order, it is important to consider the historical derivation of the notion of conscience and its emergence as an accepted alternative to a religious belief. Chapter Two therefore offers a brief history of the development of conscience as a viable belief. The Chapter is not meant to serve as a definitive history of religion nor even of conscience. Rather, the goal is to highlight the emergence of conscience as an independent belief system separate from religion. As political and social systems disentangled themselves from religious bodies, the notion of an independent conscientious belief developed without hindrance. This laid the groundwork for contemplating the possibility of upholding a conscientious belief on par with a religious belief.

Chapter Three moves into more familiar territory for international human rights by focusing on the treaties that codify the right to freedom of religion and conscience and considering the role of conscience within the normative framework of the treaties. No analysis has been conducted of the *travaux preparatoires* exclusively for the right to conscience or other forms of beliefs. The purpose of perusing the travaux preparatoires is to demonstrate through a clarification of the terms that the drafters desired to incorporate beliefs other than religious beliefs, distinguish between a conscientious belief and a more general thought or opinion, and amplify the importance of the limitations to the right. The goal is not to offer an in-depth analysis of the treaties but rather to elaborate on how the right to conscience is an inherent aspect of the human right to freedom of religion and belief.

Chapters Four and Five are a unit of sorts. The internal and external aspects of a conscientious belief are unavoidably intertwined such that it is difficult to consider or define one without the other. More particularly, there has not been any adequate analysis of the internal dimension of the right to conscience. In providing the groundwork for upholding a conscientious belief, it is imperative to consider exactly what are the implications of conscience. Hence the focus in the discussion on the relationship between an individual's conscientious belief and the surrounding social system. Asserting the human right to freedom of conscience is not only an individual endeavour, but also tends to reflect social developments and cultural idiosyncrasies. Given the essential impossibility in defining a conscientious or religious belief, one may begin to understand conscience as a result of ongoing and ever-changing communicative discourses that reflect what is important to the individual at a given moment. The implication of such an approach to the internal dimension of conscience is that, similar to religion, a conscientious belief merits manifestation because the belief relates to the individual's personal identity. Manifesting a conscientious belief is in essence comparable to manifesting a religious belief due to the importance and centrality of the belief for the individual. The book also will suggest that the possible pitfalls in manifesting a conscientious belief are not that different from those associated with supporting a religious belief.

Chapter Five further addresses the attempts to incorporate the manifestation of a conscientious belief within other human rights, generally the freedom of religion, expression or assembly. The goal is to draw out the similarities and differences with these human rights and demonstrate the importance of according a conscientious belief singular consideration in a manner analogous to a religious belief.

Expanding upon the capacity for manifesting a conscientious belief merits further consideration of the avenues currently available for such manifestation. How realistic is the right to freedom of conscience if states essentially are unwilling to acknowledge the capacity for manifestation?

What possibilities exist, if at all, for manifesting a conscientious belief while still operating within a structured rule of law? The typical example generally provided for manifesting a conscientious belief is military conscientious objection. While Chapter Six discusses the current standing of the right to military conscientious objection, the underlying idea is to draw out the significance of manifesting a conscientious belief rather than refer to external norms as the basis for an objection, such as the right to life or humanitarian law. The approach to military conscientious objection is somewhat different from the international system, which tends to merge a conscientious objection with objections based on other human rights principles. This is not to say that one may not refer to other normative grounds for asserting an objection; rather the reliance on a conscientious belief as grounds for military objection create broader opportunities for the objector.

Should an individual assert a conscientious belief in objecting to particular military orders, or against state mandates in the situation of a tax objector, it is possible that the individual may maintain the right to conscientious objection. The importance for the manifestation of a conscientious or religious belief merits consideration of these forms of objection. The focus on selective conscientious objection in Chapter Six and tax objection in Chapter Seven therefore provides the platform for amplifying the practical possibilities of manifestation of a conscientious belief.

An important element that is underlying the analysis of a conscientious belief, and that contributes to its significance in society, is the communal factor. In describing the development of a conscientious belief, the reference to external social sources and the importance of interaction when manifesting a belief are unavoidable factors for the individual believer. Furthermore, religion clearly has a communal side particularly concerning worship, education or other religious practices that merit group activity. Upon noting the similarities between a religious and conscientious belief, it also is important to consider the group dimension of the right to freedom of conscience.

Chapter Eight begins to address a group understanding of a conscientious belief and the role that such an approach can play in the human rights system. The discussion will focus on the possible integration between the rights of a minority religion and the individual's right to freedom of conscience. An additional consideration pertaining to the group dimension of a conscientious belief is in the practice of emerging belief systems that espouse external group activity such as proselytising. Given the ongoing problems associated with proselytising, it is worth turning to sociologists who have analysed the activities of proselytising organisations to assess where the boundaries could lie in providing for the manifestation of a conscientious belief. Such consideration also relates to the broader aims of the book as it begins to consider the practical application of a conscientious belief in what can be understood to be a socially disagreeable environment.

2 A Brief History of the Development of the Right to Conscience

Early Developments

In response to religious intolerance and oppression of non-believers,[1] the right to freedom of conscience emerged from the protection accorded to the minority beliefs of particular religious systems.[2] Some international commentators even ascribe the emergence of the right to freedom of conscience as an important forerunner to civil liberty.[3] While the intention of this chapter is not to provide a history of human rights or religious intolerance,[4] it will demonstrate that as the protection for minority religions

---

[1] *See e.g.* McDougal, Lasswell and Chen (1980;654 and fn. 5).
[2] Krishnaswami (1960;4-11); McDougal Lasswell and Chen (1980;663-664); Dickson (1995;331-332); Clark (1978); Walkate (1989).
[3] Bates (1945); 297-302; Richards (1986) (referring to Chapter Four of Rawls, J. (1972), *A Theory of Justice*); Lorenzen (1992); Kordig (1979) (human rights and conscience desire to uphold the individual's basic dignity through a personal moral standard); Toth (1968) (dignity, as a fundamental concept of human rights, is composed of reason and conscience).
[4] Bates (1945) quotes from the fourth edition of Jules Simon's *La Liberte de Conscience*, a nineteenth century scholar and statesman and the author of a number of influential tracts on religious liberty, who stated: 'I shall try not to write the history of intolerance; that would be to write the history of the world.' Bates nonetheless provides an excellent overview of the development of religion starting from the common era to post World War One. *See also* Kamen (1967) for a shorter, yet detailed, summary from the Reformation to the American Revolution, accounting for political as well as theological factors of religion's development; Evans, M. (1997; Chapters 1 and 2) provides a historical account of religion in Europe.
For the history of religious freedom in international law, *see generally* McDougal Lasswell and Chen (1980;Chapter 11); Lauterpacht (1945;Chapter Two) (freedom of religion as providing political theory for universal rights of man); Macartney (1934) (development of modern nation state as influenced by minority religious protection).

developed, the idea of freedom of conscience began to centre on preserving singular individual beliefs, independent of a theological standard.[5]

In the European context, with Christianity's growth in the fourth century, religious intolerance towards other beliefs was severe, as indicated by the punishment for heresy.[6] Benevolent compulsion, which forcibly converted individuals to Christianity as a mean of 'preserving' their salvation, was the method used for upholding the sole universal faith[7] and preserving the community's unity and cohesion.[8] Christian beliefs and values served as the context for approaching a concept of liberty. Even St. Thomas Aquinas, who preached liberty and tolerance, could not consider an individual notion of personal beliefs since that would have been outside the framework of the Church.[9] The predominantly Christian State forcibly imposed theological Christian beliefs that were equated with moral beliefs.

Similar developments arose in non-Christian societies outside Europe, albeit to a different degree.[10] Intolerance of other religions in the Muslim lands for example was not necessarily as extreme as in Europe, demonstrated by the toleration of minority religions, principally Christianity and Judaism, in the Muslim communities of the Near and Middle East.[11] Nonetheless, as the Muslim religion became rooted in the Middle East, Northern Africa, and the present day area of the Persian Gulf between the eleventh and fifteenth centuries, intolerance attained comparable levels to that generated by the Church.[12] The dominant religious forces imposed limitations on minority religions, exemplified by the imposition of various taxes, separation of societies such as prohibiting a Muslim from marrying outside the faith, and limiting other religions to specific social roles.[13]

The Islam religion transformed from a ruling class religion to become the dominant faith of the masses who were faced with severe economic hardships. In response, the rulers used the minorities in their

---

[5] See e.g. Maneli (1984;89-90) referring to Spinoza who believed in developing the individual's capability for independent reasoning.

[6] McDougal Lasswell and Chen (1980;663); Krishnaswami (1960;1).

[7] Maneli (1984;73).

[8] Bates (1945;133-135).

[9] See e.g. D'Arcy (1961) who defines conscience pursuant to the ideas of St. Thomas Aquinas. See also Bates (1945;140); Kirk (1948;31) for the historical context of Aquinas.

[10] Krishnaswami (1960;9-10); Bates (1945;260-280); Hourani (1991;117-119).

[11] Krishnaswami (1960;9) This possibly resulted from the notion that one religion did not possess absolute and exclusive access to the truth as well as additional social reasons, such as the economic benefits afforded by such a society.

[12] Hourani (1991;118).

[13] Hourani (1991;117-118).

lands as a scapegoat for the general problems of the society thereby deflecting the majority away from its own problems.[14] As a result, social and cultural intercourse between the different faiths diminished,[15] and persecutions, at times, ensued.[16]

A similar situation developed in India during the Muslim domination in the medieval period, when persecutions of the minority were rare.[17] Persecutions occurred however during the thirteenth and fourteenth century,[18] until the period of Akbar[19] who essentially tolerated all forms of religious beliefs. Intolerance of Hindus commenced following the end of Akbar's rule.

The common development in Europe and elsewhere was that the central authority of the state served as a means through which the dominant religion could either assert itself[20] or prevent the practice of other religious beliefs.[21] As various lands were subject to foreign influences, religious intolerance became further enmeshed with political power. Hence the Chinese referred to ethnic Confucianism as one of the grounds for intolerance of Buddhist beliefs in the second century and Christian missionaries a century later, thereby preserving the homogenous character of their people by relying on a particular belief system.[22] Japan, which only adopted Buddhism in the sixth century as the 'state' religion, did not

---

[14] See e.g. Hourani (1991;186-188) noting intolerance in Twelfth Century with emergence of Almohads.
Hourani points out that the persecutions that took place were not sanctioned by the religious spokesman. This highlights the difference with the intolerance in Europe where the basis for the intolerance derived from the rulers to entrench their power. This difference resulted in conscience emerging in a different manner in Europe, especially as it began to develop separately from religion.

[15] Hourani (1991;119).

[16] Hourani (1991;118) referring to the Fatimil Caliph al-Hakim who ruled in Egypt between 996-1021, the Almohads in the Middle East and Northern Africa, and various persecutions carried out by Mongol leaders in Iran and Iraq following their conversion to Islam.

[17] Krishnaswami (1960;8) noting the exception of the Sasanka persecution during the Fifth Century.

[18] Khawaya (1992;96, fn.15) noting various occurrences of persecution.

[19] Akbar ruled from 1556-1605.

[20] Krishnaswami (1960;9) referring to the Ottoman Empire; Bates (1945;262) referring to Europe and various Muslim lands.

[21] Bates (1945;272-279) referring to the intolerance of Christian missionary activities in the Far East.

[22] Bates (1945;272-275).

tolerate other religious identities; it imposed its political will by enforcement of religious beliefs such as requiring every household to maintain a place of worship.[23] Similarly, Muslims who were a religious minority in foreign lands such as Turkey or India asserted their belief by maintaining political control.[24]

Throughout the period of religious dominance of the political system in Europe, essentially through to the post-Reformation,[25] certain individuals attempted to question the authority of the religious power that was imposing its will at the exclusion of all other beliefs. While the state viewed these religious innovators as the social rebels of the time, their assertions nevertheless remained within the context of theology to advance their opinions.[26]

In essence, until the rise of humanism, it was almost impossible to view conscience outside a theological framework. All individuals viewed 'moral action' as arising from the objective law of God. The result was that while the minority's approach towards religious belief might have differed from the majority, thereby raising an issue of conscience, a similar oppressive outcome resulted when, or if, the minority assumed power. Each faction disallowed any deviation from the theological standard that was deemed equivalent to a religious directive.[27] For example, while Protestants might have recognised the existence of the individual conscience, it was still subject to, and in the framework of, the word of God that took precedence over all, including the state.[28]

Note that moral views were developing during the Renaissance period that, although operating within the doctrinal theistic order of the time, initiated the notion of individual moral reasoning.[29] Because it is impossible to determine conclusively the 'truth', religious innovators began to preach the idea of a more personal understanding of the Scriptures. Individuals such as Erasmus focused on the humanistic side of religion, thereby allowing future thinkers to conceive of a conscientious individual as one acting external to a formal religious framework.[30]

---

[23] Bates (1945;279).
[24] Bates (1945;262-270).
[25] Capotorti (1991;1); McDougal Lasswell and Chen (1980;665).
[26] Kamen (1967;20).
[27] Kamen (1967;190-200).
[28] Champion (1999;15); Maneli (1984;80-83). Kamen (1967;50) asserts that this also was the result of political developments, since the Protestant movement realised that the sole means of solidifying their power was to act with the state rather then against it.
[29] Richards (1986;89).
[30] Maneli (1984;85-86).

Yet, a conscientious belief still was intractable from the confines of a religious framework. Religious principles embodying an ultimate moral standard were the sole source of one's personal moral epistemology.[31] Even during the Reformation period, which adhered to the belief in a central concept of truth common to all mankind, one operated within the framework of the Scriptures without allowing for personal deviations. While the Reformation might have challenged the autonomy of the Church, the movement could not conceive the disengagement of a conscientious belief from the religious framework. Acknowledging a person's conscience as a moral authority did not disengage one's theological beliefs that served to limit a person's intellectual capacity to comprehend the conscience.[32]

Later Developments

Despite the inherent limitations on an individual's moral outlook, a key development that emerged from the religious upheaval of sixteenth century Europe was the recognition of religious liberty.[33] The ruling classes now questioned the previously inviolable religious doctrines.[34] Minority religious beliefs achieved further acceptance with the evolution of tolerant ideas within the state[35] and due to the economic necessity of maintaining a viable state.[36] States felt that allowing for a balanced economic infrastructure among all individuals would promote trade and improve the economy. Concomitant with the granting of broader autonomy to particular groups was a greater responsiveness to the various groups' interests and requests. Particularly where a group's interest might result in positive economic developments, states were keen to provide for their protection. For example, both the English and Dutch tolerated the Jews during this

---

[31] Kirk (1948;31).
[32] O'Brien (1991); Kamen (1967;160).
[33] McDougal Lasswell and Chen (1980;665); Krishnaswami (1960;11); Dickson (1995;330); Del Russo (1971;16); Robinson (1948;117).
[34] Kamen (1967;119-120) noting that the politically dominant Noble classes were afforded the luxury of questioning the Church's authority over the state while the poor and lower classes who adopted 'heretical' views felt the brunt of the Church's wrath as they received the punishments.
[35] Capotorti (1991;2) noting the build-up to the American and French Revolutions.
[36] Kamen (1967;225).

period because they realised that toleration was a necessary prelude towards promoting the state's prosperity.

The international system also reflected this developing tolerance of alternative beliefs as states began to stipulate particular protections for minority religions in a number of treaties.[37] For example, Switzerland made allowances for the Christian minority in a 1529 treaty, while freedom of religion was upheld in treaties of the Principality of Transylvania in 1538 and of Germany in 1555.[38] The Muslim world relied upon a system of capitulation, whereby foreign religions were granted a certain degree of autonomy.[39] The Muslim world created many such agreements, principally with France.[40] While these early examples emanated from a desire of the European powers to apply state law to their nationals who were travelling abroad, thereby protecting missionaries and merchants in the Ottoman Empire as the European powers extended eastward,[41] it tended to reflect an evolving trend towards religious toleration.[42]

The Emergence of Conscience as Separate from Religion

In the seventeenth and eighteenth centuries, the necessity of bridging the gap between religions, principally to end warfare,[43] provided for further development of the notion of toleration[44] and assertions of more individual beliefs.[45] The prime example is the 1648 Treaty of Westphalia that ended the Thirty Years War. It contained a stipulation protecting Protestants in Catholic States and Catholics in Reformed States.[46] The key limitation of the Treaty was that it required all minority religions to leave the state within two years or convert, thereby inhibiting development of a genuine

---

[37] Krishnaswami (1960;11); Dickson (1995;330); Robinson (1948;118-120).
[38] McDougal Lasswell and Chen (1980;665-666).
[39] Evans, M. (1997;60).
[40] Krishnaswami (1960;11) noting the 1536 treaty between France and the Ottoman Empire, which became a model for later treaties.
[41] Phillimore (1917;73-75).
[42] The doctrine of humanitarian intervention arguably developed out of these treaties since a state asserted its right to invade another state that did not allow for free practice of religion to the invader's nationals. *See* Oppenheim (1955;347) noting that the doctrine did not develop into customary law since it was subject to aberrations and inconsistent practice.
[43] Kamen (1967;129).
[44] Krishnaswami (1960;11); McDougal Lasswell and Chen (1980;665); Del Russo (1971;15).
[45] McDougal Lasswell and Chen (1980;666); Ganji (1962;153).
[46] Krishnaswami (1960;11); McDougal Lasswell and Chen (1980;668); Dickson (1995;330).

religious toleration.⁴⁷ Other treaties subsequent to Westphalia began to provide for religious freedom within their territories. However the provided protection was generally subject to the limiting proviso that the protection be accorded for 'as far as the laws' of a country would allow for such freedom. This limitation, in effect, allowed states to nullify the intended protection of the treaty.⁴⁸ Furthermore, states entered into the majority of post-Westphalian treaties due to political reasons regarding territorial conflicts between states or to create a commercial advantage.⁴⁹

The emergence of diverse religious thought during the Reformation and the disengagement of state and religious institutions following the 1648 Treaty of Westphalia weakened the influential grip of the religious authorities over the state.⁵⁰ The questioning of the Church's power, principally regarding its role within the state structure and the unyielding imposition of its principles,⁵¹ led to the acceptance of a notion of personal

---

[47] Del Russo (1971); Phillimore (1917;19) referring to Article 49 of the Treaty; McDougal Lasswell and Chen (1980;669).

[48] The typical example of such a provision is the 1763 Treaty of Paris, Article 4 that grants liberty to the 'new Roman Catholic subjects of Great Britain' (in the Canadian territories ceded by France to Great Britain) to follow their own form of worship for 'as far as the laws of Great Britain allow'. For similar treaty stipulations, *see also* 1713 Treaty of Utrecht between France and Great Britain at Article 14; 1660 Treaty of Oliva between Prussia and Sweden (only protecting co-religionists in each state); 1678 Treaty of Nijmegen between France and the Netherlands at Article 9 (which essentially relies on the capitulation regarding freedom of religion for the Roman Catholic minority living in the territory ceded by France to Holland); 1686 Treaty of Moscow between Poland and Russia at Article 9 (Poland pledged not to molest either Orthodox Church members nor try to convert same); 1697 Treaty of Ryswich between France and Netherlands (same provision as in 1678 Treaty of Nijmegen); 1699 Treaty of Carlowitz between Turkey and both Austria and Poland (protection of Roman Catholics and allowances for their visits to holy sites); 1736 Treaty Hubertsburg and 1742 Treaty of Breslau, both between Prussia and Austria; 1732 Treaty of Warsaw between Austria and Poland; 1739 Treaty of Belgrade between Russia and Turkey (same provisions as in 1699 Treaty of Carlowitz).

The aforementioned treaties can be found in Israel (1969). *See also* Del Russo (1971;16); Phillimore (1917;19); Capotorti (1991;1-2); Walsh (1990;26).

[49] Evans, M. (1997;54-55).

[50] Ganji (1962;153). Kamen (1967) and Abram (1968;44) both note that the strive for tolerance derived out of political necessity, especially as church power weakened, rather than as an altruistic drive for individual diversity.

[51] As noted by Richards (1993;66):
> In effect, the conception of religious truth, though perhaps having once been importantly shaped by more ultimate considerations of

liberty and the development of an individual conscience. The toleration of views based on reason and piety of the individual, albeit still within a theological context, became accepted forms of beliefs. Freedom of conscience was therefore inseparable from liberty since the latter provided the individual with the ability to adhere to a particular belief.[52] Furthermore, conscience in a sense served to entrench the state authority. Because the inherent requirement for authority figures was to uphold the law and religion of the land, conscience served as a social badge of political obedience towards the system.[53]

The works of two influential thinkers, Bayle and Locke, reflect the historical development of conscience as an independent notion allowing for individual approaches to ethics and morals.[54] Both recognised that the formation of reasonable moral beliefs is a matter of personal life experiences, such as parental or cultural training, which will create quite a diverse cross section of religious and moral views. Since religious questions are really a matter for God, man can only guess at the proper answer, such that a political resolution of a religious question can be just as incorrect as the views that are being suppressed.[55] Locke further developed the argument that since the ultimate truth is never attainable due to the inherent limitations of man and the omniscient nature of a deity,[56] imposing one's own ethical approach over another is a futile activity.[57] Even worse, attempting to repress the views of another serves to

---

reason, ceases to be held or understood and elaborated on the basis of reason.

[52] Maneli (1984;89-90) referring to Spinoza who asserted that an individual's reasoning served as a central basis for moral, rational, action.

[53] Champion (1999;17).

[54] Richards (1986;90) noting epistemological and circumstantial similarities between the two thinkers, with the key difference being Locke's political, republican, focus as opposed to Bayle's more philosophical approach to toleration. Bracken (1991) distinguishes Bayle's reliance on conscience as clarifying a person's moral position, versus Locke's separation of Church and State that served to regulate the individual's morality.

[55] Kilcullen (1985) noting that while both agreed that God left the search for the truth to man, Locke would allow the ruler to suppress a dangerous view while Bayle believes in corrective punishment.

[56] Kelly (1991) noting how Locke respected liberty of conscience due to the inability of distinguishing the correct from incorrect interpretation of divine law.

[57] Bracken (1991;1) The author distinguishes between Bayle's reliance on the individual conscience as the central basis for reason, as opposed to Locke's reliance on the state, when separated from the Church, as a principal source for upholding the individual's beliefs. Richards (1986;89-98) notes that the toleration espoused by Locke and Bayle did not incorporate atheistic beliefs, although such individuals were still perceived as maintaining a moral standard. Note that philosophers in the Nineteenth Century rooted

stifle the reasoning of all individuals who maintain a free conscience. Hence these thinkers created a division between beliefs in the truth, such as God-given law, as opposed to reasonable standards of beliefs that can derive from individuals.[58] Bayle in particular noted that conscience serves as an internal focal point for ethical knowledge and an external mean by which such knowledge shapes one's life and actions.[59]

As the provision for individual reasoning developed, so did the approach to conscience, particularly concerning the unnecessary link to a religious standard. The epistemological foundation of religion and morals as being dictated by the Church was now shifting to allow for reasonable inquiry by the individual, albeit still within a religious context.[60] Reliance on individual reasoning developed as a response to exclusive theistic beliefs, which had served as the basis for barbarous acts to other individuals. Individual reasoning would allow for the development of a purer form of religious and social ethics.[61]

The developing notion of liberty was based on the realisation that a person's central goal is to lead a proper and moral life rather than blindly follow theological ordinances.[62] The ability to develop one's personal orientation towards morals and ethics replaced the dominant religion's dictation of what to believe and think.[63] In essence what evolved was the idea that enforcing moral truths through political power deviates from the original intent by becoming an unreasonable assertion of views. This is particularly the case when conscience is synonymous with a religious

---

conscience in the individual's beliefs rather than in religion by relying on similar arguments made by Locke. *See e.g.* J. Bentham and J.S. Mill.

[58] Bayle held that it is a moral good to abide by the conscience, even if objectively it was incorrect, as long as the agent is intending to carry out a moral good. Kilcullen (1985).

[59] Richards (1986;94) contrasting Bayle with Locke's theo-centric mode of thought based on a just God and adherence to the Gospel's minimum ethical standards, i.e., the natural law.

[60] Champion (1999;24-25) concludes that Locke and his contemporaries still bound up conscience with pious conviction given his mistrust of atheists and others who did not believe in a deity and the necessity for a civic religion that upholds social morality.

[61] Note that the theological origins still played a role for both Bayle and Locke as they did not give credence to the atheist thinker not because such individuals were immoral, especially since atheists can act morally, but because they were non-believers in God that precluded the ability for an ethical motivation.

[62] Kamen (1967;125) noting the perspective of the Sectarians who preached a non-dogmatic ideology that centred on a separation of Church and State and linked civil with religious liberty.

[63] McDougal Lasswell and Chen (1980;664); Krishnaswami (1960;3).

belief since other forms of conscientious belief are either not tolerated or are suppressed.[64] Furthermore, the emergence of the principle of liberty led to the realisation that the state must tolerate all forms of religious beliefs and ideals since man is indivisible and retains an inherent worth that merits protection.[65] Because a concern for Enlightenment thinkers was the prospect of persecution that could arise from a tolerant attitude towards other beliefs, the goal was to displace the religious dimension of conscience from its core.[66]

Such ideals developed into political practice,[67] particularly following the French and American revolutions that provided a more effective protection for freedom of the individual and his beliefs.[68] The tolerant ideals of the United States for example were reflected in the international sphere by a variety of bilateral commerce and navigation treaties that, during the latter half of the eighteenth century, sought to ensure religious freedom for Americans abroad.[69] For example, Article 11 of a 1785 Treaty of Commerce and Amity between the United States and Prussia states:

> The most perfect freedom of conscience and of worship is granted to the subjects of either party within the jurisdiction of the other without being liable to molestation in that respect other than an insult on the religion of others.[70]

---

[64] Richards (1993;72) notes that as a result of the religious authority and individual moral autonomy distinction, the Lockean approach provides a proper basis upon which to establish authority. The individuals composing the body politic will, pursuant to reason, limit or extend the state's power as they reasonably see fit since there is no over-arching standard imposed by an ultimate authority.

[65] Maneli (1984;100-101) referring to the Eighteenth-Century Encyclopeadist movement spearheaded by Diderot who strove for peaceful co-existence, even without approval, with a focus on separating Church and State to remove opposition to minority beliefs.

[66] Fitzpatrick (1999;50).

[67] Evans, M. (1997;43) notes the shift from justifying state activity based on religious doctrine to focusing on religious liberty for the individual.

[68] McDougal Lasswell and Chen (1980;666); Ganji (1962); Krishnaswami (1960).

[69] McDougal Lasswell and Chen (1980;670-71) referring to Commerce and Amity Treaties with Netherlands (1782), Sweden (1783) and Prussia (1785).

[70] Bevans (1974;78). The Treaty was renewed in 1799 and again in 1828.
Similar language was used in the 1783 Treaty of Amity and Commerce between the United States and Sweden. Article 5 of the Treaty provides:
There shall be granted a full perfect and entire liberty of conscience to the inhabitants and subjects of each party and no person shall be molested on account of his worship provided he submits so far as regards the public demonstration of it to the laws of the country.
This treaty was renewed in 1816 and again in 1827 until it terminated in 1919. Bevans (1974;Vol.11;710).

The reference to conscience, as opposed to religion, can be a reflection of the altered role of conscience that was beginning to emerge. Protecting conscience allowed for a broader application and scope to the treaty as it was not limited to religious beliefs. Indeed, protection of internal thoughts, 'freedom of conscience', as opposed to the external manifestation of a belief, 'worship' that cannot 'insult' the 'religion of others', is reminiscent of the present day treaties' distinction between the internal and external aspect of the right to conscience.[71] Note however that the use of the term 'conscience' as opposed to religion probably derived from the strong separation of Church and State in the United States. The Establishment Clause of the United States Constitution prevents the Government from 'protecting' any religion. Hence reference to the more neutral term of 'conscience' allowed the Government to protect general, and not solely religious, beliefs.[72]

On a multilateral level, international developments provided for minority religions, along with other non-religious based minorities,[73] to assert themselves and their rights in international fora, albeit the term 'conscience' had yet to be used as the standard treaty language.[74] The multilateral treaties of the time do however reflect the emerging attitude of tolerance towards religious and other minorities. The 1814 Congress of Vienna[75] and the 1815 Treaty of Vienna exemplify this developing attitude.[76] Each document provides for blanket protection of minorities, regardless of religion or nationality. For example, Article 2 of the 1814 Congress of Vienna states:

> There shall be no change in the articles of the Fundamental Law which assure to all religious cults equal protection and privileges, and guarantee the admissibility of all citizens,

---

[71] *See* discussion *infra* at Chapters Four and Five.
[72] Bates (1945;487-88) notes that the treaties' protection of external activity related to missionary activity and erecting houses of worship.
[73] Capotorti (1991;2) notes that the protection began to focus on civil and political rights as well.
[74] The term 'conscience' began to crop up in various treaties of the League of Nations, post World War One.
[75] Which created the Kingdom of the Netherlands.
[76] Between the Netherlands, Great Britain, Russia, Austria, Prussia, Portugal, France, and Sweden. *See also* Del Russo (1971;17) who notes that individual religions, such as Jews and Catholics, sent representatives to the treaty negotiations, playing a similar role to the Non-Governmental Organisations of today.

whatever be their religious creed, to public office and dignities.[77]

Article 4 further provides for equal claim by all to fair commercial opportunities without any hindrance or obstruction. Additionally, Article 8 of the 1815 Treaty requires protection for all 'religions and creeds' along with equal access to employment. The 1830 Kingdom of Greece Treaty had similar provisions concerning free worship for Muslims[78] and eligibility of individuals from all beliefs for public office and employment,[79] as did the 1856 Conference of Constantinople, that established an independent Moldavia and Wallachia and provided for equal liberty and protection for all religions and equal civil rights for all individuals.[80] Similarly, the 1856 Congress of Paris[81] provides in Article 9 for the protection of Turkish Christians.[82]

The 1878 Treaty of Berlin proved a seminal document for further entrenching the right to freedom of religion as it applied to many states, including the Ottoman Empire, and required signatories to assure religious freedom for all.[83] The Treaty linked recognition of the newly created States with adherence to the principle of non-discrimination on religious grounds.[84] The basic language of the articles dealing with discrimination[85] provided for no differentiation, due to 'religion or creed', in employment or civil and political rights, as well as ensuring for freedom of worship.

---

[77] Mair (1928;30). *See also* Del Russo (1971;17) who refers to Article 77 of the Congress of Vienna that provided protection not only for freedom of religion but also against national and racial discrimination, as well as allowing for individual petitions to their states for protection; Phillimore (1917) refers to Article 73 that provides for protection of religious worship and overall right to equality.
[78] Capotorti (1991;2); Mair (1928;31) noting a similar declaration in 1863 concerning the Ionian Islands.
[79] Evans, M. (1997;66) noting that this treaty set the pattern for future agreements.
[80] Mair (1928;31) referring to Articles 13 and 18.
[81] Concluded between Austria, France, Great Britain, Prussia, Sardinia, and Turkey.
[82] The treaty specifically excluded any allowances for intervention, an oversight that was to be rectified at the 1878 Congress of Berlin.
[83] Krishnaswami (1960;11); McDougal Lasswell and Chen (1980;669).
[84] Evans, M. (1997;72); Mair (1928;32); Capotorti (1991;3); Phillimore (1917;94).
[85] The Treaty essentially used the same language throughout each application to the relevant states. *See* Article 5 regarding Bulgaria, Article 44 regarding Rumania, Article 27 concerning Montenegro, Article 35 regarding Serbia, and Article 62 regarding the Ottoman Empire, which was subject to additional requirements concerning protection of missionaries. Hourani (1991;297) notes that with the urbanisation of the Ottoman Empire and growth of its economy, foreign religious elements increased and they were provided with protection by their foreign country.

The key problem with these treaties however was ineffectiveness and lack of any enforcement mechanism.[86] For example, Rumania continued to discriminate against its minorities by amending its Constitution to provide that one can only become a national, and thereby acquire protection of the Treaty, through a specific legislative act. That was a virtual impossibility for a minority lacking any political power or influence.[87]

As both religious and other minority beliefs were receiving international protection, the assertion of freedom of conscience developed outside a religious context. The ideas of freedom and liberty that provided impetus for the American and French Revolutions[88] propelled philosophers to consider ethical motivation as a process distinct from theological foundations.[89] Individuals were viewed as free and rational beings who enjoyed moral autonomy and created a moral conception unique to one's personal circumstances, without pressure or influence from external sources on the person's internal sphere.[90] Upholding a conscientious belief was central to this notion of liberty since one cannot be denied the ability to exercise a moral belief once liberty is a desired outcome.[91]

The Abolitionists' reliance on conscience to buttress their attack on the slavery movement in the late eighteenth and early nineteenth century demonstrates the emergence of conscience as a moral standard separate from religion.[92] Confronted with a heavy burden of justification in a society that treated slavery as an accepted norm, the Abolitionists made an analogy between the oppression of the black slaves to the intolerance practised by

---

[86] Oppenheim (1917;366); Del Russo (1971).
[87] Phillimore (1917;95).
[88] Verzijl (1958;7).
[89] Fitzpatrick (1999;51); Richards (1986;97); Maneli (1984;133-143). The consideration was more of a tendency towards secularisation rather than an exclusive secular movement. Fitzpatrick (1999;56-57) for example notes that the obligation to conscience derived from a religious duty.
[90] Maneli (1984;144) refers to J.S. Mill, noting the constant struggle between toleration and freedom and how the latter always needs to be re-established.
[91] Bates (1945;295-297).
[92] *See e.g.* Bolt & Drescher (1980); Brown (1994). The Abolitionists' arguments in the United States essentially derived from the European sources' reasoning for abolishing slavery. The argument in the United States is interesting because it refers to conscience as a unique reasoning process with an epistemological basis external to a religious context. Richards (1993).

the Catholic Church during the Middle Ages.[93] Similar to the loss of reasonable foundations for justifying religious intolerance that eventually contributed to the downfall of the Church, the Abolitionists questioned the reasonableness of slavery from a general conscientious standpoint.[94]

The underlying contention of the Abolitionists was that slavery violated the basic inherent dignity of the individual.[95] The majority's view that slaves were not worthy of any basic rights suppressed the slaves moral, or conscientious, position. Similar to the intolerant beliefs of a dominant religion that refuses to acknowledge the beliefs of another, the narrow views of the majority deprived the slaves of any notion of conscience.[96]

The Abolitionists' argument demonstrates that conscience was not merely a concept that required a foundation in theological origins; rather the basic and inherent beliefs of the individual can serve to develop a moral belief.[97] Such personal beliefs are analogous to the minority religious beliefs that the majority neglected during the Reformation and subsequent periods.

Herein lies the crux of the proposal to disengage a conscientious belief from religious principles. Protecting a 'belief' does not necessarily imply a religious system; rather a belief can refer to an individual's understanding of a particular practice, like slavery, as determined by moral and social influences. In essence, the famous argument put forward by Thoreau at this time concerning civil disobedience, to do what one personally thinks is 'right', hinges on this very notion of conscience as an individual power above that of the state. He states that:

> The only obligation which I have the right to assume, is to do at any time what I think right ... There will never be a free and enlightened State, until the State comes to recognise the individual as a higher and independent power, from which all

---

[93] Richards (1993;63-73).
[94] Brown (1994;237) noting strong reliance by British Abolitionists on a basic moral argument due to the Quaker influence and a desire to incorporate a large cross-section of the population. He asserts that the sentiments in Britain derived from a reaction to the American revolution where each side referred to moral principles, such that an anti-slavery stance became an issue of national virtue for Britain.
[95] Daget (1980) referring to the French Abolitionists, who relied on a general moral argument, as Church influence over moral thought weakened; Anstey (1980) makes a similar point concerning British Abolitionists. Note however that both authors conclude that the eventual legal change developed due to other ancillary factors, such as economic changes, and the humanist argument was only a part of the impetus for change.
[96] Richards (1993;60-62).
[97] Richards (1993;66).

its own power and authority are derived, and treats him accordingly.[98]

Minority religious beliefs continued to receive protection in various bilateral treaties throughout the nineteenth and early twentieth centuries.[99] The 1898 Treaty of Paris between France and Spain for example provides at Article 10 for protection of the inhabitants, in the territories ceded by Spain, in the 'free exercise of their religion'.[100] The 1881 International Convention of Constantinople concluded between Germany, Austria, Hungary, France, Great Britain, Italy, Russia, and Turkey provides in Article VIII for freedom of worship for the Mohammedans and for continued existence of their religious courts and local infrastructure.[101]

Post World War One

A number of fairly broad protections for minority beliefs were instituted following the post-World War One creation of the League of Nations.[102] The key drive for creating such protection was based on the underlying desire to uphold peace, and the belief that to accomplish peace, protection must be granted to minority communities scattered throughout the world.[103] States recognised the dangers in being unduly associated with a particular religious belief since it creates friction within the state and unrest among the minority population whose interests might not be addressed.

In essence, tolerance and moral pluralism were being recognised as a fundamental concept from which to ensure for a peaceful coexistence among states. Such an approach is exemplified in a letter sent by the

---

[98] Thoreau (1849;4 and 41).
[99] Bates (1945;486-489).
[100] Phillimore (1917).
[101] Capotorti (1991;3).
[102] Krishnaswami (1960;11-12) pointing out that the protections were not universal but focused on the racial, religious or linguistic minorities found within the state.
For a more detailed explanation regarding the operation of the League's system protecting the right of minorities, *see* Stone (1932); Stone (1933) (a more focused analysis of the post-World War One conventions); Macartney (1934; Chapter Four); Capotorti (1991;Chapter II).
[103] Del Russo (1971;25); Capotorti (1991;17); Mair (1928;35) quoting President Wilson's 1919 speech addressing Rumania's protest to the minority provisions where he stated that 'If we agree to these additions of territory we have the right to insist upon certain guarantees of peace'.

French delegate M. Clemenceau to the President of Poland noting that the re-establishment of Poland's sovereignty depended on:

> the secure possession of these territories. There rests therefore upon these powers an obligation, which they cannot evade, to secure in the most permanent and solemn form guarantees for certain essential rights which will afford to the inhabitants the necessary protection, whatever changes may take place in the internal constitution of the Polish state.[104]

Additionally, the drafters of the League's Covenant proposed an article that prevented interference with the free exercise of religion and prohibited discrimination against any 'creed religion or belief' as a condition precedent for membership.[105] The basis for the proposal, as noted by Lord Cecil of Britain, was the recognition that religious persecution and intolerance were fertile sources of war and political unrest.[106] The League's Covenant did not contain such an article however as the delegates decided that it would address such issues in the future.[107] Furthermore, the issue got bogged down in attempts to include a controversial amendment regarding equality, which tended to remove the momentum for the article.[108]

Nonetheless, Article 22(5) of the League's Mandate System required a Mandatory, the power that was to oversee the dissolution of a colony, to ensure for 'conditions which will guarantee freedom of conscience and religion'.[109] Hence, various Mandates that establish the state's responsibilities for its protectorate area under Article 22[110] provide further examples of the development of conscience as an individual belief. Article 1 of the French Mandate for Togoland for example required France to:

---

[104] Mair (1928;36).
[105] Evans, M. (1997;92); Capotorti (1991;16-17).
[106] Wilson (1928;104-105). Miller (1924;Appendix 5) refers to the Smut's plan, one of the original drafts of the Covenant for the League of Nations, which provided for an automatic right to military conscientious objection, and the suspension of any forced national service as a means of meeting this underlying policy of preserving the peace.
[107] Wilson (1928;106) referring to remarks by the Greek delegate, M. Veniselos.
[108] Evans, M. (1997;100-103).
[109] Note that the terms of subsection (5) are unique to Article 22, possibly because it was drafted by the Supreme Council and not the League Committee which generally used the language of protecting 'religion and worship'. Article 22 is viewed as a policy-oriented article that established the underlying framework for a Mandate. Walters (1952;57).
[110] *See generally* Capotorti (1991;Chapter II).

ensure in the territory complete freedom of conscience and the free exercise of all forms of worship, which are consonant with public order and morality.[111]

A similar provision is found in the South African Mandate for Southwest Africa, at Article 5.[112]

In the League's subsequent treaties and mandates with various states regarding minority protection, the League used language reminiscent of the present day international human rights treaties.[113] For example, the 1919 Treaty with Poland[114] provided at Article 2, following the prohibition of religious discrimination, that:

> All inhabitants of Poland shall be entitled to the free exercise, whether public or private, of any creed, religion, or belief whose practices are not inconsistent with public order or public morals.[115]

The implementation and enforcement mechanisms of the League, which included the possibility for individual petitions to the Council, proved ineffective and cumbersome.[116] Because responsibility for upholding the treaties was left to the League,[117] the treaties were ineffectual[118] due to the absence of the more powerful states such as Germany and Italy.[119] Although the aforementioned treaties treat

---

[111] McDougal Lasswell and Chen (1980;671).
[112] McDougal Lasswell and Chen (1980;671-672).
[113] Capotorti (1991;17-18).
[114] Capotorti (1991;18).
McDougal Lasswell and Chen (1980;672) refer to similar arrangements with Czechoslovakia, the Serb-Croat-Slovene State, Rumania, Greece, Austria, Bulgaria, Hungary, and Turkey and, through unilateral League resolutions, Albania, Estonia, Latvia, Lithuania, and Iraq. The resolutions were signed by the States upon joining the League and had the same force as a treaty.
[115] McDougal Lasswell and Chen (1980;672-673) noting as well Articles 7 and 8, which provide for protection of civil and political rights without distinction of race, religion, creed, or language. Similar provisions also are found at Section IV, Articles 49-57, in the 1919 Treaty of Neuilly between the Allies and Bulgaria, and at Articles 54-60 in the 1920 Treaty of Triamen with Hungary.
[116] Evans, M. (1997;164-166).
[117] Evans, M. (1997;151).
[118] Bates (1945;490 and 500-501).
[119] Robinson (1948;123).

conscientious beliefs as worthy of protection, the rights were granted to collective entities rather than individuals[120] and manifestation of the right was limited to a narrow context usually associated with religion, such as worship,[121] which would seem to exclude any conscientious assertions.

Despite the seemingly limited protection for individual conscientious beliefs, the notion of conscience as a belief system distinct from a religious based standard was nevertheless acquiring recognition, as demonstrated in the Permanent Court of International Justice case concerning Upper Silesea.[122] The International Court was confronted with a provision of the 1922 German-Polish Convention of Upper Silesea that gave power to a parent to declare, according to one's conscience, whether he does or does not belong to a particular linguistic, racial, or religious minority. This declaration would then serve to determine the proper language course for one's child. The key issue in the case centred on whether the state's appointment of an outside expert to verify the parent's declaration violated the Convention. Recognising the development of conscience as an axiomatic assertion of a belief, the Court held that the state may not appoint an objective expert but a declarant must ensure that he is stating his 'true' position regarding his status.

Conclusion

The right to conscience was now emerging as a singular right that need not centre on religious beliefs. Rather, application of the right focused on upholding individual beliefs in a variety of situations. While the process was slow and at times not always reflective of the relevant states' true desires, the changing attitudes towards religion and conscience also had an effect on the manner in which the freedom of religion emerged. Even if not fully acknowledged or adhered to by all states, the right to freedom of religion was broadened to include a number of minority belief systems that historically had been ignored. This historical evolution of conscience as a

---

[120] Krishnaswami (1960;12); Dickson (1995;331). *Contra* Capotorti (1991;19) noting that states desired to protect themselves against the risk of dismemberment by a particular minority group.

[121] Evans, M. (1997;161) also notes the hesitation of the League's Committee to analyse critically internal rules outside the state's legal system, despite such rules playing a major part in the state's national consciousness.

[122] PCIJ Judgement No. 12, Advisory Opinion of 1928 *Rights of Minorities in Upper Silesea (Minority Schools)*.

principle distinct from religion was to be unequivocally codified with the founding of the international human rights system following World War Two.[123]

---

[123] McDougal Lasswell and Chen (1980;653 and 661); Krishnaswami (1960;15-17).

3 Analysis of the Treaties and Other Documents

Introduction

What is significant about the works that have analysed the human right to freedom of religion,[1] is the recognition that the treaties establishing the international human right to freedom of religion also include therein the right to freedom of conscience.[2] Scholarly works that analyse the international right to freedom of 'religion and belief' invariably note the distinction between religion and other forms of belief that possibly include a conscientious belief.[3] Yet the ensuing discussions generally focus on established religions as opposed to emerging beliefs, without any clarification of the significance of the right to conscience. There is no meaningful analysis of the international human right to freedom of conscience, other than in the context of military objection, nor any specific focus on the scope to be accorded to the universal treaty term 'belief' as referring to a conscientious belief.

Expanding on the *travaux preparatoires* of the principal human rights treaties can serve to clarify the relevant terms and sharpen the meaning of the text in a manner that can eventually enhance the applicability of the right to conscience.[4] The *travaux preparatoires* can

---

[1] See e.g. Tahzib (1996); Evans, M. (1997); 1992 COE Seminar on Freedom of Conscience; Edge (1996); Partsch (1981).
[2] See e.g. UDHR Article 18; ICCPR Article 18; ECHR Article 9; AmCHR Article 12.
[3] See e.g. Tahzib (1996) who discusses this issue in the introduction to the book. *Cf.* Vermeulen (1993).
[4] Gardiner (1997;643) noting that 'More often than not, tribunals look to preparatory work of a treaty, sometimes almost as a first resort rather than as a subsidiary means of interpretation'; McDougal Lasswell and Miller (1967) criticising textual approach of International Law Commission for interpretation of a treaty and contending that any meaningful textual analysis of a treaty must account for surrounding circumstances and development of the text in the travaux.

play a central role in this regard,⁵ particularly since the terms used to codify the right to freedom of conscience are general and somewhat indeterminate.⁶ Considering the obscure nature of the right to freedom of conscience in the principal human rights treaties, namely the UDHR, ICCPR, ECHR, AmCHR, and AfrCHR, analysis of the legal development of the right would seem an important exercise. As stated by Sinclair in his discussion of the Vienna Convention on the Law of Treaties:

> In any event, it is clear that no would-be interpreter of a treaty, whatever his doctrinal point of departure, will deliberately ignore any material which can usefully serve as a guide towards establishing the meaning of the text with which he is confronted.⁷

Recognising that the principal human rights treaties were the result of compromise and political considerations, particularly regarding the freedom of religion where the repeated themes of changing ones religion as well as the intended scope of the right were subject to an ongoing debate that continues until today, it is by no means certain that the *travaux preparatoires* will meaningfully elucidate the right to conscience.⁸ Further, certain treaties, notably the ICCPR and ECHR, have been subject to additional interpretation by their relevant internal bodies. For example, the HRC under the ICCPR has issued a General Comment to Article 18⁹ that assists to clarify the right to freedom of conscience. The HRC also has decided cases relating to military conscientious objection.¹⁰ The ECHR Court and Commission similarly have decided a number of cases relating to the right to freedom of conscience that assist to clarify the right.

The problem is that these sources do not adequately address the right to conscience¹¹ nor consider the broader meaning of the term as indicated by the *travaux preparatoires*. For purposes of the right to freedom of conscience, denoting the differences and highlighting the similarities of the

---

⁵ *See* Article 32 of the Vienna Convention on the Law of Treaties.
⁶ Evans, M. (1997;262) for example notes regarding the freedom of religion that it is an obscure right that merits a broader examination of the *travaux preparatoires* to further understand the meaning of the text. Surely the same reasoning equally applies to the right to freedom of conscience.
⁷ Sinclair (1984;116).
⁸ Indeed Evans, M. (1997;263) maintains that the *travaux preparatoires* highlight the differences rather than clarify the provisions.
⁹ CCPR/C/21/Rev.1/Add.4 (1993).
¹⁰ *See e.g.* 402/1990 *Brinkhof v. Netherlands* (1993).
¹¹ *See e.g.* Evans, M. (1997;210-213) noting HRC's pre-occupation with discrimination in the General Comment to ICCPR Article 18.

relevant provisions in the principal human rights treaties will provide the basis for further research and examination of the right to freedom of conscience. While the pre-occupation over the utility of the *travaux preparatoires* provides grounds for referring to other relevant sources, the cognate terms and phrases used to codify the right to freedom of conscience corroborate an underlying commonalty in approaching the right and indicate that, in certain instances, the treaties maintain like freedoms for the right to conscience. It will become apparent that the drafters of the various human rights treaties were concerned with rather similar issues concerning the right to freedom of conscience.

International Treaties

Various studies were conducted towards the end of World War Two that focused on rights to be included in a universal human rights document.[12] Between 1942 and 1944, the American Law Institute issued a document, entitled *Declaration of Essential Human Rights*, that included a provision upholding the right to freedom of religion.[13] The 1945 UN Charter however only incorporated general notions of human rights within various articles of the Charter,[14] with a view towards codifying human rights in a particular document.

At the United Nations' first General Assembly meeting in October 1945, Panama presented for discussion a draft human rights document that was being considered by the Latin American states.[15] After submitting the

---

[12] *See e.g.* UNESCO (1949) (world philosophers and scientists responded to UNESCO questionnaire and provided comments regarding general approach towards human rights); Lauterpacht (1945) (natural law basis for human rights, with heavy emphasis on importance of freedom of religion. Lauterpacht even links the overall rights of man to a coherent political theory based on free religion).

[13] The ALI solicited jurists' opinions regarding the content of human rights from countries as varied as America, Britain, Arab states, Canada, China, France, Italy, India, Latin America, Poland, pre-Nazi Germany, Russia, and Spain.

[14] *See* the Preamble and Articles 1 (UN to promote and encourage human rights), 13 (GA to assist in realising human rights), 55 and 56 (signatory countries responsible to promote respect for human rights and fundamental freedoms), 62, 64, 68 and 71 (ECOSOC's responsibility vis-à-vis human rights), and 71 and 73 (dealing with the Trusteeship System). There was no particular testimonial to human rights due to pressing time limitations and the desire to focus on general world security concerns. Samnoy (1993;17-18).

[15] The working title was *Declaration on the Rights and Duties of States* and a *Draft Declaration on Fundamental Human Rights and Freedoms*. Moller (1992;fn.1) *See also* E/CN.4/21 (Secretariat collated the various draft documents submitted for consideration which included the Panamanian submission).

draft to the International Law Commission, the General Assembly, on the recommendation of the First and Third Committees, passed the document to the Economic and Social Council.[16] ECOSOC's Nuclear Commission on Human Rights[17] reviewed the document and passed it on to the newly created Commission on Human Rights.[18]

At its first session, the CHR decided to focus on codifying an 'International Bill of Rights' and a Drafting Sub-Committee was created.[19] The CHR further decided that an initial declaration of human rights, whose legal character was subject to dispute,[20] would be drafted, followed by a more specific and more binding international covenant.[21] Hence the CHR initially focused on the UDHR.

UDHR, Article 18[22]

The final version of UDHR Article 18 pertaining to the freedom of religion and conscience states:

> Everyone has the right to freedom of thought conscience and religion; this right includes freedom to change his religion or belief, and freedom, either alone or in community with others

---

[16] Moller (1992;fn.1).

[17] ECOSOC, 1st Session, Resolution 1/5, 1946. *See also* Samnoy (1993;20 and 28-33) (discussing internal conflict regarding extent of governmental participation and the desired scope of the Commission's work).

[18] The CHR's members were the five powers at the time, US, USSR, UK, France, and China, along with Byelorussia, Iran, Lebanon, Panama, Uruguay, Ukraine, Belgium, Chile, Egypt, Australia, Philippines, and Yugoslavia. Note the absence of the defeated states from World War Two and the weak representation of the African states. The only other UN members, aside for Egypt, being Liberia and Ethiopia.

[19] The Sub-Committee was originally three states, US, China and Lebanon, but was expanded to include Australia, Chile, France, USSR, and UK.

[20] *See* E/CN.4/82 where the US. stated that the UDHR was to maintain 'considerable weight' despite the absence of any legal obligation. *Cf.* France, Chile and Lebanon who viewed the UDHR as clarifying the human rights obligations of the UN Charter. E/CN.4/SR.48.

[21] E/CN.4/57 (1947). The CHR decided to use the UK draft as a forerunner to the covenant and an in-session Working Group used the Drafting Committee's submission as a basis for the proposed draft declaration. *See* Malik (1950); Moller (1992;2); UNESCO (1950). Note that an implementation procedure was also to be drafted (and a separate committee was established for that purpose) *see* E/CN.4/SR.25, but it was eventually incorporated by the covenants.

[22] GA Res. 217A (III), GAOR Third Session, Part I.

and in public or private, to manifest his religion or belief in teaching, practice, worship and observance.[23]

An important issue confronting the drafters dealt with the focus of the article. Was it to solely protect the right to freedom of religion or also incorporate other forms of belief such as a conscientious belief? Consequently, the initial draft of ECOSOC's Secretariat provided an overview of the status of the right to free religion in various domestic systems. The focus of the participatory states' systems was to provide for free religion, such as in the US, or free worship and belief, such as in India or Panama. Those systems that did provide for a 'liberty of conscience', such as in Lebanon and Czechoslovakia, centred the right on protecting religious beliefs, although Brazil and Turkey provided protection for 'general beliefs' as well.

Despite the domestic focus on religion, the ensuing draft provided a clear provision for the individual's right to freedom of conscience. The proposal reflects the second freedom of Roosevelt's famous 'Four Freedoms' speech, 'freedom to worship God in his own way everywhere in the world'[24] but with a provision for the right to conscience. The Secretariat's draft proposal provided protection for the:

> freedom of conscience and belief and of private and public religious worship.[25]

Subsequent drafts of the article expanded on this broad approach to the right to freedom of religion by specifically incorporating the right to freedom of conscience as well.[26] As indicated in the Annex to the Secretariat's draft, the proposed amendments not only centred on protection

---

[23] The text, as submitted by the CHR, was adopted in the Third Committee by 38 votes in favour, 3 against, and three abstentions, while in the GA, it was passed by 45 votes in favour, four abstentions, and no negative votes.

[24] The speech is quoted in Samnoy (1993;11). *See also* de deZayas and Bassiouni (1994) noting the enduring influence of the speech.

[25] E/CN.4/AC.1/3/Add.1 (1947). Note the absence of any particular reference to freedom of religion since it was probably incorporated into 'conscience and belief'.

[26] The CHR draft of the article included protection for beliefs other than religious beliefs. *See* E/CN.4/56. The draft provided for:
 1. Individual freedom of thought and conscience, to hold and change beliefs, is an absolute and sacred right
 2. Every person has the right, either alone or in community with other persons of like mind and in public or private, to manifest his beliefs in worship, observance, teaching, and practice. ECOSOC, Sixth Session, Supp. 1, E/600 (1948).

for 'conscience, belief, and opinion'[27] but also included protection for 'religion or any other belief as dictated by his conscience'[28] or 'freedom of religion, conscience, and belief'.[29] This is quite significant since it demonstrates a specific intent by the drafters to protect other beliefs, including conscientious beliefs.

During the drafting process, some states were hesitant to adopt such a broad approach to the right to freedom of religion. These states argued for a more specific right focusing exclusively on protection for formal religious beliefs.[30] The argument was discredited by other states that desired a more unified right incorporating 'religion, conscience, and thought'. The intention was to interpret the latter phrase as providing protection for atheists and non-religious individuals. Some state representatives even contended that the protection for 'beliefs' should include cultural, scientific, and political beliefs and not solely religious or philosophical tenets.[31]

More tellingly, the final provision, for freedom of 'thought, conscience, and religion', derived from proposals to incorporate general notions broader then religion.[32] Acting pursuant to an earlier New Zealand proposal in the GA, the protection of religion was combined with that of conscience and thought to create a more unified right.[33] The proposals to limit Article 18 to freedom of religion only, at the exclusion of other beliefs, were rejected because they would have denied protection for non-religious believers.

Additionally, the term 'belief' was positioned alongside 'religion' to incorporate the manifestation of conceptions other than religion.[34] Reflecting this development, the French delegate altered the French translation of 'belief' from 'croyance', which has religious overtones, to

---

[27] E/CN.4/21 Annex D (1947).
[28] E/CN.4/21 Annex F (1947) a UK proposal which had initially provided for 'free thought and conscience' with the manifestation centring on worship and 'the manifestation of differing convictions'.
[29] E/CN.4/37 (1947) US proposal which eventually formed the basis for future discussion.
[30] E/CN.4/SR.60 (1948) where UK and Peru argued for exclusive protection of freedom of religion; E/CN.4/99 (1948) (similar argument by UK and India). This argument was echoed in the General Assembly as well. See A/C.3/218 (Lebanon's proposal for a separate provision for religion). See also Malik (1950).
[31] E/CN.4/SR.60 (1948).
[32] E/CN.4/85 (1948). Note as well Mexico's proposal in the GA to include manifestation of beliefs as well as religion. E/CN.4/SR.60 (1948).
[33] See E/CN.4/85 (1948); E/CN.4/82/Add.8 and 12 (1948).
[34] E/CN.4/85 (1948) based on the suggestion of Mexico, discussed *supra*.

'conviction', which reflects a more secular approach towards belief. As noted by Belgium:

> it would be unnecessary to proclaim that freedom [of conscience] if it were never to be given an outward expression; if it were intended, so to speak, only for the use of the inner man. It was necessary however to stress the external manifestation of creeds by which expression was given to beliefs.[35]

Hence, when considering the right to freedom of conscience under the UDHR, it is apparent that the drafters intended to provide for the manifestation of a conscientious belief as well. Indeed the recognition of the importance of a conscientious belief was the general reason for rejecting drafts that solely focused on the right to religion as being inadequate in scope.[36] This was to prove to be an important step since the phrase 'religion or belief' has become a summary form for describing manifestation of both a conscientious and religious belief in subsequent human rights documents.

Aside for the distinction between religious and conscientious beliefs, the drafters also focused on differentiating conscience and thought. The CHR's Drafting Committee incorporated freedom of thought into the right of freedom of religion and conscience specifically to codify thought and conscience as a unit. The proposed draft stated:

> Individual freedom of thought and conscience, to hold or change beliefs, is an absolute and sacred right.[37]

While this language is not evident in the final version of the UDHR, the drafters combined thought and conscience since thought was understood as a precursor to conscience by serving as a basis for developing a conscientious belief.[38] Nonetheless, unlike a religious or conscientious belief, the protection for thought in this article was limited to

---

[35] GA, Third Committee, Third Session, meeting 127 (1948) at 395. *See also* A/C.3/SR 127-128 at 398 where China notes that 'freedom of belief was an integral part of freedom of thought and conscience'.
[36] *See e.g.* A/C.3/SR 127-128 at 393-394.
[37] E/CN.4/21 Annex F (1947).
[38] E/CN.4/85 (1948).

the individual's 'inner freedom'[39] because this article did not provide for manifestation of all forms of thought. As stated by France:

> The opposite of inner freedom of thought was the outward obligation to profess a belief, which was not held. Freedom of thought thus required to be formally protected in view of the fact that it was possible to attack it indirectly.[40]

The term 'thought' therefore was replaced with 'opinion' in the right to freedom of expression provision to avoid an overlap of protection.[41] The indication is that 'thought' in the article upholding the right to freedom of conscience is an internal notion, whereas the thought or opinion in the article regarding the right to freedom of expression is an external action.[42]

These approaches to thought and conscience and the manifestation of a conscientious belief are important for the development of the right to freedom of conscience. Despite the difficulties surrounding the right to change a belief [43] and the debates regarding the dangers of proselytising as a practice that should be limited,[44] the *travaux preparatoires* of the UDHR indicate that a conscientious belief attained the status of a protected international human right on a par with a religious belief.

The UDHR also contains limitations to the right to freedom of conscience that address some of the fears raised by the UDHR drafters regarding an unfettered right to manifest a belief. Egypt initially had proposed that the right to freedom of conscience be subject to 'public order' as early as the Third Session of the CHR. Lebanon however refuted the suggestion, noting that the aim in drafting the article was to provide for a right above the law.[45] Recognising the necessity for some form of general limitation to the exercise of human rights, the UDHR drafters imposed a general limitation clause in Article 29. The Article provides that:

---

[39] E/CN.4/SR.60 (1948) Representatives of USSR and France noting the distinction from free expression, which is a manifested, external, opinion and therefore subject to public order limitations.

[40] E/CN.4/SR.60 (1948) at 10.

[41] E/CN.4/113 (1948) now Article 19, then Article 18.

[42] *But cf.* Evans, M. (1997;189-190) who contends that the some of drafters did not accept this commingling of religion with thought and conscience.

[43] *See e.g.* Evans, M. (1997;188); Tahzib (1991;68).

[44] Tahzib (1991;70); Evans, M. (1997;185-187) noting the USSR's attempt to limit practices contrary to the public morality and Sweden's focus on limiting proselytising that interferes with the rights of another.

[45] E/CN.4/SR.60 (1948). *See also* Scheinen (1995;266) noting that Article 29 was viewed as imposing a general form of limitation on the right; Humphrey (1985) making the same point.

> 1. Everyone has duties to the community in which alone the free and full development of his personality is possible.
> 2. In the exercise of his rights and freedoms, everyone shall be subject only to such limitations as are determined by law solely for the purpose of securing due recognition and respect for the rights and freedom of others and of meeting the just requirements of morality, public order and the general welfare in a democratic society.
> 3. These rights and freedoms may in no case be exercised contrary to the purposes and principles of the United Nations.

Article 29 of the UDHR is understood as imposing a blanket limitation on the UDHR rights.[46] Because the limitation terms stated in Article 29(2)[47] are echoed in later human rights documents that pertain to the right to freedom of conscience,[48] Article 29 merits further examination.

While initial UDHR drafts at the First Session of the CHR's Drafting Committee centred on the individual's duty to the state, society, the community, and the UN,[49] the actual limitations stated therein related mainly to abusing the rights of other individuals.[50] At the Third Session of the CHR, adherence to the requirements of morality, public order and the general welfare of a democratic society were adopted.[51]

One of the chief problems in drafting Article 29 related to the phrase 'public order', a phrase that has significance for the right to conscience. The French text required the general phrase 'public order' since a literal translation of the phrase is 'ordre public', which generally implies notions of morality and public order.[52] The English version incorporated these latter ideas through the phrase 'general welfare', with the English meaning of 'public order' implying a wider latitude of action with broad political

---

[46] Opsahl (1992;449).
[47] Article 29(1) refers to the notion of duties of the individual, which is treated as a theoretical counterbalance to rights. Daes (1990). Article 29(3) is a somewhat self-serving provision (to use Opsahl's (1992) terms) which disallows the rights to be used in a manner contrary to the 'purposes and principles of UN'. Since these paragraphs do not relate to limitations per se, they will not be the centre of analysis.
[48] Kiss (1981;290) (noting the development of the ICCPR's limitation clauses from the UDHR).
[49] See generally Daes (1990;17-18) referring to the initial drafts of the Article.
[50] See various proposals in E/CN.4/21 (1947) that resulted from the Drafting Committee's 1st Session.
[51] E/CN.4/82 (1948). See also Daes (1990;72).
[52] Spain had a similar problem with 'orden publico'. The term implied public policy and the general existence of the state. Verdoodt (1963;145).

overtones.[53] While the terms 'morality' and 'public order' presented adequate limitations, to solely base the limitation on the 'general welfare' of a democratic society was deemed too narrow as it depended on one's approach towards the implications of a democratic society. Retaining all the terms however upheld interpretations according to both the French and the English versions.[54] Furthermore, with the addition of the phrase 'prescribed by law solely for the purpose of securing...', it was believed that limitations were thereby not subject to arbitrary measures since, by definition, a democratic society is not subject to summary administrative actions.[55]

The UDHR contains an additional limitation requiring an individual to consider the 'general welfare in a democratic society'. Originally, it was drafted as the welfare of the 'democratic state' which implied a more functional characteristic to the term,[56] but the language was altered to allow for a broader understanding of democracy.[57] 'General welfare' also can serve to defuse instances of conflicts of rights, such as between the individual and society.[58] This can prove to be an imperative limitation for a conscientious belief, particularly as a minority group belief can conflict with the beliefs of other individuals.

Note that while the final draft of the UDHR was not subject to any negative votes in the GA, the right to change one's religion posed a particular problem for some states[59] leading to the abstention of some states from the final vote. This issue was to prove to be an obstacle in later documents relating to the right to freedom of religion and conscience.

---

[53] Daes (1990;72) referring to E/CN.4/SR.74 (1948).
[54] GA Third Committee, Third Session, meetings 153-155 (1948). *See also* Opsahl (1992;451-452) noting that other proposed limitations, centring on national sovereignty, solidarity, security, loyalty or good faith, were rejected since the delegates felt that they were covered by the present terms of the Article.
[55] GA Third Committee, Third Session, meeting 154 (1948). Opsahl (1992;460) notes that although the limitation is pursuant to the law of the state which is broader than a limitation granted by an international document, it is narrowed as a result of the democratic society requirement.
[56] *See* E/CN.4/SR.51 (1947) (USSR interpreting the phrase as the right of all to participate in the governmental process and gain accessibility to elected officials).
[57] E/CN.4/SR.50 (1947). *See also* Daes (1990;72) (noting that the term centres on the administrative officials of the state as being subject to the power of its peoples who elected them); Verdoodt (1963;146) (drafters had in mind democratic virtues which are greater than the characteristics of a particular state, such that governmental power is restrained).
[58] Verdoodt (1963;146).
[59] GA Third Committee, L.876.

ICCPR, Article 18 [60]

Following completion of the UDHR in 1948, the CHR turned to drafting an international covenant at its next session. The right to freedom of conscience is codified in ICCPR Article 18 and states:

> 1. Everyone shall have the right to freedom of thought conscience and religion. This right shall include freedom to have or to adopt a religion or belief of his choice, and freedom, either individually or in community with others and in public or private, to manifest his religion or belief in worship, observance, practice and teaching.
> 2. No one shall be subject to coercion which would impair his freedom to have or to adopt a religion or belief of his choice.
> 3. Freedom to manifest one's religion or belief may be subject only to such limitations as are prescribed by law and are necessary to protect public safety order health or morals or the fundamental rights and freedoms of others.
> 4. The State Parties to the present Covenant undertake to have respect for the liberty of parents and, when applicable, legal guardians to ensure the religious and moral education of their children in conformity with their own convictions.[61]

Many of the issues regarding the right to freedom of conscience discussed by the UDHR drafters were also raised during the drafting of the ICCPR. Along with the influence of the UDHR on the drafting process, the ICCPR drafters also relied upon a report from the Sub-Committee on Prevention of Discrimination and Protection of Minorities[62] drafted by A. Krishnaswami. The report was completed in 1960,[63] at around the same time that the GA Third Committee began to focus on Article 18 of the ICCPR.[64]

---

[60] 999 UNTS 171.

[61] The Article, as a whole, was adopted in both the Third Committee and the GA by a unanimous vote.

[62] Following a 1954 preliminary report on the matter by a US rapporteur. E/CN.4/Sub.2/711 (1954).

[63] *Study of Discrimination in the Matter of Religious Rights and Practices* E/CN.4/Sub.2/200/Rev.1 (1960).

[64] Indeed, the Third Committee's Secretariat specifically referred to the Krishnaswami study as a drafting tool. GA Third Committee, Fifteenth Session, meeting 1027 (1960). *See also* Partsch (1981;211) (delegates relied on the study as a means of defining belief in the broad sense, and as including beliefs held by atheists, agnostics, free thinkers, and rationalists).

The focus of discussion for the ICCPR centred on understanding what is meant by thought, conscience, religion, and belief, the implications of providing for a change to one's religion,[65] and the nature of the limitations.[66] While similar in approach and general scope to UDHR Article 18, the ICCPR incorporated some obvious differences. Most notably, ICCPR Article 18 omits any specific reference to the right to change one's religion and amplifies notions relating to thought and conscience.

The ICCPR drafters intended to distinguish conscience from religion by equating conscience with generally accepted beliefs.[67] The drafters were hesitant to define the terms for fear of creating a limited, subjective, notion of the right, which might unduly confine the concepts being protected without allowing for development of the right in the future.[68]

Similar to the assertions made while drafting the UDHR, however, some delegates desired to construe the right solely within a religious context, to the exclusion of any other form of belief. The UK delegate, for

---

Note that while the study assisted the ICCPR Third Committee drafters, it was passed to the CHR with the view towards drafting a particular covenant against religious discrimination based on the 16 principles that Krishnaswami had proposed in his report. Furthermore, the Krishnaswami study also provided impetus for UNESCO's drafting of the 1960 *Convention against Discrimination in Education* (which protects the rights of religious groups in Article 5(1)(a)) and the ILO's 1960 *Convention No. 111 Concerning Discrimination in Respect of Employment and Occupation* (Article 1 of which prohibits religious and political opinion discrimination). Dickson (1995;334 and 337-338). See also 1959 *Convention on the Reduction of Statelessness and Discrimination* that disallows deprivation of a person's nationality based on religion or political opinion. These documents do not provide for protection of belief or conscience in a manner similar to UDHR or ICCPR but centre solely on freedom of religion.

[65] See e.g. E/CN.4/SR.116 (1949) where the Commission of Churches, a Non-Governmental Organisation, identified this right, along with religious education, as being central to the freedom.

[66] See e.g. E/CN.4/SR.117 (1949) where France notes that the limitations are to apply solely to the manifestation of a religion or belief but not to inner convictions.

[67] E/CN.4/SR.116 (1949) at 3-4.

[68] Hence, when Nigeria desired to define religion in a manner that protected the general populace against sects and unduly harsh proselytising, Uruguay responded that the concepts are too difficult to actually label in any structured manner. See also GA Third Committee, Fifteenth Session, meeting 1024 (1960), Liberia (defining the right's concepts as subjective and dangerous); GA Third Committee, Fifteenth Session, meeting 1026 (1960) (France referring to Krishnaswami (1960;fn.8) who did not define religion or belief in any specific manner so as to avoid the possibility of future limitations and allow for further development of the right pursuant to changes in the future). See also GA Third Committee, Fifteenth Session, meetings 1021-1027 (1960) at 17.

example, interpreted manifestation as not including conscience because a conscientious belief is a subjective internal notion that is too intimate to even consider.[69] The delegate from El Salvador similarly reasoned that conscience only addresses man's spiritual loneliness.[70] The Saudi Arabian delegate defined conscience as the moral and intuitive ability to discern right from wrong and good from evil.[71] These definitions of conscience served to diminish the capacity for the manifestation of a conscientious belief. The delegate from Spain went even further by limiting the ability to manifest only theistic beliefs, excluding atheists or those with indifferent opinions.[72] The Venezuelan delegate acknowledged that although the right might imply the ability to not maintain any religious belief, it does not therefore mean that the right automatically provides for manifestation of atheistic beliefs or other general forms of beliefs.[73]

By contrast, other state delegates latched on to the importance of safeguarding the views of non-religious believers by comprehending a conscientious belief as an essential counterbalance to religion. This counterbalance was deemed imperative upon considering the rights of non-religious believers such that granting the ability to manifest a general conscientious belief was essential to the freedom being granted.[74] The delegate from Liberia amplified this point by noting that the role of a conscientious belief is greater than merely counterbalancing religious oppression since the belief also merits manifestation, as indicated by the wide variety of manifestations intimated in the phrase 'religion and belief'. The delegate from Ceylon referred to the broad nature of the article, especially for secular and non-religious societies, and reasoned that upholding the internal protection of conscience will, by default, uphold the external manifestation as well.[75]

Despite the different approaches aired by the states throughout the drafting process regarding the meaning of the terms and the scope of the right, inclusion of the term 'belief' illustrates a right to manifest non-religious or secular beliefs such as atheism and rationalism.[76] While the term 'belief' is not defined in any exact manner, the drafters appear to have

---

[69] GA Third Committee, Fifteenth Session, meeting 1021 (1960).
[70] GA Third Committee, Fifteenth Session, meeting 1024 (1960).
[71] GA Third Committee, Fifteenth Session, meeting 1021 (1960).
[72] GA Third Committee, Fifteenth Session, meeting 1026 (1960).
[73] GA Third Committee, Fifteenth Session, meeting 1021 (1960).
[74] GA Third Committee, Fifteenth Session, meeting 1024 (1960).
[75] GA Third Committee, Fifteenth Session, meeting 1022 (1960).
[76] GA Third Committee, Fifteenth Session, A/4625, Agenda Item 34 (1960). *But see* Evans, M. (1997;203-204) noting that the lack of any uniform understanding of the term tends to demonstrate a fundamental disagreement among the drafters.

distinguished the protection of secular thoughts from other forms of conscientious belief in a manner similar to the UDHR. For example, the USSR delegate noted, regarding the draft that included a definition of belief as incorporating atheism, that because atheism centres on natural and historical facts and not a supernatural being, it was clear that the term 'belief' was not referring to religious oriented beliefs.[77] 'Beliefs' address a different range and form of ideals than religion, as demonstrated by Pakistan's distinction between 'religion' which centres on a belief in a superhuman power and 'belief' which refers to general forms of belief, such as atheism.[78]

The approach to belief as incorporating notions outside a religious context was further endorsed by the delegate from Argentina[79] whose state delegate broadly defined beliefs as including creeds, philosophical conceptions of man and the meaning of life, and those beliefs which influence all aspects of an individual's existence.[80] The Argentinean delegate contrasted this approach to belief in religion, which relates to beliefs that are more fundamental.[81] The delegate from Cyprus also defined belief in the widest sense as incorporating every kind of faith and belief,[82] while the delegate from Ceylon viewed belief as incorporating general philosophical beliefs as well.[83] In the final report of the Third Committee to the GA, it was noted that although it is advisable not to define the terms, 'belief' includes non-religious and secular beliefs.[84]

Upon recognising that non-religious believers were worthy of protection in the same manner as religious believers, the drafters further had to provide for the manifestation of such beliefs.[85] The delegate from Brazil noted that it is impossible to really safeguard the freedom of conscience without providing for an external manifestation of the right.[86] The delegate from the Philippines also stated that once you acknowledge the right not to maintain a religion, the right to manifestation must incorporate a conscientious belief in order to protect non-believers as

---

[77] GA Third Committee, Fifteenth Session, meeting 1025 (1960).
[78] GA Third Committee, Fifteenth Session, meeting 1024 (1960).
[79] GA Third Committee, Fifteenth Session, meeting 1025 (1960).
[80] Argentina noted that the right does not protect negative beliefs, defined as those that harm another.
[81] GA Third Committee, Fifteenth Session, meeting 1025 (1960).
[82] GA Third Committee, Fifteenth Session, meeting 1025 (1960).
[83] GA Third Committee, Fifteenth Session, meeting 1026 (1960).
[84] GA Third Committee, Fifteenth Session, A/4625, Agenda Item 34 (1960).
[85] GA Third Committee, Fifteenth Session, meeting 1021 (1960) Philippines responding to remarks of UK who proposed to limit right to religious protection only.
[86] GA Third Committee, Fifteenth Session, meeting 1023 (1960).

well.[87] Consequently, similar to the interpretation accorded to the UDHR, the ICCPR provides for the manifestation of both a religious and a conscientious belief. While there was some initial doubt expressed regarding the scope of the article, it is apparent by the term 'belief' that the drafters intended to include a provision for the manifestation of a conscientious belief.[88]

Expanding on the protection accorded in the UDHR, the drafters included Article 18(2), a paragraph prohibiting coercion. 'Coercion' was defined as relating to an individual's internal mind whereby undue pressure and improper inducement, including non-physical coercion,[89] are used to adopt a different religion or belief.[90] For example, at the General Assembly's Tenth Session in 1955, the Secretary General noted that although the CHR had trouble distinguishing between thought and belief in the right to freedom of conscience, and thought and opinion in the right to freedom of expression, opinion and thought either complement one another, with free expression serving as a means of manifesting one's thought, or freedom of expression is a superfluous right. As for the internal aspect of the right to freedom of conscience which also includes thought, the Secretary General referred to it as an individual's inner thought and moral consciousness which could not be subject to restrictions.[91]

Hence, Article 18 is providing specific protection for the internal aspect of thought and conscience.[92] The right to manifest a belief however is limited to religious or conscientious beliefs, particularly since thought will manifest as an expression. Furthermore, 'coercion' involved not only physical pressure, such as forced conversion,[93] but also pressure which focused on one's internal thoughts, such as refusal to grant a state benefit on the basis of one's identification with a religion or belief.[94]

---

[87] GA Third Committee, Fifteenth Session, meeting 1021 (1960).
[88] Evans, M. (1997;206-207) assert that the purpose of the article is to tolerate different beliefs in a liberal society rather than provide a basis for the freedom of religion or belief.
[89] GA Third Committee, Fifteenth Session, meeting 1021 and 1022 (1960). *See also* GA Third Committee, Fifteenth Session, A/4625, Agenda Item 34 (1960) at 18; Nowak (1993;318) (noting that this is the reason why the term 'impair' rather than 'deprive' was used).
[90] GA Third Committee, Fifteenth Session, meeting 1023 and 1024 (1960).
[91] GA Third Committee, Tenth Session, A/2929, Agenda Item 28 (1955) at 136.
[92] E/CN.4/SR.116 (1949).
[93] Cumper (1995;370).
[94] *Contra* Cumper (1995;370-371) who limits the term to physical coercion as inferred from the HRC's General Comment to Article 18 that did not specifically refer to psychological pressure and due to the greater need to eliminate physical pressure.

The addition of Article 18(2) also derived from the desire of various states to emphasise the right to change one's belief, while balancing such a right against undue coercion by external forces, such as zealous missionaries.[95] The term 'coercion' does not prevent a third party from using moral or intellectual persuasion to appeal to an individual's internal spiritual authority.[96] Indeed, an initial proposal centred on specific protection for proselytising religious groups. While the proposal was not added to the final draft, the first paragraph of Article 18 does provide for the freedom 'either individually or in a community with others', which implies a protection for such groups.[97]

Nonetheless, the ICCPR drafters removed the specific right to change one's religion or belief.[98] Various state delegates noted the conflicts with their internal laws if the right provided for a change by further highlighting the problem of missionaries and the possibility of fraudulent changes of religion.[99] Both the delegates from Egypt and Saudi Arabia objected to the right to change a belief, reasoning that it supported improper missionary work and caused greater long-term damage to society.[100] There was no need for a specific provision regarding change, argued the Saudi Arabian delegate, by virtue of the provision for freedom of religion that implies a right to change one's religion as well.[101] If freedom really was the issue, then changing a conscientious belief or a conscious thought also should be included in the provision.[102]

The response to these assertions, summarised by the delegate from The Netherlands, was that it is difficult for any religion to recognise

---

[95] GA Third Committee, Tenth Session, A/2929, Agenda Item 28 (1955) referring to the CHR's 5th Session.
[96] E/CN.4/SR.319 (1955).
[97] GA Third Committee, Tenth Session, A/2929, Agenda Item 28 (1955) The Secretary General pointed out the lack of any specific protection for minority religious groups due to the potential conflict which could result with other religions.
[98] GA, Third Committee, Fifteenth Session, meetings 1021-1028 (1960).
[99] E/CN.4/SR.161 (1950). A memo drafted by the Secretary General prior to the CHR's next session highlighted this problem as troubling many states which disallow one to change religions. E/CN.4/528 (1951) (the Secretary General also distinguished between religion and belief as two distinct concepts).
[100] GA Third Committee, Fifth Session, meetings 288 (1950). Saudi Arabia echoed this argument at the next GA Third Committee meeting (GA, Third Committee, Sixth Session, meeting. 367 (1951)).
[101] E/CN.4/SR.319 (1952). *See also* E/CN.4/528 (1951) Memo by Secretary General who outlined Saudi Arabia's and Egypt's position on this matter.
[102] GA Third Committee, Fifteenth Session, meeting 1021 (1960).

apostasy, however that is the very nature of the freedom being upheld.[103] Another argument was that the ability to change related to the individual's capabilities and it was not a right granted to groups, such as missionaries.[104] In support of this contention was the use of the term 'coercion' at the beginning of the paragraph that implied not only a deprivation of an individual's freedom, but also applied to impairing one's freedom via improper inducements and indirect pressure.[105]

The CHR attempted to address this problem of changing one's religion by adding in the words 'to maintain or' prior to 'change' one's religion. While the alteration recognised a state's capacity to uphold a religious social construct, it did not alleviate the problem for states disallowing apostasy. The issue of providing for change of belief persisted until the end of the General Assembly's Fifteenth Session when initially the words 'to have a religion or belief of one's choice' was proposed and rejected as being too static, followed by the present language which upholds one 'to adopt' a religion or belief. As a result, it would seem that although the right to change one's belief is not as clearly provided for in the ICCPR, an individual may still assert the right to change a belief since it is an exercise of the freedom provided by the right.[106]

The ICCPR drafters also had proposed more specific recommendations regarding the right to freedom of conscience, some of which were rejected.[107] The drafters desired to avoid any specific protections within the right, especially when oriented towards a religious belief.[108] Consequently, the drafters rejected a paragraph regarding the right to conscientious objection to the military.[109]

---

[103] GA Third Committee, Fifth Session, meetings 306 (1950). *See also* GA Third Committee, Fifteenth Session, meeting 1021 (1960).
[104] GA Third Committee, Fifteenth Session, A/4625, Agenda Item 34 (1960).
[105] GA Third Committee, Fifteenth Session, A/4625, Agenda Item 18 (1960).
[106] GA Third Committee, Fifteenth Session, A/4625, Agenda Item 18 (1960). *See also* GA Third Committee, Fifteenth Session, meeting 1027 (1960) where this compromise was initially proposed by the UK.
Note that the HRC's General Comment to Article 18 interprets the phrase in paragraph 5 as 'the right to replace one's current religion or belief' and commentators have upheld the right to change one's religion or belief under the terms of the ICCPR. Clark (1978); Partsch (1981;211); Humphrey (1985;179); Nowak (1993;316); Edge (1996); Walkate (1983).
[107] *See also* earlier drafts of the UDHR that allowed for conscientious objection to acts against one's beliefs as dictated by one's conscience. E/CN.4/82/add.12(1948); E/CN.4/NGO/1 (submission by NGO to Secretary General requesting inclusion of a right to military conscientious objection).
[108] E/CN.4/SR.161.
[109] *See also* discussion *infra* at Chapter Six.

Despite this underlying policy regarding specific provisions within the right, Greece successfully inserted a provision protecting the education of children in conformity with a parents' convictions.[110] Although the proposal was previously rejected by the CHR,[111] Greece noted that Article 18(4) is based on Article 13(3) of the International Covenant on Economic, Social, and Cultural Rights[112] which did not intend to grant individuals the right to control state education or require a state to provide a particular form of education.[113] Such an approach was deemed to violate the separation of church and state.[114] Rather, the goal in drafting the provision, as originally noted in the CHR,[115] was to ensure that one's faith and customs are preserved for future generations.[116]

The term 'convictions' was used in Article 18(4) to protect individuals other than religious believers.[117] As pointed out by Canada, for purposes of paragraph 4, moral education is equivalent to religious

---

[110] E/CN.4/SR.94 and 103-104 (1949). A similar provision is found in Article 26(3) of the UDHR, which was proposed at the 3rd Session of the GA's Third Committee. See Arjarvi (1995;410) See also the 1960 UNESCO Convention Against Discrimination in Education at Article 5(1)(b) that protects education of one's children 'in conformity with their convictions'. This provision has been defined in a negative manner and not as a right to deny education to a child. Arjarvi (1995;415).

[111] Lebanon had noted a desire for a paragraph on the right to educate one's child in accordance with one's belief. See also E/CN.4/SR.160 (1950) where an NGO, the Agudas Israel World Organisation, desired a similar paragraph as a means of protecting Jewish World War II orphans who might not receive a religious education when sheltered by international charity organisations.

[112] GA Third Committee, Fifteenth Session, A/4625, Agenda Item 34 (1960); GA Third Committee, Fifteenth Session, meeting 1022 (1960). Although viewed as being somewhat repetitive between the ICCPR and ICESCR, the paragraph was included in case a state ratified only one of the two conventions. GA Third Committee, Fifteenth Session, meeting 1023 and 1027 (1960).

[113] E/CN.4/SR.285-291 (regarding the drafting of ICESCR Article 13(3)). Similarly, the ECHR, which codified the education right in the First Optional Protocol, Article 2 (as a means of avoiding any particular focus on a specific right in Article 9), also does not impose a duty on the State despite the more binding terms 'to ensure' education., Collected Edition of Travaux Preparatoires VIII (1975) at 24.

[114] E/CN.4/SR.161 (1950). The original proposal was opposed by the US, UK, and Chile because the proposal on education violated the desired separation of Church and State and was felt to be too specific for a general human rights document. See also E/CN.4/528 (1951).

[115] E/CN.4/SR.161(1950).

[116] GA Third Committee, Fifteenth Session, A/4625, Agenda Item 34 (1960) at 19.

[117] Similarly, the ECHR right is extended to 'religious and philosophical convictions'. Collected Edition of Travaux Preparatoires Vol. VIII (1978;156) (right includes all forms of beliefs) and at 172 (religious convictions incorporate all aspects of beliefs).

education.[118] This further indicates the broad scope of the article as including beliefs other than formal religious beliefs.

Concerning the limitations provided for in Article 18(3), a uniform limitation was initially proposed for ICCPR Articles 18-21 but no further action was taken towards that end.[119] Nonetheless, the interpretation given to the limitation phrases of the Article are quite similar to the other principal treaties that codify the right to freedom of conscience and consequently they maintain a similar meaning.[120]

The limitations in Article 18 of the ICCPR play an important part in understanding the scope of the right to freedom of conscience and assist to clarify what the right desires to uphold. As noted by the Russian delegate, if no limitations are imposed, a manifested belief could lead to disastrous consequences, such as committing murder on religious grounds.[121] The *travaux preparatoires* however clearly state that the limitations apply to external manifestations of a religion or belief and not to the internal protections of the right.[122]

The limitations of ICCPR Article 18(3) are narrower than the limitations found in the other articles of the ICCPR, possibly due to the high value accorded to the right.[123] The key differences between the limitations of Article 18 and other limitations in the ICCPR are the

---

[118] GA Third Committee, Fifteenth Session, meeting 1024 (1960). Similar to Canada's interpretation, Article 13(3) of the ICESCR desired to protect individuals who adhered to their general moral and spiritual values by ensuring that those values are passed on to their children. *See* E/CN.4/SR.285-291.

[119] GA Third Committee, Tenth Session, A/2929, Agenda Item 28 (1955) . *See also* E/CN.4/528 (1951) Memo of the Secretary General calling for uniform limitations throughout the Treaty.

[120] Documents and treaties drafted after the ICCPR have generally adopted the language and structure of the ICCPR's limitations. *See e.g. Convention on the Rights of the Child*, Article 14(3); *Declaration of Human Rights for Individuals not Nationals of the Country in which they Live*, Article 5(e) (despite initial, broader, allowance for limitations, the drafters altered the language to conform to the narrow limits as established by the ICCPR).

[121] E/CN.4/SR.116 (1949).

[122] E/CN.4/SR.117 (1949) (as noted by the CHR); GA Third Committee, Fifteenth Session, meeting 1022 (1960). *See also* Nowak (1993;324); Kiss (1981); Cumper (1995;373) (reasoning that *forum internum* will generally not encroach upon the rights of others); Partsch (1981;212).

[123] *See* Partsch (1981;212). Nowak (1993;326) however notes that broader limitations found in other articles can apply to Article 18 if the manifestation of a religion or belief infringes such rights.

prohibition of a derogation on the grounds of a public emergency,[124] the absence of a limitation on national security grounds because the term was deemed too imprecise to apply to the right to conscience,[125] and no limitation on the basis of the 'general welfare in a democratic society'.

The phrase 'prescribed by law' replaced the original version's term 'pursuant to law' since the latter was viewed as imposing a narrower, weaker, duty on a legislature imposing a limitation.[126] A legislature must now draft a formal and adequately constructed law[127] that provides sufficient precision in the regulation. The second requirement of 'necessity' refers to the need for proportionality between the limitation and the danger being addressed,[128] such that the limitation must be essential and inevitable.[129]

Similar to the UDHR, the phrase 'public order' posed a particular problem due to translation difficulties and overlapping meaning, particularly with public safety.[130] As discussed at the CHR's Eighth Session, the French term, 'ordre public', is closer to a meaning of public policy,[131] whereas the English term 'public order' refers to the absence of

---

[124] ICCPR Article 4(2) disallows a derogation from Article 18 in case of a public emergency. The public emergency derogation to the right to conscience is allowed in the ECHR.

[125] GA Third Committee, Tenth Session, A/2929, Agenda Item 28 (1955). *Cf.* ICCPR Articles 19-22 where the limitation is found.
Kiss (1981;296) notes that while 'national security', 'public safety', and 'public order' are at times used interchangeably, it is safe to conclude that the limitation on grounds of 'national security' was intentionally left out of ICCPR Article 18 (and ECHR Article 9). The HRC supports this conclusion by noting in the General Comment to Article 18, at paragraph 8, that the limitations are to be 'strictly construed' and restrictions are only to be applied for the grounds specified and not on other grounds, such as national security.

[126] E/CN.4/SR.119 (1949).

[127] Cumper (1995;373).

[128] HRC General Comment at paragraph 8, noting that the limitation 'must be applied for those purposes for which they were prescribed and must be directly related and proportionate to the specific need on which they are predicated'. *See also* Nowak (1993;325); Daes (1990;135); 17851/91 *Vogt v. Germany* 21 EHRR 205 (1996).

[129] Kiss (1981;308).

[130] *See e.g.* Kiss (1981;299) noting that because of the broad nature of the term, some drafters of the ICCPR assumed it incorporated public safety as well.

[131] Concerning the Spanish version, Spain defined the term as 'considerations of public order to safeguard the state's integrity and sovereignty'. Argentina noted that it is a body of political, economic or moral principles considered essential for the maintenance of a given social structure. *See* GA, Third Committee, Fourteenth Session, meeting 956 (1959).

public disorder.[132] This latter term had been criticised for its general and ambiguous nature.[133] While the UDHR and ECHR retain the term for both the English and French versions,[134] some commentators have concluded that because ICCPR Article 18(3) does not actually place the term 'public' before 'order',[135] and because in other Articles of the ICCPR, when the limitation 'public order' is imposed the French term 'ordre' public' is placed in parenthesis,[136] that the English approach towards the term as preventing disorder is the operative interpretation.[137]

The phrase 'public safety' also is ambiguous and difficult to interpret.[138] In an attempt to clarify the phrase by stating what it is not, 'public safety' differs from a 'national security' limitation since the focus of public safety is the act being conducted by the individual and the need to prevent disorder.[139] National security on the other hand relates to an external threat to the state.[140] Nonetheless, the problem of overlap remains,

---

[132] E/CN.4/SR.319 (1952). See also E/CN.4/528 (1951) Memo of the Secretary General where a similar point is noted and the broad nature of the English term is criticised; GA, Third Committee, Fourteenth Session, SR.956 (1959).

[133] E/CN.4/32 (1947); E/CN.4/85 (1948) Various NGOs criticised the term on the same grounds, noting that it was the critical limitation of the Article. See E/CN.4/SR.116 (1949); E/CN.4/SR.160 (1950).

[134] But see Kiss (1981;fn.34) who notes that while the English phrase 'public order' is used in the ECHR Article 9(2) and the French version only refers to 'l'ordre', judicial bodies have interpreted the term as 'ordre public'. He refers to 5100/71 Engel v. Netherlands 1 EHRR 647 (1976).

[135] Article 18(3) provides for 'public safety, order, health...'. The AmCHR also avoids the reference to 'public order' by structuring the limitation in a similar manner to the ICCPR.

[136] See e.g. Articles 19, 21, and 22.

[137] Cumper (1995;374); Nowak (1993;327) ('order' to be interpreted in a narrow sense); Partsch (1981;213); Kiss (1981;300-302) outlines the scope of the term 'ordre' public' under French law, pointing out that it is a tool which can also be used to defend an individual's rights, such that the term should be considered within the context in which it is being asserted and be limited to allowing the 'adequate functioning of the public institutions necessary to the collective...'.
Note that while Nowak's approach (of separating the term 'public' from 'order') might clarify the limitation, it also can unintentionally broaden the limitation since the term 'public' is disassociated from the rest of the limitations. Kiss on the other hand allows for consideration of the term within a more 'public' context. See also Verdoodt (1963;145) (when including French version in text, it becomes the operative term).

[138] GA Third Committee, Tenth Session, A/2929, Agenda Item 28 (1955) (noting the ambiguity and lack of clarity surrounding the term). For a similar contention, see also Cumper (1995; fn. 155, referring to CCPR/C/SR.1225); Kiss (1981;298).

[139] Kiss (1981;298); Nowak (1993;326). Cf. Daes (1990;121) noting the imprecise and broad nature of both terms.

[140] Nowak (1993;327).

particularly when a group endangers public safety on political grounds or because of an external threat.[141]

The limitations based on public health and public morals were not discussed in detail in the *travaux preparatoires*. It should be noted that the limitation of public morals for a right such as conscience poses an interesting conundrum, especially since the relative nature of morals prevents a state from singularly relying on this limitation.[142] It is difficult to separate individual from social morals, or even find a universal conception of morals, especially when a conscientious belief derives from an individual moral evaluation which will presumably involve, or be influenced by, considerations of underlying social morals. Both private/individual and public morals are each bound up with the unique social and cultural perspectives of the various individuals within the state.[143] In practice, it has been recognised that the actual scope of the 'public morals' limitation is difficult to define and it is largely left to the states themselves to apply the common (domestic) meaning of the term.[144]

The limitation of 'fundamental rights and freedom of others',[145] refers to a state's basic fundamental constitutional rights as well as international human rights.[146] It is generally interpreted as preventing a person from abusing one's right to harm the human rights of another person.[147]

Concerning the derogation clause of ICCPR Article 4, the drafters recognised that, at certain times, it was necessary to provide for more general human rights derogations in the interest of preserving the state.[148]

---

[141] Cumper (1995;374). Typical examples being the problems facing immigration officials who are wont to admit individuals associated with terrorist or rebel groups.

[142] Verdoodt (1963;139) notes that if a state relies solely on 'public morals', it is increasing the rule of law at the expense of morality and not, as possibly intended, upholding morality.

[143] *See e.g.* Cumper (1995;375).

[144] Kiss (1981;304), referring to the ECHR and 5493/72 *Handyside v. UK* 1 EHRR 737 (1976) (UK authorities can decide what is considered obscene materials, pursuant to limitation in Article 10 of ECHR).

[145] The ECHR and AmCHR do not contain the term 'fundamental'. Commentators have concluded that no legal distinction results from the omission. Cumper (1995;376-377).

[146] Nowak (1993;329); Daes (1990;119-120) noting the relation of human rights to other rights and of individuals to one another, such that an individual requires protection of one's rights not only from the state, but also from one's fellow man. This latter protection/limitation of one's rights is to emanate from the state.

[147] Daes (1990;128-129) refers to UDHR Article 29(3) and Article 30, which, the author notes, requires a narrow interpretation. The ECHR does not narrow the infringement of other's rights to 'fundamental', while the AmCHR does not use the 'fundamental rights' language.

[148] Daes (1990;183-184) referring to times of war or other instances of extraordinary peril and noting that the majority of state's provided for such derogations in their

The purpose of limiting the Article 4 derogation however was specifically to prevent abuses which might arise from such a general derogation clause.[149] Hence while ICCPR Article 4 is limited in scope to particular public emergencies which threaten the existence of the nation and which must be officially proclaimed,[150] the derogation cannot apply to the right to freedom of conscience.[151]

The *travaux preparatoires* of the ICCPR demonstrate the similarities to the UDHR in codifying the right to freedom of conscience, as indicated by the similar phrases used in each document. It is significant that the *travaux preparatoires* to the ICCPR note that the term 'belief' incorporates beliefs other than religious beliefs, such that the right to manifest a belief would include a conscientious belief. While the ICCPR drafters employed a rather broad understanding of the ability to manifest a conscientious belief and an altered approach to the right to change a belief,[152] the ICCPR uniquely provides a clearer understanding of the protection for the internal aspect of the right to freedom of conscience. The prohibition of coercion for example can assist in addressing problems raised by missionaries and other instances where one's exercise of the freedom of religion and belief conflicts with another individual's belief system. Furthermore, the limitations in the ICCPR offer somewhat less of an opportunity for restricting the right to freedom of conscience when compared to other rights in the document.

Regional Treaties

While the UDHR and ICCPR were being drafted, a variety of regional organisations also were working on human rights treaties specific to their regions. The first significant document to emerge was the ECHR.

---

constitutions; UN (1995;45) noting the required seriousness of a threat which threatens the life of a nation.

[149] Daes (1990;184) referring to E/CN.4/170.

[150] *See generally* Daes (1990;191-197).

[151] Because judicial fora do not acknowledge Article 18 as providing the basis for a right to military conscientious objection, the public emergency derogation might still apply to a military conscientious objection claim during a period of war. *See e.g.* Daes (1990;200-201). *Cf.* Nowak (1993;323).

[152] *But see* Report of Rapporteur on the Declaration to Eliminate Intolerance and Discrimination of Religion and Belief, E/CN.4/1997/91 at paragraphs 70-77 noting that the ICCPR provides for the right to change one's religion or belief and concluding that on the basis of the relevant treaties, religious freedom cannot be dissociated from the freedom to change religion.

ECHR, Article 9

The influence of the UDHR on the ECHR drafters is reflected in ECHR Article 9, the article codifying the right to freedom of conscience, which states:

> 1. Everyone has the right to freedom of thought, conscience and religion; this right includes freedom to change his religion or belief and freedom, either alone or in community with others and in public or private, to manifest his religion or belief, in worship, teaching, practice, and observance.
> 2. Freedom to manifest one's religion or beliefs shall be subject only to such limitations as are prescribed by law and are necessary in a democratic society in the interests of public safety for, the protection of public order, health or morals, or for the protection of the rights and freedoms of others.

Although the UDHR served as the chief source for the ECHR, the impetus for drafting the ECHR derived from a desire to create a document that better reflected the political and ideological framework of the European countries.[153] The typical example which demonstrates this point is the interpretation given to the UDHR's Article 29 limitation to a human right on the basis of necessity 'in a democratic society'. The scope of the phrase will vary depending on the underlying concepts of value within the state that can radically differ from one region to another.[154] Furthermore, the European states desired a uniform approach towards human rights. While the UDHR could exemplify the minimum level of international human rights protection,[155] an important goal of the ECHR was to achieve unity, as opposed to the UN's purpose of reflecting a host of different views in a world forum.[156] The fact that the ECHR also provides for judicial enforcement of rights indicates an intention to allow for different interpretations of the rights within the ECHR.

When considering the right to freedom of conscience, the ECHR drafters adhered to the general approach of the UDHR. The seminal Teitegen Report of 1949, which provided a drafting basis for the ECHR, quotes the UDHR in full[157] and relies on the UDHR's interpretations as a

---

[153] Schwelb (1975;510).
[154] Opsahl (1979;30 and 34); Schwelb (1975;109).
[155] Eurigenis (1979;75) noting that the ECHR has actually developed a stricter standard of rights.
[156] Schwelb (1975;510) (noting that the UDHR can still assist to interpret the ECHR).
[157] Collected Edition, Vol. I (1975;168 and 196).

means of understanding the freedom of conscience.[158] That the UDHR served as a blueprint for the right to conscience in the ECHR is evident by the first paragraph of Article 9 that duplicated, word for word, UDHR Article 18.[159]

Although the ECHR does not have a sub-section similar to Article 18(2) of the ICCPR, the 1949 Teitegen Report notes that the internal protection of Article 9 is not solely against forced confessions but to prevent 'abominable methods of police inquiry or judicial process which robs the suspected or accused person of control of his intellectual facilities and of his conscience'.

The essential difference from the UDHR is that the ECHR provides for limitations within each article. The limitations to the right to conscience are codified in Article 9(2) in response to states who desired to limit the scope and application of the right pursuant to their domestic order.[160] The ECHR retains the proviso 'necessary in a democratic society',[161] with 'democracy' being interpreted pursuant to the desired framework of the state's institutions.[162]

Concerning 'public order', the ECHR has interpreted the phrase in a similar manner to the ICCPR by upholding a dual understanding of the

---

[158] The Teitegen Report is quoted in Vol. I of the Collected Edition (1975).
[159] Evans, M. (1997;267) notes the ongoing debate between states that desired merely to enumerate the right as opposed to states that desired to define the right as well. Yet in each version, the right was based on Article 18 of the UDHR.
[160] Evans, M. (1997 ;268-269).
[161] Kiss (1981;fn.67) is ambiguous as to the significance of the omission in Article 18. He notes that it is either a mere oversight because of haphazard drafting, or reflects the drafter's treatment of the rights within the articles as 'sacrosanct'.
[162] Volume V of the *Collected Edition of Travaux Preparatoires* (1975;292). See also Kiss (1981;307). Hence the ECHR judiciary bodies have upheld various administrative decisions which have imposed limitations to the right based on protecting rights within a 'democratic society'. See e.g. 6886/75 *X v. UK* 5 D&R 100 (1976); 25522/94 *Negotiate Now v. UK* 19 EHRR CD93 (1995); 20490/92 *Ikson v. UK* 18 EHRR CD41 (1994) (pressing social needs, pursuant to interpretation of state, where state decision is proportionate to legitimate aims and are relevant and sufficient).

term.[163] Both methods of interpretation are referred to in the HRC[164] and ECHR judiciary bodies,[165] when appropriate.

Unlike the ICCPR, the ECHR provides for derogation[166] to the right to conscience in times of public emergency.[167] The derogation has however been applied in the ECHR in quite a narrow manner and with specific restrictions.[168] The public emergency exception has been defined as affecting the composition of the entire nation as a whole and not just a particular group therein. While a certain margin of appreciation is left to the state when applying the derogation, the ECHR judiciary bodies retain the power to evaluate and review the determination following the state's declaration of emergency.[169] Hence, the derogation differs[170] from a 'public order' limitation, whose purpose is to prevent public disorder or uphold public policy.

An additional provision relating to the right to conscience that caused much debate was the right of a parent to choose a child's education, as codified in Article 2 of the First Protocol. The controversy surrounded the relationship between the state and the right of the parent. What is significant about this development is that the State is to respect a parent's right to ensure education in conformity with their own religious and philosophical convictions. While some states were dubious of such general language since philosophical convictions could refer to any belief,[171] the

---

[163] Humphrey (1985;181). ECHR case law generally considers the interpretation within the context of prison rights cases, where the prison's decisions to override a particular individual's beliefs are upheld on the basis of public order. Cumper (1995;375). *Cf.* HRC General Comment at paragraph 8 noting, in quite general terms, that prisoners should 'continue to enjoy the right to manifest their religion or belief to the fullest extent compatible with the specific nature of the constraint'.

[164] 453/1991 *Aurik v. Netherlands* CCPR/C/52/453/1991 (regulation of surnames considered a matter of public order, implying a public policy approach).

[165] See e.g. 25522/94 *Negotiate Now v. UK* 19 EHRR CD93 (1995); 18748/91 *Manoussakis v Greece* 1996-IV Rep. Judg. & Dec. 1346 where public order was defined as the prevention of disorder.

[166] Humphrey (1986;64-66) (despite a limitation, the duty on the state to uphold the right remains, whereas the more powerful device of derogation temporarily removes the right in deference to a domestic law); Kiss (1981;290).

[167] ECHR, Article 5.

[168] Oraa (1992;43-45). *But see* Hartman (1981;23) noting inconsistent standard applied by judicial bodies of the ECHR.

[169] See e.g. 332/57 *Lawless v. Ireland* 1 EHRR 15 (1961).

[170] Aside for the broader functional parameters of a derogation. *See e.g.* Higgins (1976-77).

[171] See e.g. Volume VIII of the *Collected Edition of Travaux Preparatoires* (1975;108) where the UK representative feared that parents might remove their children from school at the age of 14 on the basis of a specific belief.

majority of states preferred to decrease the state's involvement with education. As a result, many states have placed reservations on this Article by generally upholding the internal education structure within the state.[172]

AmCHR, Article 12[173]

Another significant regional human rights document in which the right to conscience was codified is the AmCHR. The drafters of the AmCHR seemed to maintain a different understanding of the right to conscience, as their principal focus was on codifying the right to freedom of religion. The right is codified in Article 12 and states:

> 1. Everyone has the right to freedom of conscience and of religion. This right includes freedom to maintain or to change one's religion or beliefs, and freedom to profess or disseminate one's religion or beliefs, either individually or together with others, in public or in private.
> 2. No one shall be subject to restrictions that might impair his freedom to maintain or to change his religion or belief.
> 3. Freedom to manifest one's religion or beliefs may be subject only to the limitations prescribed by law that are necessary to protect public safety, order, health, or morals, or the rights and freedoms of others.
> 4. Parents or guardians, as the case may be, have the right to provide for the religious and moral education of their children or wards that is in accord with their own convictions.

One of the reasons for drafting a more focused document such as the AmCHR was, similar to the ECHR, based on a desire to incorporate particular regional interests in the rights enunciated.[174] Although the UDHR provided some form of direction,[175] it was viewed as 'soft' law and lacking any substantive means for human rights enforcement.[176] While some state

---

[172] Evans, M. (1997;footnotes 92-101) quoting state reservations from Greece, Sweden, Turkey, UK, Ireland, Netherlands, Portugal, Malta, Bulgaria and Romania.
[173] 1144 UNTS 123.
[174] de Abranches (1968;184).
[175] Note that Chile Cuba and Panama had submitted their own drafts for a human rights document to the ECOSOC Secretariat that reflected the results of the Inter-American drive towards creating a human rights document. ECOSOC Official Records, Second Year, Fourth Session, Supp. No. 3. The UDHR and AmCHR served to influence the other, Samnoy (1993;48-49), although the AmDHR maintains a clearer focus on individual duties.
[176] de Abranches (1968;185-187).

delegates, such as Brazil, desired to rely on UN human rights documents to uphold regional human rights,[177] the majority of states preferred a regional human rights document that could work in tandem with the ICCPR.[178]

The predecessor to the AmCHR, the AmDHR, concentrated exclusively on the freedom of religion.[179] In 1959, however the Inter-American Council of Jurists put together a draft human rights document[180] that was modelled on the CHR's draft for the ICCPR. The right to conscience was essentially the same as that found in the ICCPR, with the important difference being a change in the first paragraph of the word 'manifestation' to 'profess' a 'religion or belief'. The delegates from Chile and Uruguay also had submitted their versions of the document[181] by specifically providing for a manifested right to conscience via the terms 'manifest and profess'. The Chilean delegate also included the terms 'celebrating rituals' along with 'worship'.[182]

The Organisation of American States' Commission rapporteur, Dr. C.A. Dunshee de Abranches, recommended changes to the document in accordance with the Chile and Uruguay proposals, as demonstrated by the minor changes to the right to 'profess and disseminate' rather then merely 'profess'. The Commission also removed the term 'fundamental' before 'religion or belief' in the first paragraph.

These changes do suggest a more religious overtone to the document. 'Profess' and 'disseminate' imply specific rights for proselytising religions, a licence that was not provided for in the ICCPR. Similarly, removing the term 'fundamental' indicates a specific provision for manifesting beliefs that differ from conventional religious beliefs. The implication is that a belief need not be fundamental but can entail a more general conscientious belief harboured by an individual.

The drafters also distinguished between conscience and thought in a more obvious manner than the ICCPR drafters. In the AmCHR, freedom of thought is protected in the free expression article[183] whereas freedom of

---

[177] Sandifer (1968;175).
[178] Inter-American Yearbook of Human Rights (1968).
[179] Article 3 of the AmDHR baldly provided for the right to 'freely profess religious faith'.
[180] The Inter-American Council of Jurists drafted the first draft in 1959 at the request of the Ministers of Foreign Affairs who were members of the Organisation of American States.
[181] 1968 Inter-American Yearbook of Human Rights (1973) Appendix 3 and 4 (in Spanish).
[182] See de Abranches (1968;282).
[183] The term 'opinion' is not found in the AmCHR but it is utilised in the ICCPR right to free expression, indicating the close relation between opinion and thought as

conscience is protected alongside religion. The different approach derived from the AmCHR drafters' view of freedom of expression as a basic and essential right.[184] While the drafters recognised that conscience and thought maintain some form of internal relationship, as reflected in the ICCPR, thought was discerned as being closer to expression since the external manifestation of a general thought was via expression.

This approach to thought and expression was noted by G. Escudero in his 1967 report to the Organisation of American States. He stated that:

> Freedom of conscience presupposes the natural drive of the human spirit to act within the self on the subjective level or outside the self on the objective level of the life of the community.[185]

Escudero continued to note that when acting internally, conscience relates to the freedom of the mind, however when acting externally, conscience manifests as an expression.[186]

Indicative of the importance attached to free expression is Article 12(4) of the AmCHR which protects against limitations of indirect expression, a provision not found in the ICCPR.[187] Furthermore, Article 12(2) of the AmCHR does not centre on coercion, as in the ICCPR, but on impairing one's ability. It also retains the 'maintain or change' language of the 1955 CHR proposal for the ICCPR.

These differences indicate that the AmCHR drafters adopted a somewhat different view of the right to freedom of conscience. Rather than treat a conscientious belief as a counterbalance to a religious belief, the AmCHR seems to equate a conscientious belief with a more general thought. While Article 12 codifies the rights to freedom of religion and conscience, the focus centres on upholding religious beliefs, including minority religious beliefs. Hence the right to profess and disseminate a belief. Placing the right to freedom of thought within the context of free expression however indicates that the drafters might have intended for the manifestation of a conscientious belief within the context of the freedom of expression.[188]

---

pertaining to the internal consciousness of the person. *See e.g.* A/2929 where this same point was noted regarding thought and opinion (in Article 19) of the ICCPR.
[184] Sandifer (1968) (expression is cornerstone of liberty).
[185] Escudero (1967;119).
[186] Escudero (1967;119).
[187] de Abranches (1967;196-197).
[188] *See* discussion *infra* at Chapter Five for the distinction between freedom of conscience and expression.

As for limitations on the right to freedom of conscience, the limitations are essentially the same as the ICCPR.

AfrCHR, Article 8[189]

The Organisation of African Unity also codified the right to conscience. Article 8 of the AfrCHR offers a unique understanding of the right to conscience, as demonstrated by the different terms of the Article and the approach of the drafters. Article 8 states:

> Freedom of conscience, the profession and free practice of religion shall be guaranteed. No one may, subject to law and order, be submitted to measures restricting the exercise of these freedoms.

The AfrCHR, which emanated from a 1979 UN seminar[190] and was approved in 1981,[191] utilised unique language different from the other principal treaties when codifying the right to freedom of conscience. The AfrCHR aims to accord equal status towards both rights and duties, and thereby between the individual and the state, by protecting groups such as the community or the tribe.[192] The Organisation of African Unity endeavoured to create a distinctive human rights document which would focus on issues unique to African society, such as banning colonialism,[193] while retaining an overall African flavour regarding one's duty to others and the state.[194]

This approach of the drafters assists in explaining the structure of Article 8. The terms of the Article refer to the freedom of conscience along with the free profession and practice of religion. The drafters thereafter did not elaborate on the rights stated therein, unlike prior codifications of the right to freedom of conscience that specifically fashioned a singular right to freedom of conscience. It is possible that the drafters desired to avoid an elaboration of the individual's rights associated with the right to conscience

---

[189] 21 ILM 59.
[190] Umozurike (1983;903).
[191] Following a 1979 meeting of governmental experts in Dakar who were appointed by the Organisation of African Unity, the Council of Ministers reviewed the draft in 1980 and 1981 in Banjul (hence the Banjul Conference) and submitted it for final approval to the Organisation of African Unity's 37th Ordinary Session of Council of Ministers 1981. Gittleman (1982;670).
[192] *See* Nuituri (1995;376).
[193] Gittleman (1982;676).
[194] Gittleman (1982;677).

by providing for group-oriented aspects of the right, such as professing and practising a religion.

Yet, while Article 8 does not specifically seem to accord the right to freedom of conscience any practical external significance, it is possible to interpret the intention of the AfrCHR drafters in a broad manner. One commentator has noted that 'the right to manifest one's conscience is inherent in the freedom of conscience. What good is conscience which is not manifested?'.[195] Conscience is further considered as a right granting the ability to retain any form of belief 'be it religious, political or any other conviction'.[196] Nonetheless, because the AfrCHR does not employ the usual phrase 'religion or belief' that provided for manifestation of a conscientious belief in other treaties, such as the ICCPR, the intended scope of the freedom accorded to conscience, as opposed to religion, is not clarified.[197]

Concerning the right to education, the AfrCHR does not have any corresponding provision in Article 8. It does however provide for the right to education in Article 17(1), and Article 17(3) states that the 'promotion and protection of morals and traditional values recognised by the community' is the duty of the State. Again, the overtones of the right centre on the relationship between the individual and state, yet the result seems to be a similar right to ICCPR Article 18(4).

Regarding limitations on the right to freedom of conscience, the AfrCHR has a unique limitation in Article 8 that subjects the exercise of the right to conscience to 'law and order'. This phrase has been criticised as granting the state an almost unfettered ability to limit the right since it subjects the exercise of the right to the interests of a state's domestic policies. In essence, asserting the right would be moot once the notion of law and order are imposed, unlike the ICCPR, ECHR, and AmCHR, where limitations are subject to specific requirements which do not undermine the ability to retain the right.[198]

---

[195] Ankumah (1996;133-134). The author bases this conclusion on the general spirit of the AfrCHR and uses similar logic to imply a right to change one's religion (as deriving from the inherent freedom). Such a broad interpretation also results from the somewhat vague nature of the rights that provide for greater flexibility. *See e.g.* Rembe (1991;4).

[196] Ankumah (1996;133) (distinguishing religion which is centred on theistic notions relating to a general philosophical outlook on life).

[197] *See e.g.* Amnesty International (1991;28) defining AfrCHR Article 8 within a religious context, but noting that reference must also be made to other international treaties and standards (as required by AfrCHR Article 60) and that military conscientious objection should be considered a right under the AfrCHR.

[198] Gittleman (1982;693). The limitation in the AfrCHR could be broadened to incorporate the *forum internum* too since the right does not seem to distinguish between the internal and external nature of the right to conscience.

The AfrCHR also contains a general limitation clause similar to Article 29 of the UDHR. AfrCHR Article 27 provides:

> 1. Every individual shall have duties towards his family and society, the State and other legally recognised communities and the international community.
> 2. The rights and freedoms of each individual shall be exercised with due regard to the rights of others, collective security, morality and common interest.

Article 27 of the AfrCHR focuses on the individual's 'duties' and operates in a similar manner to a limitation clause. The duties on the individual are imposed specifically to exercise one's rights 'with due regard for the rights of others, collective security, morality and common interest'. This Article has been interpreted as providing quite a broad discretion to the state to legally restrict the rights provided for in the first part of the Charter,[199] with some commentators equating its provision with a general clawback clause.[200] This is especially due to the general language of the Article that is applicable to all the rights therein and the lack of any external control over the imposition of a limitation.[201]

Despite the broad language of the Article, the 1995 Guidelines for Submission of State Reports under the AfrCHR, as drafted by the African Commission, appear to treat the provision for limitations as derogations rather than strict clawback clauses.[202] This approach is supported by the Commission's practice to first determine whether a right has been violated before examining the derogation being asserted, and because the limitation itself is subject to specific requirements.[203] Hence, concerning the

---

[199] See e.g. Rembe (1991) referring to Tanzania's disbanding the Jehovah's Witnesses sect because the group gives the impression of being anti-establishment. See also Franck (1982;Vol.3;325) referring to a similar problem in Zambia.
[200] Gittleman (1982;690-692). Clawback clauses are broader than derogations since the circumstances for deviating from the right are not enumerated in any specific sense. A derogation is generally allowed for a particular reason, such as a public emergency, and is only temporary. A clawback is more discretionary, centres on domestic policies, and is created pursuant to a domestic legal directive.
[201] Gittleman (1982;691-692). The author does note, at 702-703, that reference can be made to other human rights documents as a means of defining the limitations.
[202] Ankumah (1996;177).
[203] Ankumah (1996;176-177) referring, in footnote 591, to Communication No. 129/94, where the Commission, without explanation, overruled the state's imposed limitation. Ankumah also refers, in fn. 587, to a Tanzanian case, *Rumbun v. Attorney General* Civil Suit No. 32 (1992) (cited in 52 Nairobi Legal Monthly 2/95) where the Court defined a limitation, subject to the proviso 'prescribed by law', as requiring adequate safeguards against arbitrary provisions in order to uphold the right being abrogated

limitations within the AfrCHR, the AfrCHR can be interpreted as conforming to ICCPR standards.[204]

Regarding the regional treaties that codify the right to freedom of conscience, it appears that the right is placed on equal footing with the freedom of religion. The treaties recognise the importance of the right and in upholding beliefs that might differ from a formal religion. Of course, given the regional nature of the documents, the right is codified in a different manner. Hence the AmCHR tends to emphasise free expression while the AfrCHR's approach to the right to conscience requires clarification. Nevertheless, what is imperative to note is that the documents generally provide for the freedom of conscience in some shape or form, and that they universally recognise the importance of upholding an individual's internal beliefs. Furthermore, bar the AfrCHR, the treaties use similar language in recognising the right to manifest a 'religion or belief'. The use of similar language to the UDHR and ICCPR, and given the context within which these treaties were drafted, it appears that the notion of maintaining and manifesting a conscientious belief is equally supported in the regional human rights treaties.

Other Significant Documents

For purposes of further demonstrating the underlying meaning of the right to freedom of conscience in international law, it is worth turning to other human rights documents that codify or address the right. Similar to the regional treaties, the significance of these additional documents is the acknowledgement regarding the right to maintain a conscientious belief and the use of the phrase 'religion and belief' to denote the right to manifestation, thereby indicating a right to manifest a conscientious belief.

The most significant of such documents is the 1981 *Declaration on the Elimination of all Forms of Intolerance and of Discrimination Based on Religion or Belief.* Although the <u>Declaration</u> is not a legally binding document, one can infer a certain level of consensus regarding the right to conscience among the state delegates who participated in the drafting of

---

from, imposing a proportional and reasonable standard in attaining the objective of the limitation, and not offending the natural justice principles. Similar phrasing is found in Articles 11-14 of the AfrCHR.

[204] *See also* AfrCHR, Article 60 which requires the Commission to 'draw inspiration' from other human rights instruments and Article 61 which directs the Commission to 'take into consideration, as subsidiary measures to determine the principles of law', other international conventions which conform to African customs and practices.

the document. Furthermore, one of the purposes in drafting the Declaration was to clarify the rights in ICCPR Article 18.²⁰⁵

*Declaration on the Elimination of all Forms of Intolerance and of Discrimination Based on Religion or Belief*²⁰⁶

The relevant provisions pertaining to the right to conscience in the Declaration are:

> *Article 1*
> 1. Everyone shall have the right to freedom of thought conscience and religion. This right shall include freedom to have a religion or whatever belief of his choice, and freedom, either individually or in community with others and in public or private, to manifest his religion or belief in worship, observance, practice and teaching.
> 2. No one shall be subject to coercion which would impair his freedom to have a religion or belief of his choice.
> 3. Freedom to manifest one's religion or belief may be subject only to such limitations as are prescribed by law and are necessary to protect public safety, order, health or morals or the fundamental rights and freedoms of others.
>
> *Article 6*
> In accordance with Article 1 of the present declaration, and subject to the provisions of Article 1, paragraph 3, the right to freedom of thought, conscience, religion or belief shall include, *inter alia*, the following freedoms:...

What is interesting about the *travaux preparatoires* of the Declaration is the drafters' focus on the same issues as the UDHR and ICCPR, that is the issue of changing one's religion and the manner in which to interpret the terms, specifically 'belief'. While this ongoing dispute among states demonstrates an inherent problem for any continued understanding and entrenchment of the right to freedom of religion, the fact that the drafters came to similar conclusions regarding the breadth of the right to freedom of conscience and the right to manifest a conscientious belief further assists to solidify the underlying meaning of the right as developed thus far.

---

²⁰⁵ *See* discussion *infra*.
²⁰⁶ GA Res36/55, 25/11/81. The GA unanimously approved the Declaration in 1981.

The significant aspect of the <u>Declaration</u> for the right to freedom of conscience is that the drafters specifically intended to incorporate protection for a conscientious belief in the same manner as a religious belief. This is exemplified by the discussion regarding the title of the document. The French delegate preferred the singular reference to intolerance in the title since, from a legal standpoint, the term incorporated freedom of conscience as well.[207] The majority of states, led by the Eastern European bloc, favoured the phrases used in the UDHR and ICCPR 'religion or belief'. These states noted that the title should not refer solely to intolerance, as intolerance could be limited to a religious context, but also to beliefs which imply more general notions of protection.[208] The Russian delegate amplified this point by noting the inclusion of atheists, non-believers, and rationalists in the ICCPR's use of the term 'belief'.[209] Indicative of this broad approach towards beliefs is the remark made by the delegate from Italy that:

> Belief, whether moral, religious, or philosophical, was a fundamental element in his conception of life. For an atheist, the important thing was of course not the negative side of believing in God [i.e., the right to deny God's existence] but the positive fact of having a moral or philosophical conviction that was undoubtedly a fundamental element in his conception of life [and therefore comparable to religion].[210]

Therefore, the title was altered to include 'intolerance' as well as 'religion or belief'.[211] This development demonstrates the broad notion accorded to the term 'belief' as incorporating a conscientious belief.[212]

On a substantive level, as the drafters of the <u>Declaration</u> began to focus on specific articles within the document, it is apparent that they intended to uphold manifestations of a conscientious belief as well. This is quite significant since the <u>Declaration</u> is a key source for interpreting ICCPR Article 18 especially since the drafters were acting with the

---

[207] GA Third Committee, twenty-second Session, meetings 1498 (1967) at 180.
[208] GA Third Committee, twenty-second Session, meetings 1497-1499 (1967).
[209] GA Third Committee, twenty-eighth Session, SR.2009-2014 (1973).
[210] GA Third Committee, twenty-second Session, meeting 1498 (1967) at 184.
[211] GA Third Committee, twenty-second Session, meeting 1505 (1967).
[212] Evans, M. (1997;229-230) criticises the title for focusing on discrimination and intolerance without any effort being made to define the terms.

intention of amplifying the meaning of that Article,²¹³ as indicated by Article 1 of the Declaration.

Focusing on Article 1 of the Declaration, the Romanian delegate stated that the draft was specifically based on ICCPR Article 18²¹⁴ such that it related to upholding an individual's right to any belief or non-belief.²¹⁵ The delegate from Spain pointed out that the Declaration was to address issues of a broader nature than religious freedom,²¹⁶ and, as noted by the German Democratic Republic delegate, was to include general moral notions greater then transcendental ideals.²¹⁷ Similar to the arguments posited when drafting the ICCPR regarding the distinction between religion and conscience, the German Democratic Republic delegate noted that to focus solely on religion at the exclusion of other, more general beliefs, would be discriminatory to those beliefs.²¹⁸

In another action reflective of the drafting process of the UDHR and ICCPR, the drafters avoided any specific definition of the terms. The underlying fear was that a specific definition could weaken the universality of the document and lead to definitions that veered from protecting non-religious beliefs as well.²¹⁹ This apprehension explains why the definition of belief as 'atheist, non-theistic and theistic' was deleted in favour of the phrase 'whatever belief', thereby upholding an even broader notion of the term than found in ICCPR Article 18.²²⁰

The phrase 'whatever belief' reflects the broad scope of protection in the Declaration²²¹ and removes the term from a religious oriented context.²²² This was necessary, according to the Bulgarian delegate, in

---

213   Declaration's general purpose as amplifying ICCPR Article 18 and its term 'belief' to provide for protection to atheists and non-believers as well. E/CN.4/1154 (1974) noting desire to enhance Article 18 but not necessarily affect the substance of the right.
214   GA Third Committee, twenty-eighth Session, meeting 2011 (1973). *See also* E/CN.4/1987/35 CHR's Rapporteur on Declaration, First Report, noting that purpose of Declaration was to clarify Article 18.
215   GA Third Committee, twenty-eighth Session, meeting 2011 (1973) (similar remarks also being made by Costa Rica).
216   GA Third Committee, twenty-eighth Session, meeting 2010 (1973).
217   GA Third Committee, twenty-eighth Session, meeting 2012 (1973). The GDR noted however that it is not allowing for the manifestation of any general feelings.
218   GA Third Committee, twenty-eighth Session, meeting 2010 and 2012 (1973).
219   *See generally* A/9134; E/CN.4/1475 (1981). The Special Rapporteur on Religious Tolerance (recently changed to the Special Rapporteur on Freedom of Religion or Belief) noted that the lack of definition is a universal problem that creates difficulties in executing his mandate. Amor (1998).
220   E/CN.4/1408 (1980) and E/CN.4/1475 (1981).
221   GA Third Committee, thirty-sixth Session, Summary Record 32-36 (1981).
222   GA Third Committee, thirty-sixth Session, Summary Record 35 (1981). *See also* GA Third Committee, thirty-sixth Session, meeting 73 (1981).

order to counterbalance the religious flavour of the Declaration, as indicated by Articles 6 and 7 that focus solely on religious manifestations.[223]

The Declaration seems to further entrench the understanding of the manifestation of a belief as including a conscientious belief. The drafters desired to amplify ICCPR Article 18 in a broad manner that includes manifestation of conscientious beliefs. Furthermore, the drafters utilised the same basic phrases found in the UDHR, ICCPR, and ECHR when describing the scope of the right to freedom of conscience.[224] Indeed, the phrases 'religion or belief' have become a watchword of sorts for implying the right to manifest a conscientious belief as well. This is demonstrated in additional documents that provide for the right to freedom of conscience.

Documents Referring to the Right to Conscience

The additional documents to be examined generally utilise similar phraseology to the UDHR, ICCPR, and ECHR when providing for a right to freedom of conscience. When internal protection of a conscientious belief is safeguarded, the general phrase 'freedom of conscience' is employed. When the broader, external, protection regarding manifestation is upheld, the phrase 'manifestation of religion or belief' is used. Indicating the influence of the UDHR and ICCPR's terminology is the fact that the documents drafted after the ICCPR was approved utilise the same phrases as a means of codifying the right to freedom of conscience. By contrast, documents drafted before the ICCPR was completed in 1966 invoke different language, such that the protection generally centres on the right to freedom of religion.

For example, the 1949 *Fourth Geneva Convention regarding the Status and Treatment of Protected Persons* provides in Article 27, *inter alia*, to respect 'their religious conviction and practices'. This document was drafted before the UDHR and contains a different form of language

---

[223] GA Third Committee, thirty-sixth Session, Summary Record 35 (1981). *See also* the reports from the Rapporteur on Freedom of Religion and Belief, E/CN.4/2000/65; E/CN.4/1999/58; E/CN.4/1998/6, where the rapporteur clearly adopts a broad approach to the terms 'religion or belief' as including all forms of beliefs. The same can be said for the CHR's resolutions regarding the implementation of the Declaration. *See e.g.* E/CN.4/RES/2000/23; E/CN.4/RES/1999/39; E/CN.4/RES/1998/18, all of which also recognise the right to change one's religion or belief.

[224] Evans, M. (1997;234) criticises this approach since it does not serve to delineate the terms in any manner but is merely repetitive.

that need not necessarily incorporate the right to conscience. Nonetheless, the Commentary to the Geneva Convention has interpreted this phrase as:

> being part of freedom of conscience and freedom of thought in general. It implies freedom to believe or not to believe and freedom to change from one religion or conviction to another. This safeguard relates to any system of philosophical or religious belief.[225]

As a means of reflection, Protocol I of the 1979 *Additional Protocols to the Geneva Conventions of 1949*, Article 75, uses the more familiar terms 'religion or belief' in the list of fundamental guarantees for individuals affected by a conflict. The key difference is that the Protocols were drafted after the ICCPR. Hence Article 75 has been interpreted in a somewhat broader fashion than the Fourth Geneva Convention as requiring the conflicting parties to respect the person's 'honour, convictions, and religious practices', with the latter being understood in the broad sense to cover 'all philosophical and ethical convictions'.[226]

Further examples are treaties that had been drafted before the approval of the ICCPR. While the UDHR might have had some influence on these documents, the UDHR had not yet attained its current influential status, arguably as customary international law, such that the language in pre-ICCPR documents centres exclusively on religious freedom. Hence the 1950 *Convention Relating to the Status of Refugees* at Article 4 protects the 'practice of religion' and 'freedom as regards the religious education of their children'. The same language is used for the 1954 *Convention Relating to the Status of Stateless Persons* (also at Article 4).[227]

The tendency to reflect the ICCPR's terms is demonstrated by the 1965 *International Convention on the Elimination of all Forms of Racial Discrimination*.[228] Article 5(d)(vii) of the Convention prohibits discrimination and requires equality in the enjoyment of the 'right to freedom of thought, conscience, and religion', language reminiscent of the ICCPR's draft then pending before the GA. While protection of the listed rights in Article 5[229] were limited to issues of discrimination

---

[225] Pictet (1958;203) noting, at 248, that the sole limitation to this right is on the basis of preserving public order and morals.
[226] Sandoz (1987;871).
[227] See also *Standard Minimum Rules for the Treatment of Prisoners* that emanated from a 1955 UN conference. Article 6 refers to the necessity 'to respect the religious beliefs and moral precepts of the group to which a prisoner belongs'.
[228] GA Res. 2106A(XX) 21/12/65; 60 UNTS 195.
[229] Which are not meant to be interpreted in any exclusive fashion.

and equality,[230] CERD has focused on substantive aspects of the right when an inequality occurs.[231] Such consideration also has included secular aspects of the right to freedom of conscience,[232] in accordance with the ICCPR's drafters intended scope of these phrases.

The 1985 *Declaration on Human Rights of Individuals who are not Nationals of the Country in which they Live*[233] provides, in Article 5(e), for the same protection as stated in the UDHR. The *travaux preparatoires* to this document explicitly note the singular nature of the right to freedom of conscience, which must conform to the right as provided in the UDHR and ICCPR, by using the same terms of these documents.[234]

---

[230] E/CN.4/SR.796-800 (1964) Remarks by Austria and UK. The Netherlands representative specifically notes that 'the purpose of the Article [5] was not to proclaim that the rights which were enumerated must be fully respected, but merely to prohibit racial discrimination with regard to their enjoyment'. The problem derives from Article 4, which prohibits 'hate speech', and the extent of overlap with the protection mentioned in Article 5 (which takes precedence over Article 4). The problem is resolved by viewing Article 5 as only applying to states which provide for such rights, that such rights must be equally upheld. Buergenthaul (1977;210-211).

[231] See e.g. CERD's response to state reports in Report to the forty-ninth Session of the GA, Supp. 18 (1994) where CERD focuses not only on the violation of Article 5 (regarding discrimination) but also on implementation of the rights therein in an equal manner (exemplified by requiring Australia to discuss the treatment of hiring Aborigines within governmental bodies, such as the police force). *See also* Buergenthaul (1977;211) noting the possibility that CERD can provide substantive protection if, as a result of a violation, an inequality occurs; Meron (1985;288-289) (noting how focus of CERD activity has been on upholding overall equality rather than racial discrimination per se'). *Cf.* Partsch (1979;225-226 and 248) (calling for restrictive approach to CERD's manner of reviewing rights and to adopt narrower view of no discrimination, along with equality, as basis for review with regard to enjoyment of rights, but not providing for such rights *ab initio*, relying on E/CN.4/Sub.2/L.344 (1964) and E/CN.4/SR.396 (1964)); Lerner (1980;150-152) (adopting non-discrimination approach since broader restrictions are placed on individuals as a means of lessening incidents of incitement - even at the expense of violating an individual's expression of thoughts); Schwelb (1966) (similar conclusion to Lerner).

[232] The State Reports to CERD and CERD's response to the States evidence this approach. See e.g. Report to the Forty-eighth GA, Supplement 18 (1993) (Zambia report required to provide information regarding ethnic groups); Report to the Forty-sixth GA Supplement 18 (1991) (Burundi's report focusing on both secular and religious allowances); A/43/18 (1988) (CERD (referred Ukraine to Declaration and required Kuwait to provide interpretation of freedom of conscience outside of a religious context. Kuwait responded in a non-committal fashion that all rights were equally upheld); Report to the forty-second GA, Supplement 18 (1987) (CERD focused on Tunisia's report with regard to foreign workers and individuals and the allowances for their right to freedom of thought and conscience).

[233] GA, Fortieth Session, Res.144 (1985).

[234] GA Third Committee, Fortieth Session, (1985) at 12, Italy noting the importance of drafting the Article pursuant to current international standards and the Working Group,

The 1989 *Convention on the Rights of the Child*, which provides for freedom of thought, conscience, and religion in Article 14,[235] also codifies a conception of conscience as a singular right separate from religion. This is apparent from the unique perspective adopted by the CRC concerning the establishment of a 'sliding scale' approach to the child's rights. The previous standard had been an all-encompassing 'best interest' of the child.[236] Hence, a court would refer to external factors and need not consider the developing beliefs or wishes of a young person. The current standard implemented by the CRC however entails a broader scope whereby a parent must consider the 'evolving capacities' of the child, especially as the child nears the majority age. Recognising that a child can develop and manifest particular individual beliefs and ideals[237] would seem to indicate that a court should 'respect' the developing beliefs of an older child that also can include conscientious assertions in a progressive manner relative to age.

This approach had been hinted at in the *travaux preparatoires* to CRC Article 14. In the 1982 and 1983 Working Group, the US proposed to incorporate ICCPR Article 18[238] but was met with resistance. Some states also felt the provision for religious education was previously codified, while others asserted that the practice of religion is not necessarily the child's right.[239] At the Working Group's next session in 1984, Canada proposed to make the freedom subject to the authority of the parents, who will provide the necessary direction to the child, pursuant to the child's evolving capacities.[240] The Holy See objected to this because it did not provide enough credence to parents to ensure for the religious education of their children.

---

at 24-25, providing for the same language as in the ICCPR. *See also* GA Third Committee, thirty-sixth Session (1981) at 11 where the Working Group's draft was revised, at suggestion of Italy, to conform to ICCPR.

[235] Note as well the 1991 *African Charter on the Rights of the Child*, Article 9, which uses similar language but has not yet entered into force, as it is pending the ratification of 15 states.

[236] *See Declaration on the Rights of the Child* (1959).

[237] *See e.g.* GA Third Committee, SR.1027 noting the broad approach towards 'religion and belief' because of a hesitation to define the terms.

The Committee on the Rights of the Child generally focuses on serious violations regarding children, such as child pornography and prostitution, and on basic survival needs of children. *See e.g.* Report to GA, Forty-ninth Session, Supplement 41 (1994).

[238] E/CN.4/1983/62; E/CN.4/1984/71.

[239] E/CN.4/1983/62 (specifically with regard to allowing for changes to a child's religious belief, a contention reminiscent of the UDHR and ICCPR drafting).

[240] E/CN.4/1984/71 Sweden also supported this approach.

The drafters were presented with a deadlock between granting greater status to the child, particularly to prevent any form of coercion on non-believers, versus recognising the importance of parental discretion.[241] The dispute was settled in the form of a compromise by deleting paragraphs that were not universally accepted by all legal systems.[242] References to other international instruments, such as the UDHR, were removed from CRC Article 14 and the general notion of 'respecting', as opposed to 'ensuring' or 'recognising' which presented problems for various secular systems, a child's 'freedom of thought, conscience, and religion' was adopted. Hence Article 14(1) requires State Parties to 'respect the right of the child to freedom of thought, conscience and religion'.

The second paragraph of Article 14 requires a state to respect a parent's desires about directing one's child,[243] with a view towards incorporating the rights of ICCPR Article 18.[244] The third paragraph makes an implicit reference to the manifestation terms of the ICCPR, 'religion or belief',[245] but in light of the compromise among the drafters, refers only to the limitations that may be imposed on the child's right.[246]

The 1990 *International Convention on the Protection of the Rights of All Migrant Workers and Members of their Families* at Article 12 essentially super-imposed ICCPR Article 18, with an adjustment of terms to reflect the focus on the migrant worker and their families.

Although not of any binding nature, the documents resulting from the Helsinki Accords and the Conference on Security and Co-operation in Europe were clearly based on Article 18 of the ICCPR.[247] The 1989 Concluding Document of Vienna provides, at paragraph 11, for respect of human rights including 'freedom of thought conscience religion or belief' and, at paragraph 16, to ensure for the freedom to 'profess and practise religion or belief'.[248] The Document has been subject to a broad reading to

---

[241] E/CN.4/1986/39.
[242] E/CN.4/1989/48.
[243] E/CN.4/1989/48. This paragraph was understood to apply to all forms of belief, not solely religious issues.
[244] See E/CN.4/1989/WG.1/WP.1/Rev.2 (Sweden notes that the Article is to be read as encompassing ICCPR Article 18).
[245] E/CN.4/1989/WG.1/WP.1/Rev.2 (Holy See equated manifestation with the right to educate following one's convictions).
[246] Tahzib (1996;85) notes the removal from the Article the right to change one's religion due to Islamic states protests.
[247] Luchterhandt (1991;162) noting the Helsinki Accords basis on Article 18 in Principle VII at Section 3 which protects manifestations of 'religion and belief acting in accordance with the dictates of his own conscience'.
[248] The Concluding Document is quoted in 10 H. Rts. L. J. 274-277 (1989) and, concerning the freedom of religion and belief, essentially adheres to the <u>Declaration</u>.

include non-religious convictions[249] and has played an influential role in the development of the right to freedom of conscience outside of a religious context within newly emerging Eastern European states.[250]

Mention should be made of *The Convention to Eliminate Discrimination Against Women*, an important human rights treaty that does *not* refer to the right to freedom of religion and conscience. This is probably due to the focus of CEDAW on eradicating gender-based discrimination. Because many religions tend to be discriminatory towards women, the CEDAW drafters had to focus on measures to prevent imposition of religious beliefs rather than consider means to buttress these beliefs.[251] Indeed there exists an inherent conflict between these significant rights, as evidenced by the extensive reservations made by states with a religious ideology pervading their socio-legal structure.[252] Some state reservations are so extensive regarding the limitations imposed on preventing discrimination that they seem to conflict with the very object and purpose of the CEDAW treaty.[253] While it is beyond the scope of this chapter to address the significant problems arising from freedom of religion and conscience and the rights of women, it seems that the absence of any provision in CEDAW relating to the former right stems from this inherent conflict.

Conclusion

In analysing the *travaux preparatoires* for the right to freedom of conscience, this chapter has focused on a number of principal issues considered by the drafters. The treaties almost universally provide protection for some form of right to freedom of conscience on

---

The limitation to the right, stated at paragraph 17 of the Document of Vienna, although liable to a possible broad reading, is 'subject to international obligations' and has been equated with the limitations provided for in ICCPR Article 18(3). *See* Tretter (1989;258); Luchterhandt (1991;168-169).

[249] Luchterhandt (1991;165) noting that the inclusion of protection for non-believers broadens freedom of religion to include free convictions.

[250] Luchterhandt (1991;174-180) discussing the broad parameters of the right to freedom of religion and conscience in Hungary and Poland whose newly drafted laws, in 1990 and 1989, respectively, appear to offer broader protection for a free conscience and non-religious believers than ICCPR Article 18, and USSR where the protection for a 'non-religious' conviction, while stated in the 1990 law, focuses mainly on religious protection. *See* Tahzib (1991;188-194).

[251] *See e.g.* An-Naim (1994).

[252] *See e.g.* Brandt and Kaplan (1996).

[253] CEDAW, Article 28.

a comparable level to that of the freedom of religion. This approach serves as a marked contrast to the secondary literature where the right to conscience is largely overlooked because the treaties provide for a broader, extra-religious, right to conscience. Additionally, the regional treaties seem to adopt different approaches to the right to conscience. In the AmCHR, free expression serves as an important right in upholding the right to conscience. The AfrCHR adheres to the group-oriented focus of the document, although the right also seems to provide protection for an individual conscientious belief. The indication is that a doctrinal diversity exists for the right to conscience, a development that can assist to entrench the right in domestic systems.

Despite the different approaches used by the treaties to uphold the right to conscience, similarities exist. The treaties provide for a distinction between conscience and thought, an important determinant for developing one's understanding of conscience. Similar language throughout the treaties is used to delineate the manifestation of a conscientious belief and the limitations to be imposed, despite the derogations provided for in the ECHR and AfrCHR. Furthermore, as the treaties achieve greater stature in the domestic sphere, principally through ratification, other documents that expand on the right to conscience, such as the Declaration, also will develop and acquire greater recognition and application.

What seems to be lacking from the treaties, as indicated in other studies regarding this particular human right, is any sense of definition or understanding regarding the desired scope of protection. This is particularly the case with the right to freedom of conscience. The term itself is somewhat amorphous. What is the latitude of one's right to freedom of conscience and can it be applied in an equivalent manner to the right to freedom of religion? How do the relevant international and domestic judiciary bodies interpret these provisions, do such interpretations conform to the *travaux preparatoires*, and how is the right to conscience actually upheld in state practice? These significant issues merit further study given the importance of alternative belief systems as a counter to an overbearing religious state or in a state refusing to recognise a particular belief system.

What has been developed thus far is that the *travaux preparatoires* indicate some form of protection for the right to freedom of conscience. While it is easy to criticise the treaties and their drafters for failing to identify conclusively any specific meaning or understanding of the term, such an approach is probably for the better. Aside for the relevant political struggles that occur in the international arena, one also has the seemingly impossible task of achieving any form of acceptable religious freedom

Analysis of the Treaties and Other Documents 71

sphere without excluding other forms of belief.[254] This latter consideration pertains to delineating the proper scope to the right and will be considered throughout the remainder of the work.

---

[254] *See e.g.* Fish (1997); Stolzenberg (1993).

4 The *Forum Internum*

Introduction

Acknowledging that the international human rights system accords a right to maintain a conscientious belief raises a host of questions. The key questions are what are the normative elements of the right to conscience, what type of activity does the right to freedom of conscience sanction, and how will the right effectively operate in a practicable sense? These issues will dominate the remainder of this work where the purpose is to analyse the international human right to freedom of conscience and provide a functional modus operandi for the right to freedom of conscience.

This chapter will focus on the *forum internum*, the internal aspect of the right to freedom of conscience. International human rights law, as evidenced in treaties and state practice, accords a rather broad view of the *forum internum* since, in contrast to the *forum externum*, the *forum internum* is not subject to limitations or derogations. This rather broad understanding of the *forum internum* possibly results in international commentators opining that there is no practical utility to this aspect of the right to conscience.[1] One can further explain the wide realm of protection that is theoretically accorded to the *forum internum* along with the lack of any practical application by the international system because the *forum internum* is an internal realm of consciousness. Hence infringement is difficult to demonstrate and the practical applications appear rather limited. Indeed, the resultant lack of social harm is the very basis for deeming the *forum internum* an inviolable sphere.[2] By contrast, the manifestation of a conscientious belief, the *forum externum*, raises a host of problems relating to the conflict between the individual's assertion of a belief and the state, as well as between the individual and other individuals and their rights. The *forum internum* does not seem to present these forms of conflicts since the

---

[1] *See e.g.* Clark (1978); Dickson (1995). The example generally referred to as violating the *forum internum* is brainwashing.
[2] *See e.g.* Vermeulen (1992;82-83); Boyle (1993).

realm of protection relates to one's internal consciousness that in a practical sense would not really conflict with another individual's consciousness. Conflicts with the state or with other individual beliefs would generally arise within the realm of the *forum externum*.

As will be demonstrated in this chapter, such an understanding of the *forum internum* is misleading. Overbearing or deliberate state action to thwart a particular belief gives rise to the *forum internum* right. Further, a variety of violations of the *forum externum* also encompass the *forum internum*, particularly when confronted with coercive actions by the state or by other groups. Indeed, the mere adherence to a belief, even a belief that has not manifested, can raise problems and cause conflicts between individuals who adopt conflicting ideologies or beliefs. Mill for example presented the case of Muslims whose prohibition of eating pork might provide grounds for the prohibition of the sale of pork in public shops. One also can think of right to lifers and their abhorrence upon seeing an abortion clinic or reading about a state execution. Construction of society also might be such that one tends to dismiss conflicting beliefs due to the state's fundamentalist stance or, even worse, belittle any form of opposing thought, thereby thwarting the individual's internal development of the *forum internum*.

Further the *forum internum* is not an altogether inviolable sphere upon considering the limitations created for the manifestation of a belief in the *forum externum*, along with the variety of cases that have broadly construed these limitations in deference to the social construct.[3] One cannot avoid the contingent framework for example of decisions from judicial bodies such as the ECHR that account for their political frameworks and subjective understanding of society's demands or desires[4] when dismissing the manifestation of a particular belief. The problem is that judicial bodies tend to overlook the effect that limiting manifestations can have on the *forum internum*. In essence, understanding the *forum internum* forces one to confront the unavoidable quandary of a tolerant society that demands, by a simple definition of the term, a certain level of intolerance at least towards intolerant views. Hence in analysing the *forum*

---

[3] See discussion *supra*.
[4] Compare 17419/90 *Wingrove v. UK* 1996-V Rep. Judg. & Dec. 1937 (Court upheld ban on video due to its insulting nature to Christians) *with* 17439/90 *Choudhury v. UK* reptd. in 12 H. Rts. L. J. 172 (1991) (ban on sale of S. Rushdie book denied despite blasphemous content for specific religion).

internum as an inviolable right, it is imperative to account for the underlying problems raised by such a right as we are forced to recognise the relative, contingent, framework within which we unavoidably operate.

Considering the practical role of the *forum internum*, it is important to understand what the *forum internum* entails and when is it violated. Examining the normative functions of a human right can provide an understanding of the right to conscience and begin to distinguish between the *forum internum* and *externum*. While the treaties and judicial decisions endorse this distinction, there is not a great deal of material that defines or expands on the meaning of the *forum internum*. J.S. Mill's analysis of liberty refers to ideas that are quite similar to the *forum internum* of a conscientious belief. Mill therefore will be referred to as a starting point for the analysis of the *forum internum*.

Further elaboration is required however since Mill, recognising that one's internal beliefs raise unavoidable social conflicts, sanctioned some limitations on the *forum internum* while international human rights law accords the *forum internum* right absolute status. Further, his notion of internal protection seems to lean towards a conception of ideas that are broader in scope than conscientious beliefs such that it is closer to the protection accorded to the free expression of an opinion or thought.[5] A conscientious or religious belief presents a narrower, more focused, framework of operation than expression of a thought or opinion.

Reference to the *forum externum* of the right to conscience will serve to refine the *forum internum* dimension of the right. Coupled with a functional understanding of conscience, at least from a consequential standpoint, the extent of the *forum internum* can begin to take shape. It will be demonstrated that one can discern the relevant beliefs of the *forum internum* by the external action one undergoes in upholding a belief and that the key focus of protection for the *forum internum* is the prevention of coercion and upholding the right to develop a conscientious belief. Further, the analysis will move away from the *forum internum* as an inviolable right, with a view towards shaping a more coherent and practical understanding of the *forum internum*.

The Notion of a 'Right' and its Implications

Referring to the normative functions of an international human right can begin to answer some of the questions referred to above regarding the right

---

[5] The relationship between the right to freedom of expression and freedom of conscience is considered *infra* at Chapter Five.

to conscience. Analysing the function of the right provides a context for creating a framework for the operation of a right and for discerning the boundaries of the right. While the practical application of human rights can at times prove difficult, the purpose of certain human rights is rather clear, as exemplified by some of the basic economic rights such as the right to housing.[6] Nonetheless, many human rights remain ill-defined or misunderstood not only in a practical sense, but also because the function of the right is unclear. When confronted with the right to conscience, a right that has not been practically applied in any clear manner nor fully clarified in international law, it is important to understand and consider the intended functions of human rights within the specific context of the right to conscience.

The basic categorisation of rights offered by Hohfeld provides a platform from which to consider the underlying implications of a right. Placing the right to conscience within Hohfeld's divisions of a right can therefore assist in understanding not only the significance of the right to conscience, once it has attained the status of a human right, but also develop the manner of its application. Additionally, Hohfeld presents an interesting analysis of rights due to his interrelationship between rights and obligations. Treating a right as an immunity, liberty, claim or entitlement also entails the removal of a correlative entitlement. The inherent link of rights with obligations is rather significant for the right to conscience given that an assertion of the right generally comes to the fore when a conscientious belief conflicts with a social duty.[7] Hence the correlative approach appears to suit the normative structure of the right to conscience.

The problem with Hohfeld's analysis is that adopting one categorisation of a right does not adequately embody the meaning and scope that was intended for the right to freedom of conscience. Conceiving human rights merely as 'immunities' appears limited in scope. Construing a human right solely as the absence of a prohibition provides an insufficient basis for exercising a human right because the immunity does not necessarily mean that all action emanating from a right is permissible.[8] In the context of the right to conscience for example, the manifestation of a conscientious belief might entail rather broad action. While the absence of

---

[6] *See e.g.* ICESCR Article 11.
[7] The conflict between belief and social duty is generally the case for the manifestation of a belief.
[8] Nino (1991;26,28).

a prohibition to believe in a conscientious ideal might provide the grounds for upholding one's *forum internum*,[9] an immunity will not provide an adequate foundation for exercising the belief, a fundamental aspect of the right, nor protect those individuals who might not want to believe yet are still subject to the persuasions of other believers.

Similarly, treating the right to conscience as an unfettered liberty or privilege implies that the right derives from an external authority. If the external authority is the state, it is possible to restrict the liberty in a broader manner than that provided for in treaty limitations, thereby removing the right from a correlative context. This is the problem for example with military conscientious objection where the liberty to exercise the right in the domestic legislation of many states emanates from a specific legislative provision and not any defined right, such as the right to conscience. The problem is further exacerbated when accounting for selective military objection given that a specific military action conflicts with one's conscientious belief. In such instances, states generally defer to their notion of state necessity for military order and limit the application of the objection to general conscientious objectors.[10] As a result, states impose various restrictions on the right to military objection that reduces the individual's privilege to the right to conscience.[11]

Another possibility is to interpret the right to conscience as a claim that intermingles with the correlative duty due to the claims of other individuals. Initially this approach would appear to be a suitable interpretation of the right to conscience given that particular applications of the right to conscience raise social duty considerations, such as military conscientious objection. Indeed, one of the central arguments of some commentators against the right to military conscientious objection is that the correlative duty on the state to honour the right is non-existent when accounting for the individual's more general social duties.[12]

Understanding the right to conscience as a claim however tends to weaken the correlatively between rights and duties. While an entitlement right to pursue one's basic needs might derive from specific correlative

---

[9] See also discussion *infra* regarding the approach to the *forum internum* as a freedom *from* state interference thereby indicating an active role for the *forum internum* as well.

[10] See discussion *infra* at Chapter Six.

[11] In particular, limiting the right for military objection to religious objectors and not conscientious objectors.

[12] See e.g. Larsen & Hess (1992) (reaching this conclusion because the right to military conscientious objection in the US derives from specific legislation and not the Constitution).

social duties,[13] a conscientious belief derives from independent permissive norms[14] that serve as a basis for creating a particular conscientious belief. As a result of such independent norms, the manifestation of a conscientious belief can affect a variety of constantly shifting correlative duties that also will incorporate the consideration of one's social duty. For example, conscientious objection to the military can derive from beliefs pertaining to a rather broad objection to any form of military participation,[15] a narrow belief in not using firearms, or a totally different belief arising from specific military actions or procedures such as orders pertaining to service in illegally occupied territories, firing on civilian areas, or other breaches of humanitarian norms. While one's social duty to military service is inherent in each instance, each form of belief also raises other personal and social duties that are correlative assertions of the right. Reliance on a belief can affect one's duty to individuals within one's military unit or other individuals who share similar beliefs to the objector. These instances indicate that one's social duty is not a necessary correlative of the right to freedom of conscience since the duty can derive from other social and political forces independent of the right.[16]

Additionally, a key factor of a claim right is the actual exercise of the right.[17] That is, the claimant assumes the existence of the right, as it would be difficult to make a claim for a right that did not exist. The practical exercise of the right comes into play once an individual asserts a claim. As a result, a claim right seems to focus on the function of a right as making a claim, but that does not necessarily define the essence or derivation of a right that would assist in understanding the significance of the *forum internum*.

The problem with focusing on the function of a right is that a host of interpretations that may serve as the basis for a claim might be at odds with other pre-defined rights, especially where state interests transcend individual interests.[18] Deriving the antecedent claim from a person's right to the necessary condition of human existence might lead to results that

---

[13] *See e.g.* Gewirth (1982;235) whose entitlement based approach to human rights, which derives from necessary action to pursue one's basic needs, discounts the right to conscience for this very reason.
[14] *See* discussion *infra*.
[15] Such as some pacifists or a Jehovah's Witness. *See* discussion *infra*.
[16] Raz (1989).
[17] Martins and Nickel (1980).
[18] Shestack (1983).

conflict with other pre-determined, basic, human rights, such as the right to housing in a crowded city versus the right to private property. A claim for the unfettered exercise of the freedom of religion inevitably conflicts with other rights such as the rights of minorities or women. Such a consequential approach to rights tends to ignore the inherent conflicts in human rights and does not assist to explain how conflicting claims are to function.

An approach to rights that appears adequately to incorporate the right to conscience as intended by the international human rights framework is one that integrates the various Hohfeldian characteristics of rights. For example, recognising that a liberty right can exist even if the right is not being enforced,[19] one can understand the derivation of a belief from the individual's exercise of a non-interfered with liberty right to adopt some form of belief. The liberty centres on the underlying object or purpose of the right to conscience in forming a belief, where the state does not define the right in any positive sense. The liberty granted by the right lays the groundwork for the rights holder to make a claim to that entitlement in a specific context. An individual can make a claim to a range of individual actions that have as their source a particular conscientious belief.

Two principal characteristics of a right then can at times clarify one's understanding of a right - the underlying entitlement or purpose in maintaining the right, and the actual conduct or claim towards exercising the right.[20] The normative validity of a right provides the foundation for the entitlement, in essence to create or develop a particular conscientious belief, while the normative autonomy or function of a right provides for its operation, by having the individual adhere to a belief.[21] Each aspect of the right maintains a particular significance, principally for assisting the other in providing for the exercise of the right.

The importance of such an approach towards a human right like the right to freedom of conscience is that it recognises some form of relativity within different legal systems. The right itself can remain fixed as a constant, while its application will vary depending for example on social, economic or political conditions or even personal circumstances.[22] While

---

[19] Donnelly (1985;16) comparing a right with a stolen car. Even if the stolen car's owner does not actually use the car, he still retains the right to enjoy it.
[20] *See also* Eleftheriadis (1996;37) (noting the difference between legal relations, that define the content of a legal rule, and legal remedies, that describe the actual enforcement of these rules).
[21] Bickenbach (1989).
[22] Panichas (1985).

the human 'right' unconditionally exists, its application can differ depending on the social and cultural background of the individual or the state.[23]

The structure of the international human right to freedom of conscience reflects this distinction between the existence, or entitlement, of a right and the application, or claim, of a right. The right to conscience comprises two principal provinces that provide a framework of protection for the right to conscience - the internal source of the right and the external manifestation of the right. The distinction between the *forum internum* and *forum externum*, while not specifically delineating the terms, is the manner in which the right to conscience operates. The *forum internum* relates to the formation of a conscientious belief. For the internal aspect of conscience, the *forum internum*, the importance lies in recognising one's entitlement to develop and harbour a conscientious belief. The focus of the right is on upholding a person's internal, mental, framework that shape and forms the conscience.[24] For the external aspect, the *forum externum*, the important role is the exercise of the right to conscience. The *forum externum* centres on the claim aspect of the right because it entails manifesting or applying one's beliefs.

Before elaborating on the entitlements developed in the *forum internum* and questioning the proposed division between the *forum internum* and *forum externum*, the chapter will offer a comparative look at the relationship between the *forum internum* and *externum*. The interplay between these two aspects of the right to conscience will assist in delineating the desired protection accorded to the *forum internum*. Furthermore, it will highlight the manner in which the *forum internum* and *externum* are intertwined since a limitation imposed on the claim to manifest a belief also can, in certain circumstances, infringe upon the individual's internal entitlement to create and adhere to a specific belief.

The Internal and External Right to Conscience

Referring to the normative functions of an international human right can begin to answer some of the questions referred to above regarding the right

---

[23] A communal society for example will inherently account for local traditions and social considerations. Alexy (1991).
[24] See discussion *infra*.

to conscience. Analysing the function of the right provides a context for creating a framework for the operation of a right and for discerning the boundaries of the right. While the practical application of human rights can at times prove difficult, the purpose of certain human rights is rather clear, as exemplified by some of the basic economic rights such as the right to housing.[25] Nonetheless, many human rights remain ill-defined or misunderstood not only in a practical sense, but also because the function of the right is unclear. When confronted with the right to conscience, a right that has not been practically applied in any clear manner nor fully clarified in international law, it is important to understand and consider the intended functions of human rights within the specific context of the right to conscience.

The basic categorisation of rights offered by Hohfeld provides a platform from which to consider the underlying implications of a right. Placing the right to conscience within Hohfeld's divisions of a right can therefore assist in understanding not only the significance of the right to conscience, once it has attained the status of a human right, but also develop the manner of its application. Additionally, Hohfeld presents an interesting analysis of rights given his interrelationship between rights and obligations. Treating a right as an immunity, liberty, claim or entitlement also entails the removal of a correlative entitlement. The inherent link of rights with obligations is rather significant for the right to conscience given that an assertion of the right generally comes to the fore when a conscientious belief conflicts with a social duty.[26] Hence the correlative approach appears to suit the normative structure of the right to conscience.

The problem with Hohfeld's analysis is that adopting one categorisation of a right does not adequately embody the meaning and scope that was intended for the right to freedom of conscience. Conceiving human rights merely as 'immunities' appears limited in scope. Construing a human right solely as the absence of a prohibition provides an insufficient basis for exercising a human right because the immunity does not necessarily mean that all action emanating from a right is permissible.[27] In the context of the right to conscience for example, the manifestation of a conscientious belief might entail rather broad action. While the absence of a prohibition to believe in a conscientious ideal might provide the grounds

---

[25] *See e.g.* ICESCR Article 11.
[26] The conflict between belief and social duty is generally the case for the manifestation of a belief.
[27] Nino (1991;26,28).

for upholding one's *forum internum*,[28] an immunity will not provide an adequate foundation for exercising the belief, a fundamental aspect of the right, nor protect those individuals who might not want to believe yet are still subject to the persuasions of other believers.

Similarly, treating the right to conscience as an unfettered liberty or privilege implies that the right derives from an external authority. If the external authority is the state, it is possible to restrict the liberty in a broader manner than that provided for in treaty limitations, thereby removing the right from a correlative context. This is the problem for example with military conscientious objection where the liberty to exercise the right in the domestic legislation of many states emanates from a specific legislative provision and not any defined right, such as the right to conscience. The problem is further exacerbated when accounting for selective military objection given that a specific military action conflicts with one's conscientious belief. In such instances, states generally defer to their notion of state necessity for military order and limit the application of the objection to general conscientious objectors.[29] As a result, states impose various restrictions on the right to military objection that reduces the individual's privilege to the right to conscience.[30]

Another possibility is to interpret the right to conscience as a claim that intermingles with the correlative duty due to the claims of other individuals. Initially this approach would appear to be a suitable interpretation of the right to conscience given that particular applications of the right to conscience raise social duty considerations, such as military conscientious objection. Indeed, one of the central arguments of some commentators against the right to military conscientious objection is that the correlative duty on the state to honour the right is non-existent when accounting for the individual's more general social duties.[31]

Understanding the right to conscience as a claim however tends to weaken the correlatively between rights and duties. While an entitlement right to pursue one's basic needs might derive from specific correlative

---

[28] See also discussion *infra* regarding the approach to the *forum internum* as a freedom *from* state interference thereby indicating an active role for the *forum internum* as well.
[29] See discussion *infra* at Chapter Six.
[30] In particular, limiting the right for military objection to religious objectors and not conscientious objectors.
[31] See e.g. Larsen & Hess (1992) (reaching this conclusion because the right to military conscientious objection in the US derives from specific legislation and not the Constitution).

social duties,[32] a conscientious belief derives from independent permissive norms[33] that serve as a basis for creating a particular conscientious belief. As a result of such independent norms, the manifestation of a conscientious belief can affect a variety of constantly shifting correlative duties that also will incorporate the consideration of one's social duty. For example, conscientious objection to the military can derive from beliefs pertaining to a rather broad objection to any form of military participation,[34] a narrow belief in not using firearms, or a totally different belief arising from specific military actions or procedures such as orders pertaining to service in illegally occupied territories, firing on civilian areas, or other breaches of humanitarian norms. While one's social duty to military service is inherent in each instance, each form of belief also raises other personal and social duties that are correlative assertions of the right. Reliance on a belief can affect one's duty to individuals within one's military unit or other individuals who share similar beliefs to the objector. These instances indicate that one's social duty is not a necessary correlative of the right to freedom of conscience since the duty can derive from other social and political forces independent of the right.[35]

Additionally, a key factor of a claim right is the actual exercise of the right.[36] That is, the claimant assumes the existence of the right, as it would be difficult to make a claim for a right that did not exist. The practical exercise of the right comes into play once an individual asserts a claim. As a result, a claim right seems to focus on the function of a right as making a claim, but that does not necessarily define the essence or derivation of a right that would assist in understanding the significance of the *forum internum*.

The problem with focusing on the function of a right is that a host of interpretations that may serve as the basis for a claim might be at odds with other pre-defined rights, especially where state interests transcend individual interests.[37] Deriving the antecedent claim from a person's right to the necessary condition of human existence might lead to results that conflict with other pre-determined, basic, human rights, such as the right to housing in a crowded city versus the right to private property. A claim for

---

[32] See e.g. Gewirth (1982;235) whose entitlement based approach to human rights, which derives from necessary action to pursue one's basic needs, discounts the right to conscience for this very reason.
[33] See discussion *infra*.
[34] Such as some pacifists or a Jehovah Witness. See discussion *infra*.
[35] Raz (1989).
[36] Martins and Nickel (1980).
[37] Shestack (1983).

the unfettered exercise of the freedom of religion inevitably conflicts with other rights such as the rights of minorities or women. Such a consequential approach to rights tends to ignore the inherent conflicts in human rights and does not assist to explain how conflicting claims are to function.

An approach to rights that appears adequately to incorporate the right to conscience as intended by the international human rights framework is one that integrates the various Hohfeldian characteristics of rights. For example, recognising that a liberty right can exist even if the right is not being enforced,[38] one can understand the derivation of a belief from the individual's exercise of a non-interfered with liberty right to adopt some form of belief. The liberty centres on the underlying object or purpose of the right to conscience in forming a belief, where the state does not define the right in any positive sense. The liberty granted by the right lays the groundwork for the rights holder to make a claim to that entitlement in a specific context. An individual can make a claim to a range of individual actions that have as their source a particular conscientious belief.

Two principal characteristics of a right then can at times clarify one's understanding of a right - the underlying entitlement or purpose in maintaining the right, and the actual conduct or claim towards exercising the right.[39] The normative validity of a right provides the foundation for the entitlement, in essence to create or develop a particular conscientious belief, while the normative autonomy or function of a right provides for its operation, by having the individual adhere to a belief.[40] Each aspect of the right maintains a particular significance, principally for assisting the other in providing for the exercise of the right.

The importance of such an approach towards a human right like the right to freedom of conscience is that it recognises some form of relativity within different legal systems. The right itself can remain fixed as a constant, while its application will vary depending for example on social, economic or political conditions or even personal circumstances.[41] While

---

[38] Donnelly (1985;16) comparing a right with a stolen car. Even if the stolen car's owner does not actually use the car, he still retains the right to enjoy it.

[39] *See also* Eleftheriadis (1996;37) (noting the difference between legal relations, that define the content of a legal rule, and legal remedies, that describe the actual enforcement of these rules).

[40] Bickenbach (1989).

[41] Panichas (1985).

the human 'right' unconditionally exists, its application can differ depending on the social and cultural background of the individual or the state.[42]

The structure of the international human right to freedom of conscience reflects this distinction between the existence, or entitlement, of a right and the application, or claim, of a right. The right to conscience comprises two principal provinces that provide a framework of protection for the right to conscience - the internal source of the right and the external manifestation of the right. The distinction between the *forum internum* and *forum externum*, while not specifically delineating the terms, is the manner in which the right to conscience operates. The *forum internum* relates to the formation of a conscientious belief. For the internal aspect of conscience, the *forum internum*, the importance lies in recognising one's entitlement to develop and harbour a conscientious belief. The focus of the right is on upholding a person's internal, mental, framework that shapes and forms the conscience.[43] For the external aspect, the *forum externum*, the important role is the exercise of the right to conscience. The *forum externum* centres on the claim aspect of the right because it entails manifesting or applying one's beliefs.

Before elaborating on the entitlements developed in the *forum internum* and questioning the proposed division between the *forum internum* and *forum externum*, the chapter will offer a comparative look at the relationship between the *forum internum* and *externum*. The interplay between these two aspects of the right to conscience will assist in delineating the desired protection accorded to the *forum internum*. Furthermore, it will highlight the manner in which the *forum internum* and *externum* are intertwined since a limitation imposed on the claim to manifest a belief also can, in certain circumstances, infringe upon the individual's internal entitlement to create and adhere to a specific belief.

Mill and the Forum Internum

In *On Liberty*, Mill addressed the issue of state regulation of an individual's inner domain. He defines this inner domain as solely affecting the individual only and the 'inward domain of consciousness, demanding liberty of conscience in the most comprehensive sense.'[44] When considering

---

[42] A communal society for example will inherently account for local traditions and social considerations. Alexy (1991).
[43] *See* discussion *infra*.
[44] Mill (1859;11).

the necessity for regulating this inner-sphere of liberty, Mill centred on the difference between opinions and actions that might emanate from the inner-sphere.[45] Opinion relates to the beliefs and internal moral values of a person.[46] Opinion however can change in the 'marketplace of ideas' by way of discussion and integration of the opinion into the social system.[47]

While an opinion, or internal thought or belief, can entail social consequences for another,[48] such as concerning their understanding or view of another individual's belief, Mill focuses on protecting others from a person's external actions. He defines the 'interest' of another as a pre-existing, socially created, obligation or duty. Social control limiting one's actions operates when a person raises a claim for protection. This protection is similar to a claim right that creates an obligation on the state to protect that person.[49] An action resulting from a belief that affects the interest of another, with interest defined as another person's *de facto* claim to a right, merits social protection and the imposition of limitations on one's liberty.[50]

The distinction presented by Mill between opinions and actions seems to equate opinion with the *forum internum*. Both Mill's opinion and the *forum internum* are contingent ideas that centre on internal beliefs and, while prone to external influences, do not singularly violate the rights of another. Further, due to the internal nature of an opinion or the *forum internum*, there is no infringement of another individual's interests or rights.

Mill further notes the difference between violating personal dignity as opposed to violating a personal right.[51] One can be apathetic towards one's dignity since the only person whom it will affect in any substantive sense is yourself. One can therefore dress in a slovenly manner or practise boorish manners. An individual cannot be apathetic towards a right since it could result in a violation of an entitlement either to another or oneself. Hence one cannot contract to become a slave since this will entail a violation of a right.

---

[45] Rees (1985;146-149).
[46] *See generally* Rees (1985;Chapter Two).
[47] Rees (1985;121-122). *See generally* Ten (1980;Chapter Three).
[48] *See e.g.* Ten (1980;16); Gray (1983); Rees (1985;138).
[49] Rees (1985;146-148).
[50] Rees (1985).
[51] Mill (1859;77).

Concerning one's personal dignity, a sphere that is seemingly wholly personal and internal, Mill imposes limitations pursuant to his harm principle. If one's dignity or opinion creates such a pernicious effect as to harm the rights of another, infringement of the individual's liberty may occur. The example he raises is a drunken Father who neglects to care for his household. While a person is entitled to become a drunk, that person cannot thereby neglect the rights of his family by not providing food, shelter, and education, as required by social convention. In that instance, society may infringe the individual's liberty, presumably by forcing the drunk to mend his ways. Mill considers the greater 'public order and morality',[52] using terms similar to the limitations enunciated in the human rights treaties, because one cannot ignore the general duty owed to society. By contrast, Mill notes that in a Muslim society, the prohibition of eating pork should not inhibit the individual from doing so in his private domain.

Even upon factoring in his utilitarian tendencies, Mill's protected 'inner-sphere' of liberty can be analogous to the *forum internum*.[53] Gray for example categorises Mill's approach as indirect utilitarianism that entails an intermingling of utilitarian principles, as a justifying basis for action, with individual moral notions that serve as secondary considerations.[54] He concludes that utilitarianism only applies to actions and not opinions such that an opinion would still have relevance for the individual even if not acted upon. More revisionary approaches towards the sphere of liberty, exemplified by Ten, place utilitarian considerations to the side when conflicting with individual moral considerations of the inner domain.[55]

Similarly, when a person internally harbours a moral value or belief, society cannot attempt to alter such knowledge. The human rights system therefore prevents a state from tampering with an individual's internal beliefs, as indicated by the absolute nature of the *forum internum*. Even if an internal belief engenders a general dislike for a minority belief, one need not inhibit the belief as long as no infringement occurs to the rights of the minority. One can therefore harbour racist views internally without being subject to regulation. Manifesting the belief might result in their curtailment, especially if social convention deems such views immoral or contrary to public policy.

Recognising that the right referred to by Mill also relates to the *forum internum*, some of the questions to consider when according the

---

[52] Mill (1859;86).
[53] Note that some commentators dismiss the utilitarian issue by considering Mill in an historical light. *See e.g.* Rees (1985) (Rees distinguishes his view from Himmelfarb who divided Mill into distinct historical periods).
[54] Gray (1983;13).
[55] Ten (1980;18).

forum internum a functional status are the manner of identifying an internal belief and, given such an identification (if possible), how is one to uphold a *forum internum* belief. While Mill's understanding of opinion provided a means of initially identifying the *forum internum*, he clearly was not solely referring to conscience but to a host of conscious opinions and thoughts. The *forum internum* of conscience might differ from other forms of conscious thought given its role in establishing the framework for a conscientious belief. Therefore, to explicate further our understanding of the *forum internum* and its practical application in the international human rights system, it is necessary to identify the internal conscientious ideal developed in the *forum internum* and attempt to differentiate some of the characteristics of the *forum internum* from other general forms of thought.

Dimensions of the *Forum Internum*

Identification Problems

Article 18(2) of the ICCPR indicates an approach towards identifying the *forum internum*. Before providing for the manifestation of the right to conscience, Article 18(2) requires that:

> No one shall be subject to coercion which would impair his freedom to have or to adopt a religion or belief of his choice.[56]

It is apparent from the travaux preparatoires that part of the focus of this subsection is on the forum internum. The travaux note that the intention of the phrase 'to have or adopt' is to sanction the ability of the individual to change a religion or belief, a freedom to which various states severely objected.[57] The drafters linked the ability to change a belief with the forum internum because the change focuses on the internal, cognitive, abilities of the individual. Hence the travaux preparatoires also refer to the

---

[56] *See also* ST/HR/SER.A/16 at paragraph 26 which prohibits a state from using both physical and psychological coercion due to one's religion or belief. The other principal treaties that codify the right to conscience, the UDHR, ECHR, AmCHR, and AfrCHR, do not contain such a provision.

[57] Tahzib (1996); Shaw (1992).

issue of proselytising and the protection of missionaries from coercing individuals into changing their belief.

While one's external actions also might change as a result of adopting a new form of belief, the change itself occurred within the internal sphere due to a conscious decision to adopt a new form of belief. Alternatively, one can be coerced into changing one's external actions without altering one's internal beliefs. A state might unduly limit the manifesting of a belief due to overriding national security interests or internal interests that cause the state to interpret the belief as threatening. Indeed, coercive state tactics might even strengthen one's internal resolve. Such coercion of external actions however results in a violation to the forum externum of the right to freedom of conscience.

Coercion principally focuses on preventing a hindrance to the internal development of ideas and beliefs. The HRC's General Comment to Article 18 defines coercion as incorporating:

> the use of threat or physical force or penal sanctions to compel believers or non-believers ... to recant their religion or belief or to convert. Policies or practices having the same intention or effect ... are similarly inconsistent with Article 18(2).[58]

The General Comment refers not only to preventing the external practice of a belief, the *forum externum*, but also to coercing one to recant a belief, the domain of the *forum internum*. Even if one maintains a *forum internum* belief, one can interpret the coercive actions of the state as violating the *forum internum* right to freedom of conscience, particularly where the state is coercing an individual to alter the internal belief.[59]

Commentators also have interpreted Article 18(2) as centring on the *forum internum*. Coercion appertains to the individual's private, spiritual, or moral existence that cannot be subject to undue persuasion. The prohibited form of coercion differs from influences found in external forces, such as daily exposure to the media and advertising.[60] While 'appeals' to change a belief can include material inducements, the key factor is to avoid coercing the individual's freewill.[61]

---

[58] General Comment to ICCPR Article 18, paragraph 5.
[59] See discussion *infra*.
[60] Nowak (1993;314); Sullivan (1988;494).
[61] Cumper (1995;370) citing to Sullivan (1988;494). Of course, advertising can be coercive as well. See e.g. 7805/77 *Church of Scientology v. Sweden* 16 D&R 68

Both the Indian Supreme Court[62] and the ECHR Court[63] also have distinguished between propagating a religion through missionary work, such as engaging a person in a general discussion, versus forcibly converting a person to another religion. Although not explicitly stated by the ECHR Commission in *Larissis v. Greece*, the prevention of coercion can be a reason for upholding an Air Force member's proselytising to civilians while prohibiting proselytising to fellow Air Force officers.[64] The Commission recognised the concern of the state that the inherent trust between Air Force personnel could be compromised to appease the desires of a superior officer,[65] thereby avoiding the potential for coercion.

Commentators further have noted the illegality of state brainwashing or other inhumane inquisitorial methods that rob the intellectual facilities and conscience of a person.[66] Coercion in this sense is comparable to losing one's autonomous ability to be a person.[67] Additional examples centre on denying the existence of personal moral or religious norms, such as coercing one to follow a particular religious belief system.[68]

Krishnaswami's approach to the *forum internum* also focused on upholding the freedom of one's internal beliefs to prevent compulsion or coercion to belong or not to belong to a certain group.[69] As described by Krishnaswami when studying the right to freedom of religion, a method for violating the *forum internum* is:

> any instance of compelling an individual to join or of preventing him from leaving the organisation of a religion or a belief in which he has no faith must be considered to be an

---

(1979) (restrictions on wording of advert for an 'E-meter', arguably a religious item, was upheld due to commercial nature of transaction).

[62] *Stainslaus v. M.P.* AIR 1977 SC 908.
[63] 14307/88 *Kokkinakis v. Greece* 17 EHRR 397 (1993)(Greek law limiting proselytising exceeded permitted limitations on the right to conscience).
[64] 23372/94 *Larissis v. Greece* VII(1) H.R. Case Digest 60 (1997).
[65] Note as well that limiting the beliefs of a particular group also affects the *forum internum* of other individuals who might have developed their beliefs by being exposed to the suppressed group. This broader aspect of the right shall be considered *infra* regarding the *forum internum* of groups.
[66] Vermeulen (1993;82) relying on the ECHR Travaux Preparatoires at 222.
[67] Shapiro (1983;1289).
[68] McDougal, Laswell and Chen (1980;655-660) discussing mistreatment of individuals identified with a particular religious belief.
[69] Krishnaswami (1960;24-27).

infringement of the right to freedom of thought conscience and religion.[70]

Pursuant to these comments, the protection accorded to the right to conscience in the *forum internum* is to prevent outside forces from violating an individual's internal thoughts and conscientious or religious views. The focus is on prohibiting the compulsion of an individual's internal thought or belief system, with the purpose of altering such a view. For example, brainwashing an individual is not so much concerned with a particular external practice or activity of the individual, but with a desire to change a belief or unit of knowledge harboured internally. The act of brainwashing, which also can entail a physical, external, action that invokes other human rights violations, consists of a desire to impose one's own beliefs or thoughts on the internal structure of the individual.

To further understand the *forum internum* and the protection accorded to an individual's *forum internum* in international human rights law, the prohibition against mental or psychological torture merits scrutiny. Article I of the *Convention Against Torture and other Cruel Inhuman or Degrading Treatment or Punishment* defines torture as including physical *and* mental torture with an intention to coerce or intimidate an individual. The intention of adding the term 'mental' to the Torture Convention was to incorporate actions that force an internal change in the tortured individual's psyche.[71] Instances of such torture include implied threats or creating fear in the victim, thereby altering the victim's perception and forcing a change in one's will or conscience.[72]

Although the ICCPR Article 7 does not specifically prohibit mental torture, the drafters discussed incorporation of the terms 'moral and mental' torture and indicated the prohibition against methods that paralyse the individual's will through non-physical, psychological, methods.[73] While the HRC has not always seized the opportunity to incorporate a prohibition against psychological torture when defining the term,[74] it has acknowledged that psychological torture is an important consideration.[75]

---

[70] Krishnaswami (1960; 16).
[71] Macdonald (1989).
[72] *See also Report in the Greek Case* 12 Ybk of the ECHR 1969 where the European Commission defined torture as driving an individual to act against his will or conscience.
[73] *See e.g.* E/CN.4/SR. 141(1950) that indicates a broad reading for Article 7.
[74] McGoldrick (1991;368).
[75] McGoldrick (1991;376) referring to *Quinteros v. Uruguay* A/38/40 who suffered psychological torture following the disappearance of her daughter.

Mental torture focuses on instances where authorities desire to alter or change the internal belief of a person to extract information or convince the person of their guilt.[76] This understanding of mental torture is similar to the HRC's General Comment to Article 18 regarding the definition of coercion. Both torture and coercion centre on altering the internal conscientious framework of the individual to either extract information or force a change to a person's belief.

Analogous to the prohibition of brainwashing and the prohibition of mental torture may be a host of measures that oppress internal beliefs. Upholding the *forum internum* includes protection from dubious state practices against particular beliefs, especially a belief that need not be asserted in the *forum externum*. Because a person might internally adhere to a particular belief or ideology, as exemplified by external action such as associating with a group or engaging in various protests, the state authority not only opposes the belief, but also desires to alter the belief.

State harassment, such as constantly being followed by a state security agent due to one's association with a contrary belief or religion, is an example of a violation. For example, the African Commission held that Zaire violated AfrCHR Article 8 right to freedom of conscience when the Zaire Government continually harassed Jehovah's Witnesses.[77] The African Commission found that the State targeted the Jehovah's Witnesses for harassment because they were associated with a different form of belief.

By contrast, the ECHR Commission did not find a *forum internum* violation when teachers subjected a pupil to psychological pressure to persuade her to attend religious classes, which she eventually did contrary to the wishes of her parents.[78] The teachers would for example suggest that it would be better for the student to attend the classes and leave blank spaces on her school reports pertaining to religious education. The Commission did not find a *forum internum* violation since there was no indication of indoctrination or force. The Commission held that the

---

[76] Burgers and Danelius (1988).
[77] 56/91 *Les Temoins de Jehovah v. Zaire* reported in 4(1) IHRR 89 (1997) The Commission also accounted for the State's denial of access to education.
[78] 23380/94 *C.J. v. Poland* 84 D&R 46 (1996). *See also* 21787/93 *Valsamis v. Greece* 1996-VI Rep. Judg. & Dec. 2312 involving a student from a Jehovah's Witness household being forced to participate in a parade commemorating National Day that signifies the end of the war with Italy.

exemption from classes sufficed to protect the *forum internum* of the student.[79]

Similar results occur in the United States. For example, in *Mozert v. Hawkins*,[80] parents lost a challenge to their local School Board regarding the liberal reading content of the required textbooks. The claim that the books violated their fundamentalist teaching was dismissed because of the books liberal content that exposed the students to more free thinking forms of thought.

The overall problem with these aforementioned cases is that in deferring to the social system, or to some limitation on the *forum externum* by extrapolating a supposedly neutral social or pubic concern, an infringement occurs to the *forum internum*. The desire not to have a child attend specific classes, even so called neutral classes that address social issues regarding sexual practices, overlooks the parent's reference to a specific belief in protesting the attendance of the child at the classes.[81] While this *forum internum* sphere still requires clarification, it is important to recognise the breadth of the right as accorded by the international human rights system. Although a state might not be coercive in infringing or inhibiting a belief, the actions undertaken to limit a belief clearly will affect the *forum internum*.

The significance in broadening the understanding of the right to conscience in the *forum internum* is that it provides an expanded protection for beliefs that the *forum externum* or other human rights might not uphold. Even in instances where the making of a statement or the manifestation of a belief might not merit protection, the absolute protection accorded to the *forum internum* of a conscientious belief seems to provide some protection, particularly in cases where the state desires to alter the belief as well.

The Broad Scope of the Forum Internum

Noting the link between the *forum internum* and external actions such as torture demonstrates that the protection accorded to the *forum internum* is not exclusively limited to prohibitions against intrusive 'internal' action by an outside party, such as psychological as opposed to physical torture.[82]

---

[79] The Commission also dismissed the claim of emotional distress on the basis of ECHR Article 3 and not Article 9.
[80] *Mozert v. Hawkins Cty. Bd. of Education* 827 F.2d 1058 (6th Cir. 1987).
[81] *See e.g.* Stolzenberg (1993;650) noting how deference to the liberal tradition, no matter how open-minded, tends to inhibit other beliefs that deem liberal thought a threat to their beliefs.
[82] *Contra* Dickson (1995;328).

The protection also can extend to prohibiting external actions that lead to a violation of the *forum internum* since that is the forum where one forms a belief and from which emanates an individual's direction for external action. Alternatively, just as the external actions of an individual need not be an actual manifestation of a belief, a *forum internum* violation can result from merely targeting an individual for identifying with a particular belief. The violation of the *forum internum* develops as the authority or external source acts to alter the internal belief. The key factor is the focus on altering the individual's adherence to a particular thought or belief.

The description however demonstrates the fine line inherent in identifying a violation of the *forum internum*. Many instances of a violation will spill over into the domain of the *forum externum* or other rights, especially where external state action might mask the underlying intentions of a state. As noted in the HRC's General Comment to Article 18, for example, ICCPR Article 17 (right to privacy) and Article 19(1) (right to hold opinions without interference) serve to buttress the unlimited protection accorded to the *forum internum*.[83]

ECHR cases also tend to link ECHR Article 8 (right to privacy) with instances of conscientious assertions centring on altering a belief. For example, the case of *Kjeldsen, Busk, & Pederson v. Denmark*[84] entailed a challenge before the ECHR Court regarding the teaching of sex education in public schools. The applicants contended that such education violated a belief in privately educating one's children on the matter of sex. The ECHR distinguished between religious education, as involving private matters, and a sex education course, as relating to social public morals. The ECHR Court considered the right to privacy issue that the case raised in tandem with the asserted challenge to the applicant's belief regarding sexual education. Although the outcome of the case hinged on privacy grounds, the Court noted the inherent relationship between these rights.[85] From a standpoint that accounts for the *forum internum* however the case is merely

---

[83] HRC General Comment to Article 18, paragraph 3. *See also* Nowak (1993;294-295;314-315) making a similar point regarding privacy and concluding that the private sphere is not subject to any limitations.

[84] 5095/71 *Kjeldsen, Buck. & Pederson v. Denmark* 1 EHRR 711(1980).

[85] *See also* 8811/79 *X Y & Z v. Sweden* 5 EHRR 147 (1984) (right to privacy not violated after state imposed restrictions on religious sect that believed in beating their children); 12875/87 *Hoffman v. Austria* 17 EHRR 293 (1994) (Commission held that Articles 8 and 14 - right against discrimination - were violated for Jehovah's Witness' right to custody. The Court decided the case solely on the basis of Article 14).

a contingent decision based on the subjective understanding of the ECHR Court of sexual mores because one may treat sex and religion as a public or private matter. Indeed one's attitudes towards sex and religion are generally linked, such that internally asserting a belief on a matter, even if not entitled to manifestation, still demands some form of entitlement.

Another typical example would be discrimination against an individual for identifying with a group that professes a particular belief. While the state might be interfering with the individual's *forum internum* if the state desires that an individual alter a belief, the violating state action generally entails a claim of discrimination against the state.[86] Thus even if initially a state might focus on an individual in a manner that seems to violate the *forum internum*, i.e. with a specific intention to alter the internal belief system of the individual, the eventual violation will centre on more explicit human rights breaches, such as torture or the right to security.[87]

The odd result seems to be that while the protection accorded to the individual's *forum internum* is quite broad, the actual illegitimate activity is limited. This narrow application of the right derives from the difficulty in identifying violations of an internal belief when dealing with more extreme state action such as discrimination or right to security, the general conflict between social interests and individual interests, and the ease in focusing on identifiable actions of the *forum externum*.

The lack of any practical application of the *forum internum* indicates the impossible situation that an unfettered right creates. That is, a state that recognises a particular belief system, and provides for the belief system's operation, will by definition be excluding other forms of beliefs that either conflict with the prior approved belief system, in the freedom *to* sense, or cannot provide the belief system the ability to adhere to their own practices, in the freedom *from* sense.[88] While the state may defer to the limitations provided in the human rights treaties, the limitations do not apply to the *forum internum*, an area that also will seemingly be violated should a belief be suppressed even on a legitimate basis.

Additionally, it is difficult to define the scope of the *forum internum* of a conscientious belief because it relates to all forms of thought and mental processes.[89] This is especially the case when considering the broad manner in which external authorities can influence or violate an individual's thoughts. An authority might cause an alteration of the *forum internum* by forcing an individual to divulge certain information.

---

[86] *See e.g.* ICCPR Article 26.
[87] *See e.g.* 195/1985 *Delgado v. Columbia* (1990).
[88] Fish (1997).
[89] *See* discussion *infra* regarding the distinction between thought and conscience.

Alternatively, an authoritative influence can result unintentionally by limiting an individual's education that will hinder one's mental processes or by encouraging an excessively competitive society that can create frustrated individuals who cannot cope with social demands.[90] One's internal thoughts also will be a reflection of one's own intellectual limitations that can hinder a person's overall mental perceptions. Such a drawback can result exclusive of any external authority. For example, it can derive as a result of one's upbringing or unduly traumatic childhood.

Obviously it was not the intention that an international human right would hold the state accountable for all forms of *forum internum* alterations, even if they might be due to state oversight or error, such as not adopting a structured education policy.[91] The examples of brainwashing and coercion however suggests a more active role by the authority, one that seems to adopt a teleological approach towards the authority's actions. The indication is that while the international human rights system accords the *forum internum* an unlimited scope of protection, the actual violation of the right by state activity is subject to a rather specific set of circumstances. While such an approach is practically sound, it does raise questions regarding the requirement on the state to protect all forms of beliefs, even beliefs that are inherently contradictory to the state's basic tenets. As a result, it seems that a limitation on the manifestation of a belief in the *forum externum* also results in a limitation on the *forum internum*.

Analogy to Forum Externum

There remains a host of questions to consider regarding the *forum internum* right. What if the mere existence of the belief harms another, for example believing in homosexuality or abortion might create feelings of disgust in another person? The question is especially relevant if the disgusted person is of a particular religious persuasion. Further, how is one to then achieve a balance between the individual's liberty and social interests? Can one limit pornography merely because one believes that it is indecent? Will that person's internal beliefs then be 'harmed' upon observing a pornographic book for sale in a local shop? What if the internal belief centred on a religious principle, such as the one cited by Mill regarding a Muslim not

---

[90] Scharr (1967).
[91] *See also* ICCPR Article 18(4).

eating pork? Could the local butcher sell pork even if the sale might infringe the Muslim's internal belief system?

While the *forum internum* differs from the *forum externum* principally as a result of the physical realm of the right, one can analogise between the two to clarify the *forum internum*'s scope. The freedom of conscience in the *forum externum* has been grouped into two fundamental sections. The right applies to freedom *to* a belief, meaning to practise according to the beliefs' directives, as well freedom *from* a belief, meaning to prevent applications of a belief's requirements on a non-believer. While this division does not alter the practical application of the right, international commentators use the approach to clarify the dimensions of the right.[92]

One also may divide the *forum internum* along similar lines, despite operating within a different context than the *forum externum*. Indications for this approach to the *forum internum* are found in ICCPR Article 18(2), where the terms 'have or adopt' have been interpreted as protecting the individual's right to change a religion, freedom *to*, as well as limiting the actions of excessively zealous missionaries, freedom *from*.[93] The HRC also has noted that 'coercion' applies to not only impairing one's right to a belief (freedom *to*) but also to protecting non-believers from compulsion to believe (freedom *from*).[94] The next two sections will amplify these distinctions by considering freedom *from* and *to* within the context of the *forum internum*.

Freedom To

The principal considerations of the freedom *to* for the *forum internum* relate to situations where it is not necessarily the physical practice of the belief that merits protection but the ability to mentally adhere to a belief or thought. In such a case, the state might be imposing its will through various avenues that need not necessarily entail a physical violation but affect the person's psyche or mental process. The key factor here is the consequential desire of the state to alter the internal beliefs or thoughts of a person, even when associating the state violation with another form of human rights violation.

For example, a state's suppression of a person's freedom of expression also can violate one's *forum internum* if the state desires that the

---

[92] *See e.g.* Krishnaswami (1960).
[93] Scheinen (1992;267).
[94] HRC General Comment to Article 18, paragraph 5.

person alter the expressed belief rather than solely suppress the expression. It is one thing for a state to close the offices of a particular journal or limit the political abilities of a group that the state deems a public danger. It is quite a graver violation however for a state also to attempt to alter the internal beliefs of the journalists or the dissident group making the expression by way of mental or physical coercion.[95]

That a particular external action occurred need not disqualify the violation of the *forum internum* vis-`a-vis freedom *to*. As noted above, the scope of the *forum internum* right is quite broad such that the analysis of the violation will generally focus on more explicit or violent violations that emanate from the underlying goal of altering the internal belief. This distinction in degree of state action can reflect instances in which states can suppress other human rights, such as in national emergencies. The difference exists when considering the need for maintaining state stability during instances of internal strife,[96] versus quashing a liberation movement with a view towards altering the views of the movement's members.

A 1990 case before the HRC demonstrates the manner in which to apply the freedom *to* right. In *Delgado v. Columbia,* the state demoted the plaintiff, a teacher, from his position in a state school as a result of his insistence on teaching liberation theology along with the required curriculum mandated by the State's Church authorities. The School system forced the plaintiff to teach in areas not relating to his expertise, threatened him with criminal prosecution on false charges, and he was subjected to harassment and duress, for example, receiving threatening, anonymous, telephone calls.[97]

---

[95] Coercive state tactics to alter a belief sometimes serve to strengthen the belief rather than diminish it. This result does not change the fact that the state is committing a *forum internum* violation.

[96] Fox & Nolte (1995) (contending that a newly formed democratic state might be entitled to breach certain rights in order to sustain the viability of the state).

[97] *See also* 314/1988 *Bwala v. Zambia* (1993) where the HRC found a violation of the right to security for a political party member who was prevented from campaigning, was continually harassed, and was denied employment.
A similar case was also raised before the AmCHR Commission after the Nicaraguan Government published false information regarding the leader of the opposition political party. The applicant claimed that the Government violated AmCHR Article 12 because their actions effectively stifled his beliefs. *See* Res. No. 29/86 OAS Doc. OEA/Ser.L/V/II.68, Doc. 8 Rev. 1 (1986). The AmCHR Commission however decided the case on defamation grounds, AmCHR Article 5.

The HRC held that ICCPR Article 9 (right to security) was the applicable provision as it is a State's duty to safeguard individuals who are subject to such threats. The HRC limited its examination of ICCPR Article 18 to the manifestation of the belief, the *forum externum*, and held that there was no violation since the government can control state education of religion.

Considering the case from the *forum internum* standpoint however the state exerted pressure on the individual as a result of his identification with a set of beliefs. Granted that the manifestation of the beliefs might have been properly curtailed by not allowing the plaintiff to preach his minority beliefs in a state school classroom.[98] However the subsequent treatment of the plaintiff as a result of his beliefs, including the alteration of his position from religious educator to teaching shop mechanics and ongoing harassment through bogus telephone calls, created a different violation than a breach of the right to security.[99] The violations of the plaintiff's rights resulted in the State oppressing the plaintiff due to his internal beliefs that conflicted with the authorities. This is especially the case for the State Church that had withdrawn initial support for the plaintiff as a religious teacher despite being aware of his liberation-theology beliefs. The State's actions indicated a desire to alter the plaintiff's belief before allowing him to continue teaching the religious course.

Freedom From

Freedom *from* in the *forum internum* involves the imposition of an outside belief with the purpose of impelling the individual to adopt a particular belief. The underlying objective of the imposing force is to replace one belief for another; however a person need not identify with a particular ideology to have this aspect of the *forum internum* violated. Freedom *from* primarily relates to developing a proper and fair social divide that provides for the existence of beliefs while preventing imposition of these beliefs on another. Individual beliefs should be granted the ability to develop independently of undue influences from ancillary sources, such as an

---

[98] *Cf.* 23991/94 *Ergul v. Turkey* 84 D&R 69 (1996) (Commission upheld denial of judicial service due to claimant's membership in a political party. State policy was deemed a necessary condition established by law).

[99] Some commentators limit the right to security to circumstances surrounding detention, such as an individual facing an unfounded threat of detention. *See e.g.* Dinstein (1981;128); Niemi-Kiesilainen (1992;150). The HRC decisions seem to refute their conclusions.

authority's ideologically derived desire to entrench a particular thought in the psyche of its populace.[100]

The freedom *from* aspect of the *forum internum* is generally easier to identify than freedom *to* because a state is targeting a specific belief or mode of thought with a view towards changing it. Since the state is acting as an overseer of thought, the compulsion on the individual's *forum internum* is more recognisable. The state is acting in a pro-active manner by creating a policy of desired change and forcing modification of one's internal thoughts and beliefs. Even if the targeted individual does not adhere to a belief, a violation occurs when a state acts to alter or instil a particular belief. For example, a state violates the right to free expression by requiring its teachers to accede to a 'duty of loyalty' oath to the state, even if a teacher is a member of a dissident political faction.[101] In such a case, a violation to the *forum internum* also occurs. The state desires to alter the views of political dissent groups by imposing state ideology at the expense of an internal belief. The same standard would conceivably apply even when a state relies on the loyalty oath pursuant to a treaty limitation, such as state necessity in times of political unrest. Given the broad right of the *forum internum*, a violation of the right can occur. Even factoring in the limitations of the *forum externum* does not discount a possible violation of the *forum internum*.

Of course, the distinction between freedom *from* and *to* in the *forum internum* is not a strict division. The lines eventually merge as a result of social and individual forces. While the thoughts or beliefs of an individual serve to structure the overall social and cultural construct, such thoughts and beliefs originated from objectively accepted knowledge that the individual had acquired from external sources. Culture is a multi-directional process that provides a social framework for operation; a person objectifies one's inner thoughts into an external reality and the thoughts are subsequently internalised back into the subjective consciousness. Each aspect of culture is equally important since the definition of reality transpires by how other members of society view one's thoughts, especially since one defines reality by a comparison with the external objective world.[102]

---

[100] A similar problem is raised when internal groups within the state impose their views with the goal of altering the individual's *forum internum*.
[101] 17851/91 *Vogt v. Germany* 21 EHRR 205 (1996).
[102] Berger (1969;16).

The result is that without referring to the expressive symbols of the external reality, one's internal thought patterns become meaningless. As noted by Geertz, culture defines the individual because the individual is dependent on culture to adequately define his or her behaviour.[103] External influences on a person (freedom *from*) also shape and form a person's beliefs (freedom *to*),[104] particularly when considering a person's development in a closely knit social, religious, or group context. As a result, whatever a person believes (freedom *to*) will, to a certain extent, indicate the social and communal arrangement of that society (freedom *from*) that influenced, to varying levels of degrees, the individual's beliefs.

Significance for the Forum Internum

There is an even greater significance to the blurring of the freedom *from* and freedom *to* divide that will further enlighten our understanding of the *forum internum*. In forming a belief in the *forum internum*, the individual is subject to a host of internal and external influences that derive from constant interaction with society. The implication seems to be that this bilateral relationship between the individual and society highlights the importance of *how* we go about acquiring knowledge or shaping a conscientious standard. Therefore, what is important for the conscientious process is not an understanding of the relationship between conscience and morals (or some other 'universal' form of ethical standard), but an analysis of the dynamic of the relation between conscience with the external world.

For example, in discussing the epistemology of a person, Foucault indicated similar considerations even in more objective fields such as the natural sciences. Foucault noted that discoveries solely do not occur because of scientific, empirical, experiments, but as a result of changes in the political and social arena that alter our perception and understanding of certain processes; discoveries happen as different discourses become acceptable and society removes previous social or language barriers.[105] Hence one may interpret a belief or ideology not as a truism, but as resulting from the 'effects of truth [that] are produced within a discourse which in themselves are neither true nor false'.[106] The knowledge at one's

---

[103] Geertz (1973;43-44) contends that one should grasp the unique nature of each culture rather than attempt to construct universal, and somewhat shallow, generalisations about overall culture.
[104] Hence the right to educate ones child pursuant to one's beliefs. *See* ICCPR Article 18(4).
[105] Foucault (1980;115).
[106] Foucault (1980;118).

disposal produces what the individual or society understands to be the truth.[107] The significance of such an approach is that the internal development of a belief is the result of a host of influences based on our particular regime of understanding; a belief need not relate to the truth of one's existence nor to some lofty ethical standard.

Additionally, Foucault can shed some light on the relationship between the *forum externum* and the *forum internum*. For Foucault, thought is not necessarily a subjective, interior, process, but is an external transgressive idea that defines an attitude of what we are ontologically.[108] Consequently, it is possible that certain essential considerations regarding the manifestation of a conscientious belief can assist in clarifying the scope of protection granted to the *forum internum*. While the difference between the *forum internum* and *forum externum* is that the exteriority is limited for the *forum internum* since it emanates from the individual's subjective understanding of the changes and discourses surrounding him, social factors, or transgressive considerations, will influence and shape one's internal belief structure. For example, understanding knowledge as a transgressive notion can result in a comprehensive shift regarding the individual's reliance on conscience. Relying on a conscientious belief need not entail an individual's strive for the search for a universal truth, but rather can be understood as an ongoing search for a new understanding of one's position in the world and a sharper focus on the freedom that defines an individual's distinguished role in life.[109] The key factor is to acknowledge our derivation of knowledge and understand our social interactions, with a view towards shaping a new understanding of ourselves.[110] This is rather significant for the *forum internum* since it assists to identify the underlying goal when considering a conscientious belief. As the external world shifts and different alternatives become available, one's approach to the truth of a particular belief also will be subject to change. Beliefs then become contingent ideas, given different levels of knowledge and understanding in societies.

---

[107] For Foucault, this was a rather important point given the inherent relation between one's acquisition of knowledge and one's use of power.
[108] Simons (1995;89).
[109] Bernauer and Mahon (1995;153).
[110] Rouse (1995;111) noting that understanding Foucault as striving for an ongoing process of attaining truth can begin to address critics such as Taylor and Rorty, whose analyses were tied to the epistemic or political sovereign such that they could not avoid the conclusion that Foucault was caught in a never-ending cycle of power.

While the classification of the *forum internum* into freedom *to* and *from* assists to understand descriptively the right, and begins to categorise it, one is still left with a rather broad scope for the *forum internum*. Internal thoughts and beliefs refer to essentially anything, particularly when considering the subjective quality of thoughts as well as the difficulty in creating an objective, justifiable, basis for beliefs. One qualifying factor is that a particular aspect of the individual's *forum internum* has been the focus of discussion, namely conscience. From a relational standpoint, conscience, as defined *infra*, refers to more precise beliefs that create the groundwork for particular external action. A general conscious thought does not necessarily require a particular manifestation because it can 'exist' within one's psyche without ever being manifest. While this distinction is somewhat superficial, given that conscientious beliefs also can exist internally without manifesting, the purpose in upholding the *forum internum* of a conscientious belief is to lead to a manifestation of such a belief as a result of the nature and content of conscience and its implications for the individual's belief system. From a phenomenological standpoint, the sufficiency of a conscientious belief essentially requires its eventual manifestation. A more general thought also can have external implications, but it is not a necessary result of all conscious thought.

Such an approach explains why one can commingle the freedom *from* and *to* given the relation between the individual and society. Social agents are linked because as we attain knowledge, we acquire greater control over the individuals around us.[111] Yet, such control is not a uni-directional assertion of power by a sovereign over his subjects, but is a multi-layered process that involves approval and sanction from a host of agents.[112] Hence developing a conscientious belief entails external relations as well as eventual manifestation. As a conscientious belief reflects the individual's acquisition of knowledge and understanding, so too the role that the belief will play in social interaction will have a significant effect on one's actions.

Because a conscientious belief might require specific external action, one may consider the *forum internum* for such particular beliefs alongside the manifestation of the belief or the exercise of another right. For example a state violates the right to free expression by requiring its teachers to accede to a 'duty of loyalty' oath to the state, even if a teacher is

---

[111] Rouse (1995;105).
[112] Hence Foucault's disillusionment with the notion of sovereignty since the analyses of sovereignty tended to focus on the relationship of the subjects to the sovereign, when the relationship was more complex and dynamic. *See e.g.* Constable (1991).

a member of a dissident political faction.¹¹³ In cases where the refusal to accede to an oath stems from a belief, be it political or otherwise, a violation of the *forum internum* also occurs. The state desires to inhibit the views and actions of political dissident groups as a result of a specific belief that has not manifested or the state has prevented manifestation pursuant to a limitation.¹¹⁴ Yet one can discern a *forum internum* violation particularly should one's belief be infringed.

To fully comprehend the protection being granted to the *forum internum* of conscience, it is essential to analyse conscience and the implications of a conscientious belief for the individual, as well as begin to point out some practical differences between a conscientious belief and other forms of thought.

Forum Internum and Conscience

Dual Notion of Forum Internum *Beliefs*

As noted, the treaties that codify the right to conscience describe the *forum internum* as protecting 'religion conscience and thought' but use the terms 'religion and belief' to codify the manifestation of the right in the *forum externum*. While the next chapter will address the meaning of the term 'belief' vis-à-vis the *forum externum*, apparently the *forum internum* relates to a range that includes all forms of thought.

'Thought' implies an infinite realm of ideas that a person might internally harbour. These can range from a general opinion, such as the merits of the colour blue in a bedroom, to a more developed form of knowledge, such as one's understanding of the laws of nuclear physics. By contrast, the protected *forum internum* beliefs are closely aligned to a psychological conception of the term. A 'belief' in that sense refers to an internal unit of knowledge deriving from specific mental processes. The unit of knowledge acquires its importance because individuals' attribute to such knowledge some level of truth, even for a non-scientifically justified

---

113   17851/91 *Vogt v. Germany* 21 EHRR 205 (1996) (case decided within the context of the 'necessity' limitation of ECHR Article 9, which was deemed inapplicable to a teacher of languages).
114   Note that if a state utilises the loyalty oath on the basis of an allowed limitation, such as state necessity in times of political unrest, a *forum internum* violation can still occur.

belief,[115] which in turn leads to some form of compelling external action. The *forum internum* then encompasses all forms of thought and knowledge since it is internally unlimited, is subject to constant change and development as one considers new inputs of knowledge that institute the thought process, and is unique to each individual since each person's social experiences and particular environment will result in different thoughts and knowledge.[116]

Furthermore, *forum internum* thoughts need not manifest themselves as *forum externum* beliefs since more general forms of expression could suffice.[117] For example, one's thought as to the merits of painting a prison wall bright red as opposed to brown based on the psychological benefits to the inmates can manifest itself through a number of general avenues. The typical mode might be by expressing one's opinion in governmental reports or professional journals relating to prisons. While the underlying 'belief' originates from an internal thought developed in the *forum internum*, the manifested action does not derive from a mandate to 'adhere' to the belief but results from a decision to express an opinion stemming from a thought. The thought itself does not demand any particular action from the person, even if it influences a person towards taking some form of external action, such as testifying to the benefits of the colour red before a governmental prison committee.

Of course, the individual is free to engage in particular actions that might be equivalent to the manifestation of a belief. Adhering to the belief that all prison walls are to be red might mandate a psychologist to personally paint all such walls or demand that it be carried out according to his beliefs. Just as a doctor's Christian belief is grounds for not performing an abortion based on the specific mandates of the belief, a psychologist also can refer to an internal belief as grounds for performing a particular action. The treaty terms 'to manifest his religion or belief in worship, observance, practice, and teaching' indicate such an approach, as the treaty drafters' were referring to cognitive beliefs that the individual relates to an underlying truth through one's existence.[118] Unlike a general thought, the manifestation of a 'belief' mandates specific modes of action pursuant to particular principles from which it is difficult to deviate. The narrower *forum externum* sphere of beliefs then derives from structured internal

---

[115] Any form of criticism will result from inter-subjective thought thereby preventing any true form of objective criticism. *See e.g.* Popper (1945;213).
[116] Bar-Tal (1990;Chapter One).
[117] The typical example is freedom of thought manifesting via the freedom of expression. Van Dijk and Van Hoof (1990;398).
[118] Partsch (1981); Lillich (1981); McDougal, Laswell, and Chen (1980); Benito (1989).

obligations that differ from the general units of knowledge protected in the *forum internum*.

Because a manifested *forum externum* originates from particular internal processes, the *forum internum* of such beliefs also take on a different character than the more general notions incorporated by thought. Granted that all internal beliefs derive from a host of influences and justifications. The internal conscientious process takes a belief a step further by shaping and developing a belief into a more structured set of conative directives or imperatives that mandate particular action. The direction of the internal mental process that shapes and forms the belief is towards specific external action. A Christian doctor for example is relying on specific internal directives as developed by basic tenets of her religious or conscientious belief when refusing to perform an abortion. Similarly, a prison psychologist might be relying on an internal belief regarding the virtues of red walls in prison as a basis for painting the walls red. This is not to say that one may manifest all religious or conscientious beliefs;[119] however highlighting the belief does clarify the distinction between a conscientious belief and a general thought because of the importance of the eventual manifestation of the belief to uphold a belief's underlying tenets or directives through particular action.

The distinction between a conscientious belief and a general thought indicates a broader freedom for the right to conscience. Recognising that a conscientious belief relates to a specific form of action that differs from a general thought provides a focus not only on the protection accorded to the manifestation of the belief, but also augments the possibility for *forum internum* protection. If one recognises the development of a conscientious belief as a distinct process because the belief develops into specific external practices, the protection accorded to the internal aspect of the belief is similarly entitled to specific protection.

One of the problems with this approach is that it relies on the *ex post* manifestation to define a conscientious belief. Not all beliefs manifest or need to be manifested. Especially when considering the freedom *from* notion, where a belief is maintaining a passive role, there is no clarification regarding the scope of positive protection; rather the state's actions are to be limited to protect or preserve a particular belief. Discerning the belief might be difficult if it has not manifested, yet state action might require curtailment if a state's edicts or policies infringe the individual's *forum*

---

[119] *See* discussion *infra* at Chapter Five.

internum. Alternatively, the *forum internum* might be so broad as to prove unworkable. Mill's example of pork being sold in a local shop as infringing the sensibilities of local Muslims clearly relates to the *forum internum*. No particular external action or manifestation of the belief is being infringed, yet one can conceive an infringement of an internal belief by the public sale of pork.

An additional problem with relying on the manifestation of a belief to discern the *forum internum* is that as the state imposes limitations on the *forum externum*, the limitations will no doubt affect the *forum internum*. Preventing the practice of a belief, even when justified, tends to internally inhibit the belief itself given that the belief mandates particular action. Hence in instances where a state imposes limitations on social or public policy grounds, such as sex education or a 'neutral' religious education, an infringement on the *forum internum* of individuals who maintain contrary beliefs nevertheless can occur.[120] The infringement is not only in a personal sense, such as Muslims who cannot bear the sale of pork given their particular belief, but also one finds limitations of beliefs due to the infringement upon particular principles of one's belief.[121] Preventing the manifestation cannot but avoid some form of internal harm to the belief itself.

These problems identified with the *forum internum* suggest that its inviolability might be a practical impossibility. Yet, the *forum internum* merits some form of protection given its seminal epistemological role in shaping and creating an individual's beliefs. Focusing on the manifestation of a belief might still assist to define the contours of the *forum internum*, or at least indicate the framework of that sphere. One way to achieve this elusive definition is to further elaborate on how a conscientious or religious belief differs from a 'belief' that derives from a general unit of knowledge or from a more particular thought that encompasses a person's external actions. One might believe in the necessity for prison reform and the need for painting prisons the colour red as an example of manifesting a belief at the expense of one's employment or personal relationships. Even if such a belief does not relate to the 'truth of one's existence', at best a narrow, subjective and somewhat stilted understanding of a belief, a psychologist might desire to adhere to the belief because for her it reflects the

---

[120] This contention regarding the violation of a person's belief seems to be the point raised by the dissent in 21787/93 *Valsamis v. Greece* 1996-VI Rep. Judg. & Dec. 2312.

[121] A similar contention is raised by the cognitive dissonance theory since a religion will attempt to structure external actions pursuant to social demands in order to maximise the internal consistency of one's cognitive system. Hence, social policy can restructure religious beliefs. *See e.g.* Harmer-Dionne (1998) (discussing the US ban on polygamous marriages for Mormons).

truth. Acknowledging that a conscientious belief merits specific protection that differs from that provided to a thought, how is conscience different, if at all, from a thought? The next section will begin to address this issue by focusing on the *forum internum* of conscience and the foundational role it can play in upholding the manifestation of the belief in the *forum externum*.

Development and Meaning of Conscience

Understanding Conscience

The term 'conscience' can imply a host of internal or external reactions depending on one's approach towards the meaning of the term.[122] Some commentators treat conscience as an emotive based response to a dilemma,[123] or adopt a psychological approach.[124] Conscience then preserves the individual's inner harmony based on apprehensive thoughts - internal disharmony - should the conscience be violated. Conscience need not be an emotive reaction but a reflexive action motivated by an egoistic desire to prevent a person's apprehension arising from a loss of harmony. Such an understanding also removes conscience from any moral context.[125]

Other approaches to conscience view a conscientious belief as creating some form of Kantian categorical imperative. This approach is somewhat analogous to the historical link between conscience and religion whereby conscience was to reflect an objective notion of morals based on theological principles. In each instance, one associate's conscience with pre-determined cognitive beliefs that involve particular manifested action.

The various approaches accorded to conscience demonstrate that, from a phenomenological standpoint, it is virtually impossible to adequately define the meaning or implications of conscience. When

---

[122] See e.g. Bahm (1964) grouping conscience into a number of categories, centring on the innate - such as biological, acquired - such as apprehension, and a combination of the two - such as a personal, spiritual, experience.
[123] See e.g. Arendt (1971).
[124] Freud, who links conscience with the superego.
[125] May (1983) notes that the 'inner harmony' approach favours harm to oneself rather than another as a means of reducing apprehension if confronted with the choice. This results in the individual deferring to the interests of another pursuant to a pre-conceived conscientious standard, the very action which the approach was attempting to avoid.

considering one's subjective nature of comprehension, which is accompanied by an inherent personal agenda,[126] attempting to identify the underlying conscientious reasoning of a person seems an impossibility.

For example, equating conscience with an emotion[127] at first glance seems valid when considering the subjective nature of conscience as being governed by one's emotional whims. A similar approach relies on a psychological definition of internal reasoning, such as Freud's linking of conscience with the superego. Each equates conscience with other human phenomenon, such as a desire for inner harmony, and attempts to incorporate a wide range of internal mental processes.

On a functional level, however, these views do not cover the range of beliefs associated with conscience. Despite conscience being a process that derives from internal reasoning,[128] one must not lose sight of the derivation of such reasoning. An individual acquires an understanding of the world and the ability to reason from a host of social and communal factors. Conscience also must account for the broader social and moral considerations before undergoing any external action. One couples the 'inner morality' of conscience with an evaluation of the person's overall condition of existence as influenced by society and distinct personal experience.[129] A conscientious determination is to relate to one's destiny both individually and socially.[130] As noted by Fuchs:

> The subject, in the realisation of the object world,... must on account of his goodness attempt with personal responsibility to act according to the proper meaning of the human object world.[131]

Hence the 'moral' approval involved in the conscientious process, even if not universal, incorporates some form of social value for the individual within the social group.[132]

Additionally, equating conscience with a categorical imperative or moral duty, such as noted by Kant or a latter-day theologian, creates a problem when confronted with a moral uncertainty. Reference to pre-

---

[126] Taylor (1985) (consideration of the self in the moral space is quite vast due to a person's particular identifications).
[127] See e.g. Arendt (1971).
[128] See e.g. Richards (1986;71).
[129] Virt (1987).
[130] Kordig (1979).
[131] Fuchs (1987:36) (note that since the author is a theologian who relies on St. Thomas Aquinas, he assumes that goodness exists prior to conscience); Harvey (1970).
[132] Garnett (1965).

determined moral principles for an individual confronted with a moral dilemma will not necessarily resolve the conflict. Focusing on the maxims of conscience and not the motivations for action cause conscience to become a blind duty that ignores the broader effects of one's actions[133] and seems to overlook the possibility for relative human action. Indeed such an overbearing belief is what the international human rights system desired to avoid. Furthermore, rationality is only a necessary, but not a sufficient, condition for conscience since referring to logic does not identify what is to be adhered to.[134] Such an approach is a contingent process that is subject to speculative reason, a problem associated with humanism in general.

Note however that one should not discount the descriptions accorded to conscience by these views as they represent internal mental processes meriting *forum internum* protection, particularly when acknowledging that conscience is a peculiar combination of both feelings, a psychological fact, and claims.[135] The underlying problem with these descriptive approaches when considering the manner in which to practically apply the *forum internum* right to conscience is that no one can unequivocally prove or demonstrate what this internal conscientious process entails or consequentially creates. The conscientious process appears to entail broader considerations, such that examining the moral ontology of a conscientious belief in the same manner as a rule of natural science appears misplaced.

Conscience and Moral Action

The problem then is obvious for the *forum internum* right given the seemingly impossible absolute protection accorded to the right by the international system. How is one to consider exactly what is being upheld in the *forum internum*? Further, is it possible that the difficulty in applying the *forum internum* right derives not from the inability to adequately identify the internal belief, but rather because of an authority's need to exclude other beliefs simply by default? Recognising this inherent conundrum for a supposed tolerant system that desires to uphold all forms of the *forum internum*, the critical approach presents a seemingly insurmountable problem.

---

[133] Teale (1952) (noting that Kant adhered to a strict duty of conscience as a means of avoiding the erratic or incorrect conscience).
[134] MacIntyre (1981;Chapter Five).
[135] McGuire (1963).

Adopting an understanding of a belief that operates in a setting similar to Foucault's understanding of the truth might begin to suggest a resolution to the problem. Foucault proposed that the issue regarding the truth is one's striving to acquire knowledge, and not necessarily the struggle between what is and what is not the truth. Rather, the truth is subject to the social regime's understanding of the truth, which will in turn influence the individuals understanding of it as well. The truth, or for our purposes, a conscientious belief, is not an achievement of a final goal that definitely states what the truth is; rather, it is an ongoing social process based on external discourses and what society deems is important at a given moment. Similar to the eighteenth and nineteenth century class struggle, where the battle was not between the powerful 'haves' and the resisting 'have-nots' but was a series of ongoing clashes that formed the social body of the time,[136] a belief system can result from, or be a response to, the surrounding social regime. As we accept novel uses of ideas and words given different time periods and developments, so too the social understanding of belief or the truth will be contingent.[137] Hence one's subjective understanding of discourse regarding the truth or a belief can become a powerful tool in shaping and influencing society and producing a particular effect.[138] Even in the natural sciences, where exact empirical proof is an imperative element, one notices the importance of specific social language as reflected in political and social changes. The alterations in language also force a person to think differently and approach an issue from a different angle.

The use of available language tools to focus on the desired *result* of a conscientious assertion, and not the more formal, descriptive, definition of the ideas invoked by a conscientious assertion,[139] can begin to allow for a clearer understanding of what conscience entails. What is important is not whether a conscientious assertion reflects the truth. Rather, it is the recognition that an assertion of a conscientious belief is a performative utterance whereby, in the words of Searle 'an action is performed just by saying literally we are performing it'.[140] The world changes to match the context of the utterance given a pre-configured cognitive capacity. Hence

---

[136] Foucault (1989;187-188).
[137] Foucault (1989;52) Hence his interpretation of history centred on demonstrating the underlying or inherent social rules regarding words and ideas that in turn influenced an individual's understanding of the truth.
[138] Foucault (1977;123) noting that politics becomes the continuation of war given the importance of discourse and not, as Clausewitz states, war as the continuation of politics.
[139] *See e.g.* Searle (1969:15).
[140] Searle (1991;374).

for a conscientious belief, one actually has the intention to externally adhere to the belief rather than merely make a commitment to have such an intention because 'the manifestation of the intention in the utterance does not require any further causal effects...it simply requires recognition by the audience'.[141]

Deeming an assertion of a conscientious belief as a performative utterance highlights the significance of such a belief for an individual believer. While conscience obviously does not provide a universal justification for action, it can at least provide a window from which to view a person's moral approach towards a particular matter.[142] As contended by Neibuhr,[143] a person attempts to objectively consider personal feelings when forming an opinion about one's actions or other individuals. Since 'we know ourselves only in the presence of another',[144] the self is both the subject and object because it is influenced by many 'others', such as social background, culture, family, profession, et al. As a result, a person will attempt to make a personal judgement about oneself in a mature and fair fashion. Conscience then retains its importance for the individual by focusing on the individual's striving for moral action and to better understand their social and individual practices.[145]

What emerges then from a conscientious decision is that conscience forms an essential component of one's self identity. Conscience is part of an important element of one's internal framework from which one shapes and forms qualitative discriminations regarding the good. Such qualitative discriminations are a necessary and constitutive condition for human agency since what I deem to be fundamentally important determines 'who I am'.[146] In the words of Taylor:

---

[141] Searle (1991;383). *See also* discussion *infra* regarding the distinction between freedom of expression and freedom of conscience.
[142] Childress (1979) for example defines conscience as a reflection of the individual's approval or disapproval of a particular action on the basis of personal moral convictions.
[143] Neibuhr (1945).
[144] Neibuhr (1945).
[145] Rorty (1989:58).
[146] Taylor (1989).

> My identity is defined by the commitments and identifications
> which provide the frame or horizon within which I can try to
> determine from case to case what is good...[147]

The conscientious process is part of this internal framework as the instinctual and intuitive qualitative discriminations that a person creates assist in making sense of one's life and in shaping one's self identity. A person will strive to achieve this self-imposed standard of good since it composes an essential element of one's identity on an instinctive plane and as a morally conscious human agent.[148]

Conscience then is part of a process that allows the individual to make sense of one's life and define what is important and what is not. It entails a component of self reflection and moral understanding[149] that develops into a cognitive responsive action.[150] One's identification of the good, which also will consider the role of the individual within the social group,[151] serves as the initial motivating force for conscience to ascertain the proper action for a particular circumstance.

The international human rights system appears to adopt an understanding of conscience that is quite similar to the aforementioned description. Conscience is not merely awareness of a moral dilemma. If morals created a conscientious obligation, the ensuing conscientious directive would seem superfluous as the obligation would exist because of the moral standard.[152] Conscience moves beyond the moral standards by conceiving a broader social context that entails external action.

The international human rights treaties indicate this distinction between morals and conscience by the 'public morals' limitation to the right to conscience. The implication is that conscience differs from a process that compiles public moral choices or identifies subjective moral imperatives that are influenced by social or environmental factors. Rather, one develops judgements whose binding directives then provide the basis for external actions.[153] Conscience creates a motivation for individual action by reference to fundamentally important qualitative discriminations.

---

[147] Taylor (1989;27).
[148] In the words of Taylor (1989;34) 'What I am as a self, my identity, is essentially defined by the way things have significance for me'.
[149] Garnett (1965).
[150] Clarke (1987:135).
[151] Sibley (1970) (with the relative differences arising out of the various applications of the objective moral order).
[152] Wallace (1978).
[153] Bourke (1966) (distinguishing cognitive determination from a practical judgement where one's practical reasoning determines *how* one should act in a particular situation,

While conscience might entrench moral norms, it does not create moral norms.[154] The applied moral standards that serve as a conduct-regulating facility for conscience generally arise antecedent to the conscience.[155] One can adopt a host of views regarding the derivation of morals depending on one's identification with natural law, positivism, rationalism or any other view. The conscience however assesses and applies these moral standards to a particular situation.[156]

The importance of the application of conscience for international law is that it entails a manifestation of self reflection. The *forum internum* joins awareness, which is consciousness, or 'thought', with a subjective understanding of moral sanction. As stated by Rotenstreich:[157]

> Even if we interpret the position of conscience as a subjective phenomenon, ... we cannot be oblivious to the phenomenological component that we find two levels in conscience - one of awareness and one of evaluation.

An individual will form an opinion regarding the morality of one's actions that influences the decision making process and evokes a certain external response.[158] The eventual action that derives from one's conscience implies that an individual has no internal justification for acting against the conscience, cannot forget the act in question if compelled to perform the act, and has no excuse to avoid responsibility for the act.[159]

The important role of conscience is that the ensuing conscientious decision to act personifies that person's approach towards moral action for both that particular action and similar future situations. The ongoing revision involved in the conscientious process is encouraged to improve upon one's moral standards, especially since such action will serve as a basis for individual moral norms in future decisions.[160]

---

once 'conscience' has determined the moral action). *See also* Clarke (1987); Wand (1961).
[154] Kordig (1979;376).
[155] Childress (1979;319).
[156] Rotenstreich (1993); Fuss (1974).
[157] Rotenstreich (1993;3).
[158] Broad (1969).
[159] Childress (1982).
[160] Wand (1961): Ryle (1954). Rotenstreich (1993:33) notes that 'we learn from our experience,...and turn it [conscience] into a motive which goes beyond the particular

The incorporation of subjective and objective factors shapes the individual's moral practice and influences the individual's conception of morality. Conscience in essence becomes an element of the individual's character and moral beliefs. As part of our self identity, the conscience will assist in identifying our constitutive moral self. This ideal moral self will always be a sought after goal since it serves as a basic mean for classifying our self identity.

One may understand conscience then as operating on two different levels. One is the internal development of the conscience, which will include an assessment of moral standards, to create the foundation for a conscientious belief. The other level relates to the manifestation of the conscientious belief following the internal assessment and development of the belief. The conscientious decision and conscientious action highlight the *forum internum* and *forum externum* distinction.[161] The internal conscientious decision does not decisively direct the individual towards action since it might appear too narrow or conflict with other social or moral criteria. While the eventual manifestation could deviate from the original conscientious decision,[162] the manifestation of a conscientious belief will reflect the standard developed in the *forum internum*. The internal standards are readily definable as a result of the externally manifested action.

Conscience and Thought

Although a host of factors influences the open-ended mental process that forms the conscience, it differs from thought both in the *forum internum* and the manner in which each concept arises in the *forum externum*. Rotenstreich distinguishes conscience from thought as follows:

> Conscience is characterised by the foci; it differs from consciousness because it does not just point to a content but points to two interrelated directions of human behaviour - approval or disapproval...Judging is not just awareness but an application of criteria to specific situations or deeds.[163]

The key difference between conscience and thought is that, similar to a religious belief, conscience directs the individual towards taking a

---

occurrence to become an element of our constant attitudes and thereby of our character'.
[161] Wallace (1978): Nowell-Smith (1957).
[162] Clarke (1987) (one retains the option of rejecting the conscientious decision where it is morally commendable to do so).
[163] Rotenstreich (1993;30-31).

particular action through the application of internal conscientious norms.[164] These norms focus on an individual's orientation towards the good which in turn play a central role in defining and constituting one's basic self identity, as exemplified by external action. While a general cognitive thought might account for similar considerations and lead to external action, the external action is not necessarily a result of the thought itself. Fish stated it thus:

> Belief is not what you think about but what you think with...there can be no distance between them [i.e., one's beliefs] and the acts they enable.[165]

A belief provides an epistemological framework for the individual, from which the individual considers and then conducts specific actions. Although there might not be any infringement to a Muslim's formal beliefs upon seeing pork being sold in a local shop, there is a certain level of internal disturbance that might arise for a believer to different degrees. Because a belief provides the cognitive framework for assessing external occurrences, the belief will alter one's reactions and direct one's responses to what one sees around him. Similarly, an animal rights protector or a vegan might have a negative reaction upon seeing the public sale of pork or any other form of meat. The belief systems that influence or shape their forms of thought and evaluation also will influence their external reactions to a variety of public practices. While from the *forum externum* approach one cannot discount the social and public right to sell meat, one's response to external actions also can determine the existence of belief.

When viewed from the approach of the *forum externum*, a rather broad understanding of conscientious belief emerges. The importance of a conscientious belief is the manner in which it affects one's life or influences one's actions. Hence a psychologist might initially understand the need to paint the prison walls red as based on scientific studies or personal empirical analysis. However such actions are the reflections of the truth and serve a strong function as a prelude to eventual external action. Similarly, an individual who despises meat as a matter of taste also might have his external actions to be swayed by such internal feelings. The degree by which the individual adheres to the feeling will be determined by

---

[164] *See* Robert (1993:24).
[165] Fish (1997;2257) referring to his 1989 book, *Doing What Comes Naturally*, at 326.

the range of external actions to be taken. While society might not have a duty to bar all sales of meat, or alternatively, a religious state might desire to bar the sale of particular type of meat, the individual will either adhere to such edicts or attempt to deviate from the law according to the internal beliefs. In essence, it is the external actions, that are subject to limitations, that serve as a gauge for determining the distinction between thought and conscientious belief.

The travaux preparatoires for the ICCPR clarify this distinction between thought and conscience. The drafters equated religious beliefs with conscientiously held moral directives and beliefs as a contradistinction to more general thoughts. The drafters deemed the manifestation of a conscientious belief as an essential facet in providing for the freedoms delineated in the right.[166] As noted by the delegate from Brazil, it is impossible to maintain a 'conscientious directive' without recognising the ability to manifest that ideal.[167]

Furthermore, the GA's Third Committee delegates noted that despite the association between conscience and religion, conscience includes philosophical and scientific concepts that relate to belief, as opposed to religion that is an act of faith.[168] The drafters understood conscience as a morally based process that focuses on the individual's intuitive ability to subjectively discern right from wrong and good from evil, and they equated the manifestation of conscience with a religious belief.[169]

Thought on the other hand was limited solely to the protection of an individual's internal conscious process. Thought encompassed a broad range of internal, individual, thoughts,[170] with its manifestation being placed within the confines of free expression.[171] The AmCHR indicates such an approach by separating thought from conscience and religion and upholding its protection, along with opinion, in the right to free expression.[172] Hence the relationship between thought and free expression,[173] since free expression can protect a broad range of manifested

---

[166] See e.g. GA 15th Session Third Committee, mtg. 1024-1025, in particular, the statement by the El Salvador representative.
[167] GA 15th Session Third Committee, at mtg.1023.
[168] See e.g. A/C.3/218.
[169] See e.g. GA, 15th Session, Third Committee, mtg. 1021, remarks by Saudi Arabia.
[170] GA, 15th Session, Third Committee, mtg. 1021.
[171] See e.g. A/2929 regarding UDHR Article 4(2) (which prohibits any derogation to Article 18) where the drafters note the similarities between thought, as protected in Article 18, and opinion, as protected in Article 19 (freedom of expression).
[172] AmCHR Articles 12 and 13.
[173] See e.g. Van Dijk and Van Hoof (1990;413) equating the freedom to hold opinions (Article 10 of the ECHR) with freedom of thought (Article 9 of the ECHR).

thoughts and not solely an expression that reflects the conviction of a person asserting the expression.

While the aforementioned distinction focuses on the *forum externum* aspect of conscience, it provides for a better understanding of conscience as a concept that implies something more compelling than thought. The protection of conscience centres on upholding one's moral integrity and autonomy to adhere to a belief, such that the protection will generally arise in the context of the *forum externum*. The manifestation of a conscientious belief clarifies its internal basis for action such as to also provide for protection of the *forum internum* of the belief. Of course, a conscientious belief need not always manifest; however the belief will be of such a nature that it affects an individual's pre-determined external actions pursuant to the internally developed directives.

The tendency to refer to the *forum externum* to discern the *forum internum* raises the issue regarding the absolute nature of the *forum internum*. Because our operative understanding of the *forum internum* belief is within the context of an external action, a state's imposition of limitations on external actions, as provided in all the human rights treaties, also will affect the internal belief. For example, a doctor who subscribes to the right to life might be required to perform an abortion or lose his employment. While a state possibly may impose such a limitation on the manifestation of the belief pursuant to the treaties, an infringement on the internal belief system of the doctor also is occurring. The doctor has created a specific internal framework of belief that in turn has significance for her external actions. Similar reasoning would seem applicable to the prison psychologist who has created a specific and personal form of belief regarding the colour of prison walls. Although limitations may be imposed on the manifestation of the belief, the effect on the *forum internum* is unavoidable.

While such an understanding of the *forum internum* might narrow the *forum internum* right to conscience, in another sense it tends to strengthen the practical application of the *forum internum*. Considering the proposed distinction between thought and conscience, it seems that a conscientious belief serves a specific purpose for the individual. The conscience highlights the qualitative discriminations of the individual; what the individual deems to be important in developing oneself and what is important when relating to other individuals and to society. Further, conscience entails an evaluation that will have a clear effect on one's external actions. Given such an understanding of conscience, an understanding that seems plausible merely to distinguish between the treaties' approach towards conscience and thought, the consequence that some limitations also might occur to the *forum internum* seems a necessary evil when considering a practical role for the *forum internum*. While the limitation might not be justified, given the role of conscience as assisting in shaping and forming one's identity, the reference to the *forum externum* certainly defines what it is that the individual deems to be important and what are one's underlying beliefs.

Conclusion

The discussion thus far has attempted to identify the possible sphere for the exercise of the right to the *forum internum* of a conscientious belief. While the treaty drafters granted the *forum internum* absolute protection, analysis of the meaning of the *forum internum* right has been largely overlooked, possibly due to the broad concepts that are raised by the *forum internum*. As a result, this chapter focused on understanding the internal nature of a conscientious belief and the importance of maintaining the internal, cognitive, abilities of the individual to provide for the development of an internal belief.

It was contended that one of the significant aspects of the *forum internum* is the seminal role it plays in developing the grounds for manifesting a conscientious belief. The *forum internum* differs from other conscious thought because it evaluates and develops particular conscientious beliefs, with a view towards upholding the beliefs in particular situations. Unlike a general thought, one can comprehend the *forum internum* by examining the manner in which an individual manifests the conscientious belief in the *forum externum*. Taking advantage of this two way process provides the framework for elaborating upon the *forum internum*. While not all beliefs will manifest, the key factor is the manner in which a conscientious belief tends to influence an individual's external actions.

From the perspective of violative state action, the *forum internum* of the individual is generally violated by coercive action. Coercive action involves not only the suppression of a belief, but also the intention to alter a belief. This aspect of intent can assist to define the parameters of the *forum internum* since not all actions are considered coercive. A state might have to limit the beliefs of an individual without any intention of creating a change to the *forum internum* belief where, for example, the belief might unduly interfere with the belief's of others or for other reasons of public policy.

This chapter also elaborated on conscience as an internal phenomenon and the effect that has on one's external actions, in contrast to more general thoughts. Conscience is not a moral standard or a strive for universal truth but relates to the very essence of a person and the individual's understanding of the world. Indeed, this relationship between the individual and the surrounding society is what assists an outside party in identifying a conscientious belief and distinguishing it from thought.

While the distinction between thought and conscience is not fully resolved, the resultant protection is not affected given the treaties' general commingling of thought and conscience in the *forum internum*. What this chapter attempted to demonstrate is that the issue of practical protection can arise when considering the manifestation of a conscientious belief. Indeed, the chapter does not conclusively identify the exact boundaries of the conscientious *forum internum* as distinguished from thought since both are entitled to similar protection. Rather, the focus has been on ways to identify the conscientious *forum internum* and expand on avenues that uphold the right. The broader issue regarding the boundaries of a protected belief, as intended by the principal international human rights treaties, will be considered in the next chapter when analysing the *forum externum* of a conscientious belief.

5 The *Forum Externum*

Introduction

Upon considering the relationship between the *forum externum* and the *forum internum*, the external manifestation of a belief appears to be an easier right to explain. From a purely functional standpoint, the external nature of the *forum externum* presents a more readily assessable occurrence that eases the practical identification of the belief in question. Hence Krishnaswami for example defined manifestation of a religious belief as incorporating a host of external actions that a religion may demand of its followers, such as worship, pilgrimages, burials according to the religion, celebrating holidays, marriage and divorce, and dietary practices.[1] What is apparent is that Krishnaswami, and the treaties that followed his report, understood manifestation as external actions that are taken in pursuance of a belief. In the context of a pacifist belief, for example, manifestation would seem to include specific instances that are mandated by the belief, such as not conducting military service, rather than broader applications of pacifism that derive from the belief's principles, such as distributing pamphlets at an army base that espouse one's pacifist views.[2]

Nonetheless, similar to the *forum internum*, an immediate problem is with the scope that the treaties accord to the external exercise of a belief. Recognising that the absolute protection accorded to the *forum internum* derived from the locus of the right, i.e. an internal phenomenon with little social implications, the *forum externum* will demand some form of limitation on its application because of the external, sometimes public, realm within which the right is manifesting. Even with an easier form of identification for the *forum externum* when compared with the *forum*

---

[1] Krishnaswami (1960;31-36).
[2] See e.g. 7050/75 *Arrowsmith v. UK* 3 EHRR 218 (1978) discussing the scope of manifestation of pacifist beliefs. Note that the example can be included under the ECHR right to freedom of conscience. See 11567/85 *Fritz v. France* 11 EHRR 67 (1988).

internum, not all manifestations of a belief are desirable or mandated under the treaties.[3] Military conscientious objection highlights the problem of manifestation because the objection could result in rather broad conduct that might entail a host of actions, such as not working at a military installation, refusing alternative military service, or not paying portions of one's income tax that the state has budgeted for the military.

Given the potential for an interminable right to manifest a belief, commentators generally refer to the specific terms of the treaty regarding manifestation when considering the scope of the right. That is, pursuant to treaties such as the ICCPR and ECHR, manifestation is generally for 'practice worship teaching or observance'[4] of a 'religion or belief'.[5] The treaty terms describing manifestation seem to focus on religious oriented manifestations, such as 'worship' or 'observance'. A religion mandates specific actions such as worshipping a certain number of times during the day or observing a specific religious holiday.[6] Given such a textual approach towards defining the meaning of manifestation of a belief, it is possible that the term 'practice' also could encompass the manifestation of conscientious beliefs. 'Practising' a manifestation relates to externally adhering to principles that derive from a belief. For example, practising a pacifist belief dictates specific actions relating to one's involvement with the military. A host of beliefs therefore can manifest even if not associated with religion, including veganism and pacifism.[7] Furthermore, the travaux preparatoires along with the HRC's General Comment to ICCPR Article 18 clearly understand the right as according some form of manifestation for non-religious based beliefs.[8]

The problem is that the treaty terms do not provide any substantive basis for defining the term 'belief' *ab initio* nor do they assist to delineate what forms of belief are manifest. Determining the scope of manifestation is a vexing issue given problems associated with proof regarding the status or existence of a particular conscientious belief, as well as demonstrating

---

[3] Hence the USSR's point when drafting ICCPR Article 18 regarding the necessity to limit the manifestation of religious beliefs of certain sects that mandate dangerous actions, such as mass suicide.

[4] The AfrCHR uses the term 'profess' to describe manifestation of a belief, indicating a religious-oriented form of exercise. Furthermore, it is not entirely clear whether the right under the AfrCHR also includes manifestation of a conscientious belief. *See* discussion *supra*.

[5] *See e.g.* Article 18 ICCPR; Article 9 ECHR.

[6] The term 'teaching' is understood under ICCPR Article 18(4) as well as ECHR Protocol.

[7] *See e.g.* 18187/91 *H v. UK* 16 EHRR CD44 (1992).

[8] *See* discussion *infra*.

some form of 'actual belief' in the principles being asserted. The notion of practising a belief such as veganism or pacifism is rather dubious and unclear. Furthermore, analogising a conscientious belief to a religious belief is a troubling method for delineating principles given the relativity problems inherent therein and the subjective application that would result.

In attempting to expand on the manifestation of a conscientious belief, it is essential to focus on the notion of belief as intended by the treaties. The objective is to achieve a general understanding of the meaning of manifestation of a conscientious belief. Is there a necessity for some type of formal or doctrinal link between the belief and the action being asserted, such as a pacifist's non-performance of military service, or does manifestation of the belief extend to bombing military bases or physically blocking their entrances?[9] What of less extreme actions such as handing out pamphlets extolling the moral prohibition of killing another human being[10] or refusing to pay a tax because it is supporting the military[11] in a manner similar to an atheist refusing to pay local church taxes?[12] Would it matter where the individual protest occurs or on what basis the individual was acting when relying on a belief as a basis to protest against the military?[13]

Some individuals manifest their pacifist beliefs by even refusing to conduct alternative service that is associated with the military. Other objectors develop a conscientious belief while serving in the military or object to specific actions taken by the military on grounds of a conscientious belief. Are these actions' manifestations of a conscientious belief or do they fall under the guise of other human rights? In essence, is manifestation only an action taken pursuant to a particular directive of the belief or does it incorporate all action derived therefrom? Further, what of a negative exercise of the right that might manifest by avoiding identification with the actions of the military, such as refusing to attend a parade commemorating a military victory? If only the negative aspect of the right - may one rely on a belief, in the freedom *from* sense, to avoid the imposition of a state's religious or ideological beliefs? How broad is that right and does it, in the end, differ from an assertion of a right to a belief?

---

[9] Of course, such action would be subject to the limitations that are stated in the treaties. *See* discussion *infra*.

[10] 7050/75 *Arrowsmith v. UK* 3 EHRR 218 (1978).

[11] *See e.g.* 446/1991 *JP v. Canada* (1992). *Cf.* 20747/92 *Bouessel v. France* 16 EHRR CD 49 (1993) (refusal to pay social security tax because it supported publicly funded abortions. The Commission summarily rejected the contention).

[12] *See e.g.* 11581/85 *Darby v. Sweden* 13 EHRR 774.

[13] 2238/93 *Van den Dungen v. Netherlands* 80 D&R 147 (1995) (Commission upheld injunction on claimant from handing out anti-abortion materials near abortion clinic).

Additionally, what of the *forum internum* as a means to explicate the direction and scope of the *forum externum*, particularly if the prevention of manifestation will in turn infringe the *forum internum*?[14]

Given the likelihood that manifestation of a broader form of beliefs will lead to inevitable social clashes, it also is imperative to focus on the limitations provided for in the articles. There seems an inherent confusion in the variety of decisions that have addressed this right resulting from the inadequacy in defining the meaning and scope of manifestation, such that the distinction between situations of manifestations as opposed to proper application of limitations becomes confused.[15] At times, it seems that in deciding what form of belief is manifest, judicial bodies avoid the minefield of addressing the right by commingling the lack of manifestation of a belief with the provided treaty limitations.[16]

Clearly one should be operating within a specific context of belief, as elaborated upon in the chapter regarding the *forum internum*. The purpose of this chapter on the *forum externum* is to develop a broader understanding of belief in accordance with the intention of the treaties. One can avoid the quagmire of distinguishing between conscientious and religious beliefs, or choosing randomly between conscientious beliefs, while providing an operative and realistic application of the international human right to freedom of conscience.

In examining the manifestation of the right, the key example to be referred to will be military conscientious objection. The reason for this approach is that military conscientious objection is an acknowledged form of manifesting a belief, even if its status as a codified right under the treaties is unclear.[17] Judicial bodies and commentators acknowledge pacifism, the secular form of asserting a right to military conscientious objection,[18] as a valid

---

[14] *See* discussion *supra* at Chapter Four.
[15] *See e.g.* Evans, M. (1997;330); 14307/88 *Kokkinakis v. Greece* 17 EHRR 397 (1993).
[16] *See e.g.* 16278/90 *Karaduman v. Turkey* 74 D&R 93 (1993) (ECHR Commission upheld university's requirement that Muslim student remove head scarf for an identification photo based on lack of manifestation as well as limitation).
[17] *Compare* HRC General Comment to Article 18, CCPR/C/21/Rev.1/Add.4 (1993) *with* 11850/85 *G v. Netherlands* 51 D&R 180 (1987). *See also* 1997 HRC Report regarding comments on France's report where it is noted that 'the right to conscientious objection to military service...is a part of freedom of conscience under Article 18 of the Covenant...'; 1996 HRC Report regarding comments on Spain's report that preventing the claim of in-service conscientious objection to the military 'does not seem to be consistent with the requirements of Article 18 of the Covenant, as pointed out in the Committee's General Comment No. 22(48)'.
[18] As opposed to a religious based assertion of military objection, such as a Jehovah Witness' refusal to serve in the military.

belief.[19] A pacifist belief nevertheless serves as a good example because the scope of the manifestation remains unclear and because such an objection is sufficiently different from a 'typical' manifestation of a religious belief where a believer might be relying on clearly delineated principles as a basis for manifestation. Furthermore, military objection maintains a strong normative status given the putative emergence of conscientious objection to military service as a customary norm.[20] While a pacifist is asserting a particular belief by not engaging in military service, there are no specific guidelines or formal dictates that derive from the belief, as found by a more formalised or established religious belief.

Forum Internum and *Forum Externum* Compared

As described *supra*, the significance of the *forum internum* is not only that it is an inviolable forum, but also it serves to compel a believer to abide by the conscientious belief in the *forum externum*. Non-adherence to the internal conscientious decision would result in undermining the belief itself, in a manner similar to preventing the performance of a religious practice.[21] Hence the importance of the treaty term 'practice' when considering a conscientious belief. As the phrase is currently understood, one only may manifest beliefs that dictate a pre-ordained, mandated, practice such as pacifism and objection to military service, as opposed to other forms of general beliefs that seemingly derive from personal preferences, such as refusing to serve the military in an alternative capacity. Commentators focus on the required practice emanating from a belief, such that manifestation of a conscientious belief is analogous to a religious person's requirement for worship at specific times of the day; upholding the conscientious belief demands the guarantee of specific practices that serve to maintain the belief.[22]

By contrast, it would be difficult to violate the *forum externum* of a general thought that does not mandate particular external action as a necessary condition for the maintenance of the thought. Hence an uncomfortable solicitor refusing to wear the court-mandated attire, such as a wig, as a condition precedent for representing a client before the court,

---

[19] 7050/75 *Arrowsmith v. UK* 3 EHRR 218 (1978).
[20] *See* discussion *infra* at Chapter Six. *See e.g.* Marcus (1998).
[21] *See e.g. Texas v. Bullock* 489 US 1 (1991) (comparing conscience to religion); *US v. Seeger* 380 US 163 (1965) (belief as occupying a parallel position to religion); Loschelder (1992;30) (regarding German law).
[22] Robert (1993;24-25) concluding that the right to conscience is not simply a matter of internal faith.

does not seem to be asserting a conscientious belief, per se, even though she is internally harbouring a thought. Here the attorney can maintain her desire through other avenues, such as requesting more frequent court recesses in which to remove the wig, raising the thermostat controls on the air conditioner, or conducting protests outside the courtroom to persuade other attorneys to alter the regulation, without undermining the ultimate objective of remaining comfortable. However, there is no explicit principle regarding the 'belief' that mandates any form of manifestation. In this instance, she would do better to manifest the thought by way of an expression[23] because it is the result that is important to maintaining the assertion, i.e. to be comfortable or to change the mode of courtroom attire, rather than the desire to uphold a particular principle or belief.

The 'practice' of a pacifist, or any other religious or conscientious believer, is to uphold the asserted belief no matter what the outcome.[24] Whether the legislative branch will alter military service or create changes to its military structure is not the central goal of a military objector. What is important is the manifestation of a specific pacifist belief that results in a conflict with a state directive regarding military service.

The *forum internum*, which can include a general thought or opinion, differs in that no specific form of mandated action need arise therefrom. Personal desires are the driving force for the external action rather than the underlying directives of a specific belief. Hence in the ECHR, the judicial bodies have hesitated to uphold external actions under Article 9 where the assertion did not involve an overriding belief but entailed the expression of ideals or desires.[25] The tendency is to deem an action as expressing an ideal, rather then a belief, where there is no particular exercise of a mandated action or the focus is on a desired result. Similarly, US Courts have not accorded the right of manifestation to new forms of 'religious' beliefs that are based on informal creeds or that do not

---

[23] Loschelder (1992;30) refers to this case regarding a German attorney. *See also* discussion *supra* at Chapter Four regarding the distinction between conscience and thought.

[24] Hence the distinction between civil disobedience, where the protester desires a change in the law, and conscientious objection, where the individual relies on a conscientious belief without necessarily demanding a change to the law.

[25] *See e.g.* 16616/90 *Vereniging v. Netherlands* 46 D&R 200 (1986) (organisation assisting prisoners on basis of ideals and not a specific belief, especially since other means exist to uphold the organisation); 8741/79 *X v. Germany* 24 D&R 137 (1981) (scattering of ashes over grave is a desire rather than manifestation of a belief).

evoke any formal binding directives for practice nor an underlying ideology.[26]

Note however that given a different set of circumstances, a so called personal desire can still manifest as a belief. For example, instead of a military objector relying on a personal desire to avoid the military, one may interpret the objector's actions as harbouring a pacifist belief regarding the use of weapons. Similarly, the basis for a solicitor's objection to wearing a wig could be that the mandatory courtroom wigs are made from the fur of endangered species. The manifestation of such a 'belief', as opposed to being based on the opinion that the wig is uncomfortable, could fall under the guise of a conscientious belief. The action of not wearing the wig is linked to a particular belief regarding the importance of preserving endangered species that dictates to an individual not to wear such accoutrements. Forcing an attorney to buy and wear the wig then can raise a *forum externum* problem,[27] while certainly entailing a violation of the *forum internum*.

Recognising that one may deconstruct the understanding of the term 'belief' to incorporate a wide variety of ideas or desires, it would seem that the international system is referring to something more distinct. As delineated in the discussion regarding the *forum internum* of conscience, manifestation relates to an application of specific principles deriving from the belief. Hence, one can recognise the ability to manifest certain forms of secular beliefs, such as veganism[28] or pacifism.[29] The supposed distinction seems to be that these beliefs mandate specific forms of action, *ex ante*, that relate to a believers' conduct, as opposed to assertions based on singular opinions or thoughts that do not affect the individual in any over-

---

[26] *See e.g. US v. Myers* 95 F. 3d 1475 (2d Cir. 1996) (church of marijuana deemed personal philosophy and not a religion due to lack of formality); *Randall v. Orange County Council* 952 P.2d 261 (1997) (Boy Scouts deemed a social organisation); *Jacques v. Hilton* 569 F.Supp. 729 (N.J.Dist.Ct. 1983) prisoners' creation of a new religion was not entitled to Free Exercise protection. The Court compared the new religion to a general code of an organisation, like the Boy Scouts, as opposed to a belief which provides direction and an 'ordering of one's life' relating to ultimate rewards which focus on fundamental issues of life.

[27] Whether forcing the attorney to wear the wig is an *actual* violation of the belief will be discussed *infra* where the 'actual practice' of a belief is distinguished from other forms of conscientious assertions.

[28] 18187/91 *H v. UK* 16 EHRR CD44 (1992); *Jenkins v. Angelou* 948 F. Supp. 543 (E.D. Va. 1996). Both cases involved prisoners, such that limitations were applied due to their particular circumstances.

[29] 7050/78 *Arrowsmith v. UK* 3 EHRR 218 (1978).

arching or universal manner. Particular 'beliefs' or personal desires[30] generally have not benefited from the protection accorded by the right to freedom of conscience. Even in the US, where courts might confer constitutional protection to a sincere assertion of a belief,[31] the courts do not grant much credence to manifestations of more general beliefs.[32] Judicial bodies consider these assertions to be individual desires for which the legal system cannot cater in the context of the right to conscience.[33]

Two key criteria for identifying the *forum externum* are emerging that at this point are necessary, but not sufficient, to demarcate its boundaries. First, the conscientious decision emanating from the *forum internum* leads to definitive action or inaction in the *forum externum*. The internal belief provides specific direction for external action according to the belief's underlying directives. Second, the action or manifestation of the *forum externum* relates to a crucial aspect of the belief being asserted. Prevention of the desired action or inaction will therefore not only impede its performance, but also generate an unyielding predicament that can serve to thwart the belief itself.[34] This internal dilemma is in essence comparable to a violation of a religious belief. Hence the right to military conscientious objection as reliant on pacifist beliefs because the action relates to specific directives of the belief, such that denying the claim to military objection infringes a basic principle of the belief.

This categorisation also can begin to explain the distinction in the ECHR between manifestations that are or are not 'actual' expressions of the belief. For example, the ECHR Commission has held that a pacifist must pay taxes even if the funds are for military purposes because there is no connection between the action of tax payment and the asserted belief. Refusal to pay taxes is not viewed as any formal 'practice' of a belief, even if the state uses the funds for purposes contrary to one's belief. Similar arguments are raised concerning paying child support even if the payments

---

[30] Such as the scattering of ashes over one's grave, 8741/79 *X v. Germany* 24 D&R 137 (1981).

[31] See e.g. *Jacques v. Hilton* 569 F.Supp. 729 (N.J.Dist.Ct. 1983).

[32] *US v. Myers* 95 F. 3d 1475 (2d Cir. 1996); *Randall v. Orange County Council* 952 P. 2d 261 (1997).

[33] Of course, preventing the practice of a belief does not necessarily undermine the basis for the belief itself. The *forum internum* need not be violated by a state's prevention of an external practice, save for where the intention of the state in preventing the practice is to alter or eradicate the belief. *See* discussion *supra* at Chapter Four.

[34] Edge (1996); Loschelder (1992;30); Marshall (1995) (relying on this same point as a means of equating the 'Free Exercise' of conscience with religion); Childress (1979).

inhibit one's religion by preventing attendance at one's house of worship[35] or infringe a religious principle.[36]

Nonetheless, the noted division between *forum internum* and *externum* also brings to the fore two essential issues regarding the required boundaries for manifestation in the *forum externum*. If, as noted by the attorney who objected to wearing the courtroom wig, a belief protecting endangered animals is a basis for an assertion, why cannot a 'belief' in being comfortable also be protected? Surely such a belief can derive from a person's *forum internum* as a belief, and not merely a thought or desire, which can structure one's life in a particular direction pursuant to specific applications of the belief, i.e., to be comfortable? One may even define as 'actual practice' specific forms of behaviour, such as refusing to wear a wig at all times, much like a Sikh's requirement to always don a turban.[37]

Belief systems that use illegal narcotics to practise their beliefs reflect this problem. Although public policy serves as a limitation to the practice,[38] some decisions focus on the underlying 'belief'. For example, the HRC held that a belief that consists primarily in the distribution of narcotic drugs is not a 'belief' for purposes of the ICCPR Article 18.[39] The HRC did not refer to the limitations of Article 18 in reaching its conclusion, thereby indicating some form of narrow definition for the meaning of a belief. Hence even if only a particular form of belief merits preservation, protecting a belief merely because it entails a particular practice is not a sufficient standard. Otherwise, courts would uphold any form of practice deriving from the directives of a 'belief', such as keeping comfortable or ingesting drugs.

One should not conclude from this point however that the right to manifest a religion or belief is of a limited nature or referring to specific beliefs at the exclusion of other forms of belief. The world is too diverse to rely on another individual's subjective understanding of belief or religion

---

[35] 24875/94 *Logan v. UK* 1 EHRLR 83 (1997).
[36] *Karakuzey v. Germany* 23 EHRR CD92 (1996).
[37] See e.g. 7992/77 *X v. UK* 14 D&R 234 (1978). *Cf.* UK law that exempts Sikhs from the statutory requirement to wear a motorcycle helmet. Motorcycle Crash Helmets (Religious Exemption) Act 1976.; 208/1986 *Singh Binder v. Canada* (HRC upheld Canadian requirement to wear a hard hat as condition of employment on grounds of protecting public health); *Singh v. British Rail* [1986] ICR 22 (similar case involving removal of a safety helmet); *Van Schaik v. Neuhaus* (S.Ct. of Canberra, 1/5/96) (asserted belief against wearing a bicycle helmet denied as being unreasonable in light of contrary legislation). *Cf. Goldman v Weinberger* 475 US 503 (1986) (preventing Military Rabbi from wearing a 'Kippah' to uphold military directive to remove all headgear while inside a building).
[38] See e.g. *Employment Division v. Smith* 494 US 872 (1990).
[39] 570/1993 *M.A.B. v. Canada* (1994).

that would seem to unduly limit the human right under discussion. Furthermore, such an understanding would not conform to the treaties and the intentions of the drafters.[40] Rather the distinction between a conscientious belief and personal desires or other assertions demands further elaboration. In certain instances, manifesting a personal desire like keeping comfortable might entail the application of a different human right, such as the right to privacy or freedom of expression. Other human rights present a judicial body with an easier avenue for applying a belief without having to delve into the quagmire that is presented by the freedom of religion and conscience.[41]

Furthermore, one must not overlook the *forum internum*. Can the manifestation of a belief derive from a seemingly non-existent *forum internum* that requires manifestation? For example, what of an individual who might not identify with atheism yet also not believe in the religion supported by the state? May the local parish force her to pay Church taxes as is the accepted practice in some states[42] or should she be entitled to forego payment because she does not identify with any 'belief'? On the positive side of exercising a right, are IRA prisoners' assertions to wear special prison clothes unique to a POW[43] entitled to manifest their protest as a conscientious belief? What of an individual's desire to forego a burial due to a belief mandating the scattering of his cremated remains over his grave?[44] Are such random 'beliefs', seemingly deriving from political or personal desires that nevertheless entail specific action, suitable for manifestation or should they be classified as random thoughts deriving from an innate idea developed in the *forum internum*? Indeed, one may even assert that military conscientious objection is a random occurrence rather than a reliance on a belief mandating specific practices. A pacifist belief seems to provide even less guidance regarding a specific form of external action than a belief requiring one to scatter ashes over a grave or refusal to don a wig in the courtroom.

---

[40] *See* discussion *supra* at Chapter Three.
[41] *See e.g.* 20390/92 *Tinnelly v. UK* 1998-IV Rep. Judg. & Dec. 1633 (considering the unfavourable treatment accorded to a building contractor, who also was a religious minority, under the context of ECHR Article 6).
[42] Capotorti (1991;73) noting practice in Norway and exemption for non-believers. *Cf.* 1979 HRC Report, A/34/40 Report of Finland stating that church tax served a secular purpose in funding the local census as well as assisting with the upkeep of the church buildings.
[43] 8317/78 *McFeely v. UK* 3 EHRR 161 (1979) (Commission held that it was not equivalent to a 'belief').
[44] 8741/79 *X v. Germany* 24 D&R 137 (1981) the contention was not deemed a belief.

The basic problem with the aforementioned delineation of a manifested conscientious belief is that it is based on a descriptive distinction between decision and action. Merely acknowledging a right for action in the *forum externum* however does not solve the initial query regarding the prescriptive breadth for the manifestation of a conscientious belief. If acting according to the belief is the determinant, how do we deal with all other action that might derive from a conscientious decision or create a motivation for action? Must the manifestation centre solely on action taken pursuant to a belief that establishes specific and identifiable directives? What if one's belief system did not establish specific directives for action, such as belief in protecting endangered animals that can lead to a variety of manifestations or an anthroposophic's refusal to join a mandatory welfare scheme?[45] Must a judicial system not accord these belief systems the right of manifestation because they are not structured in a manner equivalent to a formal religious belief?

Alternatively, what if a belief system, such as pacifism, includes actions motivated by the belief, as illustrated by blocking shipments to armament plants or refusing to participate in alternative army service that need not entail discharging military weapons? The problem also can arise in a religious context, such as relying on Church doctrine to claim that one's belief entitles a refusal to undergo a breathalyser test on the Sabbath[46] or that a state should ban the publication of a book that blasphemes one's religion.[47] Is such a contention an actual 'manifested' action of the conscientious or religious belief or is it too removed from the underlying belief to be excluded from the protection created by the right to conscience?

Upon considering this issue in the framework of the international human rights system, the question becomes one of interpretation. While it is apparent from the travaux preparatoires that the definition to be accorded to religion and belief was unclear and subject to controversy,[48] a consequential approach to the human right at issue indicates that the goal is to uphold the assertion of a belief in some form or manner. Yet a succinct definition for the term raises a no-win situation since any decision limiting a belief will create consequences for other forms of belief systems that a formalised definition might exclude. The remainder of this chapter

---

[45] *See e.g.* 10678/83 *V. v. Netherlands* 39 D&R 267 (1984) (refusal to join state pension scheme on basis of anthroposophic beliefs was not considered an 'actual practice' of the belief).
[46] *Chaousie v. Police Commissioner* 1995 Aust. SASC Lexis 4.
[47] 17439/90 *Choudhury v. UK* reptd. in 12 H. Rts. L. J. 172 (1991).
[48] *See* discussion *supra* at Chapter Three.

therefore will consider the different approaches to understanding what type of 'belief' merits *forum externum* protection, and what is the scope of manifestation of a belief under the treaties providing for the right to conscience.

Defining 'Belief'

Introduction

The international human rights treaties that codify the right to conscience provide for the manifestation of 'religion and beliefs'. There is no reference to manifestation of conscience, unlike the *forum internum* where conscience merits specific protection. For example, ICCPR Article 18 codifies the ability 'to manifest his religion or belief' in contrast to the initial *forum internum* protection of 'freedom of thought, conscience and religion'.[49]

The shift in treaty terminology raises an essential question for the manifestation of a conscientious belief. Simply put, does the term 'belief' include a conscientious belief as well? The answer will initially entail a demonstration that the treaties' provision for the external manifestation of 'beliefs' refer to a particular, conative, application of beliefs. The asserted belief is linked to an axiomatic belief system developed in the *forum internum* that is comparable in status and importance to religious beliefs. Indeed the underlying utility of the term 'belief' in the treaties is to afford protection for conceptions that differ from religion.[50] Commentators have taken a common sense approach towards interpreting belief by defining the term in a broad manner that includes beliefs other than merely formal religious beliefs.[51] International documents have similarly distinguished between religion and belief.[52]

---

[49] *Cf.* AmCHR Article 12; Declaration Article 2, which uses the terms 'religion or *whatever* beliefs' [emphasis supplied] as a means of underscoring beliefs to include notions external to religion, such as atheism, agnosticism, and rationalism. See discussion *supra* at Chapter Three.

[50] See e.g. E/CN.4/SR.116 at 3-4 (right to conscience need not be equated with religion but beliefs in the general sense).

[51] Partsch (1981;214); Boyle (1993;41); Edge (1996); Cumper (1995); Nowak (1993); Krishnaswami (1960;1); Sullivan (1988). *Cf.* Vermeulen (1992) and (1993); Humphrey (1985).

[52] See e.g. ST/HR/SER.A/16 *Seminar Encouraging Understanding Tolerance and Respect in Matters Relating to Freedom of Religion and Belief* (1984; paragraph 22) 'beliefs' defined as 'beliefs other than religious beliefs according to the individual's conscience'.

From the travaux preparatoires, it appears that the drafters intended that the term 'belief' includes beliefs other than religious beliefs. When codifying the right to freedom of conscience in the ICCPR, the CHR delegates relied on the 1960 Krishnaswami study that advocated a broad definition for belief.[53] The definition incorporated beliefs held by atheists, agnostics, free thinkers, and rationalists, in contrast to the delegates who desired to focus solely on the manifestation of the religious aspect of right. The Secretary General's 1960 memorandum further supports this approach. The memorandum states that even though the first part of the paragraph of ICCPR Article 18(1) that provides protection for freedom of 'thought, conscience, and religion' did not include belief, the terms 'religion and belief' of ICCPR Article 18(3) refer to two distinct ideas; formal religious beliefs as opposed to beliefs that exist outside the context of the religious sphere. The policy reason for adopting a broader approach to 'religion and belief' in Article 18(3) was the risk that defining belief or religion in any structured sense would unduly confine the right without providing for different approaches towards the right in the future.[54]

The HRC's General Comment to Article 18 further supports the approach to 'belief' as a term with different connotations than its counterpart term 'religion'.[55] The HRC specifically supports a broad construction of the term 'belief',[56] by not limiting the application of Article 18 to:

> traditional religions or to religions and beliefs with institutional characteristics or practices analogous to those of traditional religions.[57]

---

[53] See A/4625, 8/12/60, item no. 34, where the CHR delegates noted specific reliance on the Krishnaswami study.

[54] Krishnaswami (1960;1). See also UN./GA./15th Session, Third Committee, mtg. 1024, remarks by Liberia advising not to translate the term 'religion' since the result would be too subjective; Edge (1996) (noting similar considerations regarding ECHR Article 9); E/CN.4/1475, at 140 (travaux preparatoires to Declaration making same point regarding definition of 'religion and belief').

[55] McGoldrick (1991;100) noting that General Comment of HRC is generally of a sharper nature since they do not focus on a particular state; Shelton (1986) (presumption that General Comment are final word for interpreting ICCPR).

[56] Similar to the drafters of the treaties, the HRC did not define the term, so as to include all forms of religion and belief. See CCPR/C/SR.1162 (travaux preparatoires to HRC's General Comment to Article 18).

[57] General Comment to Article 18, paragraph 1.

While this statement is more a description than a definition of the term, it indicates that the HRC is applying an interpretation of the term 'belief' that can incorporate belief systems that differ from religion.

Whether the interpretation also will incorporate a manifestation of conscience depends upon the implications of the term 'belief' as interpreted in judicial fora. One can categorise the approach towards the manifestation of conscience as either being of a narrow or broad nature. The narrow approach limits manifestation to the 'actual practice' of a particular doctrine by pre-determined beliefs.[58] For example, limiting pacifism, a protected conscientious belief,[59] to manifestations that only entail an 'actual practice' of pacifism. Manifestation of the belief therefore would seem to include conscientious objection to military service. General actions deriving from the belief are not construed as 'actual practices', such as refusing to pay taxes supporting the armed services or refusing to engage in alternative military service that does not involve the use of weapons. The manifestation of a conscientious belief refers to a narrower, internal, aspect of the right, essentially limiting the right to a negative, freedom *from*, context. Yet, as will be demonstrated, the narrow approach to the manifestation of a conscientious belief does not adequately encompass the rights accorded to conscientious beliefs under the treaties.

The broader approach recognises the right to manifest beliefs that derive from an individual's conscience, without necessarily being an 'actual practice' of the belief. An individual in the US, for example, can rely on pacifist ideals to refuse employment in an armaments' factory and still be entitled to unemployment benefits.[60] Pursuant to the broader approach, it is at times possible to claim that the manifestation emanates from a general motivation that derives from a conscientious belief.[61] Of course, not all forms of motivations deriving from a belief can manifest. Rather it is imperative to focus on the belief being asserted to determine the

---

[58] Beddard (1993;114); Edge (1996); Vermeulen (1993;84) noting that it is not the personal motivation, but the 'objective characteristics of the relevant act' which determine whether the act falls within the scope of the law.

[59] See e.g. 7050/75 *Arrowsmith v. UK* 3 EHRR 218 (1978).

[60] *Thomas v. Review Board* 450 US 707 (1980). *Cf. Employment Division v. Smith* 494 US 872 (1990) where Justice Scalia limits this case to the domain of employment benefits.

[61] Edge (1996); Rimanque (1993;157) (distinction between manifestation and motivation is unfair and superfluous in light of derogation inherent in article which protects against arbitrary reliance on the right); 7050/78 *Arrowsmith v UK* 3 EHRR 218 (1978) (Opsahl for dissent) (requirement for conscience need not be 'clearly manifesting a belief' if action is based on a genuine belief which provides motivation for the action).

importance of the asserted conduct and its relevance to upholding the asserted conscientious belief.

As will be discussed in the next few sections, a narrow reading of the right that limits manifestation to 'actual expressions' of a belief is the favoured approach in international fora. While such an interpretation might make sense simply as a practical matter, the narrow approach tends to exclude the manifestation of a variety of conscientious beliefs. The remainder of the chapter therefore will compare and contrast the narrow and broad approach towards the meaning of belief, with a view towards understanding the implications of each approach.

Narrow Approach Towards Conscientious Belief

It is difficult to succinctly identify the criteria for manifestation of a religion or belief from the case law. Nonetheless, it seems that the key factor that delineates a narrow approach towards the right is that the belief in question is of a universal nature whose principles are practised within a particular pre-defined framework. An additional criterion that appears important is that the belief's directives serve a uniform function for all individuals who identify with the belief. Hence when considering the ECHR and the right to military conscientious objection, states can distinguish between religions such as Jehovah's Witnesses that mandate that their believers cannot serve in the military, even in an alternative service capacity, and secular conscientious objectors who attempt to rely on their pacifist beliefs as grounds for refusing alternative military service.[62]

Despite the narrow understanding of belief as implying a more formalised and structured setting, the right to manifest a general conscientious belief can occur in limited instances. The freedom *to* manifest the right to conscience[63] provides for actions according to a belief's directive that adhere to particular 'practices' of the belief.[64] Hence a pacifist has the right to assert the freedom to believe in pacifist ideals, such as not using deadly weapons and foregoing military service.[65] Because

---

[62] *Cf.* HRC Report of 1998 noting Finland's preferential treatment of Jehovah's Witnesses over other military conscientious objectors seemed to conflict with ICCPR Article 26.
[63] Krishnaswami (1960;29-46) proposed the distinction between freedom *from* and freedom *to* the exercise of the right to freedom of religion.
[64] Krishnaswami (1960;32).
[65] *Cf.* Krishnaswami (1960;43) who deemed military conscientious objection as a freedom *from*. Since his report, pacifism has been accepted as a conscientious belief

freedom *to* is a positive assertion of a right to conscience, it affords the individual the ability to manifest only particular beliefs. Freedom *to* therefore would not include the right to object to other actions that support the military, such as alternative military service[66] or payment of a military tax.[67]

Upholding the right to freedom of conscience also can derive from the freedom *from* approach towards a belief. The freedom *from* a belief centres on limiting applications of religious beliefs supported by the state, such as forced participation in religious ceremonies or taking an oath.[68] If a state supports a particular ideology, it must not impose the ideology on those who do not identify with the belief, such as an apostate in a fundamentalist Muslim state.[69] The freedom *from* then applies to prevent coercive state practices when a state 'requires individuals to support the practices of a faith with which they do not agree'[70] such as mandating all public school students to participate in prayers[71] or salute the flag.[72]

Some commentators favour defining the right to conscience solely within the context of the freedom *from* approach.[73] Because manifestation of a conscientious belief can be quite broad and, at times, indeterminable, the freedom *from* aspect of the right can protect non-believers without having to delve into their internal beliefs.[74] Indeed, ECHR case law

---

which is entitled to manifestation. 7050/78 *Arrowsmith v. UK* 3 EHRR 218 (1978); 1567/85 *Fritz v. France* 11 EHRR 67 (1988).

[66] See e.g. 20972/92 *Raninen v. Finland* 84 D&R 17 (1996).

[67] 446/1991 *JP v. Canada* (1992).

[68] Krishnaswami (1960;42).

[69] See e.g. E/CN.4/1994/79, CHR, 50th Session, where the rapporteur to the Declaration noted that the prohibition of apostasy in Muslim states posed a central problem for non-believers and the overall right to freedom of religion.

[70] *Marsh v. Chambers* 463 US 783 (1983) (dissent to opinion which upheld practice of opening each state legislative session with a prayer from a publicly funded chaplain).

[71] 21787/93 *Valsamos v. Greece* 1996-VI Rep. Judg. & Dec. 2312 (Jehovah Witness student forced to participate in parade); *Lee v. Weisman* 112 S.Ct. 2469 (1992) (non-sectarian prayer at public school graduation); *D.A.U. College, Jullunder v. State of Punjab* AIR 1971 SC 1737 (religious college did not possess right to mandate teaching of religious principles to all students).

[72] HRC report of 1996 regarding Zambia where students are required to sing the national anthem and salute the flag as a condition precedent for attending a state school, even for those who conscientiously object to such practice; *West Virginia v. Barnette* 319 US 624 (1943) (Jehovah's Witness foregoing pledge of allegiance); *Bijoe Emmanuel v. Kerala* AIR 1987 SC 748 (similar decision by Indian Court).

[73] Vermeulen (1993; 82-83); Scheinen (1992;271); Evans, M. (1997).

[74] Humphrey (1985) (conscience as an internal right, with external manifestation relating solely to religion or other, similarly identifiable, beliefs); Vermeulen (1993) relies on ECHR case law to establish 'beliefs' as being the equivalent to religious beliefs.

indicates such an approach as it generally favours upholding the *forum internum*[75] while hesitating to sustain the *forum externum*.[76] Conscience is therefore considered solely as a *forum internum* principle with only a limited entitlement to manifestation.

Note that for the freedom *from* approach, the determination is whether the state or religious authority is imposing its beliefs on individuals outside the accepted religious framework. Whether the individual is exercising a particular form or aspect of a belief is not at issue. The resultant protection for the right to conscience is limited to the *forum internum*, as a non-believer is responding to an overbearing religious assertion.[77] Such was the basic reasoning of the ECHR Court in *Valsamis v. Greece* in denying a Jehovah's Witnesses' protest to attending a school parade commemorating a military victory. The Court held that there was no imposition of beliefs by the government nor was there any form of forced indoctrination.[78] As a result, when considering the right to conscience pursuant to the freedom *from* approach, the assertion of the right would seem to be confined to states that maintain an over-arching ideology or particular religious belief that attempts to limit the development or assertion of other forms of belief.[79]

Nonetheless, one may still manifest a conscientious belief as a freedom to assertion pursuant to the narrow approach to the right to conscience. One avenue for such manifestations is pursuant to a specific pre-determined principle, or 'actual practice', of a belief system. This would include a pacifist maintaining a conscientious objection to the military. The objector is practising a conscientious belief pursuant to the belief's specific principles. Religion also is a prototype form of belief for

---

[75] 23380/94 *C.J. v. Poland* 84 D&R 46 (1996) (focus of Article 9 protection is upholding the *forum internum* aspect of a belief).

[76] See e.g. 22838/93 *Van den Dungen v. Netherlands* 80 D&R 147 (1995) (belief against abortion and right to disseminate literature); 10295/82 *C v. UK* 37 D&R 142 (1983) (pacifist's objection to paying military taxes).

[77] Rather then existing as a right of the individual to assert/manifest a conscientious belief, outside of a religious context.

[78] 21787/93 *Valsamis v. Greece* 1996-VI Rep. Judg. & Dec. 2312. Note that the majority did note in *dicta* that it was rather strange to require all pupils to attend a parade outside of school hours. The dissent held that the views of the child were violated by attending the parade. *See also* 24095/94 *Efstratiou v. Greece* 1996-VI Rep. Judg. & Dec. 2347 (similar decision).

[79] See e.g. 1979 HRC Report A/34/40 regarding Bulgarian practice to teach ideology of communism, at exclusion of all other forms of religion; 1982 HRC Report, A/37/40 regarding Moroccan limitations imposed on non-Islamic beliefs; 1983 HRC Report A/38/40 regarding Catholic majority in Peru, where Peru noted it was 'willing' to cooperate with other forms of beliefs.

the narrow approach, at least in the manner in which the international system has seemed to interpret religion, because it is an over-arching belief system that provides a lucid, assessable, doctrine for the 'actual practice' of the belief. For example, pursuant to the principles of a religious belief prohibiting abortions, a physician or nurse may refuse to participate in an abortion procedure, even when mandated by the state. It is doubtful however whether religious grounds provide for further forms of objection under the narrow approach. Hence, a religious adherent cannot object to a tax payment made to support local abortion clinics[80] since the action is not an actual practice of a belief's directive.

An additional method for manifesting a conscientious belief under the narrow approach is by way of another human right, notably the right to freedom of expression or assembly.[81] While the narrow approach recognises the existence of a host of *forum internum* beliefs, manifestation of a conscientious belief is generally linked to other human rights that provide a clearer, and more focused, method of assessing the action.[82] Assessment of the manifestation of a belief then can occur within the context of freedom of expression, such as the refusal of a Jehovah's Witness to pledge allegiance to the flag in the US,[83] or freedom of assembly, such as protesting due to an infringed belief.[84] Conscientious beliefs similarly will fall under free expression protection, such as a pacifist's dissemination of peace pamphlets,[85] or the right to assembly, such

---

[80] See e.g. 20747/92 *Boussel v. France* 16 EHRR CD49 (1993).
[81] There also exists additional means for asserting a conscientious belief however such cases do not necessarily focus on the right to manifestation. See e.g. 20390/92 *Tinnelly v. UK* 1998-IV Rep. Judg. & Dec. 1633 (violation of ECHR Article 6 for building contractor who was denied a public contract on basis of religious beliefs).
[82] Beddard (1993;115); Humphrey (1985) (noting parallel between right to religion and assembly); ST/HR/SER.A/16 (protection of secular beliefs generally derives from right to free expression, such that context for considering freedom of conscience is 'actual practice' standard); *Church of Lukumi v. City of Hialeah* 508 US 520 (1993) in a concurring opinion, Justice Scalia notes in a rather understated manner that examining the link between expression, assembly, and religion poses an issue of vast proportions.
[83] *West Virginia v. Barnette* 319 US 624 (1943). Cf. *Bijoe Emmanuel v. Kerala* AIR 1987 SC 748 (Indian Supreme Court deciding same case on free religion grounds).
[84] *Platform Artze v. Austria* 44 D&R 65 (1985).
[85] Van Dijk and Van Hoof (1990) noting how right to conscience is supported by free expression. Note however that the ECHR cases deferring to free expression in lieu of the right to conscience have denied the free expression assertion as well. See e.g. 11567/85 *Fritz v. France* 11 EHRR 67 (1988) (Commission held that distribution of pamphlets should be banned since they incited incorrect military conduct); 22838/93 *Van den Dungen v. Netherlands* 80 D&R 147 (1995) (free expression against abortion limited due to legitimate and necessary aim of government).

138 The International Human Right to Freedom of Conscience

as publicly protesting against fascist views,[86] due to the broad scope of actions that these rights can encompass.

Upon re-considering the questions mentioned *supra* regarding the scope of the right to conscience and the type of belief being protected, the narrow approach furnishes an initial answer. The belief in question must be linked to an over-arching doctrine that provides a universal direction for the individual pursuant to clearly defined principles. Under the ECHR for example a belief must mandate an actual practice that is an expression of a 'coherent view on fundamental problems' in order for an action to amount to a protected manifestation.[87]

Some states also seem to adopt a similar approach. For example, the Indian courts refer to acts done in pursuance of religion that are integral parts and practices of the religion.[88] While the US maintains a somewhat subjective standard due to a focus on the individual's sincerity, US Courts define belief as a conviction equivalent to religion that centres on an ultimate goal, distinguishes between right and wrong on moral, ethical or religious grounds, and the individual sincerely adheres to the belief as determined by expressions and actions.[89]

An asserted belief deriving from a 'personal' desire or conscientious standard will not necessarily meet these criteria. The asserted belief will not provide an over-arching doctrine or mandate specific actions for the practice of the belief. Hence a personal belief, such as removing an uncomfortable wig, or a more general belief, such as protecting endangered species, does not manifest as a belief because of the lack of a pre-determined means for upholding the belief. These assertions do not entail prayer or particular observances of actual practice as mandated by pre-determined directives of the belief system. Rather, the narrow approach will acknowledge the belief within a freedom *from* context of the right. Alternatively, the narrow approach would consider manifestation of such

---

[86] See e.g. 8440/78 *Christians Against Racism v. UK* 21 D&R 138 (1981) (although assembly was central right for manifestation of group's anti-racist and anti-fascist views, the state had a legitimate security consideration in limiting the protest); 25522/94 *Negotiate Now v. UK* 19 EHRR CD93 (1995) (assembly to support peaceful negotiations with Ireland was banned due to public order limitation); 19601/92 *Ciraklion v. Turkey* 80 D&R 46 (1995) (free thought and expression deemed subsidiary to right to assembly).

[87] 8741/79 *X v. Germany* 24 D&R 137 (1981); 7050/75 *Arrowsmith v. UK* 3 EHRR 218 (1978); 8317/78 *McFeely v. UK* 3 EHRR 161 (1981).

[88] *HRE v. LT* AIR 1954 SC 282; *Swami v. TN* AIR 1972 SC 1586.

[89] See e.g. *US v. Ward* 989 F.2d 1015 (9th Cir 1992); *International Society for Krishna v. Barber* 650 F.2d 430 (2nd Cir 1981) (using similar criteria with regard to Krishna faith).

beliefs as deriving from other human rights, such as free expression where the belief is equated with a more general form of thought, or freedom of assembly where the belief is understood as representing a movement for change.[90] These rights[91] provide a more practical context for assessing the scope for the manifestation of an asserted belief and make it easier for a judicial body to consider an assertion of a belief without making a final determination regarding the adequacy of a belief.[92]

The key characteristic of a narrow approach to the right to conscience then is the comparative role to religion that the conscientious belief must play. A manifested conscientious belief is one where the individual is relying on clearly pre-determined principles that are comparable to a religious directive. Hence one can understand the manifestation of a pacifist's belief against military service because it entails a conflict with the central directive of the belief regarding the self imposed prohibition of the use of weapons.

A pacifist's assertion of military objection differs however from an objection to alternative military service. In the latter instance, it is not entirely clear from a doctrinal standpoint that all pacifists would object to alternative service or even acknowledge the existence of a conflict with a pacifist belief given the option of non-military alternative service.[93] Yet, when compared to a more orderly or doctrinal form of religious belief, such as Jehovah's Witnesses who also object to alternative service, one can understand the narrow approach as upholding their right to object even to alternative service.[94] The basis for the assertion of the Jehovah's Witness is a specific religious directive that prevents any form of association with military activity.

Because conscience and religion present the strongest link both historically[95] and in practice,[96] the distinction will serve as the initial focus

---

[90] See discussion *infra* for an elaboration of the relationship between the right to conscience, expression and assembly.

[91] Note other rights also can entail a conscientious assertion, such as the right to privacy or the right to life. See e.g. Marcus (1998) (discussing the grounds for conscientious objection to the military).

[92] See e.g. 17419/90 *Wingrove v. UK* 1996-V Rep. Judg. & Dec. 1937 where the ECHR Court considered blasphemy laws within the context of free expression.

[93] Note *Thomas v. Review Board* 450 US 707 (1980) (Court upheld free exercise for an individual assertion of a a belief, even when other members of religion might not have acted in same manner as believer).

[94] See e.g. 10410/83 *N v. Sweden* 40 D&R 203 (1984) (upholding distinction between Jehovah Witness' objection to alternative military service versus a secular objection to same). *Cf.* 402/1990 *Brinkhof v. Netherlands* (1993).

[95] See discussion *supra* at Chapter Four.

[96] See discussion *infra*.

of consideration, principally to determine the adequacy of the narrow approach as a means of upholding the *forum externum* right to conscience. A variety of domestic legal systems also will be considered to contrast and further explicate the proposed distinction between religion and conscience. The two key state systems to be considered are the United States, where the notion of separation of church and state is subject to a great deal of doctrinal confusion, and India, where the attempt to impose a secular system raises a host of methodical problems for a legal system that is dealing with a religious populace.

Conscience and Religion

One may associate the narrow right to manifest a conscientious belief with a religious belief because manifestation is limited to actions that derive from a particular doctrinal directive of a belief. This generally results in a limited form of manifestation pursuant to a particular practice that the belief system dictates, a difficult component to demonstrate for a conscientious belief. Additionally, or, one might contend, as a result of this limited approach, some legal systems tend to constrict the right of manifestation to the negative confines of a freedom from approach to the right to conscience, thereby limiting any positive assertions of a manifested belief. These approaches to the *forum externum* right to conscience will be examined in turn, with a view towards demonstrating that such applications of the right derive from a misunderstanding of the significance of a conscientious belief as well as the application of a religious belief.

In the context of the ECHR, a link must be maintained between the manifestation of a belief, be it religious or otherwise, and the 'actual practice' of a belief. The standard utilised in the ECHR framework is somewhat illusory due to the difficulty in creating distinctions between beliefs that can manifest and beliefs that cannot. The basic requirement imposed by ECHR judicial fora is to uphold a generally recognisable, and particular, practice that has been pre-determined as a central element of the belief, or the action is necessary to fulfil the belief.[97] For example, the Commission indicated that a 'belief' that one's ashes be scattered over the grave is not a formal belief since it does not present a 'coherent view on fundamental problems' but a personal view regarding the manner of burial.[98] Even in situations where the Commission has recognised a formal belief that maintains particular direction, such as anthroposophy, the belief

---

[97] Evans, M. (1997;311).
[98] 8741/79 *X v. Germany* 24 D&R 137 (1980).

can only manifest as an 'actual practice'. Hence the Commission has interpreted a refusal to join a state pension scheme as being motivated by one's anthroposophic beliefs and not representing an 'actual performance' of the belief.[99]

Manifestation of a conscientious belief in the ECHR occurs within a limited context where the principles underlying the belief serve a purpose that is analogous to religious principle. A pacifist belief can manifest in circumstances entailing a practice of the belief, such as military conscientious objection, but not in other instances where the action is not a 'generally recognisable form' of practice, such as refusing to pay part of income tax that supports the military.[100] This leads to decisions such as *N. v. Sweden*[101] where the petitioner claimed that granting Jehovah's Witnesses an exemption from alternative service was discriminatory, and in violation of ECHR Article 14, since all other conscientious objectors were subject to alternative service. The Commission held however that the state had an objective basis for discriminatory treatment since Jehovah's Witnesses adhere to specific guidelines through strict principles and religious convictions, thereby providing a basis for complete exclusion. The secular military conscientious objector cannot refer to any objective standard to demonstrate sincerity, thereby allowing for different treatment.[102]

Similarly, the ECHR Commission has held that an architect's refusal to join a mandatory professional organisation, because the organisation's political views were at odds with his conscientious beliefs,[103] was not an 'actual expression' of the objector's personal beliefs.[104] Rather the Commission interpreted the assertion as a general refusal that is not linked to any pre-determined practice of a belief. The narrow nature of the right also applies to religious manifestations. For example, state-mandated external actions do not necessarily translate into inhibitions on one's right to manifest belief, such as paying state regulated child support even if the payments might deprive one of sufficient funds to travel to a house of worship.[105] Similar reasoning is applied to objections to alternative service since the objection does not relate to any specific aspect of the belief.

---

[99] 1067/83 *V v. Netherlands* 39 D&R 267 (1984).
[100] 10358/83 *C v. UK* 37 D&R 142 (1983) (tax being deemed a neutral activity).
[101] 10410/83 *N v. Sweden* 40 D&R 203 (1984).
[102] See also 11595/85 *Suter v. Switzerland*, 51 D&R 160 (1986) (military could distinguish between penalties imposed on conscientious objectors who act based on secular or religious reasons, as long as law is applied fairly).
[103] 14331/88 *Revert Legallais v. France* 62 D&R 309 (1989).
[104] *Cf.* the ECHR's treatment of individuals who object to paying dues to trade unions. See e.g. 16130/90 *Sigurjonsoon v. Iceland* 16 EHRR 462 (1993).
[105] 24875/94 *Logan v. UK* 1 E.H.R.L.R. 83 (1997).

Additionally, the ECHR further seems to limit the right to manifest a belief, aside for the limitations provided for in the treaty,[106] if the state determines that the situation warrants it.[107] For example, the Commission has upheld instances whereby the authorities deem it necessary to inhibit manifestation because the individual placed oneself in a particular position. Hence the military may dismiss a soldier who has adopted fundamentalist views,[108] and a university may deny admission to a Muslim student who refused to remove her head covering for an identification card photo.[109] Courts apply similar reasoning to in-service conscientious objectors, whereby a soldier might adopt a pacifist belief during his military service.[110]

Because the freedom to manifest a conscientious belief is limited to narrow instances of 'actual practice', it is difficult to interpret a conscientious belief as creating any traditional form of pre-determined practice in a manner comparable to a structured religion. The result is that in the framework of the ECHR, the majority of decisions regarding this right have focused on religious, rather then conscientious, principles,[111] and many commentators have even questioned whether there exists any right to manifest a conscientious belief.[112]

In the US, the courts adopt a similar understanding of the scope of manifestation, although the debate occurs within a different context given the constitutional structure. Essentially, part of the determination regarding the right to manifest a conscientious belief hinges on the attempt to achieve a balance between the Establishment Clause, the prohibition regarding the entanglement of the government into religious affairs, and the Free Exercise Clause, the right of all individuals to practise their beliefs.

Granting too much credence to the establishment side tends to weaken the free exercise right to the point that an individual may not

---

[106] Article 9(2) and the margin of appreciation accorded to a state in certain instances. *See* discussion *infra*.
[107] *See also* Cullen (1997) noting the tendency towards the social justification for manifestation of the right.
[108] 20704/92 *Kalac v. Turkey* 1997-IV Rep. Judg. & Dec. 1199 (Judge Advocat forced to retire due to his fundamentalist views where the Court noted that in exercising a right, one must account for the specific situation at hand); 14524/89 *Yanoeik v. Turkey* 74 D&R 14 (1993) (similar decision regarding a soldier).
[109] 1627/90 *Karaduman v. Turkey* 74 D&R 93 (1993).
[110] *See e.g.* 11595/85 *Suter v. Switzerland* 51 D&R 160 (1986).
[111] *Compare* 14307/88 *Kokkinakis v. Greece* 17 EHRR 397 (1993) (proselytising upheld as part of religious belief) *with* 11308/84 *Utrecht v. Netherlands* 46 D&R 200 (1986) (organisation's mandate to assist prisoner's not considered a belief that can manifest in any practical sense).
[112] Evans, M. (1997); Vermeulen (1993); Harris, O'Boyle and Warbrick (1995).

manifest a conscientious belief due to limited governmental involvement. Alternatively, acknowledging the Free Exercise Clause as the driving force could lead to policy problems relating to the over breadth of assertions, create a difficulty in delineating the form of beliefs to be protected, and diminish the Establishment Clause.[113] What this debate demonstrates however is that aside from the underlying constitutional policy decision confronting a US court, there exists an inherent difficulty in creating an adequate form of protection or right for an individual who does not identify with a formal religion. Indeed, a problem that some US commentators have with the First Amendment's freedom of religion is the focus on preventing the imposition of a religious standard on the state, rather than an attempt to provide for the manifestation of a belief or 'exercise' of the right in any meaningful sense.[114]

When confronted with a free exercise issue, the US Courts tend not to analyse the merits of an individual's pre-determined religious beliefs.[115] Rather, the Courts associate the determination to the strength of the belief that the individual harbours, with the focus on how a belief creates an uncompromising moral issue for the person.[116] Upon considering the Establishment Clause within this context, the US Supreme Court focuses on the importance of neutral action by the Government rather than imposing a blanket prohibition regarding governmental involvement in religious affairs. Hence a tax exemption for a religious publication violated the Establishment Clause since the exemption did not extend to other groups that focus on accommodating reflection and discussion about 'ultimate values or the contours of a meaningful life'.[117] The Court used similar reasoning to uphold the religious sacrifice of animals, despite state law indicating that the ritual was contrary to the wishes of the local public.[118]

---

[113] Levine (1997); Davis (1995;251) (noting that Rhenquist has adopted a narrow construction of the clauses, thereby making it easier for greater government involvement in a non-discriminatory fashion). Note that prior to the Supreme Court's overturning of the Religious Freedom Restoration Act, courts were swamped with requests to uphold a variety of belief systems. Geoly and Gustafson (1996;462).
[114] See e.g. Eisgruber and Sager (1994).
[115] *Thomas v. Review Board* 450 US 707 (1981).
[116] *Seeger v. US* 380 US 163 (1965) (key aspect is the manner in which the asserted belief plays a central role in one's life); *Torasco v. Watkins* 367 US 488 (1960) (Court defines belief system in broad manner).
[117] *Texas v. Bullock* 489 US 1 (1991) at 16.
[118] *Church of Lukumi v. City of Hialeah* 508 US 520 (1993). A key basis for overturning the law was due to its specific focus on this form of practice, excluding other forms of ritual practice on animals such as slaughter for Kosher meat. Note that the *Lukumi* majority attempted to distinguish *Reynolds v. US* 98 US 145 (1879), which involved a

A superficial difference between the approach of the US and the ECHR is that US laws seem to protect individual practice deriving from particular beliefs, whereas the ECHR might not. For example, US Courts upheld a Christian's refusal to work on Sunday based on a personal interpretation of Scriptures although other Christians would work on Sunday.[119] Similarly, US Courts have upheld an Amish's claim to remove a red triangle from his horse-drawn cart despite the practice of other Amish who used the triangle,[120] or a Native American's refusal to cut his hair despite a prison regulation to the contrary and the lack of any scriptural evidence.[121]

A key factor in the US that might imply a broader understanding of belief is the focus on the 'sincerity' of an individual, as determined by prior adherence to the asserted belief and the individual's current assertion of faith.[122] This was the test applied to a Church of God member who relied on prayer instead of surgery to heal a cancerous tumour, even though her religious sect did not advocate such an approach. The Circuit Court nevertheless granted the woman state assisted benefits.[123] In a more general sense, US Courts might uphold the manifestation of a conscientious belief when a connection exists to an over-arching standard of a sincerely held belief deriving from an individual's moral approach.[124] A typical example would be the right for non-religious military conscientious objectors to manifest their beliefs by refusing military service.[125]

---

challenge to the Congressional banning of polygamous Mormon marriages, because the legal focus in Reynolds was of a more general, public, nature. Nonetheless, the Mormons in *Reynolds* treated polygamy as an 'actual practice' of their beliefs, thereby raising a Free Exercise violation. Harmer- Dionne (1998) (asserting that *Reynolds* created a change in the Mormon's manner of practice). *See also* Moens (1989).

[119] *Frazee v. Illinois* 489 US 829 (1989).
[120] *State v. Miller* 538 N.W.2d 573 (Wis. App. 1995).
[121] *Gallahan v. Holyfield* 516 F.Supp. 1004 (E.D.Va. 1981).
[122] Of course, this raises an inherent conflict for a system that asserts it will not delve into religion since an analysis of sincerity would seem to require some form of understanding or evaluation of the religion as well. Coffman (1997).
[123] *Lewis v. Califano* 616 F.2d 73 (3rd Cir.1980).
[124] Marshall (1995); Smith (1993) (criteria centre on both subjective views towards belief and broader, more abstract, conceptions); McConnell (1998) (outlining historical precedent for individual belief approach); Killilea (1973) (belief creates an uncompromising moral issue in a manner equivalent to a religious belief).
[125] Note however that the US Court did not seem to acknowledge the right to military conscientious objection on constitutional grounds but rather based its decision on a specific statute. *Welsh v. US* 398 US 333 (1970).

One reason for this individual approach is that the US derives protection for freedom of religion from the 'norm of liberal neutrality'.[126] Such an approach, which comprehends religion as an individual and secular process, upholds a religious belief that is consistent with secular constitutional norms[127] such as free expression.[128] A court therefore will be hard-pressed to uphold general assertions of a conscientious belief that might be unfair to other individuals. This develops not because of a pre-determined limitation, but as a result of the underlying secular nature of the system as derived from the Establishment Clause. For example, the US Supreme Court denied First Amendment 'Free Exercise' protection to an American Indian who refused to register his daughter for a social security number. The Indian claimed that the registration would 'rob her spirit'. The Court decided however that upholding the belief would create a unique right for a religious belief in violation of the principles of establishment and neutrality.[129]

Note however that the US Courts apply rather similar criteria to the ECHR bodies when considering the form of belief to be protected. That is, the ECHR distinction between actual practice and mere motivations appears to apply in the US as well. Upon determining which beliefs to consider as falling under the protection of the Free Exercise clause, the US Courts generally favour structured beliefs that are analogous to religious beliefs. Courts distinguish between assertions that reflect a way of life or a philosophical outlook rather than a belief system that is analogous to a religion. For example, courts have held that 'nuclearism', a group of individuals who do not believe in any reliance upon nuclear energy or nuclear weapons, is a political judgement and does not reflect a belief system.[130] Similarly, in denying Free Exercise protection to the Church of Marijuana, the Court adopted a rather functional understanding of religion

---

[126] Gedicks (1995) referring to a variety of critical legal studies proponents such as Kelman and Unger.
[127] See e.g. Tushnet (1988) (noting as well cases where it was socially inexpensive to grant an exemption, such as allowing Amish to teach their own children); Marshall (1983) (protection for free exercise of religion granted in situations analogous to free expression).
[128] See e.g. *Heffron v. Krishna Consciousness* 452 US 640 (1981) (regulation of distribution of pamphlets, including religious pamphlets, upheld on basis that free expression be applied equally to all). Note that linking the free exercise with other constitutional values can serve to overly constrict the free exercise right. See Garvey (1986) (asserting that the Free Exercise clause must incorporate values beyond those of other constitutional rights). See also discussion *infra* distinguishing free exercise of religion from freedom of expression.
[129] *Bowen v. Ray* 476 US 693 (1986).
[130] *US v. Allen* 760 .2d 447 (2nd Cir. 1985).

in holding that the so called 'Church' merely reflected a philosophy regarding the virtues of marijuana rather than any formalised system of behaviour.[131] Courts similarly have decided that the Boy Scouts are a charitable organisation operating for a social purpose rather than a formalised belief system.[132]

Furthermore, the US Supreme Court has adhered to the *forum internum/forum externum* distinction up to a certain extent. For example, some commentators contend that the Court imposes a belief/conduct distinction.[133] The Court seems to uphold assertions of a belief that relate to an internal aspect of the individual and the state's attempt to control the mind, such as in the school prayer cases. In such instances involving the *forum internum*, the Supreme Court is wary and tends to uphold the belief. Yet when a court considers the connection between the external conduct and the asserted belief, the tendency is to consider other factors as grounds for limiting the exercise of the right, such as social costs or establishment issues.[134]

As a result, the seemingly broad exemption for secular conscientious beliefs in the US seems to be the exception rather then the rule. Courts uphold the manifestation of a belief in the US when the action will either not entail severe social costs by granting undue deference to a particular belief,[135] or the individual brings to the fore other constitutional rights.[136]

India serves as a rather interesting contrast to the US. The Indian State will actively involve itself in matters of religion. In India, where the underlying governmental policy of secularism operates in what is a largely religious populace, courts have focused on the proper degree of state entanglement with religious policy. Hence the state may require a sect to provide for entrance and prayer by all individuals, including lower caste untouchables,[137] or prevent discrimination towards untouchables.[138] When

---

[131] *US v. Myers* 95 F.3rd 1475 (10th Cir. 1996). *See also State v. Balzer* 954 P.2d 931 (1998).

[132] *Randall v. Orange County Council* 952 P.2d 261 (1997) (holding that the local civil rights laws regarding religious discrimination did not apply to the Boy Scouts).

[133] Hamilton (1993) (concluding that such an approach derives from socially inherent Christian values); Pritchard (1990).

[134] *See e.g. Jenkins v. Angelou* 948 F. Supp. 543 (E.D.Va. 1996) (Court recognised vegan's right to assert belief but, given prison context, Court deferred to prison's evaluation regarding costs and security reasons for denying the claim).

[135] *See e.g. Frazee v. Illinois* 489 US 829 (1989).

[136] Gedicks (1995;112-113) noting the general lack of success for individual free exercise challenges before the Supreme Court.

[137] *Yagnapurushdasji v. Muldas* AIR 1966 SC 1119.

[138] The [Central] Untouchability (Offences) Act 1955 (No. 22 of 1955) (law banning discrimination towards untouchables).

confronted with a conflict between a religious belief and state law, an Indian court will not hesitate to examine the underlying religious principles that formed the basis for the belief[139] and attempt to find available alternatives.[140] India therefore poses an interesting contrast to the US and ECHR because the Indian Courts confront issues of religious conflict that have invaded the state's domain and superimpose the social goal of equality and secularism. Indeed, it seems that the social policy goals provide a more focused determination of genuine action (or sincerity) since the Indian Courts readily refer to the doctrine and practice of the belief.[141]

The state will actively regulate society in a manner that will conflict with, and even create a change to, a particular religious practice, such as providing divorced women with larger maintenance sums contrary to a religion's practice.[142] A key goal of the state is to address various inequalities in society to remedy the situation of the under-class.[143] Hence while a religion might require hereditary priesthood as a central tradition of its belief, the state will act in the guise of a social reformer to alter the practice, especially if a priest is serving a secular role while acting as a servant to the Temple.[144]

A case involving a Hindu believer who objected to the use of a photo on a voter registration card highlights the different approach to freedom of religion in India. The determination regarding the practice centred on whether, historically, there existed a religious basis for the asserted belief.[145] The focus of attention for the Indian judiciary was the religion itself and the particular demands that emanate therefrom.[146]

Such a case serves as a rather interesting contrast to the ECHR where the Commission rejected an assertion to wear a head scarf for a university photograph based on the fact that the individual had placed

---

[139] *Rajasthan v. Sajjanlal* AIR 1975 SC 706 (Court analyses Jain scriptures to determine whether state regulations regarding management of a Jain temple's trust funds violated the religious requirements).

[140] *Faruk v. State* AIR 1970 SC 93.

[141] *Bijoe Emmanuel v. State of Kerala* AIR 1987 SC 748 (Court upheld the right of a child of Jehovah's Witnesses to refuse to sing the National Anthem in school since it infringed a genuine religious belief).

[142] *Kahin v. Shah Bono* AIR 1985 SC 945 (Court upheld law regulating maintenance payments in amounts greater then the pre-determined amount in Muslim law). *See also* Dhavan (1978).

[143] Bharatiya (1987); Chatterjee (1994); Dhavan (1987).

[144] *Swami v. T.N.* AIR 1972 SC 1586.

[145] *Kuman v. CEC* AIR 1961 Cal. 289 (Court held no historical basis for the assertion). *Cf. Saheb v. Special Officer* AIR 1988 Andh. Pra. 377 where the Court held that taking photographs violates the religious principle of haram.

[146] *See also Narayanan v. State of Madras* AIR 1954 Mad. 386.

herself in the position of attending a secular institution (as well as the surrounding public policy considerations pursuant to the limitations). The Indian case also is analogous to the US Supreme Court decision regarding an American Indian's refusal to register his daughter's social security number on grounds that it would breach the dictates of his religious belief; the US Supreme Court relied on public policy grounds of administrative necessity rather than consider the significance of the refusal for the Indian's belief system.

Galanter[147] further clarifies India's approach by distinguishing between the US, as a limitation system, and India, as an intervention system. The US participates in 'shaping' religion since the government influences religion by:

> promulgating public standards and by defining the field in which these public standards shall prevail, overruling conflicting assertions of religious authority.[148]

Hence the US Supreme Court decisions upholding the legislative ban of polygamy[149] or requiring the use of social security numbers[150] as violating the public standards that centre on the strive for a secular, independent, state. Regarding the positive exercise of the right, the US courts also will incorporate socio-religious influences, as exemplified by the decision upholding a Christmas tree and Menorah display in a public square, while banning the display of a crèche depicting the birth of Jesus[151] or upholding Sunday Closing laws as representative of a secular holiday that enhances family life.

India, on the other hand, is interventionist according to Galanter since the issue is:

> more explicit and more complex. The Constitution attempts a delicate combination of religious freedom in the present with a mandate for active governmental promotion of a transformation of India's religions...[it is] an attempt to grasp

---

[147] Galanter (1992;250-252).
[148] Galanter (1992;250).
[149] *Reynolds v. US* 98 US 145 (1878).
[150] *Bowen v. Ray* 476 US 693 (1986).
[151] *Allegheny v. ACLU* 492 US 573 (1989). As noted by Galanter, 'The American legal setting, [for example,] has made and presumably will continue to make a profound contribution toward shaping religion in the United States.' *See also* Greenawalt (1988) (while government should not promote religion, religion will still play an unavoidable role in society and in political decisions).

the levers of religious authority and to reformulate the religious tradition from within, as it were.[152]

Hence an Indian court upheld a Jain festival not only because it was a secular holiday celebrated by all, but also because the state wished to propagate minority beliefs and tolerate, as well as identify with, all forms of faiths.[153] While both legal systems will unavoidably engage in decisions involving a balancing of religious practices against the secularist foundation of the state, India intentionally desires to create a pluralist society[154] composed of diverse views and thoughts.[155] Hence in the *Shirur Mutt* case,[156] the Court upheld a state's appointment of a manager to oversee funds of a bankrupt religious institution as long as the manager only dealt with the secular actions of the institution, such as economic or political decisions, and not the funds that the institution had designated for religious purposes.[157] The state plays a more active role in balancing its maintenance of a plural society with equality for all individuals[158] and an attempt to uphold equality and non-discrimination for all religions.[159]

On a more practical level however the Indian Courts seem to structure the right to freedom of religion and conscience in a comparable

---

[152] Galanter (1992;250).
[153] *Chandra v. Irdui* AIR 1975 Delhi 168. *Cf. Estate of Thornton v. Caldor, Inc.* 472 US 703 (1985) (Court upheld Sunday Closing Laws, despite religious overtones, since Sunday had become a universal day of rest).
[154] Bharatiya (1987; Chapter 1). *See also* Chatterjee (1994) noting importance of accounting for overall minority representation in policy-level/national sphere as a means of ensuring for a secular state which reflects all forms of the population.
[155] Bharucha (1994) (Indian secularism is respecting all religions within a framework of equality). The author notes that the strive for equality should be based on a cultural framework which lies between religion and politics, so as to address the instability and differences inherent in relying on any one force to determine the equal position; Bhargava (1994) (noting necessity for a number of ideals in a neutral state); Cossman & Kapur (1997) (calling for a move towards upholding cultural diversity rather than a strict interpretation of neutrality as inaction).
[156] *HRE v. LT* AIR 1954 SC 282.
[157] *See also Sri Venkataramana Devaru v. State of Mysore* 1958 SCJ 382 regarding the opening of Hindu temples to untouchables, which clearly was a religious matter. The Court upheld their right to enter, yet granted the temple certain periods upon which to exclude entry by the general public; *Kahn v. Shah Bono* AIR 1985 SC 945 where the Court referred to the Criminal Procedure Code to overturn Muslim religious law that mandated a limited period of maintenance payments. The government subsequently passed a law that side-stepped the court decision. Baird (1998;346).
[158] Galanter (1992;249-250) noting the profound contribution made by the state towards shaping religion; Baird (1998;342-344).
[159] Cossman and Kapur (1997) (noting that toleration as equality, rather than neutrality, is the driving force for India).

manner to the ECHR. Pursuant to the interventionist nature of the State's secular policy, the Indian Supreme Court has interpreted Article 25 of the Indian Constitution to incorporate an internal and external dimension. Religion is not only a code of ethics or set of beliefs that an individual may harbour internally, but also includes rituals and ceremonies conducted by a person in furtherance of the religion.[160] Courts also have upheld acts done in pursuance of the 'essential matters' of religious beliefs[161] that are viewed as 'genuine assertions' of an essential religious belief or practice.

The broad scope accorded to the right to freedom of religion in India seems to include conscientious beliefs as well. Courts have interpreted the right to freedom of religion and conscience as including non-theistic principles which centre on a conscious duty to obey certain rules of conduct. In *Mittal v. India* for example, the Supreme Court interpreted 'religious activity' as a conscious duty to obey rules restricting one's conduct that need not be theistic. In deciding whether the State could appoint an administrator for a town, the Court held that while the establishment of the town was a secular multi-cultural experiment, the asserted belief, derived from a Yogic ideal, was equivalent to a religion since it maintained a collective system of beliefs, as exemplified by the town's tax provisions, that included adherence to moral practices resulting from the belief.[162] The minority opinion, which agreed that operating a town was a secular activity, noted that 'religion' encompassed thought, belief or faith 'as involving the conscience' and included profession or practices in a particular manner even if different from the original intentions of belief.

Commentators also have equated the right to conscience with minority beliefs,[163] noting that the manifestation be an essential and integral part of the belief.[164] Religion then is a doctrine that also concerns

---

[160] *Swami v. State of TN* AIR 1972 SC 1586 (right extends not only to doctrines or beliefs but to actions that are an integral part of the belief).

[161] Bharatiya (1987; Chapter Four) noting key requirement for Article 25 (constitutional basis for freedom of conscience) is that the asserted belief be an 'essential matter' for the religion.

[162] For purposes of Article 26, ('religious denomination') the Court found a common organisation and distinctive name.

[163] Bharatiya (1987) (although subject to state interest, Article 25 relates to manifesting a general belief as well).

[164] Jain (1987;635); Khawaya (1992;95) (concept of tolerance applies to a host of different beliefs and ideals). *Cf.* Basu (1988) noting that manifestation of conscience only occurs within the context of free expression, with Article 25 protection relating solely to the *forum internum*.

the conscience and underlying spirit of the person as long as it is capable of being overtly expressed and relates to an essential practice.[165]

Of course recognising the seemingly broad treatment towards the manifestation of a belief raises the issue of scope that a state is to accord to manifestation. Similar to other legal systems, courts generally limit the individual's manifestation of a belief to a particular mandated practice. Hence in banning polygamy for both Muslims[166] and Hindus,[167] the decisions focused on the distinction between a religion allowing for polygamy, as opposed to requiring a religious adherent to be polygamous. Because polygamy was not a specific practice mandated by the respective religions, there was no violation by the state in restricting the practice. Similarly, in *Quareshi v. State of Bihar*[168] the court held that the Quran did not specifically mandate the sacrificing of a cow on a Muslim ceremonial day, a practice prohibited by law, such that the Court could require that the religious adherents sacrifice a different animal instead. By contrast, and recognising that Indian courts would not hesitate to delve into religious practices, in deciding the merits of a state's decision to restrict a religious dance in public, the Court focused on the historical importance of the dance for the religion, as the dance forms an essential and integral part of the religion's practice.[169]

What emerges is that in the legal systems examined thus far, a conscientious belief can manifest when the belief requires a particular form of practice. Even if a legal system will consider motivation, one must discern a link between the action and the particular practice demanded from the belief system. Furthermore, each system appears to lean towards the narrow approach for the right to freedom of conscience. From a teleological standpoint, different legal systems might maintain different goals in their approaches towards the relationship between the state and religion. Nonetheless, the consequential outcome as pertaining to the right to manifest a conscientious belief appears to be similar. Even in the US, which recognises some manifestations of non-traditional conscientious beliefs, the Courts' uphold the constitutional freedom by associating it with other constitutional rights or entangling the right in the difficult balance between the Establishment Clause and the Free Exercise Clause.

---

[165] Bharatiya (1987) (religion as being based on the adherence to moral and ethical rules that, conceptually, incorporate the right to conscience as well).
[166] *Badhuddin v. Aisha Begum* 1957 All.L.J. 300.
[167] *Bombay v. Narasu Appo* AIR 1952 Bom. 84.
[168] *Quareshi v. State of Bihar* 1959 SCJ 985.
[169] AIR 1990 Cal. 336 (D.B.).

It is possible that due to the difficulty in delineating the scope of manifestation, similar, practical, policy considerations pertain to the breadth accorded to the right to avoid the slippery slope problem of unfettered exercises of all manner of beliefs. From the standpoint of international human rights however, the status of the right to freedom of conscience, particularly regarding its link with the freedom of religion under the narrow approach, merits further examination. The problem is twofold. Conscience operates in a different manner than religion, such that deferring to the 'actual practice' standard or solely referring to traditional practices of a belief might not provide for the proper manifestation of a conscientious belief. Putting aside a conscientious belief because an individual need not practise the belief in the traditional sense or in a manner similar to a traditional religion does not translate as a categorical prohibition of the manifestation of conscientious beliefs. It seems that what is important is the status of the belief to the individual asserting the belief, in the same manner that a religious belief serves an important and fundamental purpose to the individual. Furthermore, a closer examination of the narrow approach demonstrates that it does not avoid the pitfalls raised by a broader approach, even when applying the narrow 'actual practice' test. The practice of religious or conscientious principles occurs in a variety of ways and is subject to a host of interpretations and applications, such that the 'actual practice' standard does not adequately address the concerns pertaining to an unfettered right.

Distinctions Between Religion and Conscience

The consequences for the right to conscience, when considering an approach that centres on religion as a basis for the right, are manifold. The association with religion tends to dilute the right to manifest non-theistic and atheistic beliefs and can exclude the beliefs of formative or socially 'unacceptable' religious minorities.[170] Because an accepted 'universal' belief such as pacifism is not formally subject to specific tenets of action in a manner comparable to a religious belief, the manifestation is subject to stricter limitations and restricted protection.[171] The result is that one might

---

[170] *See e.g.* Perotti (1993;179) (discussing problems relating to education of Muslim minority in France).

[171] *Compare* 14307/88 *Kokkinakis v. Greece* 17 EHRR 397 (1993) (ECHR upheld right to propagate religion as a form of practice thereof); *Stainislaus v. MP* AIR 1977 SC 908 (propagation, as opposed to conversion, was upheld as a form of religious practice) *with* 11567/85 *Fritz v. France* 11 EHRR 67 (1988) (pacifist limited in ability to distribute peace pamphlets as a form of manifesting the belief).

overlook or accord secondary status to the significance of a conscientious belief. Merely upholding the *forum internum* aspect of conscience and focusing solely on manifestation of religious beliefs disregards the importance of the individual's desire to abide by a belief, especially when the manifestation derives from a protected *forum internum* belief.[172]

Furthermore, holding a conscientious belief to a religious standard demonstrates a misunderstanding regarding the objective of conscience for an individual and for the subjective nature of a conscientious belief. The tendency to limit manifestation to a negative, freedom *from*, context highlights these problems and illustrates how similar problems regarding identification and motivations deriving from a conscientious belief equally apply to a religious belief.

Disregarding the motivation behind the act can lead to a misunderstanding of the liberty for the manifestation of a belief. For example, there is a distinction between a Christian who kneels and cites the Lord's prayer as opposed to an atheist doing the same action on a film set.[173] A similar problem arises for the military objector because it is not clear whether an individual's pacifist belief directs one to refuse military service or merely motivates a person in the direction of this form of objection.

A reviewing body can generically interpret many 'acts' as being religious in nature, with the difference arising from the motivation for the actions. Motivation certainly seems to play a role when an individual's external action appears genuinely based on a particular belief. Opsahl noted in his *Arrowsmith v. UK* dissent that the key criteria for manifestation should be a genuine motivation deriving from the belief, even if not clearly manifested, when the action entails expression of the belief. The second dissenting opinion of Klecker clarified this point regarding the role of motivation by noting the necessity for harmony between the motivation and the act under scrutiny.[174]

Approaching conscience as both a cognitive and conative process,[175] manifestation of the conscientious decision is an essential aspect thereof.

---

[172] Lorenzen (1992) (conscience marks the individual dignity and integrity of the human person); Kordig (1979) (denial of conscientious belief can be equated with denying the individual's fundamental existence and underlying human dignity).
[173] *See e.g.* Edge (1996).
[174] Of course, this raises the issue regarding the difficulty of recognising a sincere motivation. The next section that discusses the broader approach shall amplify the relationship between motivation and belief.
[175] *See* discussion *supra* at Chapter Four.

The underlying utility of conscience is not solely to protect free thought,[176] but also to root the individual's conscientious norms in a particular situation.[177] In essence, preventing the practice of a belief, especially a practice that is essential to the belief, infringes the belief itself and creates an internal change.[178] Limiting the manifestation of the conscientious decision therefore tends to undermine the right to conscience *ab initio* by preventing an exercise of a conscientious belief. This can in turn violate the *forum internum* as well because prevention of the external practice leads to a change in the internal understanding of the belief.

The problem with determining 'practice' further highlights a fundamental distinction between religion and conscience in consequential and utilitarian terms. Logical reasoning or a deep-rooted moral conviction need not be a basis for religion; it is a matter of faith in objective principles that require particular action by the individual based on a specific duty. Religion is an assertive process that dictates the required action *ex ante*. One's religious faith results in particular actions that reflect that faith as required by the religion.

The focus then for examining a religious assertion can be the extent, or sincerity, of belief rather then the actual basis of the belief. The proof will relate to the degree of faith or duty one feels towards a religion as demonstrated by one's actions. When coupled with the general judicial policy of avoiding any assessment of a religious belief's underlying validity, as is common in the ECHR,[179] the US,[180] and India,[181] the key factor becomes the sincere assertion of an objective standard of religious doctrine.[182]

---

[176] The distinction between freedom of thought and conscience is apparent in the treaties which separately codify the two freedoms. *See also* discussion *supra* at Chapter Four.

[177] *See e.g.* Boyle (1992) noting that 'Freedom of thought is the internal freedom of the mind. From that freedom of the mind flows the freedom of conscience which is the moral resource of the individual'.

[178] *See e.g.* Harmer- Dionne (1998) (referring to Fetsinger's cognitive dissonance theory to demonstrate the changes that occurred to the Mormon religion following the US Supreme Court's decision outlawing polygamy).

[179] *See* 17086/90 *Autio v. Finland* 72 D&R 245 (1991).

[180] *Hobbie v. Unemployment Appeals* 480 US 136 (1987) the US. Supreme Court declared that it would not determine the truth of an underlying belief which is being asserted.

[181] *Bijoe Emmanuel v. Kerala* AIR 1987 SC 748 (key goal is not to assess the belief but to ensure that the belief is held in a genuine manner). The Court also referred to *Jamshedi v. Soonabai* 23 Bombay ILR 122.

[182] Note that relying on sincerity also can be interpreted as creating a new form of limitation.

The focus for a conscientious determination is different, especially since demonstrating one's sincerity towards personal moral beliefs is quite difficult. The problem is that due to the subjective nature of a conscientious belief, one may have to demonstrate sincerity by bearing the negative consequences of an action that the believer took to avoid a breach of a conscientious belief. Such a test then creates a tautology since it undermines the very freedom that one is striving to protect by forcing an individual to demonstrate their sincerity.[183]

As noted by the discussion regarding the *forum internum*,[184] conscience derives from a host of internal thoughts and personal beliefs that can manifest in a variety of ways. The different process associated with conscience indicates that focusing on sincerity towards a conscientious principle will not suffice by merely demonstrating faith in a belief. A link to an over-arching belief is not necessary for conscience since it can derive from subjective evaluations or be based on personal moral principles that need not dictate a particular course of action. The General Assembly's Third Committee alluded to this aspect of the right in associating conscience, but not equating it, with religion since conscience includes philosophical and scientific ideas that relate to a more general understanding of belief, as opposed to religion that is an act of faith.[185]

As a result of the subjective nature of the conscientious process, demonstrating 'sincerity' in the same manner as a religious assertion would be meaningless. One may only assess a 'sincere' conscience within the cognitive moral framework of the individual making the assertion. Proving sincerity towards a conscientious belief then will entail clarifying the underlying principles of the conscientious assertion since such principles, similar to the idea of faith in religion, provide the impetus for the individual to act or refrain from acting. For example, Australian case law regarding conscientious objection to trade union membership requires an individual not merely to demonstrate belief in particular views, but also:

> it must be shown that there is a deep-seated conviction that those views are right and that the conviction represents something more than persuasion and in a general sense operates to influence the actions of the applicant.[186]

---

[183] Vermeulen (1993;79-80).
[184] *See* discussion *supra* at Chapter Four.
[185] *See e.g.* A/C.3/218.
[186] *Wright v. Minister for Labour and National Service* 14 F.L.R. 91 (1969).

Demonstrating one's sincerity for a conscientious claim will focus on the underlying basis for the belief rather than a determination of the principles of the faith. Hence proving a 'sincere' objection to military service in the US entails a demonstration of one's prior non-violent or non-militarist behaviour.[187] Similarly, a conscientious objector to jury service in Australia must prove the genuineness of the claim based on past behaviour, affidavits from friends and family, as well as provide 'an explanation of their conscientious beliefs.'[188] Such evidence relates just as much to the basis for one's conscientious conviction as it does to the sincerity of one's beliefs. Unlike religion, where prior behaviour involves adherence to a particular tenet of the religion, thereby allowing for the possibility of an objective evaluation of an individual's sincerity,[189] a prelude to the proof of a sincere conscientious belief requires one to first state what that belief entails, especially since a conscientious standard derives from subjective evaluations of particular principles.

The Negative, Freedom From, Aspect

The narrow approach to the right to conscience tends to limit the right to a freedom *from* context, whereby the state cannot act to infringe or inhibit the believer's ability to believe. Yet the right will not accrue to any external manifestation of a conscientious belief. The basic reason for such an approach is that it removes the necessity to refer to subjective conscientious beliefs, thereby providing a more functional form of right.

Upon considering the application of the freedom *from* aspect of the right to conscience, however, it appears unavoidable that such a conscientious assertion will entail a focus on the underlying asserted belief. If a state imposes a religious belief on its population, the conflict with the individual's freedom *from* aspect of the right to conscience will arise because the individual adheres to another form of belief.[190] This is the common ground for preventing minority sects from the ritual slaughtering of animals for non-consumption purposes.[191] The state imposes the

---

[187] As codified in 32 C.F.R. Ch. XVI part 1636.
[188] *New South Wales Jury Report* (1984) page 40 paragraph 4.7.
[189] Usually involving a demonstration that an individual is a member of a particular religious order. *See e.g.* New South Wales Law Reform Commission (1984) at paragraph 4.37, where proving a sincere objection to jury service for a member of the Christadelphian sect entails a demonstration that the claimant is an avowed member of the religious order.
[190] *See e.g.* Nowak (1993;317).
[191] *Church of Lukumi v. City of Hialeah* 113 S.Ct. 217 (1993); *Faruk v. Pradesh* AIR 1970 SC 93.

majority's principles under the guise of public policy as a result of an individual assertion to abide by a belief. The argument is similar to that raised by US constitutional scholars when they note that any attempt to balance the Establishment Clause with the Free Exercise Clause will unavoidably raise the issue of establishment because the state will be making a value judgement regarding the type of beliefs, both religious and conscientious, that it desires to protect in its society.[192]

When considering the right to conscience solely from a freedom *from* standpoint, it is difficult to ignore the freedom *to* element that also plays a role in determining the boundaries of the right. In the typical freedom *from* example, a religious state banning apostasy,[193] the state not only violates the freedom *from*, to be free from the imposition of an external belief system, but also infringes the individual's freedom *to* believe or not believe in another religion or belief. The individual might desire to become an apostate not only to remove oneself from a religious framework, but also to practise another religious or conscientious belief or not to practise any belief at all. In each of these instances, asserting the freedom *from* aspect of the right entails an identification with another form of belief. This identification with a different belief is a desire to assert the right to believe as well, which is in essence a freedom to harbour a belief.

Krishnaswami hinted at this relationship between freedom *from* and freedom *to* when discussing the freedom *from* protections.[194] He refers to not taking an oath or engaging in military service[195] because the objection against such actions derives from the person's internal belief system. If the basis for freedom *from* is that a state infringes an individual's belief because of a particular law, the protection deriving from the right to conscience is an assertion of the right to freedom *to*. Each instance of freedom *from* manifestation then will entail an understanding of the individual's belief upon which she is relying to assert the freedom *from* claim.

A US case involving a Native American forced to register his daughter's social security number as a pre-condition for receipt of welfare

---

[192] *See e.g.* Hauerwas & Baxter (1992) The authors refer to Charles Taylor who asserts that the US doctrine regarding separation of church and state was not to preclude religion from public life but to combine the two to create a better civic freedom.

[193] A disputed right that probably can be derived from the UDHR, ECHR, and ICCPR. *See* discussion *supra* at Chapter Four.

[194] Krishnaswami (1960;42-45).

[195] Krishnaswami also refers to not participating in religious ceremonies (the basis for which can be adherence to atheist beliefs) and compulsory treatment of a disease (the basis of which is a particular belief against external, or non-natural, medical treatment).

alluded to this symmetrical relationship between freedom *from* and freedom *to*. The plaintiff contended that the social security number would 'rob the spirit' of his child.[196] The concurring opinion of Justice O'Connor noted that the Supreme Court's attempt to distinguish between an individual not receiving a benefit due to a belief, such as unemployment benefits for leaving employment that violates one's beliefs,[197] as opposed to forcing the government to practise pursuant to the complainant's belief,[198] such as not registering a social security number, is meaningless. Whether the individual is practising a belief, as a freedom *to* the right, and thereby losing a benefit, or desires to avoid required governmental action, as a freedom *from* another belief, by demanding particular governmental practice, does not avoid the violation to that individual's system of beliefs. The result is that limiting the right to freedom of conscience solely to a freedom *from* notion implicitly acknowledges the right to a freedom *to* manifest a conscientious belief.

Additionally, as a result of the open-ended nature of conscience, manifestation of conscience can apply to a host of varied situations and depend on a number of factors, such as the scope of the principle being asserted or the surrounding events that caused the conscientious conflict. For example, an individual can conscientiously oppose abortion in a number of ways ranging from a refusal to perform the act to more general protests such as not paying welfare taxes that support abortions[199] or refusing to type medical forms recommending an abortion.[200] By contrast, because of the link between a religious belief and a particular directive to which a believer will faithfully adhere, a religious objection to participating in an abortion is a clear manifestation of a religious belief. A religion will specifically forbid the taking of life or broadly define when life begins such as to create a bar to performing or participating in an abortion. Indeed, this problem of adequately identifying the belief is why military conscientious objectors who also refuse to perform alternative service because of its connection to the military, a claim that is analogous

---

[196] *Bowen v. Ray* 476 US 693 (1986).
[197] Referring to *Sherbert v. Verner* 374 US 398 (1967) and its progeny, such as *Hobbie v. Unemployment Commission of Florida* 480 US 136 (1987) which uphold receipt of unemployment benefits following a voluntary dismissal for not working on the Sabbath.
[198] As the majority contended in *Bowen v. Ray* 476 US 693 (1986).
[199] *See e.g.* 20747/92 *Bouessel v. France* 16 EHRR CD49 (1993) (conscientious belief in the right to life will not allow withholding of social security tax payments that support state-sponsored abortions).
[200] Grubb (1988;162) (discussing *R v. Salford* [1988] 2 WLR 442 which involved a secretary who refused to type a doctor's referral letter recommending an abortion).

to Jehovah's Witnesses, are precluded from the claim due to the general and seemingly illusory nature of the claim.

Yet this difficulty in identifying the principles of a conscientious believer equally seems to apply to an assertion of a religious belief as grounds for an objection. Religion will not always provide a pre-defined basis from which to assess the right to manifest a belief. If the particular action under consideration is not a pre-conceived manifestation of a dictated religious belief, the assertion of the 'belief' seems closer to a conscientious assertion. Hence Jehovah Witnesses objecting to alternative service, a recognised right in some states,[201] are in essence asserting a similar claim to a military conscientious objector by extrapolating from the principles of their belief as the grounds for refusing even alternative service.

Instances also can arise involving motivated actions from religious principles, despite the link to a pre-conceived set of universal beliefs. For example, refusing fiscal support for publicly funded abortions might derive from a religious belief prohibiting one's participation in an abortion, however because the manifested action is not an 'actual practice' of a religious belief, it is closer to an assertion of a conscientious belief. Religious standards motivate the individual and, similar to a conscientious assertion, provide a reason for acting.

The Indian Courts demonstrate this difficulty in cases that examine the underlying religious principles being asserted, where the courts are to separate the non-religious or wholly economic aspects of the belief. Scriptures might be ambiguous[202] or reference to other forms of beliefs might be necessary without a clear understanding of the religion under review.[203] Hence while the criterion for manifestation of a belief is 'actual practice', ambiguities inevitably arise since the actual 'practice' will depend on personal insights of the religion's requirements in a manner comparable to a subjective conscientious assertion.

Nonetheless, the affinity of epistemological sources between conscience and religion indicates the possibility for comparable treatment when considering that both involve the manifestation of particular beliefs. That is, both conscience and religion incorporate transcendent and

---

[201] 11595/85 *Suter v. Switzerland* 51 D&R 160 (1986).
[202] See e.g. *Rajasthian v. Sajjanlal* AIR 1975 SC 706 (state management of temple did not violate religious requirements to manage the temple as a result of ambiguity in the scriptures).
[203] See e.g. *Yagnapurushdasji v. Muldas* AIR 1966 SC 1119 (court compared beliefs of petitioners to that of Hindus to demonstrate similarities of religion, despite assertions to the contrary, on the basis of particular philosophies and scriptures).

immanent factors.[204] The transcendent factors relate to the abstract principles that form the basis for the underlying obligation. This can derive from a host of ideas, such as belief in a god, in pacifism, or in what type of food to consume. The individual places the abstract principles within the context of an action based on one's immanent, subjective, perceptions.[205]

While the similarities in which both religion and conscience operate does not necessarily mean that they should be accorded the same treatment, the indication is that they entail similar problems concerning the manifestation of a belief. A transcendental view might base religion on over-arching or universal principles, yet the manifestation and degree of adherence will, as with conscience, depend on the individual's approach to the doctrine. Hence the broad provision in US law for the free exercise of individual views of a religious directive. The US Courts recognise the individual derivation and interpretation of religious directives that can in turn lead to a variety of manifestations. Similar to a conscientious belief, religious principles can influence a person in a variety of ways ranging from a strict, positivist, account of religious directives to using religion as a source of inspiration for further reflection. Acknowledging the broad, subjective, range in which religion acts as a belief system indicates that its manifestation does not radically differ from a conscientious directive. Religion does not really assist to distinguish, in any substantive manner, a religious assertion from a conscientious one; the considerations for a court are essentially the same such that the 'actual practice' doctrine does not create a definitive framework for the right to freedom of religion and conscience.

Conscience and Freedom of Expression and Assembly

It seems that the narrow approach to the right to freedom of religion and conscience can unduly limit the exercise of the right at the expense of the underlying belief being asserted. Yet, there are other avenues for upholding a conscientious belief that merit examination before discussing a broader approach to the right to conscience.

When attempting to broaden the manifestation of the right to freedom of conscience apart from the religious context, courts and commentators tend to incorporate conscience within other rights, particularly freedom of expression and assembly.[206] Commentators have

---

[204] Smith (1993).
[205] *See e.g.* Greenawalt (1988) noting how religious sources incorporate our perspectives on human nature and society which in turn influence our ethical judgements.
[206] Note as well other rights, such as the right to the family.

equated the right to hold opinions of ECHR Article 10 with the Article 9 right to freedom of thought.[207] Some commentators on India and US laws only consider the manifestation of the right to conscience through free expression by interpreting the right to conscience solely as an internal right.[208] This is similar to the AmCHR approach given its focus on combining expression and thought in a more explicit manner than the ECHR and ICCPR. The analytical focus shifts to viewing conscience as manifesting through these rights that tend to more readily entail external conduct, thereby avoiding the necessity of examining the internal basis for the asserted belief.[209]

Turning for example, to the right to free expression as an avenue for manifesting a conscientious belief can assist to address issues regarding the scope and breadth of manifestation. A court need not consider whether handing out pamphlets against the use of military or nuclear weapons, or refusing to pay taxes to the military, is a manifestation of a belief. Given an approach to manifestation through free expression, it is irrelevant whether a person desired to abide by the underlying belief because the context for the external action is freedom of expression rather than manifestation of a belief.

Recognising that all forms of speech involve the performative use of symbols to convey ideas as well as information,[210] assertion of externally manifested conduct based on conscientious principles can occur through free expression. Speech is the key avenue for manifesting a conscientious belief since the expression ensures for an equal communicative integrity in the formation and exercise of the conscience, such that any restrictions on

---

[207] Beddard (1993); Scheinen (1992;266) (both freedom of expression, UDHR Article 19, and freedom of assembly and association, UDHR Article 20, strengthen the right to manifest one's religion or belief); van Dijk & van Hoof (1990;398&413) (noting the close relation between ECHR Articles 9, 10 and 11 and that the manifestation of conscience is 'shored up' by freedom of expression and assembly since the manifestation of these latter rights is not limited to actual expression of a belief); Benito (1989) (right to freedom of religion and conscience is closely linked with other human rights, particularly freedom of expression and assembly).

[208] Basu (1988); Richards (1993).

[209] *See e.g.* Cohen-Almogovar (1994) (expression as incorporating action, thereby serving as a means from which to measure tolerance of others); 10126/82 *Platform Artze v. Austria* 44 D&R 65 (1985) (outward appearance of action, being the assembly, is favoured over the intrinsic significance of the action for the individual).

[210] Searle (1969) who defines speech based on acts which are thereby produced or carried out as a result of the speech (due to the impossibility of actually defining a word via any linguistic avenue). *See also* Searle (1991).

speech would hinder the individual's conscience.[211] An analogous example is a case in India, the *Maneka Ghandi* [212] case, that involved an assertion of the right to travel under the guise of free expression. The Court held that free expression is a fundamental right with narrow limitations that can uphold other rights where the latter are an integral part of free speech or represent an instance of same due to the basic nature and character of the action.

Freedom of expression also is a right that can protect a broad range of expressions that incorporate one's conscientious belief.[213] For example, while an individual might object to joining an organisation whose creed conflicts with her conscience, the assertion could manifest as a negative speech claim to the right to silence because the requested 'speech', joining the organisation, would appear to an outsider as an expression of identification with the organisation's beliefs.[214] Hence in *Bowman v. UK*,[215] there was no ground to assert a right to freedom of religion or conscience based on the distribution of pamphlets that highlighted the abortion positions of local election candidates because it would not appear to be a manifestation of the right. Yet, it is easier to comprehend the case as an instance of free expression, as the ECHR Court did, by considering the importance of free expression and the limitations placed thereon by the state authorities.

Similarly, concerning the right to assembly, a court will focus on the invocation of the right to assembly rather than the asserted belief.[216] Hence the right to freedom of conscience becomes an element of the right to

---

[211] See e.g. Richards (1993). Cf. Barendt (1992;42) disagreeing because not all acts are entitled to free expression (the example he refers to is a terrorist attack whose purpose is to communicate an idea).

[212] *Maneka Ghandi v. India* AIR 1978 SC 597. The authorities had confiscated plaintiff's passport and denied her a right to appeal. The basis of her claim was that denying the right to travel without an appeal was equivalent to a denial of the fundamental right to free speech.

[213] Van Dijk and Van Hoof (1990) (can express a belief as well as an opinion); Dimitrijevic (1991) (free expression as an absolute right under ICCPR).

[214] Barendt (1992;63-64). Cf. 14331/88 *Revert Legallais v. France* 62 D&R 309 (1989) (applicant's ideological conflict with professional organisation did not preclude him from paying dues on basis of the right to conscience); *R v. Secretary of State* Queens Bench Division, 12/1/96 (dismissal of police officer upheld due to possibility that public will identify him with Orange Brigade following his disclosure of membership in the group).

[215] 24839/94 *Bowman v. UK* 1998-I Rep. Judg. & Dec. 175.

[216] 8440/78 *Christians Against Racism and Fascism v. UK* 21 D&R 138 (1981) (right to assembly deemed central right for anti-abortion protest march, rather then underlying belief).

assembly[217] especially if the issue pertains to the very substance of the right to assembly.[218]

Concentrating on the freedom of expression and assembly also is more practical since it avoids an assessment of the merits of a conscientious belief. The focus is on the invocation of the particular right and not whether an asserted 'belief' lies within the framework of the right. Individuals who refuse to salute a flag because it violates a particular belief, religious or otherwise, demonstrate this advantage. If the analysis is within the framework of the right to free speech, as in the US, the focus is on whether the right to free speech incorporates the act of saluting the flag.[219] If however one comprehends the refusal to salute the flag as a right of freedom of religion, as in India, the analysis will shift from determining whether the right to free expression incorporates such an action, to an assessment of the belief and whether the action derives from a genuine 'actual practice'. Hence the court in India had to delve into the question of whether Jehovah's Witnesses harbour a belief not to pledge allegiance to the flag.[220] The latter approach can prove quite awkward, as demonstrated by *Valsamos v. Greece*[221] where a school parade violated the beliefs of a participant and yet the ECHR Court found no violation of the right to freedom of religion or belief even in the freedom *from* context. By contrast, deciding the case within the realm of free expression might have inclined the Court to uphold the ban on the parade.

Free speech therefore is referred to as an alternative method for manifesting a conscientious belief since it allows for a more direct application of a belief in a manner that avoids any reference or assessment of the asserted conscientious belief. Courts also would be inclined to consider more radical beliefs, such as burning the flag,[222] or decide issues involving conflicts between beliefs. In India for example a court upheld a ban on using loudspeakers for prayer based on the applicant's right to

---

[217] See e.g. 10126/82 *Platform Artze v. Austria* 44 D&R 65 (1985) (Commission considers right to conscience and expression as elements of right to assembly); 16130/90 *Sigurjonsoon v. Iceland* 16 EHRR 462 (1993) (analysis of right to expression and conscience precluded by examination of right to assembly); 2522/94 *Negotiate Now v. UK* 19 EHRR CD93 (1995).

[218] 26695/95 *Sidiropoulos v. Greece* 1998-IV Rep. Judg. & Dec. 1594 (Macedonian minority party was entitled to representation and did not pose a security threat to the state); 21237/93 *Socialist Party v. Turkey* 1998-III Rep. Judg. and Dec. 1233 (1998) (one of objectives of freedom of assembly is to protect opinions and free expression).

[219] *West Virginia v. Barnette* 319 US 624 (1943).

[220] *Bijoe Emmanuel v. State of Kerala* AIR 1987 SC 748.

[221] 21787/93 *Valsamis v. Greece* 1996-VI Rep. Judg. & Dec. 2312.

[222] See e.g. *Street v. New York* 394 US 576 (1969).

negative speech, i.e., not to listen to calls for prayer.[223] It is contended that political speech or negative speech provides a better context for considering the issue rather than focusing on the underlying belief that drove the individual towards such action.

Linking free expression with the right to conscience is particularly suitable for the US where speech is a mechanism for refining and developing the communicative integrity of the individual. Free communication upholds the democratic ideal of evaluating ideas. Hence the broad grant of free speech in the US, since the right incorporates forms of action that relate to the 'communicative integrity' for the critical conscience. This basis justifies 'hate speech' because individuals, and not the state, are to use their inherent conscientious powers of rational conduct and reasonableness to assess the credibility of various expressions, even if the expression tends to offend the audience.[224] Additionally, courts uphold acts such as burning the US flag or wearing black armbands to protest the Vietnam War because they relate to a symbolic communication that affects the conscientious perceptions of the greater community.[225]

Nonetheless, while the inclination of a court might be towards free expression and assembly when analysing a particular conflict or upholding the manifestation of a belief, these rights do not universally encompass the full range of manifestation as intended in the international human rights system. Fundamental distinctions between the rights exist[226] so that the reasons for originally turning to the right to expression and assembly to expand the manifestations of a conscientious belief in the *forum externum* are not necessarily effective.

Distinctions Between Expression, Assembly and Conscience

Considering the underlying justifications for free speech and the manner in which conscience can or cannot conform to such theories will demonstrate the problem of incorporating conscience as an aspect of free expression or assembly. The identified grounds for free speech, particularly the search

---

[223] See e.g. *PA Jacol v. Superintendent of Police* AIR 1993 Ker. 1.
[224] Richards (1986;180).
[225] Richards (1986;194).
[226] See e.g. Dimitrijevic (1991;64) noting the difference between merely harbouring an opinion or thought, which is linked with freedom of expression, as opposed to manifesting a conscientious belief. *See also* discussion *supra* at Chapter Four (difference between thought, which incorporates a host of ideas, as opposed to conscience, which is focusing on specific individual standards of action).

for, and development of, truth in society,[227] the right to democratic participation,[228] and the need to allow for self fulfilment and communicative integrity,[229] only provide for a limited manifestation of conscience. These cardinal grounds for free expression overlook the underlying assertions and personal ideals involved in a conscientious decision and do not retain the capacity to incorporate all forms of conscientious manifestation.

A central ground for upholding free speech is the role it plays in the search for social truth.[230] Encouraging free expression assists society in achieving a broader understanding of what individuals view as the truth, thereby allowing for a more reasoned and measured approach to the truth. The link between this justification and the assertion of a belief derives from the focus on preserving the vitality of an individual's belief by tolerating its outward expression.[231]

The problem with this approach is that the right to conscience is not a consequential notion but a rights-based freedom that morally autonomous individuals may heed their personal, moral, beliefs. The search for truth basis of free speech does not recognise the importance of a conscientious assertion nor that such an assertion derives from a need to adhere to personal conscientious belief. Rather the basis involves a social oriented goal of allowing for an open society that encourages expression of a broad range of ideas, to enable society to make their own reasoned determination of the truth.

Furthermore, not all conscientious assertions involve a desire to have others agree or identify with the asserted belief. A vegan's belief in

---

[227] This basis can be viewed either as an argument that all assertions are fallible and therefore require a free speech challenge or that free expression ensures for the development of truth in the free marketplace of ideas, whereby all beliefs are ensured of vitality and guarded against undue suppression. *See* Cohen-Almogovar (1994).

[228] The notion is that a rational public should decide which ideas to accept or identify with and that free expression is a necessary component of democracy.

[229] Cohen-Almogovar (1994) understanding this basis as a means of preserving autonomy, whereby one can advocate ideas and beliefs, protect one's moral sovereignty and general spirit, and challenge accepted social standards. *See also* Barendt (1992;8-23).

[230] Barendt (1992;8-13) referring to Mill. Barendt notes however that this approach will not incorporate all aspects of free speech, such as emotive speech or pornography, and is not supported by the various interpretations of the right in domestic courts, especially because the restraints on free speech due to other, public policy or social, reasons. *See also* Richards (1994;35) (noting how this basis does not conform to US law).

[231] Cohen-Almogovar (1994) who understands the truth basis as central to free expression. He relies on Mill to form a balancing of striving for the truth versus allowing for respect for others, thereby imposing limitations on free expression where its sole purpose is to incite and cause harm, rather than communicate an idea.

not using printing dye tested on animals typifies such a conscientious manifestation.[232] The reason for only using synthetic printing dye results from the adherence to a belief and not to engage in social discussion or convince society of the merits of a belief.

The truth aspect of expression highlights the distinction between the manifestation of a thought and the manifestation of a conscientious belief.[233] Adherence to a conscientious belief invariably derives from internal directives formed in the *forum internum*. Communicating a thought can entail an attempt to convince others of the merits of a belief, but it need not raise an action that manifests the belief. Additionally, this distinction highlights the problem surrounding proselytising. While a proselytiser certainly is attempting to express a belief, the additional key factor is that a proselytiser also is acting pursuant to the belief's directives to convince others of the religion's merits.[234]

The eventual outcome in interpreting conscience within the context of the search for social truth could result in a dismissal of conscientious assertions that do not relate to a social search for the truth. This is particularly the case when equating speech with conscientious conduct since the criteria for deeming 'action' as speech concentrates on the intentions of the actor and whether the public views the actor as communicating the particular idea.[235] Such factors will limit the manifestation of a conscientious belief to specific actions involving communication, while overlooking the underlying reasons for acting.

A related rationale to the social truth basis for free expression is the importance of free speech as providing for full participation by all individuals in the democratic process.[236] In such a case, expressing one's conscientious beliefs is a form of exercising one's democratic entitlement by familiarising the greater society with one's individual moral conceptions.

Such an argument however is difficult to uphold when considered within the context of an assertion of a conscientious belief. Preserving a democratic society could diminish the very values of the individuals that the society is attempting to support as a result of utilitarian calculations[237] by not focusing on the individual's conscientious calculation and the basis of the assertion. For example, courts in India limit the reliance on free

---

[232] 18187/91 *H v. UK* 16 EHRR CD44 (1992).
[233] See discussion *supra* at Chapter Four.
[234] See 14307/88 *Kokkinakis v. Greece* 17 EHRR 397 (1993).
[235] Barendt (1992;47).
[236] Barendt (1992;20).
[237] Barendt (1992;16); Machan (1989).

expression to buttress other rights to actions that retain the 'character and nature' of the right to expression. Hence in the *Maneka Ghandi* case, the Indian Court compared interference with the right to travel to a more specific prevention of speaking at a conference.[238] However linking the right to travel with free expression might cause a problem when a person is not travelling to lecture at a conference, but desires to undergo a pilgrimage to a holy site.[239] In such an instance, considering the right within the context of free expression could tend to dilute the right to freedom of religion and conscience by ignoring the belief being asserted.

One must still consider the individual making the assertion and not solely the desired effect that the communication is to have on other individuals within society,[240] otherwise the belief itself would be quashed. For example, the Inter-American Court of Human Rights has entitled journalists to a broader scope of objection to joining a compulsory professional organisation when compared with individuals in other professions because journalists are engaged in the communication of ideas.[241] The proposed distinction, which centres on the connection of the right to expression with association, could limit the conscientious assertions of professionals who do not engage in the communication of ideas but whose beliefs dictate that they not join an organisation should the manifestation of a conscientious belief be considered within a policy context of free expression. Additionally, pursuant to such reasoning, the military might deny a claim for military conscientious objection due to the potential effect the objector's actions can have on other individuals within the military unit. If the conscientious assertion is an expression that is to affect others, the military might have grounds to quash the assertion without considering the importance of the belief to the conscientious objector. Alternatively, a state might grant a military conscientious objector the ability to express his views but deny the ability to manifest the belief by not granting an exemption from the military.

There also is a problem resulting from the negative right to free expression. A person might not want to identify with a belief by uttering an

---

[238] *Maneka Ghandi v. India* AIR 1978 SC 597.
[239] *See* Mason (1993) discussing the right to make a religious pilgrimage.
[240] Even an 'absolutist' such as Richards (1986;184) recognises this distinction when discussing the provision for subversive advocacy in a democratic society. He notes the difference between expressing subversion (which is subject to First Amendment free speech protection) versus actually carrying out the action (which is not protected).
[241] No OC-5/85 *Request by Costa Rica Regarding Compulsory Membership in an Association for all Journalists* Inter-American Court of Human Rights, November 13, 1985.

expression,[242] such as refusing to take a loyalty oath as a pre-condition for employment.[243] The problem is that it is not clear whether the negative free expression right also applies to not engaging in particular conduct. The latter instance, which can raise the more important issues regarding manifestation of conscience, is not necessarily a protected form of expression under the right not to speak. If covering a motto on a licence plate is a form of free speech, where is the doctrinal limitation to free expression?[244] Would a negative speech right also apply to not paying taxes? Referring to the right to conscience for such actions moves the determination into a venue where understanding, but not assessing, the underlying belief is essential, rather than examining the issue solely from the view of free speech.

A similar argument also is relevant to the incorporation of the right to conscience with free assembly.[245] The freedom for an employee's conscientious objection to union membership is narrower when considered within the context of the right to assembly. Courts have dismissed the claim where other unions are willing to take the employee.[246] However, such a systematic approach to the objection being made tends to overlook the underlying reason for making the objection, such as asserting a conscientious belief against any form of participation in a union. [247]

---

[242] Barendt (1992;63-66) (noting distinction between withholding ideas and opinions, as opposed to imparting beneficial information to the public).
[243] 17851/91 *Vogt v. Germany* 21 EHRR 205 (1996) (loyalty oath to state for language teacher who was a member of a dissident political party was violation of right to expression despite claims by Germany of internal political unrest). *See also Wooley v. Maynard* 430 US 705 (1977) (Court upheld Jehovah's Witness' covering motto 'Live Free or Die' on New Hampshire licence plate since state, by requiring motto, unconstitutionally abridged right *not* to speak). The dissent (Rhenquist) did not deem such action as 'speech'.
[244] Barendt (1992;67).
[245] *See e.g.* Leader (1992;175).
[246] *See e.g.* 14327/88 *Sibson v. UK* 17 EHRR 193 (1994) (the plaintiff's basis for objection was loss of honour stemming from being accused of robbery by co-workers. The plaintiff was dismissed following refusal to join dominant union or switch to another, lower status, position); *Application of Aper* 35 FLR 388 (1978) (Australian Court rejected selective conscientious objection of independent contractor to particular employee organisation).
[247] The dissent in 14327/88 *Sibson v. UK* 17 EHRR 193 (1994) held that the plaintiff was denied a right to conscience by being forced to either join a union to which he objected or trade his self esteem for a lower paying job.

It also is imperative to note that the rights to free expression and assembly are subject to broader limitations than the right to conscience.[248] Linking the right to conscience with expression or assembly can thereby create broader grounds for limiting a belief when considered within a different rights context.[249] Furthermore, freedom of expression and assembly are derogable rights in both the ICCPR and ECHR; the right to conscience by contrast is non-derogable in the ICCPR.

An alternative approach to free speech, one that seems closely affiliated with conscience, is viewing speech as a means to self-fulfilment, such that restrictions on speech will inhibit the personal growth and moral sovereignty of the individual.[250] Free expression can serve to uphold the individual's right to freedom of conscience by engaging in arguments against the state based on the exercise of independent reasoning.[251] This ensures a free conscience as well since expression incorporates 'sincere convictions about matters of fact and value in which a free people reasonably has a higher-order interest'.[252]

The question, then, is why limit the right to conscience to the confines of free expression when other avenues exist to preserve the individual's personality, specifically by granting the right to adhere to the conscientious belief? The question seems particularly relevant upon noting that applications of the right to free expression do not support the preservation of one's self fulfilment. For example, other ancillary grounds might limit speech, such as restricting advertising to protect the public, which seems to relate to paternalistic grounds rather than the individual's self-fulfilment.[253]

---

[248] *Compare* ICCPR, Article 19(2) *with* Article 18(3). *See e.g. Hertzberg and Others v. Finland* Doc A/37/40 where the HRC gave wide discretion to the state to determine the extent of 'public morals' concerning the right to assembly.

[249] Indeed, the broader limitations on the right to free expression in the ICCPR was one of the reasons why the US reserved its adherence to Article 19. *See* Stewart (1993).

[250] Barendt (1992;19); Cohen-Almogovar (1994) referring to this view as the autonomy basis; Richards (1994) referring to this view as the toleration model.

[251] Richards (1994;42).

[252] Richards (1994;38).

[253] *See e.g. 7805/77 Church of Scientology v. Sweden* 16 D&R 68 (1979) (restrictions in advert for E-meter on grounds of protecting public. The Commission denied Article 9 protection since the case centred on a commercial issue involving the sale of an item). Note as well the issue of racial speech which is essentially limited for political reasons. Barendt (1992;167). *Cf.* Cohen-Almogovar (1994) who bases the limitations of racial speech on the inherent paradox that to allow for toleration of ideas or beliefs, one must be prepared to impose limitations on one's own freedom. His reasoning, which centres on the communication of ideas, is linked to the Kantian notion of respect for others and mutuality among society members such that intolerant members need not be tolerated.

The very purpose of upholding the right to conscience is to preserve the individual's personality and moral dignity, such that turning to free speech seems superfluous and awkward. This seems to be one of the reasons why commentators call for a more focused application of the right to conscience, independent of free expression, since the right to conscience is not a privilege that a state is to weigh against a state interest, but is a right to manifest in the *forum externum* to maintain the belief.[254] Indeed, pursuant to ECHR cases, interpreting the right within a freedom *from* context tends to equate the right to conscience with that of negative speech. Within such a limited context, the focus of analysis is not on the individual's belief, but on the state's avoidance of any indoctrination. Hence in *Valsamos v. Greece*,[255] the Court solely considered whether participation in a state mandated parade celebrating a military victory was a form of indoctrination or identification by the parents and child, rather than account for the belief being asserted by the parents and child. While refusing to participate might be a freedom *from* issue, it is not solely a matter of lack of identification with the marchers, but also that identification with the march conflicts with one's beliefs.[256]

Further, one can contend that combining free expression with religious aspects creates a murkiness in court doctrine. For example, the ECHR *Otto Preminger* case relied on the margin of appreciation doctrine when the assertion of free expression conflicted with the socio-religious construct. Yet the ECHR Court's focus on the manner in which such expression might injure other believers appears to impose an additional standard beyond the confines of the right and its limitations.[257] Further, it has been contended that the Court is less inclined to defer to the state where the issue entails an aspect of religious pluralism.[258] Nonetheless, it is possible that the margin of appreciation for the state would be broadened for other instances entailing assertions of a minority belief, or where a

---

[254] Barendt (1992;64) noting that the existence of a right to conscience essentially moots the notion of referring to free expression when considering the distinction between conduct (or external action) and speech, since any attempt to distinguish the concepts leads to equivocal results. *See also* Eisgruber and Sager (1994) (arguing that the US Free Exercise Clause should be treated, like free speech cases, as a vulnerable right which merits protection).

[255] 21787/93 *Valsamis v. Greece* 1996-VI Rep. Judg. & Dec. 2312; 24095/94 *Efstratiou v. Greece* 1996-VI Rep. Judg. & Dec. 2347.

[256] *Cf.* 14307/88 *Kokkinakis v. Greece* 17 EHRR 397 (1993) (right of Jehovah Witness to proselytise considered a manifestation of a belief and not a free expression case).

[257] Evans, M. (1997;331). A similar contention applies to 17419/90 *Wingrove v. UK* 1996-V Rep. Judg. & Dec. 1937.

[258] Prebensen (1998) noting that a lower standard for the margin of appreciation might be imposed when relating to different issues regarding the right.

state's social morals or fundamental believers are prone to being affected, without regard for the belief being asserted because of the free expression context. For example in *Wingrove v. UK*, the Court upheld the restriction on freedom of expression because a blasphemous home video was likely to cause outrage to a majority religious group. Although the case did not entail an assertion of a belief, the decision was reached despite the uneven application of the domestic blasphemy laws that are not applied to other instances whereby a minority religion might be slighted by the exercise of a free expression.[259]

The basic problem with the narrow approach as outlined herein is that it does not prevent the unfettered manifestation of the right to freedom of religion even when excluding the right to conscience or when linking the right to freedom of expression or assembly. Rather such fusion of rights tends to create doctrinal confusion between the rights, particularly for a right subject to controversy like the freedom of religion and conscience, and a tendency to rely on one right at the expense of another, such as overlooking the underlying religious or conscientious belief being asserted. This does not mean that one should never consider conscience within the context of freedom of expression or assembly because, at times, it certainly is unavoidable.[260] However, the narrow approach inadequately upholds a conscientious belief because the right is almost wholly confined to the *forum internum*, with only a limited right to manifest a conscientious belief. A conscientious belief seems to merit broader protection particularly since the international human rights system has codified the right to conscience and accorded it fundamental status on a par with the freedom of religion. The remainder of this chapter will consider the broader approach to the right to conscience and the practical considerations presented by a broad understanding of the right to conscience.

---

[259] 17439/90 *Choudhury v. UK* reptd. in 12 H. Rts. L. J. 172 (1991) (blasphemy raised by a Muslim in UK following publication of S. Rushdie's book).

[260] *See e.g.* 7511/76 *Campbell and Cosans v. UK* 4 EHRR 293 (1982) (must account for freedom of religion and expression when considering merits of human social behaviour); 5095/71 *Kjeldsen, Buck and Pederson v. Denmark* 1 EHRR 711 (1980) (same consideration in context of evaluation of all subjects, not just sex or religious education, in school syllabus); 24839/94 *Bowman v. UK* 1998-I Rep. Judg. & Dec. 175 (distribution of abortion literature during election campaign); *Allegheny v. ACLU* 492 US 573 (1989) (US Supreme Court links Establishment Clause determination with underlying expression that plaintiff desires to communicate, comparing religious context of crèche display with neutral, secular, display of Christmas tree and Menorah).

Broader Approach

Before discussing the implications that ensue from a broader approach and the manner in which to address such problems, it is important to note that the international system does not completely deny a broader understanding of the right to conscience. A positive indication of the movement towards a broader understanding of the term 'belief', specifically as incorporating the manifestation of conscientious beliefs, is the HRC's General Comment to Article 18. The HRC's summary record noted that the underlying purpose in drafting the Comment was to expand the right to freedom of conscience and thought to place these rights on par with the right to religion.[261] The impetus for drafting the General Comment was that the HRC felt that the state reports were focusing attention exclusively on the right to religion.[262] As noted by Dimitrijevic, the Yugoslav HRC member and principal drafter of the General Comment:

> With regard to the freedom to manifest one's religion or belief, freedom of religion implied the right to have or to adopt a religion or belief of one's choice and such freedom applied to thought conscience and religion alike. As for the right to manifestation, it applied solely to religion or belief. It was for that reason that the term 'belief' was interpreted very broadly in the draft general comment in order to encompass all forms of thought and - to use terms which had obviously been avoided in drafting the covenant - beliefs which are not expressed as being the affirmation of a truth. That, indeed, was how religion was defined, since it was based on a belief and not on a scientific premise.[263]

The HRC further distinguished between the *forum internum* and *forum externum*. Focusing on the *forum internum*, the main point of the first paragraph of the General Comment to Article 18 is to equate the right

---

[261] CCPR/C/SR.1162 where the drafters to the General Comment note the lack of attention to the right to conscience and a desire to expand on the manifestation of the right.

[262] CCPR/C/SR.1162.

[263] CCPR/C/SR.1162 at paragraph 10. *See also* Dimitrijevic (1991;64) noting, at a Council of Europe sponsored conference on the right to conscience, that:
One of the efforts the (ICCPR) Human Rights Committee is making is to show that in addition to the religious dimension of the freedom of conscience and thought, there is a non-religious secular dimension, ideological dimension, from which many problems stem.

to freedom of thought and conscience with that of religion. However the summary record notes that the internal protection of thought and conscience is not merely to support toleration, but also to provide for the manifestation of the belief.[264] The General Comment expands on this idea by adopting what appears to be a considerable definition of conscience that is to be 'broadly construed' and include non-theistic and atheistic beliefs, in accordance with the travaux preparatoires of the ICCPR. The intention was to encompass all religions and beliefs in all their diversity, even if not regarded as a religion by the state.[265]

Yet despite this rather lofty approach towards the notion of manifestation and the meaning of the term 'belief', the General Comment does recede somewhat from the original broad interpretation when considering the specific instances of manifestation. For example, the HRC referred to the Declaration[266] to explicate the terms used to delineate manifestation in Article 18 - 'worship, observance, practice and teaching' - by simply quoting the various forms of religious manifestation stated in Article 6 of the Declaration.[267] In particular, the HRC did not provide a singular interpretation of the term 'practice'. Rather, the HRC associated the term with 'observance' and did not distinguish, in any meaningful manner, between manifestation of a religious practice as opposed to a conscientious practice.[268]

While the Declaration might be a valid starting point from which to interpret the scope for manifesting religious beliefs, the *travaux preparatoires* to the Declaration note that Article 6 is not an exhaustive interpretation of ICCPR Article 18 rights. The intention of the Declaration was to provide only a partial listing of what the right can include, with a prime focus on protecting religious beliefs.[269] State reports submitted to the

---

[264] CCPR/C/SR.1162.
[265] CCPR/C/SR.1162 at paragraph 67.
[266] See Declaration Article 6. Note however that the Declaration had accorded a broad definition to the term 'belief'. See E/CN.4/SR.1522 (broad understanding of belief, as including theistic, atheistic, and non-theistic beliefs); E/CN.4/SR.1636 (drafters discussed broad interpretation of the term); Benito (1989) (belief being explanation of meaning of life and 'how to live accordingly'); Boyle (1992) (interpreting Article 1 of Declaration as incorporating a broad range of beliefs and not solely religious standards); Walkate (1989) (belief being interpreted in first Sub-Commission report, E/CN.4/Sub.2/711, as entertaining 'a belief which may be regarded as a system of philosophy.').
[267] See Paragraph 4 of the General Comment to Article 18.
[268] Cumper (1995).
[269] See e.g. E/CN.4/1154 CHR 30th Session (1974).

rapporteur created under the Declaration support this understanding[270] although recent rapporteur reports commingle religion and belief to incorporate all forms of practice.[271] Yet it seems odd that the HRC would rely on a document whose focus is religious protection, when one of the seminal reasons for drafting the General Comment to Article 18 was to rectify the tendency to refer exclusively to religious beliefs at the exclusion of other beliefs.[272]

There has been some evidence of a shift towards recognising a broad role for the right to conscience following the 1993 drafting of the HRC's General Comment to ICCPR Article 18. The HRC has referred states to the General Comment to clarify their reports regarding protections for secular beliefs.[273] State reports also have, at times, begun to incorporate considerations of additional aspects of the right, including the protection of secular, individual, beliefs.[274]

A further indication of this broad understanding of the right is the HRC's approach towards including various forms of conscientious objection other than military objection, such as a doctor's conscientious refusal to perform an abortion. The HRC noted that such instances were already accounted for by the General Comment's amplification of the

---

[270] See e.g. Report of Rapporteur from 1990 - E/CN.4/1990/46; 1991 - E/CN.4/1991/56; 1992 - E/CN.4/1992/52 as typical examples regarding the focus on religious manifestations.

[271] See e.g. Report of Rapporteur from 2000 - E/CN.4/2000/65 at paragraphs 171-175; Report of Rapporteur from 1999 - E/CN.4/1999/58 at paragraphs 104-108, each report noting the necessity for toleration towards all forms of manifestation in a manner that clearly distinguishes between religion and beliefs.

[272] When Committee Member Dimitrijevic was asked why the General Comment did not provide for manifestation of conscience, especially when attempting to develop the right to conscience would seem to imply the need for manifestation, he responded that the HRC desired to adhere to the language and composition of the Article.

[273] GAOR 49th Session, Supp.40 A/49/40 1994 Report of Jordan that focused on the requirement to register 'non-recognised' religions or beliefs; 1994 Report of Slovenia (which had problems pertaining to religious education); CCPR/C/28/Add.7 1995 Report of Libya.

[274] CCPR/C/81/Add.4 - 1995 Report of US referring to general manifestation of conscience as well as religion; CCPR/C/94/Add.2 1995 Report of Ireland, noting change in domestic law to provide for freedom of more general, secular, convictions; CCPR/C/84/Add.3 1995 report of Paraguay, noting that general beliefs are protected by various articles in the Constitution; CCPR/C/84/Add.1 1995 Report of Tunisia noting free conscience is defined as providing for any belief or religion; CCPR/C/81/Add.6 1995 Report of Brazil noting toleration and upholding of general, secular, beliefs; CCPR/C/81/Add.5 - Report of Estonia (general discussion regarding right to belief and opinions); CCPR/C/81/Add.2 - 1995 Report of Azerbaijan noting allowance for any beliefs or 'own convictions' even if not in common with other individuals.

manifestation of conscience.²⁷⁵ Additionally, the HRC's interpretation of the ICCPR as incorporating a right to military conscientious objection, despite the prior rejection of the right to military conscientious objection under the ICCPR by the HRC,²⁷⁶ further hints at a broader approach. Indeed, paragraph 11 of the General Comment to ICCPR Article 18 states that while the:

> covenant does not explicitly refer to a right of [military] conscientious objection, the Committee believes that such a right can be derived from Article 18, inasmuch as the obligation to use lethal force may seriously conflict with the freedom of conscience...

The term 'lethal force' refers to any act of aggression that will lead to homicide and is broad language that relates to more general notions regarding an aversion to taking the life of another person. The indication is that the HRC did not limit military conscientious objection solely to individuals who do not desire to use firearms.

Recent HRC cases also have alluded to a broad right to military conscientious objection under the ICCPR. For example, in a case involving a conscientious objector to military taxes,²⁷⁷ the HRC noted that Article 18 provides for manifestation of one's conscience, which includes military conscientious objection. While made in passing, the statement reflects the change occurring in the HRC's approach to Article 18, particularly as the HRC was drafting the General Comment to Article 18 at around the same time. The indication is that one may apply a broader understanding of the right to manifest a conscientious belief, not necessarily as a motivation driving the belief, but as deriving from the specific principles of a belief that indicate the proper manner in which to act.

Other systems also have hinted at a broader understanding of the right to conscience, albeit the underlying doctrine still remains unclear. For example, in the ECHR system, the Commission has upheld the manifestation of 'acts intimately linked to the [conscientious] attitude',²⁷⁸ a standard that appears somewhat detached from the 'actual practice' of a particular directive. While the assertion of a belief must still be within the context of some over-arching or universal system, the acts which stem from the belief can be of a broader nature. Hence a belief system linked to

---

[275] General Comment at Paragraph 8.
[276] CCPR/C/SR.1237.
[277] 446/1991 *JP v. Canada* (1992).
[278] 18187/91 *H v. UK* 16 EHRR CD44 (1992).

specific acts, such as a vegan's belief towards eating requirements, can manifest in a general manner, such as not working with printing dye tested on animals.[279]

The ECHR Court also has hinted at a broader notion of manifestation without addressing the issue by upholding the right of a Jehovah's Witness to proselytise.[280] While the Court focused on the limitations of the right,[281] the Court seemed to allude to a broader conception of protected forms of manifestation.[282] A subsequent Commission case amplified *Kokkinakis* for example in upholding the right of Pentecostal Church members to proselytise.[283]

It is interesting that the stance adopted by the *Kokkinakis* Court regarding a Jehovah's Witness' manifestation of a belief is similar to the dissent's position in *Arrowsmith*, where the Commission upheld a ban preventing a pacifist from distributing literature.[284] The dissent in *Arrowsmith* maintained the protection for any genuine assertion of a belief, including the expression of a pacifist belief by distributing pamphlets. The key factor for the dissent was a genuine motivation deriving from the belief, rather then an 'actual practice' of the belief. In *Kokkinakis*, while the Court did not directly discuss the right to manifest a belief, the decision did centre on the applicant's desire to express his belief by distributing pamphlets and engaging in discourse.

Note further a 1988 case with similar facts to *Arrowsmith*[285] where the Commission upheld the prohibition of the distribution of anti-military pamphlets at an army base because the material incited a lack of military discipline. Using rather odd reasoning, the decision regarding the right to conscience hinged on the contents stated within the pamphlets rather than the action taken by the pacifist. The Commission held that the pamphlets contained material targeting servicemen to ignore orders, which posed a

---

[279] 18187/91 *H v. UK* 16 EHRR CD44 (1992). Note that the case recognised the basis for the belief but denied the claim on security grounds, as the applicant was in prison, a forum which has generally resulted in denial of such claims due to the security interests involved. See e.g. 8231/76 *X v. UK* 5 EHRR 162 (1983).

[280] 14307/88 *Kokkinakis v. Greece* 17 EHRR 397 (1993).

[281] The Court seemed to apply a standard that is not provided for in the ECHR by balancing state latitude to regulate the right to religion with oversight by the ECHR.

[282] The concurrence noted that the Court should have upheld the applicant's action as a proper manifestation of his belief.

[283] 23372/94 *Larissis v. Greece* 1998-I Rep. Judg. & Dec. 362 (Pentecostal Church members allowed to proselytise while serving in Air Force, save for attempting to convince their fellow officers).

[284] 7050/75 *Arrowsmith v. UK* 3 EHRR 218 (1978).

[285] 11567/85 *Fritz v. France* 11 EHRR 67 (1988) (pacifist handed out leaflets on military base stating objection to French military presence in Federal Republic of Germany).

danger to military discipline at the base. The implication is that if the pamphlets merely stated the pacifist's position, the Commission might have treated the action as a manifestation of the belief, in a manner similar to a proselytising Jehovah's Witness, despite the absence of any formal directive or mandated actual practice.

Yet one should not interpret the aforementioned decisions out of context since it is likely that the equivocal attitude towards the right to manifest a belief stems from an overall misunderstanding regarding the protection of the right.[286] Hence the hesitation in applying the right, as indicated either by deferring to other rights, such as the freedom of expression and assembly,[287] or by intermingling the right to manifest a belief with the limitations that a state may impose under Article 9(2).[288] Indeed, reference to the provided for limitations, a prevalent occurrence in recent ECHR decisions,[289] has caused a gap in the analysis regarding the right to manifest a belief. The ECHR organs too readily refer to the limitations and the inherent balancing between the individuals and the state interests that are at stake, thereby glossing over the determination pertaining to whether a belief has even manifested.[290] This is not to say that limitations to the right do not play an important role. On the contrary, limitations assist the broader approach by accounting for social interests and public policy. The problem is that the limitations should not be the means used for defining the right, but only considered following an analysis of the right to manifest a belief.[291]

The proposed standard does not necessarily mean that all 'motivations', the favoured phrase to describe the broader approach, deriving from a belief are to manifest under the right. Such an understanding of the broader approach tends to remove any hopes for recognising the manifestation of conscientious beliefs in a manner comparable to religious beliefs. Indeed, many instances occur whereby a judicial body will deny manifestation to 'motivations' that derive from

---

[286] Evans, M. (1997;311).
[287] See also 25528/94 *Canea Catholic Church v. Greece* 1997-VIII Rep. Judg. & Dec. 2843 where the Court preferred to rely on the right of access to a court along with article 14 rather than determine the case under the joint umbrella of articles 9 and 14, as the Commission had decided.
[288] See discussion *infra* regarding limitations.
[289] See e.g. 14307/88 *Kokkinakis v. Greece* 17 EHRR 397 (1993); 24645/94 *Buscarini v. San Marino* decided 18/2/99.
[290] Evans, M. (1997;330).
[291] *Cf.* Cullen (1997;33-34) who maintains that the right in the ECHR has an underlying social dimension rather than an individual basis for asserting a belief. *See also* discussion *infra* at Chapter Eight.

religious beliefs as well.[292] Furthermore, the treaties do not propose an uninhibited right for manifesting a motivation, as indicated by the distinction between thought, conscience, and religion, whereby individuals are entitled to harbour illicit views in the *forum internum* without any unfettered right to manifest same.[293]

A broader approach to the right to freedom of conscience however provides for the manifestation of one's conscientious beliefs in the *forum externum* even when the underlying belief does not specifically dictate the required action. Manifestation of a belief relates to the importance of a belief to the individual and the role that a belief plays in shaping the contours of the individual. It is in essence a commingling of the emerging conscientious belief from the *forum internum* with the *forum externum*, and the necessity to manifest the principles deriving from such a belief via definitive action.

Pursuant to the understanding of a conscientious belief in the *forum internum* as shaping a belief that is bound up with the individual's personal identity, it is imperative to examine the assertion and determine whether the manifestation is being conducted in pursuance of the belief. One's right to act in pursuance of one's belief is the key factor, where the belief is the driving force for the external actions, even if the actions that are to uphold the asserted belief are not entirely clear or pre-determined. Rather the individual is attempting to manifest a belief in a manner that maximises the internal consistency as developed in the *forum internum*.

Additionally, the focus of an external body reviewing the manifestation is not whether the belief mandates specific action, but rather to determine and ascertain what is the driving force behind the individual's assertion for conducting an action. The key question is whether there is a definitive connection between the asserted belief and the action to be undertaken, where the action is an attempt to uphold an aspect of the belief. For example, it is understandable why a pacifist does not conduct military service given the possible belief regarding the use of weapons and that undergoing military service will entail the discharge of weapons. Such

---

[292] See e.g. 24875/94 *Logan v. UK* 1 EHRLR 83 (1997) (Buddhist's maintenance payments resulted in an inability to attend religious services).

[293] See *International Convention on the Elimination of all forms of Racial Discrimination* Article 4. Although the Article bans racial hatred and discrimination, it is to be applied 'with due regard' for the 'rights expressly set forth in Article 5 of this Convention'. Article 5(d)(vii) provides for the right to freedom of thought, conscience, and religion. *Cf.* US. case law which generally upholds racial speech on Free Speech grounds. *See e.g. Collin v. Smith* 578 F.2d 1197 (7th Cir. 1978) (local ordinance deemed unconstitutional for prohibiting dissemination of literature which promoted racist views).

an objection is a recognised form of manifestation of the belief despite there being no specific directive regarding the expected external actions of a pacifist believer. A pacifist also might be abhorred at any form of association with the military, in the same manner that a religious individual would not be associated with an action that is directly contrary to an underlying belief, such as conducting, or assisting with, an abortion.[294] Hence the connection between the manifestation of the belief and the specific action that is undertaken is not whether the belief specifically mandates such actions, but rather whether the action is conducted, or refrained from, in pursuance of a belief and the principles that are derived from such a belief.

The broader approach to manifestation of a conscientious belief in the *forum externum* also is not a matter of erring on the side of the individual's assertion of a belief, specifically by upholding any form of action that is claimed to be within the confines of a belief system. Rather, it is an acknowledgement of the importance and the central role that a conscientious belief plays for the internal construct and development of a person. Hence while a pacifist might refuse military service, or even alternative service, due to the association between the action that is demanded and the possible infringement of a belief, it is not entirely clear that blocking shipments of weapons also should be deemed a matter of a conscientious belief. Similar to the Zen Buddhist who claims that maintenance payments prevent him from attending religious services,[295] or the anti-abortionist who resorts to firebombing abortion clinics, the pacifist would have a difficult time demonstrating that pacifist beliefs mandate the blocking of shipments, or partaking in other violent acts, as a matter of belief.[296] Blocking armament shipments might be a desirable outcome, and even be an outcome that in a certain sense derives from, or is motivated by, the belief system; but the action itself does not appear to be a manifestation of the belief. An individual would be hard pressed to demonstrate that blocking the shipments derives from a specific belief, or that the underlying goal is not necessarily an assertion of a belief but closer to a

---

[294] See e.g. Hammer (1999).
[295] 24875/94 *Logan v. UK* 1 EHRLR 83 (1997).
[296] Even if one were to analogise to the *Kokkinakis* case by asserting that a belief system might mandate the preaching of one's edicts to others, there is still a distinction between proselytising and physically conducting the action, where limitations to the right might apply as well.

desire to create a social change[297] or alter the behaviour of other individuals.

Recognising the importance of focusing on the belief however does not diminish the initial problem regarding the potential for broad assertions. For example, instead of relying on pacifism to block armament shipments, an individual may choose to block such shipments due to a belief in protecting all individuals from deadly weapons, a contention that is similar to the anti-abortionists' stance that they are protecting the unborn foetus. In such a case, to summarily determine that one's actions in the public sphere are limited because not all beliefs can manifest does not adequately address the individual's claim to abide by the belief in the *forum externum*. As discussed *infra*, one could rely on a conscientious belief to object to a tax payment that had been specifically created to fiscally support a programme that is contrary to one's beliefs.[298] Such a contention against tax payments is closer to an infringement of the belief itself given the purpose of tax payments as serving to provide fiscal support to the military.

Additional examples can include an attorney who refuses to don courtroom attire because it is made from the fur of an endangered species. To the individual making the claim, the assertion is a manifestation of a belief. It is similar to a Muslim's refusal to pay maintenance since the ex-spouse is not 'recognised' by the religion following the ex-spouse's post-divorce return to Christianity.[299] It is not simply a matter of creating a new right by virtue of a reference to a belief. Rather a belief dictates specific principles that have been deemed important and that provide grounds for taking the action, thereby requiring a believer to acknowledge and uphold a belief.

Such actions can be distinguished from instances whereby a religious or conscientious belief might serve a motivational role, but the so-called manifestation does not necessarily relate to a specific directive or principle of the belief. A belief as a motivation is exemplified by an individual's claim that high child maintenance costs deprive him from attending Zen Buddhist services[300] or a pacifist blocking armament shipments. Granted that one's belief might mandate the attendance of religious services, but that does not relate in any manner to the action of

---

[297] *See e.g. US v. Allen* 760 F. 2d 447 (1985) ('nuclearism' was not a belief but a reflection of a political judgement).
[298] *See* discussion *infra* at Chapter Seven.
[299] 26568/95 *Karakuzey v. Germany* 23 EHRR CD92 (1996).
[300] 24875/94 *Logan v. UK* 1 EHRLR 83 (1997).

paying the child benefits.³⁰¹ Similarly, the pacifist might not believe in using deadly weapons but that does not automatically mandate the prevention of manufacturing such weapons. The claim relates to a specific desired result from an external action that does not involve the belief in any substantive manner. The belief does not seem connected to the manifested action, save for the possibility that the action might ultimately benefit the underlying belief.

In this sense, one can begin to discern the distinction between motivations and manifestations. Motivation is a matter of personal stimulation, where the individual is provided with an incentive for conducting an action. Such an incentive can derive from a belief, but not in any necessary manner. For example, the incentive for blocking an armament shipment or for firebombing an abortion clinic is to prevent the continuation of a particular activity by other individuals. It is not solely a matter of relying on a belief as an *ex ante* cause of action, but the action is taken with a view towards creating an *ex post* change in the actions of others. Such instances therefore relate to the connection between the freedom of belief and freedom of expression and assembly.³⁰² Although the underlying goal is bound up with a belief because the belief might have provided the incentive and drive for taking the action, the eventual purpose is to prevent others from taking action that might infringe the principles of the believer.³⁰³

While the movement away from a positive framework of norms, such as found in a formalised religion, is difficult to comprehend for a legal system, manifestation of the right to conscience can occur in a manner that need not endanger the underlying fabric of a society. The contention is that one also could provide for a broad understanding of belief and manifestation by accounting for the limitations provided in the right. Acknowledging various social ramifications or other considerations of public protection³⁰⁴ raised by the manifestation of a belief serve to

---

301 An argument that has been applied, incorrectly in the views of this author, to the conscientious objection to certain tax payments. *See* discussion *infra* at Chapter Seven.
302 *See e.g.* 17419/90 *Wingrove v. UK* 1996-V Rep. Judg. & Dec. 1937.
303 The distinction between proselytising and other forms of action that can affect individuals will be addressed in the discussion pertaining to the group notion of a belief. The key difference is that proselytising derives from specific directives of a belief. Similarly, the notion of public protest or attempting to alter the actions of others in a broader social sense will be considered and contrasted in the discussion regarding conscientious objection to tax payments.
304 *See e.g. Panesar v. Nestle Co. Ltd.* [1980] ICR 144 (Indian who worked in a food processing plant required to remove all facial hair in the interest of public health). The UK Court of Appeals referred to ECHR case law for support.

enhance the ability to apply the right even if the right eventually is curtailed. For example, one can acknowledge that a belief mandates scattering the ashes of a deceased over his grave, or even to not recognise the existence of one's ex-spouse pursuant to religious norms, however the inherent limitations would serve to diminish the potential social harm that might ensue.[305] Additionally, with the development of a rather wide margin of appreciation accorded to states, a margin that would probably be deferred to in instances involving moral determinations,[306] there appears to exist an adequate cushion against indiscriminate beliefs. Limitations can assist in conceiving of a broader form of belief, as a state may continue to operate within the confines of the right without sacrificing public order or its control over the rule of law.

Limitations

Limitations generally apply to instances of religious manifestations that might endanger other individuals, such as prohibiting the use of dangerous knives for public ritual dances[307] or curtailing public 'calls for prayer' on loudspeakers in the interest of non-adherents living in residential areas.[308] Similarly, conscientious beliefs have been subject to limitations for comparable reasons. Abatement of a belief system that prohibits the purchasing of automobile insurance[309] or registering one's cattle with the Health Service[310] transpire on grounds of public health protection or to prevent harm to third parties. A conscientious belief against the payment of taxes also has been limited on the grounds that a belief should not interfere with various state functions.[311]

---

[305] See HRC General Comment at paragraph 8 noting that limitations should not vitiate the rights guaranteed under Article 18.

[306] Cullen (1997;43). The HRC's General Comment to Article 18 alludes to such protection when defining 'morals' as deriving from a host of sociological and philosophical traditions, such that a limitation for moral reasons must 'be based on principles not deriving exclusively from a single tradition'. HRC General Comment at paragraph 8. Cf. CCPR/C/SR.1209 where the HRC members debate the merits of a pluralist society, especially if a society is rooted in a single religious doctrine.

[307] See e.g. Jagdishwaranand v. Police Commissioner AIR 1984 SC 51 (knife was also deemed non-essential to the celebration ceremony).

[308] Cumper (1995;378) (referring to UK law); PA Jacol v. Superintendent of Police AIR 1993 Ker. 1.

[309] 2988/66 X v. Netherlands 10 Ybk. ECHR 476 (1967).

[310] 1068/61 X v. Netherlands 5 Ybk. ECHR 278 (1962); Jacobson v. Massachusetts 197 US 11 (1905) (compulsory vaccination of animals).

[311] See e.g. Loschelder (1992;39-40) (referring to German decisions).

The important aspect of the limitations is that the state must demonstrate some form of pressing social need, such as protecting the rights of others or preserving a basic social value unique to the state. Hence limitations can address instances whereby an assertion of a belief might affect other individuals, such as refusing to vaccinate one's cattle on religious grounds or asserting the right to proselytise.[312] In essence, the limitations provide the opportunity to the state to balance the individual's assertion of the right against the state's ability, as derived from the limitations, to limit such assertions.[313]

Upon considering the application of the limitation aspect of the right, judicial bodies also acknowledge a certain margin of appreciation towards the state. The state is to shape a definable social construct, with only a limited infringement of the individual's belief system. The margin of appreciation doctrine then serves an important role for defining public morals and the desired construct of a state. Hence in *Buscarini v. San Marino*,[314] the ECHR Court acknowledged the importance of an oath for newly elected governmental officers as a device that upholds public order and ensures the citizens' trust in governmental institutions. Yet, the Court also held that the religious character of the oath violated ECHR Article 9, despite the fact that the oath's religious significance had waned with time.

Limitations to the right to freedom of conscience serve to enhance the development of a broader approach. An individual may manifest a host of beliefs in the *forum externum* not just as a matter of doctrinal application pursuant to specific directives, but also as a result of the importance attributed to the belief and the concomitant necessity to uphold the principles derived therefrom. While such an approach grants rather wide discretion to the individual, the imposition of limitations forces to the fore the notion of social duties and the state's goal of protecting its citizens and underlying social mores. In *Larissis v. Greece*[315] for example, the ECHR Court upheld the ban on a Pentecostal Church member from proselytising to fellow military personnel under his command as opposed

---

[312] 14307/88 *Kokkinakis v. Greece* 17 EHRR 397 (1993). Note that when considering the religious pluralism issue, it is possible that the margin of appreciation standard will be subject to a strict scrutiny test given the underlying goal of the right as promoting religious pluralism. *See* Prebensen (1998).

[313] Evans, M. (1997;331). *Cf.* Yourow (1996;47-48) noting that the margin of appreciation should not entail a balancing of interests but should be treated as a narrow exception to the right. Yourow might have reached his conclusions prior to a variety of recent cases pertaining to the margin of appreciation doctrine in the ECHR.

[314] 24645/94 *Buscarini v. San Marino* decided 18/2/99.

[315] 23372/94 *Larissis v. Greece* 1998-I Rep. Judg. & Dec. 362.

to civilians near the base.³¹⁶ An important factor was that the case occurred in a military context,³¹⁷ thereby providing grounds to the state to limit the manifestation of the belief.³¹⁸

When confronted with a broad form of manifestation of a conscientious belief, it is conceivable that a state may impose limitations based on public policy or public morals to preserve the overall social structure. Not only will international bodies defer to the state in such instances, but such an approach can acknowledge the asserted belief while not hindering the greater society. Furthermore, treaties can be subject to a broad interpretation yet acknowledge some sort of order regarding the limitations on applying the right.

Conclusion

As noted at the outset when referring to the *forum internum* as a reference point from which one's beliefs emanate, conscientious beliefs inevitably result in external manifestations as well. The international human rights system recognises such a necessity and accords protection to the *forum externum* right to conscience in the form of a negative right, freedom *from*, and positive right, freedom *to*. The majority of this chapter has focused on the matter of demonstrating how the current, narrower, understanding of the right to conscience is inadequate. Linking manifestation with the 'actual practice' of a belief makes it difficult for an individual conscientious believer to assert a more general belief that might not dictate any specific form of practice. Further, it seems to incline a reviewing body to assess the asserted belief, a task that most judicial assemblies are wont to undertake. Associating a conscientious belief with a religious manifestation also creates an inoperable right. Linking the right with other human rights, such as expression or assembly, fails to encompass the full range of the right as intended by the treaty drafters and as is necessary for a proper manifestation of a conscientious belief.

Upon considering the broader application of the right, the key factor to consider is that an individual is attempting to manifest a belief in a manner that maximises the internal consistency as developed in the *forum*

---

[316] *Cf.* dissent who held that any action greater than the mere exchange of ideas and that is intended to alter the targeted person's belief is not considered a manifestation under the treaty.
[317] *See e.g.* Evans, M. (1997;328) noting broad margin of appreciation towards public order in prison and military contexts.
[318] *See also* 14524/89 *Yansik v. Turkey* 74 D&R 14 (1993).

internum. Recognising that a belief dictates specific principles that have been deemed important and that provide grounds for undertaking an action indicates the importance of upholding a belief, with the scope of the manifestation depending on the clarity of the asserted belief. The focus should be on the asserted principles of the individual and the importance that such principles might play for the believer, with a view towards determining whether the asserted action relates to, and upholds, the underlying belief.

While this chapter addressed some of the issues raised at the outset, particularly concerning the interpretations to be given to the treaties, more needs to be said regarding the overall scope of the right to conscience. The treaties codifying the right to conscience and various international resolutions and declarations interpreting the right have hinted at a broader approach to conscience. Broadening the scope of the *forum externum* right to conscience by examining the formal or doctrinal link between the asserted belief and external actions however merits further examination. A more particular analysis that considers the mechanics of the right to conscience in various contexts along with the relationship between the *forum internum* and *forum externum* would assist to clarify the manner in which the broader form of the right should be applied. The next few chapters will focus on different kinds of conscientious manifestation that can assist to demonstrate the broader form of the right. The topics include the right to selective military conscientious objection and objecting to the payment of taxes. Furthermore, a group approach to the right to conscience will be examined not only to consider additional potential applications, but also account for additional areas of conflict that are raised by a broader application of the right to freedom of conscience.

6 Military Conscientious Objection

Introduction

The two key spheres for considering the application of the human right to freedom of conscience, the *forum internum* and the *forum externum*, assist to provide contours to a conscientious belief and to create a framework for application of the right. Particularly when considering the scope of manifestation for a conscientious belief, one must account for the seemingly impossible distinction between actual manifestations of a belief, as opposed to mere actions that might somehow be linked to a belief system.[1]

Recognising such process-oriented difficulties for the right to manifestation of a conscientious belief, it is rather odd that the usual example for the manifestation of a conscientious belief is the right to conscientious objection to military service. International fora regularly consider the status of the right to military conscientious objection, with most declaring that the right emanates from the treaty provision pertaining to the freedom of conscience. States generally recognise the ability to assert a conscientious objection to the military in some shape or form. Indeed, a number of commentators contend that the right to military conscientious objection has attained the status of a customary international law, following the acceptance of the right in state practice and recognition in international bodies.[2]

The focus on military conscientious objection is a rather interesting development when considering that it seems to present the same degrees of difficulty as any other form of manifestation of a belief, particularly in

---

[1] The common issue noted in the ECHR context, where a distinction is proposed between manifestation of a belief versus actions that are motivated by a belief.
[2] *See e.g.* Marcus (1998); Moskos and Chambers (1993); Major (1992); Lippman (1990); Weisbrodt (1988); Wolff (1982); Schwelb (1975).

proving one's beliefs and determining the scope of the objection.[3] Furthermore, military conscientious objection involves broader issues than some other forms of manifestation due to the extensive social effects an individual's manifestation of a belief can have on the military process. Granted the diverse approaches to military conscientious objection might limit the implementation of the right,[4] but even that the state recognises the individual's ability to object to military service on the grounds of a conscientious belief is a rather significant acknowledgement.

Military conscientious objection therefore seems to be a proper starting point for considering the practical application of a conscientious belief. Given the right circumstances, such as a pacifist believer objecting to military service, military conscientious objection can embody a typical example of exercising the *forum externum* right to freedom of conscience. A military conscientious objector is asserting a conscientious belief, such as against the bearing of arms, whereby the requested action by the state, participating in the military, entails a direct conflict with the belief.

Yet, despite the international clamour regarding the right[5] and the calls for equating it with a customary international norm, applications of the right to military conscientious objection vary to such an extent that there seems to be a lack of appropriate normative development for customary law purposes. The right is subject to much ambiguity in treaty committees and other international and regional bodies when delineating the framework of military objection. The right to military conscientious objection is considered as deriving from the right to freedom of conscience, yet the application of the right is not always equated with a manifestation of a conscientious belief. For example, international bodies also associate the right with humanitarian norms or the right to life. The

---

[3] The general reason for its acceptance is that military conscientious objection presents a rather stark dilemma for the military conscientious objector confronted with the taking of a human life. However this would only seem to apply to specific objectors and not necessarily other forms of objection based on a conscientious belief, such as a selective objector. Further, such an approach could weaken the argument for an objector who is not serving in any front line unit or using military weapons.
[4] See discussion *infra*.
[5] The Commission on Human Rights requested the Secretary General to prepare reports and then issue a biennial resolution regarding conscientious objection to military service. See e.g. E/CN.4/RES/2000/34 for the most recent resolution by the Commission on Human Rights.

objection is then linked to specific normative standards and not necessarily to the capacity to manifest a conscientious belief.

State practice regarding the scope of the right to military conscientious objection also differs in ways that can affect the very essence of the right. Examples include discrimination towards military conscientious objectors even if the ability to object is recognised, excluding alternative service in place of military service, or distinguishing between religious and secular objectors. Objecting to the military might be a state provided option to a potential conscript, or a state might afford an individual the capacity to appeal to a higher military authority, but that is not necessarily translated as the creation of a *right* to military conscientious objection nor the capacity to manifest a conscientious belief. Rather, an individual challenge to military participation can be a legislative grant based on a military judgement pursuant to specific internal criteria.[6]

Given the inherent difficulties associated with defining the right to military conscientious objection, this chapter will refer to the basis for asserting that military objection is a recognised customary right under international law. In doing so, the discussion will highlight the problems associated with such a contention and the normative consequences that one may derive from such developments. The problems associated with the emergence of military conscientious objection and creating a standard that adequately defines the contours of the right in a sense reflects the overall problems associated with the application of the right to freedom of conscience.

This chapter also will consider the significance of an individual's assertion of a right to military objection by focusing on the right to selective conscientious objection to the military. A selective conscientious objector is one who objects to a particular military action on the basis that the requested military action violates a conscientious belief.[7] States generally do not acknowledge such a right despite the groundwork for recognising the right to an overall military conscientious objector. It is necessary then to analyse the contentions of a selective conscientious objector and demonstrate how the assertion of a selective objector is comparable to a general military objector, such as to refute any distinction

---

[6] See discussion *infra*.
[7] Note that one also may define a selective objection in a context outside of a conscientious belief, such as objecting to a military action that violates international law or the humanitarian norms relating to the manner of warfare. Such an objection could be linked to a conscientious belief in some manner but does not necessarily raise the form of objection linked to a specific violation of a conscientious belief as described in the previous chapter.

between them. In essence, once one derives the right to military conscientious objection from the freedom of conscience, it is difficult to understand how such a right would not include selective objection.

Note that along with selective conscientious objection, there also are other forms of objection that might not be fully incorporated into the right to military conscientious objection. For example, the right to military conscientious objection for those already serving in the military or objection to alternative military service are additional applications of the right to military conscientious objection.[8] Some of these forms of military conscientious objection might be relevant to the development of customary international law, as well as important to an understanding of the manner in which a conscientious belief can manifest. The focus on selective objection however will suffice to begin to demonstrate the importance of developing an individual right to freedom of conscience as grounds for military objection and to delineate how other forms of military conscientious objection can further entrench military conscientious objection as a right.

Military Conscientious Objection and Customary Law

While there might be a host of *opinio juris* regarding the right to military conscientious objection emanating from international bodies and non-governmental organisations, and although the state practice element indicates some consensus, there is no universal understanding or approach that is suggested for the right. The key problem is that not all states acknowledge the ability for military conscientious objection as a right and even those states that do recognise some form of military conscientious objection, the right does not always emanate from the freedom of conscience but from other sources.

The purpose of this section is not necessarily to undergo an analysis of the customary status of the right to military conscientious objection. There have been a number of more than adequate analyses and studies of

---

[8] These forms of military conscientious objection are fully analysed in the Secretary General's reports to the Commission on Human Rights and are recognised as valid assertions of the right in the CHR's resolutions.

military conscientious objection in international human rights law.[9] Rather, this section will demonstrate that the right to military objection can emanate from the principal human rights treaties, has achieved recognition as a right in international fora and among some states, and is best understood as deriving from the right to freedom of religion and conscience as a form of manifesting an individual's conscientious belief.

Sources Within the Treaties

The ICCPR and ECHR[10] would seem to provide the perfect underpinning for upholding military conscientious objection as an exercise of the right to freedom of conscience. Codification of the right to conscience and interpretation of its form of manifestation indicates the possibility for permitting some type of right to military conscientious objection.

One structural problem in relying on these treaties as a source for the right to military conscientious objection is the inherent indication in other treaty articles that military conscientious objection is *not* a recognised right under the treaties. In ICCPR Article 8, which abolishes slavery, Article 8(3)(c)(ii) defines 'forced or compulsory labour' as not including:

> any service of a military character and, in countries where conscientious objection is recognised, any national service required by law of conscientious objectors.

Similarly, Article 4(3)(b) of the ECHR provides for:

> any service of a military character, or, in case of conscientious objectors in countries where they are recognised, service exacted instead of compulsory military service.

The implication from these treaty provisions, as defined by the HRC and ECHR judicial bodies,[11] is that legislatures tolerate military conscientious objection but the right does not derive from the framework of the treaties.

---

[9] Marcus (1998); Moskos and Chambers (1993); Major (1992); Lippman (1990); Weisbrodt (1988); Wolff (1982).

[10] The ICCPR and ECHR are discussed herein, at the exclusion of the AmCHR and AfrCHR, because the issue has been raised under the aegis of their respective judicial bodies.

[11] See discussion *infra*.

Additionally, the drafters of ICCPR Article 18 proposed to incorporate the right to military conscientious objection into the Article. The Philippines for example proposed the following:

> Persons who conscientiously object to war as being contrary to their religion shall be exempt from military service.[12]

The drafters however did not accept the amendment, thereby serving as a further indication that the treaties do not provide for the right to military conscientious objection.

Upon a closer examination of the travaux preparatoires however the implication that the right to freedom of conscience does not incorporate a right to military conscientious objection is somewhat dubious. Concerning the definition of 'forced and compulsory labour', the drafters inserted the phrase 'in countries where conscientious objection is recognised' in deference to those countries who did not recognise the right to military conscientious objection.[13] Furthermore, the ILO based the insertion on its understanding of military service as unforced labour[14] rather than any indication against the right to military conscientious objection. France also pointed out that some states would refuse to ratify the treaty if states did not insert such a phrase defining forced labour.[15]

Similarly, Article 8 concerned some drafters as being too broad to exclude the option for military conscientious objection. A debate within the Commission on Human Rights ensued concerning the Drafting Committee's intentions to uphold the right to military conscientious objection.[16] The Lebanese Representative desired to focus on the treatment accorded to military conscientious objectors. He proposed that they receive equal service and remuneration and be treated in a proper and humane manner[17] or at least in a non-retributive manner of

---

[12] E/CN.4/353/Add.3 and E/CN.4/SR.119. *See also* E/CN.4/NGO/1 (submission to Secretary General regarding status of military conscientious objection in various countries).
[13] A/2929.
[14] *See* ILO *Forced Labour Convention*, 190, No. 29, Article 2, section 2(a), that excludes 'any work or service exacted in virtue of compulsory military service laws for work of a purely military character' from being considered forced or compulsory labour.
[15] E/CN.4/SR/104.
[16] E/CN.4/SR.94 CHR Fifth Session.
[17] E/CN.4/SR.94.

employ.[18] Furthermore, deference to those countries that did not provide for military conscientious objection was unnecessary because military conscientious objection was a developing trend.[19] Hence the Commission on Human Rights noted at its Seventh Session that the wording of the article could conceivably deprive protection for military conscientious objectors.[20] Israel even suggested that the wording be altered to include compulsory 'alternative' military service, thereby upholding the possibility for deriving the right to military conscientious objection under the ICCPR.

The problem was that some state representatives were apprehensive of a burgeoning of claims from insincere military conscientious objectors should the ICCPR provide an explicit provision for alternative military service. Other representatives felt the provision regarding fair employment went too far and was unnecessarily specific for a general article.[21] While the proposals were rejected due to the inappropriateness of discussing rights not related to the prevention of slavery, the indication is that the clause was not meant to remove the possibility that other treaty articles can serve as a source of military conscientious objection.

Regarding the Philippines' proposal for military conscientious objection in Article 18, Uruguay noted that because Article 8 already recognised the right to military conscientious objection, there was no need to provide for it in the article pertaining to the freedom of religion and conscience.[22] India protested the proposal's focus on the religious aspect of military conscientious objection without accounting for a secular based military conscientious objection right.

Nonetheless, the majority of drafters, including the UK and US, objected to the inclusion of a specific privilege in such a general right.[23] The drafters rejected the proposal because they desired to maintain a certain level of generality in Article 18 rather then refer to specific rights emanating from the right. Note as well the Krishnaswami study, which served as a background for the ICCPR Article 18 drafters,[24] that had referred to the right of military conscientious objection under the proposed article.

---

[18] E/CN.4/SR.103.
[19] E/CN.4/SR.104.
[20] E/CN.4/528.
[21] E/CN.4/SR.104.
[22] E/CN.4/SR.161. The comment was rather odd considering that the present discussion took place a year after that regarding Article 8. It is possible that the amendments to Article 8 were pending final approval.
[23] E/CN.4/SR.161.
[24] See discussion *supra*.

The indication is that it is incorrect to imply that the terms 'forced or compulsory labour' and the absence of a specific provision in the right to conscience discount any right to military conscientious objection under the treaties. Contrary to the subsequent interpretation of the clauses in the case law, the treaty drafters clearly desired to recognise the right to military conscientious objection without specifically providing for the right in stated terms. Rather, the articles were drafted in a manner that would realistically allow for adoption of the treaty by all states. Hence, referring to the treaty right to freedom of conscience seems to provide grounds for manifesting a conscientious belief against military service.

Recognition in International Fora

Decisions

Decisions and recommendations of international bodies have generally held that the treaties do not unequivocally provide for the right to military conscientious objection. For example, the ECHR Commission and Court have not upheld military conscientious objection as a right due to the ECHR's definition of 'forced or compulsory labour' in Article 4. In essence, the ECHR Court has qualified Article 9 by the terms of Article 4[25] commencing with the initial military conscientious objection case that arose before the European Court regarding a Jehovah Witness' objection to alternative service on conscientious grounds.[26] The Court has interpreted ECHR Article 9 by reference to Article 4(3)(b) of the Convention such that alternative service of a non-military character is not granted. A number of subsequent cases before the European Commission have upheld this reasoning.[27]

As a result, the different treatment accorded to military conscientious objectors by states under the ECHR is not considered

---

[25] See e.g. 18206/91 *Faclini v. Switzerland* 16 EHRR CD13 (1992); 5591/72 *X v. Austria* 43 Collection of Decisions of ECHR 161 (1973); 7565/76 *Conscientious Objectors v. Denmark* 9 D&R 117 (1977); 7705/76 *X v. Germany* 9 D&R 196 (1977); 10600/83 *Johansen v. Norway* 9 EHRR 103 (1987); 10410/83 *N. v. Sweden* 40 D&R 203 (1984).

[26] 2299/64 *Grandrath v. FRG* 10 Ybk. of the ECHR 626 (1967).

[27] See e.g. 10600/83 *Johansen v. Norway* 9 EHRR 103 (1987) (applicant's refusal of civilian service on grounds that it contributed to military activities was denied under Article 9).

discriminatory since it is not a protected right under the treaty.[28] When the Commission considers the issue of discrimination because a domestic system might differentiate between religious or conscientious beliefs as grounds for the right to military conscientious objection, the Commission defers to the state's legal framework, even if the domestic law is discriminatory towards certain military conscientious objectors. For example, in *N. v. Sweden*,[29] the objector claimed that granting Jehovah's Witnesses an exemption from alternative service violated ECHR Article 14 since all other conscientious objectors were subject to alternative service. The Commission held however that the state had an objective basis for discriminatory treatment because Jehovah's Witnesses adhere to specific guidelines through strict principles and religious convictions, thereby providing a basis for complete exclusion. The secular military conscientious objector cannot refer to any objective standard specifically to demonstrate sincerity, thereby justifying the different treatment.[30] By comparison, the Commission upheld the reliance on Article 14 where the domestic law discriminated against a particular religion whose tenets disallowed military service.[31] The result is that while it is possible to rely on provisions such as ECHR Article 14 to prevent discrimination against a military conscientious objector, the liberty being recognised by the ECHR Commission stems from the freedom provided by the domestic law and not because military conscientious objection is a protected right under the ECHR.

The HRC has adopted similar reasoning in finding that Article 18 of the ICCPR does not provide for military conscientious objection by inferring from ICCPR Article 8 that military conscientious objection is a voluntary right. In a decision involving the admissibility of a claim, the HRC noted that there is no inherent right under Article 18 requiring a state to grant the right of military conscientious objection.[32] The HRC arrived at

---

[28] 11850/85 *G v. Netherlands* 51 D&R 180 (1987); 10640/83 *A v. Switzerland* 38 D&R 219 (1984); 7565/76 *Conscientious Objectors v. Denmark* 9 D&R 117 (1977); 5591/72 *X v. Austria* 43 Collection of Decisions of ECHR 161 (1973); 7705/76 *X v. FRG* 9 D&R 196 (1977).

[29] 10410/83 *N v. Sweden* 40 D&R 203 (1984).

[30] See also 11595/85 *Suter v. Switzerland* 51 D&R 160 (1986) (military could distinguish between penalties imposed on conscientious objectors who act based on secular or religious reasons, as long as law is applied fairly); 22956/93 *Spottl v. Austria* 22 EHRR C88 (1996) (objector to both military and alternative services based complaint on grounds of sex discrimination. Commission found distinction between men and women was justified on objective grounds and also due to margin of appreciation in area of national defence).

[31] 19233/91 *Tsirlis and Kouloumpas v. Greece* 21 EHRR CD 30 (1996).

[32] 185/1984 *LTK v. Finland* (1986).

this conclusion by referring to Article 8(3)(c)(ii) that prevented construing Article 18 as implying a right to military conscientious objection.

Subsequent HRC cases involving military conscientious objection have centred on the equality of treatment accorded to objectors pursuant to ICCPR Article 26. The HRC has upheld distinctions concerning the application of a right to military conscientious objection, such as a state denying a military conscientious objector the right to appeal.[33] The HRC based its reasoning on the premise that the limitation equally applies to all individuals within the military and that a state may impose military service even if it results in the limitation of an individual's rights.

Nonetheless, there have been indications by the HRC that the right to military conscientious objection could derive from Article 18. Recent cases have alluded to military conscientious objection as being a right provided for in the ICCPR. For example, in a case involving a conscientious objector to military taxes,[34] the HRC noted that Article 18 provides for manifestation of one's conscience, which includes military conscientious objection. Furthermore, the General Comment to Article 18[35] states that the treaty provides for the right to military conscientious objection.

Declarations and Resolutions

An additional indication of the customary status of the right to military conscientious objection is activity in international fora. Attempts to codify the right to military conscientious objection by relevant international bodies assist in entrenching the right. Yet, there seems to be an inherent distinction between developing the ability to object to the military as opposed to recognising an individual's assertion of military conscientious objection as a form of manifesting a conscientious belief. In attempting to build a basis for the right to military conscientious objection, international bodes tend to lump together a number of human rights to solidify the normative grounds for recognising military conscientious objection, possibly at the expense of the right to freedom of conscience.

A key indication of the status of the right to military conscientious objection in the ICCPR is the General Comment to Article 18. In the

---

[33] 267/1987 *MJG v. Netherlands* (1989); 245/1987 *RTZ v. Netherlands* (1989).
[34] 446/1991 *JP v. Canada* (1992).
[35] See discussion *infra*.

General Comment, the HRC focused on military conscientious objection and not other forms of conscientious manifestation due to the prior rejection of the right to military conscientious objection. The HRC decided that it was time to recognise the right under the Covenant.[36] Hence the HRC considered proposals to include other forms of conscientious objection, such as a doctor's conscientious refusal to perform an abortion, as being already accounted for by the General Comment's amplification of the manifestation of conscience.[37] Military conscientious objection however merited specific mention to ensure for the right under the Covenant and has been a concern of the HRC.[38]

Despite the HRC's preference for military conscientious objection, it is important to note the form of manifestation that is being acknowledged. Paragraph 11 of the General Comment to ICCPR Article 18 states that while the:

> covenant does not explicitly refer to a right of conscientious objection, the Committee believes that such a right can be derived from Article 18, inasmuch as the obligation to use lethal force may seriously conflict with the freedom of conscience...

The term 'lethal force' is referring to any act of aggression that will lead to killing, such that military conscientious objection is not limited to individuals who do not desire to use firearms. The HRC noted that although using this broader term also allows for a military conscientious objection opposed to killing, one should not interpret the phrase as equating military service with murder.[39] Rather, one must object to lethal force, language that relates to more general notions regarding an aversion to taking the life of another person.[40]

Such an approach seems a somewhat confined understanding of the right to conscience since it narrows the scope of the right to specific belief systems pertaining to taking life, without accounting for other forms of conscientious objection. One might maintain a belief system that prohibits

---

[36] CCPR/C/SR.1237.
[37] General Comment at Paragraph 8.
[38] *See e.g.* Comments to the State Report of Libyan Arab Jamahariya, CCPR/C/79/Add.45 (1994) at paragraph 13, noting the HRC's concern at the lack of any provision for conscientious objection to military service.
[39] CCPR/C/SR.1237.
[40] The General Comment also requested states to report on the right to alternative service and noted the desire for ensuring equality of such service with one's military counterparts.

any connection whatsoever with the military, including alternative service, or possibly a religion that forbids service in a secular military. These instances of objection pertain to the manifestation of a belief and should be grounds for military conscientious objection. In a sense, the HRC's limiting language towards other forms of beliefs as grounds for military conscientious objection highlights the problems of the treaty drafters when refusing to define the treaty terms 'religion or belief' given the possibility for excluding various belief systems outside of the defined framework.

Nonetheless, other international fora acknowledge a broader approach to the right to military conscientious objection, most significantly the Commission on Human Rights that has addressed the issue in the most extensive manner.[41] In 1981, the Commission on Human Rights passed a Resolution requesting the Sub-Commission on the Prevention of Discrimination and Protection of Minorities to prepare a report on the issue of military conscientious objection.[42] The final version of the report, presented in 1983,[43] seemed to equate military conscientious objection with violations of international law, such as using the military to enforce apartheid, genocide, illegal occupations, gross violations of human rights, illegal weapons, or weapons of mass destruction.[44] The reporters also mentioned the right to life as a basis for military objection[45] and the

---

[41] The Commission on Human Rights initially broached the issue under the agenda item *Study of the Question of Young People all over the World for the Development of its Personality and Strengthening of its Respect for the Rights of Man and Fundamental Freedoms* beginning with its 27th Session in 1971. See e.g. E/CN.4/1068 (1971). The Commission on Human Rights discussed military conscientious objection throughout the 1970's, requesting the Secretary General to issue semi-annual reports regarding the status of the right in various states. See e.g. E/CN.4/1118/Add.1-3 (1973); E/CN.4/1118/Con.1 (1974); E/CN.4/12-13 (1976); E/CN.4/1408 (1980)

[42] Resolution 40 of 37th Session of CHR (1981).

[43] Asbjorn Eide and Chama Mubanga-Chipoya prepared the report, entitled *Conscientious Objection to Military Service* E/CN.4/Sub.2/1983/30/Rev.1 (1983). See also E/CN.4/Sub.2/1982/24 (preliminary report). The Report also summarised the status of military conscientious objection in various countries. It recommended that, at a minimum, states recognise a general right to military conscientious objection to any form of warfare. Upholding the common good of society should not be a basis for a summary rejection of the right.

[44] E/CN.4/Sub.2/1983/30 at 7.

[45] Eide and Mubanga-Chipoya *Conscientious Objection to Military Service* E/CN.4/Sub.2/1983/30/Rev.1 at 8, referring to the UDHR Article 3, ICCPR Article 6, ECHR Article 2, and the AmCHR Article 4.

Nuremberg Principles that hold individuals responsible for breaches of international law.[46]

The problem in looking to other rights or to international law violations as a basis for military conscientious objection is that it can result in a limited scope to the right to military conscientious objection. For example, one of the key grounds commonly asserted for military conscientious objection is the right to life.[47] Referring to the right to life as a basis for military conscientious objection narrows the focus of the right to the prevention of arbitrary killing. While prevention of random killing includes that of state security forces such as the military, the focus for the right to life is to place a burden on the state to control the actions of its forces.[48] Granted that because a state might inadequately address the arbitrary deprivation of life by its military, a military conscientious objection issue can arise for one refusing to carry out such illegal actions. However that does not necessarily encompass the broad form of military conscientious objection that the international human rights system intended, especially when deriving the right from the right to freedom of conscience. Rather it equates the notion of a conscientious belief with the laws of war. While this might be a desirable outcome, it is not necessarily driven by a belief system but is linked to external rules pertaining to warfare and the individual's obligation not to deviate from such rules.[49]

Furthermore, the HRCs First General Comment to ICCPR Article 6 refers to a state's obligation to engage in the legal use of force. The focus for the discussion is the inherent tension between a state protecting the right to life while also maintaining the ability to take life in given circumstances. There is no reference to the responsibility of the individual actors in the military. Indeed, the state reports to the HRC rarely mention the connection between warfare and Article 6.[50] Hence, it would seem unrealistic to interpret the right as prohibiting warfare or providing a unitary basis for military conscientious objection because they involve the prevention of taking a life.[51] In a sense, similar to considering freedom of

---

[46] Eide and Mubanga-Chipoya *Conscientious Objection to Military Service* E/CN.4/Sub.2/1983/30/Rev.1 at 9.
[47] Major (1992); Wolff (1982). The Commission on Human Right's resolutions also refers to this basis, along with the right to security. *See e.g.* E/CN.4/RES/2000/34 at first preambular paragraph.
[48] *See e.g.* General Comment(I) 6/16 to Article 6.
[49] Such an approach to the right seems to be more in the form of civil disobedience rather than relying on a specific conscientious belief.
[50] McGoldrick (1991;334).
[51] Dinstein (1981;120). *See also* Fawcett (1987) noting that the ECHR upholds the right to life and not life itself.

expression and assembly in tandem with the manifestation of conscience, the right to life is a right that works in tandem with the right to conscience to form the groundwork for the right to military conscientious objection.[52] That does not mean however that the right to life is the exclusive basis for asserting a conscientious belief given the possibly broad implications of a conscientious belief.

Yet, the Commission on Human Rights report did note that military conscientious objection is broader than pacifism as it incorporates genuine ethical convictions reflected in international and domestic law.[53] The right to military conscientious objection can be based on both religious and ethical grounds, albeit the latter claim requires a high standard of proof to demonstrate the veracity of one's ethical convictions.[54] Hence the report referred to Articles 18 of the UDHR and ICCPR, Article 9 of the ECHR, Article 12 of the AmCHR, and Article 8 of the AfrCHR. Furthermore, the report noted that although ICCPR Article 8 is a specific provision that prevents objection to military or alternative service on grounds of forced labour, one should not interpret the Article as discounting a general right to military conscientious objection.[55]

In 1987,[56] the Commission on Human Rights adopted a resolution[57] that 'appealed' to states to recognise military conscientious objection as a legitimate exercise of UDHR and ICCPR Article 18.[58] The Commission on Human Rights acknowledged however that military conscientious objection derives from reasons of conscience and profound convictions

---

[52] Particularly regarding selective conscientious objection and nuclear weapons. The General Comment II to ICCPR Article 6 regards nuclear weapons as a threat to peace. *Cf. Advisory Opinion on the Legality of the Threat or Use of Nuclear Weapons*, July 8, 1996, in 35 ILM 809 (1996).

[53] E/CN.4/Sub.2/1983/30 at 4-6.

[54] Eide and Mubanga-Chipoya *Conscientious Objection to Military Service* E/CN.4/Sub.2/1983/30/Rev.1 at 18-19.

[55] Eide and Mubanga-Chipoya *Conscientious Objection to Military Service* E/CN.4/Sub.2/1983/30/Rev.1 at 7-8.

[56] The Secretary General received additional information in the mid-1980s. E/CN.4/1985/25. The Secretary General's report reviewed the status of the right in some states and considered submissions by various NGOs. The Commission on Human Rights then proposed a resolution in 1985 but it was withdrawn. E/CN.4/1985/L.33/Rev.1.

[57] Resolution 1987/46 *See* E/CN.4/1987/60.

[58] CHR Resolution 1987/46 at paragraph 1; E/CN.4/1987/SR.54/Add.1 CHR 43rd Session.

based on religious, ethical, moral, or similar motives.[59] Twenty-six members of the Commission on Human Rights adopted the Resolution. Fourteen states abstained[60] due to their approach to military service as an honour and duty to be undertaken by all citizens[61] or because they provided for military service in their constitution.[62] Iraq and Mozambique voted against the Resolution claiming that continuing conflicts with Iran and South Africa, respectively, prevented them from supporting the Resolution.[63]

Following more submissions to the Secretary General by various countries and Non-Governmental Organisations,[64] the Commission on Human Rights passed additional resolutions without a vote. The 1989 Resolution[65] explicitly recognised the right to conscientious objection based on Articles 18 of the UDHR and the ICCPR.[66] The grounds for military conscientious objection however were reasons of conscience arising from 'religious or similar motives'. Although the 1989 Resolution did not mention ethical or moral grounds,[67] the preamble to the 1993 Resolution[68] included ethical as well as religious motives as grounds for military conscientious objection, although no reference was made to moral motives.[69]

---

[59] Resolution 1987/46, Preamble. It also recommended that states adopt an alternative service system and impartial review tribunals. Resolution 1987/46 at paragraphs 3-4. The resolution also placed the matter officially on the agenda of the Commission on Human Rights under the title *The role of youth in the promotion and protection of human rights, including the question of conscientious objection to military service.*

[60] Algeria, Bulgaria, Byelorussian Soviet Socialist Republic, China, Congo, Cyprus, Ethiopia, German Democratic Republic, India, Mexico, Nicaragua, Union of Soviet Socialist Republics, Venezuela, and Yugoslavia.

[61] *See e.g.* remarks by Yugoslavia in E/CN.4/1987/SR.54/Add.1.

[62] *See e.g.* remarks by the Congo, Algeria and Venezuela E/CN.4/1987/SR.54/Add.1.

[63] E/CN.4/1987/SR.54/Add.1. *Cf.* Nicaragua who used the same reasoning to abstain from the voting.

[64] E/CN.4/1989/30.

[65] 1989/59.

[66] Resolution 1989/59 at paragraph 1.

[67] The resolution also expanded the notion of alternative service, noting that such service should be of a non-combatant or civilian character and not a punitive measure, and recommending alternative service and an impartial tribunal to review conscientious objector's claims. Resolution 1989/56 at paragraphs 3-5.

[68] Resolution 1993/84.

[69] Resolution 1993/84 at Preamble. It did include a direct reference to the possibility that individuals may develop an in-service objection to military duty in Paragraph 2 and Paragraph 8 affirmed the importance of providing conscripts with information about the right to military conscientious objection.

By contrast, the 1995 Commission on Human Rights Resolution[70] refers to the HRC's General Comment that recognised Article 18 as a basis for military conscientious objection.[71] Other changes were the inclusion of ethical and humanitarian, along with religious, motives as grounds for military conscientious objection.[72] The subsequent two resolutions from 1998[73] and 2000[74] further entrench the conclusion that the right to freedom of conscience serves as the basis for military conscientious objection.[75] Although the 1998 resolution is a more comprehensive statement regarding the scope of the right to military conscientious objection,[76] both resolutions refer to ICCPR Article 18 and the General Comment to the Article as grounds for invoking the right.

The indication is that for the Commission on Human Rights, the right to military conscientious objection is a right emanating from the freedom of conscience, along with a number of other human rights. Furthermore, the Commission on Human Rights acknowledges that the decision for the objection can derive from an individual's conscientious belief, a rather broad approach to the right of manifestation and an expansive recognition of the meaning of belief.

Similar to the Commission on Human Rights, the Council of Europe also has addressed the right to military conscientious objection. In 1966, the Parliament of the Council of Europe proposed a motion for a

---

[70] Resolution 1995/83.
[71] E/CN.4/1995/SR.59.
[72] E/CN.4/1995/SR.62. and reference to UDHR Article 14 regarding the right to asylum that is to serve as a basis for a military conscientious objection facing persecution.
Paragraph 2 of the Resolution improved on the 1993 version by removing the term 'compulsory', thereby extending the right to an in-service objection for voluntary military services. Paragraph 4 was a new addition urging states not to differentiate in their treatment of military conscientious objectors who maintain different forms of beliefs. The Commission on Human Rights also altered Paragraph 7 to incorporate an emerging practice among some states whereby the military conscientious objector's claim is accepted as 'valid without inquiry'.
[73] E/CN.4/RES/1998/77.
[74] E/CN.4/RES/2000/34.
[75] The Resolutions followed reports by the Secretary General, E/CN.4/1997/99 and E/CN.4/2000/55. Following submissions by a number of states, the Secretary General concluded that most countries recognise the right to military conscientious objection on the grounds of the right to freedom of religion or belief, although a minority of states either did not provide for the right, or limited the right solely to those whose objection was based on religious beliefs.
[76] Following a more detailed report by the Secretary General. E/CN.4/1997/99.

recommendation on military conscientious objection[77] and the following year, the Consultative Assembly passed Resolution 337. The Resolution specifically referred to Article 9 of the ECHR as a basis for military conscientious objection on grounds of 'religious ethical moral humanitarian philosophical or similar motives'.[78]

In 1977,[79] the issue was again raised before the Consultative Assembly[80] who adopted Recommendation 816 that urged the Committee of Ministers to introduce the right of military conscientious objection into the ECHR and consider Resolution 337. The Committee of Ministers again replied that several members had settled the question of military conscientious objection within their own laws, while other states could not provide for such a right.[81]

The Council of Ministers consulted with the Assembly in 1987[82] and, at its 906th meeting, adopted Recommendation No. R(87)8.[83] The document recommended that conscientious objection be recognised as a right[84] albeit without any reference to ECHR Article 9 due to the existing

---

[77] Doc. 2076 (1966).
[78] It required that notification be given to all conscripts regarding the right to military conscientious objection, Resolution 337 at paragraph B.1, that the decision making tribunal be separate from the military, Resolution 337 at paragraph B.2.and 3, and that alternative social service be provided on equal terms with military service. Resolution 337 at paragraph c.1. – 3.
[79] Previous action in the Council of Europe generally centred on suggestions to consider military conscientious objection. *See* Appendix to Resolution 683 (1972) - suggestion by Amnesty International at the 1971 Parliamentary Conference on Human Rights to consider resolution 337; 1974 Opinion of Committee of Experts on Human Rights to consider issue of Military Conscientious Objection.
[80] Previously, the Committee of Ministers received the Resolution by way of Recommendation 478. The Recommendation requested the Committee to give effect to the principles of Resolution 337 through a Recommendation or Convention and further requested all member states to adopt similar legislation.
[81] The Steering Committee for Human Rights then took control of the matter. The key problem noted by the Steering Committee was that although many member states had adopted provisions for military conscientious objectors, the solutions were extremely diverse. The central focus of the Steering Committee's activity in devising a draft Recommendation therefore was harmonisation of domestic laws and practices. In 1986, the Steering Committee turned the matter over to the Committee of Ministers and transmitted a draft Recommendation to the Committee of Ministers.
[82] Opinion No. 132 (1987).
[83] Reported at 9 EHRR 529 (1987).
[84] The Recommendation also noted that individuals be informed of the right to object before enlistment, the military allow for conscientious objection during military service and provide an impartial tribunal or right to appeal to such a tribunal, allow for alternative service and ensure that military conscientious objectors receive benefits on an equal scale to those granted to other military personnel.

case law that does not recognise military conscientious objection as a right under the ECHR.[85] Nonetheless, the terms 'reasons of conscience' were used to imply that 'all compelling reasons dictated by conscience against being involved in any use of arms are to be considered as a basis for granting conscientious objection status',[86] thereby encouraging states to avoid a precise definition or unduly restrictive attitude towards military conscientious objectors.[87] Furthermore, the Ministers noted that while the Recommendation refers to compulsory service, the terms could also be applied to voluntary service as well.[88]

The Ministers categorically stated as a Basic Principle in paragraph 1 that all compulsory conscripts are entitled to release from service if 'for compelling reasons of conscience' they 'refuse to be involved in the use of arms'. The reference to 'use of arms', as opposed to the HRC's language of 'lethal force' implies an even narrower basis for military conscientious objection. The HRC's General Comment phrase of 'lethal force' can refer to military actions other than using arms, such as participating in a military manoeuvre, while Recommendation (87)8 centres on individuals opposed to personally being involved in 'using' arms. Hence the term 'compelling', which was meant to discount selective military conscientious objectors who object to the use of particular arms.[89]

Following the Resolution, the Parliamentary Assembly requested a formal report on the right to military conscientious objection that was completed in 1993.[90] The report centred on recognition of military conscientious objection as a right under the ECHR and provided for a very broad approach, including the capacity for selective military conscientious objection as being based on religious philosophical ideological or political grounds for objection.[91] Indeed, the report even noted recognition of conscientious objection in other contexts, such as to abortion or military

---

[85] Explanatory Report to Recommendation No. R(87)8, at paragraph 13.
[86] Explanatory Report to Recommendation No. R(87)8, at paragraph 15.
[87] Explanatory Report to Recommendation No. R(87)8, at paragraph 16.
[88] Explanatory Report to Recommendation No. R(87)8, at paragraph 11.
[89] Explanatory Report to Recommendation No. R(87)8, at paragraph 16. *See also* discussion *infra*.
[90] Doc. 6752 29/1/93 *Report on the Right to Conscientious Objection to Military Service*.
[91] The reporter also called for a reasonable duration of non-military alternative service and the right to appeal to a non-military tribunal. As to an in-service right to military conscientious objection, the report upheld such a right due to the possible introduction of new forms of warfare or development of one's beliefs after joining the military.

taxes simply because the treaty right provided for the existence of all forms of beliefs.

The European Union's European Parliament also has promoted the right to military conscientious objection. Following a commissioned report in 1982 outlining the status of the right,[92] the Parliament passed a Resolution in 1983 stating that the right to military conscientious objection is a form of the right to freedom of conscience[93] and should be accepted as such within the ECHR.[94] Due to lack of further activity, the European Parliament passed a 1989 Resolution on military conscientious objection.[95] The Resolution states that because it is impossible to examine one's conscience, a potential conscript 'must' be entitled to conscientious objection, whether armed or unarmed,[96] based on a declaration setting out the individual's motives[97] and should be recognised as a right in the ECHR.[98]

What emanates from the aforementioned bodies is the derivation of the right to military conscientious objection from the treaties providing for the right to freedom of religion and conscience. While the ECHR and HRC have not been as clear in their decisions when considering the right to military conscientious objection, nor have the HRC's General Comments necessarily accorded a broad based approach to the right, there certainly appears to be some form of developing consensus on this matter pursuant to the declarations and resolutions of other international bodies. The notion that the right to military conscientious objection derives from the right to freedom of conscience certainly is becoming entrenched, and the broad

---

[92] 1 Doc. 1-546/82, referred to as the Macciocchi Report, after its author.
[93] OJ No C68 14/3/83.
[94] Resolution OJ No C68 14/3/83 at paragraph 9. The Resolution went on to affirm the importance of alternative service, which should not exceed the duration of military service, Resolution at paragraphs' 4-5, and that a written statement regarding one's objection should suffice as proof for a military conscientious objection claim. Resolution at paragraph 3.
[95] Doc A3-15/89; OJ No C 291/123.
[96] Resolution c291/123 at paragraphs A.-B.
[97] Resolution c291/123 at paragraph 4. The Resolution uses broad language to allow for in-service military conscientious objection 'at any time', paragraph 1, and 'calls on' states to provide military conscientious objection information for all potential conscripts, paragraph 2, along with a proper national appeals procedure, paragraph 8. It further required that the granting of alternative service be on equal terms with military service and should not exceed more than fifty per cent of the period for military service to compensate for reserve periods, paragraphs 3,5,6, and 10.
[98] Resolution c291/123 at paragraph 11.

meaning accorded to a conscientious belief appears to be the common approach.[99]

The disparity between the legislative mechanisms such as the Commission on Human Rights or European Parliament, and the decision making bodies could be due to the lack of any binding power resulting from declarations and resolutions while the decisions of the judicial bodies carry greater weight and involve specific instances of military objection that directly affect the state. Similarly, the General Comments, while not binding on the states, certainly serve a seminal role in interpreting the ICCPR. Hence the judicial bodies might hesitate before issuing a broad decision, something that might not be the case for non-binding declarations and resolutions. While some decisions might have hinted at the right to military conscientious objection, and although the HRC's General Comment to Article 18 gives credence to the link between military conscientious objection and the right to freedom of conscience, the hesitancy in deriving the right from the relevant treaties remains.

At the very least, the declarations and resolutions carry some weight towards demonstrating an *opinio juris* among states and have some form of influence given the change in attitude by the HRC and possibly the ECHR.[100] Note however that even the declarations and resolutions that uphold the right to military conscientious objection contain ambiguities such as to suggest a misunderstanding regarding the significance of referring to the right to freedom of conscience. The right might be based upon the freedom of conscience, yet the reports also refer to humanitarian norms, other *jus cogens* norms such as genocide, and other human rights like the right to life, as grounds for an objection.[101] Such an approach makes the basis for the right unclear. Is military conscientious objection a result of an individual's conscientious belief or must it be linked to some external norm, such as the prevention of genocide? If the latter is the preferred option, a result that the subsequent resolutions do not support, then it seems to be closer to a selective conscientious objection, a right that is generally denied to military conscientious objectors.[102] If however the

---

[99] *See also* Marcus (1998) making a similar conclusion.
[100] *See e.g.* dissent in *Tsirlis v. Greece supra* noting that Article 9 should be read as recognising the right to military conscientious objection subject to the limitations of 9(2). *See also* Cullen (1997;HRC/40).
[101] *See e.g.* Eide and Mubanga-Chipoya *Conscientious Objection to Military Service* E/CN.4/Sub.2/1983/30/Rev.1.
[102] *See* discussion *infra*.

basis for objection is a conscientious belief, then it should not matter whether the objection is reflected in humanitarian norms or not since the important element is to prevent violations of a conscientious belief. Military conscientious objection then is similar to other forms of manifestation of a conscientious belief. Even if the grounds for the belief do not relate to using arms or lethal force, the belief could derive from other sources, such as a religious mandate against killing a fellow religious believer or concerns pertaining to the environment. These issues are further clouded upon considering the variety of approaches that are suggested by state practice.

State Practice

Similar to the resolutions and declarations developed in international fora, domestic state practice indicates some universality regarding the right to military conscientious objection. A cursory review of the Secretary Generals 1997 report[103] indicates that a majority of states provide for the right to military conscientious objection in some shape or form.[104] Yet the diversity in approach demonstrates the scope of the problem facing UN bodies like the Commission on Human Rights when attempting to draft a resolution favourable to all participant states. That is, although 48 states did not recognise any right to military conscientious objection, some of the 114 states that were examined and that did provide for the right recognised a general right not to serve while other states merely provided for a right to abstain from a combatant role. Nonetheless, the Report noted that the majority of states adopt the basis of conscientious objection on the grounds of the right to freedom of religion and conscience, although some states do limit the right to a religious belief or do not necessarily consider the foundation for the right.

The key difference between the domestic protection and the international protection seems to be that the right to military conscientious objection in the domestic context sometimes derives from particular legislative action rather then a recognition of a particular right to the freedom of religion or conscience. For example, a legislative enactment serves as the basis for military conscientious objection in the US rather

---

[103] E/CN.4/1997/99. *See also* Marcus (1998;527-531) for a detailed discussion of the report.
[104] The Council of Europe's review of the domestic state systems also noted a majority consensus among states providing for the right to military conscientious objection based on a review conducted in AS/JUR (36)4 and corrigenda; AS/JUR (38)3; AS/JUR (41)17.

than a Constitutional right.[105] While commentators generally agree that one can infer the right to military conscientious objection from the Free Exercise Clause,[106] the legislative provision of the right has made the issue irrelevant for a court deciding a military conscientious objection case.[107]

By contrast, Article 4(3) of the Basic Law of the German Grundgesetz provides that:

> No one shall be forced to perform armed military service against the dictates of his conscience.[108]

This is quite a unique constitutional right, given that there is a mandatory draft in Germany. Note however that the phrase 'armed military service' implies a specific form of military conscientious objection where the claim centres on opposition to killing another human being against his conscience via the use of weapons. It does not necessarily incorporate all instances of military conscientious objection that derive from a conscientious belief.

It therefore seems that many domestic jurisdictions acknowledge the right to military conscientious objection for individuals who object to all forms of military service.[109] The differences arise in the application of the right to specific situations. While this certainly assists to demonstrate the emergence of a customary norm, it also creates problems when considering the application and scope of such a norm. Should a state recognise all beliefs as a basis for an objection, limit the objection only to those whose belief systems mandate that they cannot use lethal weapons, or only recognise religious rather than secular believers? Is a state to recognise the conscientious belief of the individual as the basis for the right or does it

---

[105] For the history of the right within the US, *see* Brown, Kohn and Kohn (1985-86); Kohn (1986); Russell (1951-52).

[106] *See e.g.* Brown, Kohn and Kohn (1985-1986) (analysing approach of the drafters of the US Constitution towards military conscientious objection and concluding that it is a constitutional right); Davis (1991) (military conscientious objection is a constitutional right since dealing with a fundamental interest); Landskroen (1991); Fogarty (1983).

[107] 50 USC app. sections 451-471(a).

[108] Kuhlman and Lippert (1993;98). Note as well Portugal, Spain, Austria, Croatia, Slovenia, Estonia, Slovakia, Czech Republic, Russia, Brazil, Uruguay, Guyana, Surinam, and Zambia also have constitutional provisions regarding the right to military conscientious objection. *See* Sousa e Brito (1999;612).

[109] Moskos & Chambers (1993); Marcus (1998).

suffice merely to create some form of narrow legislative arrangement for military conscientious objection? What of the ancillary rights associated with military conscientious objection, such as alternative service instead of the military? May a state impose lengthier periods of alternative service or is that considered a punitive measure rather than an acknowledgement of the individual's ability to uphold their conscientious beliefs? Must a state recognise the ability for in-service objection, a likely development if the right is based on upholding an individual's belief that is subject to constant reassessment, or could the state defer to its own policy reasons for limiting the right? What if a state distinguishes between a religious as opposed to a conscientious objector? May a state accord such objectors different treatment?

Upon considering the variety of forms that exist for military conscientious objection, apparently the basis for the right is instrumental in dictating the scope of the right to be accorded. Basing the right on domestic legislation provides the state with the opportunity to limit the scope of military conscientious objection. The objector is essentially subject to the policy decisions of the legislature rather than being afforded the ability to rely on a conscientious belief. Similarly, recognising the right to military conscientious objection as a constitutional right might entrench the right, but the state could narrow the capacity for objection, such as only to those objectors opposed to using lethal force.

Because the international declarations and resolutions pertaining to military conscientious objection agree that the right is based upon the human right to freedom of religion and conscience, it is imperative to consider the implications of such a development. Even in domestic state systems that have codified a narrow capacity for military conscientious objection, the human right to freedom of conscience still provides the opportunity for manifesting a conscientious belief. Hence other forms of military conscientious objection might still fall under the right to freedom of conscience. This is the case for selective conscientious objection, one who objects to a specific military conflict or form of warfare based on a conscientious belief. The selective conscientious objector need not necessarily object to participating in the military. Rather, the objection relates to a particular action that the individual deems will violate a conscientious belief as a result of carrying out a particular military directive. If the basis for military conscientious objection is the human right to freedom of conscience, then subject to the treaty limitations, the belief should manifest. If however the basis for military conscientious objection is domestic legislation or narrow forms of constitutional rights, then the ability for selective conscientious objection generally will be limited.

Similar consequences apply to other forms of military conscientious objection, such as alternative service or in-service objection. Understanding these objections as assertions of a conscientious belief lead to a different result than when suggesting that a state adopts these options to accommodate an objector. Selective conscientious objection presents a rather telling example of this distinction given that it is linked both to the manner of warfare and the rules of war as well as an individual conscientious belief.

Selective Conscientious Objection

Selective Objection in Resolutions and Declarations

In passing various resolutions on the right to military conscientious objection, international organs have never specifically provided for the right to selective conscientious objection. For example, the Council of Europe in the Explanatory Notes to Recommendation 87(8) clearly does not include selective conscientious objection.[110] The Council of Europe however did recognise that the military conscientious objection right is to apply to 'all compelling reasons of conscience against being involved in any use of arms'.[111] While this might discount a right for a selective conscientious objection claim to particular forms of military action, it does seem to provide for objections entailing a conscientious objection to any use of a form of weapon, such as a nuclear device or other violations to the standards of *jus in bello*. The Explanatory Notes to the Recommendation however do not allude to this interpretative distinction.

By contrast, the 1983 CHR Report referred to the possibility of selective conscientious objection. The Report noted that a selective conscientious objector determines that a form or method of military action breaches an internal moral that is equated with international law. Nonetheless, following analysis of the state reports on military conscientious objection, the Report concluded that selective conscientious objection is not an acknowledged form of the right.

---

[110] Recommendation 87(8) at paragraph 16.
[111] Explanatory note to Recommendation 87(8) at paragraph 15.

In the CHR's Resolutions that followed the Report, the basis for military conscientious objection was a 'genuinely held conscientious objection to armed service'.[112] The phrase can arguably provide the basis for selective conscientious objection to particular methods of armed service such as nuclear weapons, particularly when contrasted with the Council of Europe's language of 'use of arms'. Nevertheless, such an interpretation would be difficult to construe. There is no indication that the CHR intended such a broad understanding of 'armed service' as referring to particular forms of such service. Furthermore, state practice, which the CHR was attempting to reflect, generally does not provide for the right to selective conscientious objection.

The right to selective conscientious objection possibly can be derived from the HRC's provision for military conscientious objection in the General Comment to Article 18. The notion of objecting to 'lethal force', rather then using language regarding the bearing of arms, centres on the manner of warfare being conducted. A broad interpretation of the term 'lethal' can include selective objections to particular lethal weapons, such as using chemical weapons in warfare, even though the same person might not object to handling a gun or bearing arms.

On the domestic front, some states recognise the right to selective conscientious objection. Examples of such states are Australia,[113] Denmark,[114] and the Netherlands.[115]

The majority of states however do not recognise selective conscientious objection as an option. This is principally because the right to military conscientious objection is subject to the factoring in of more practical considerations regarding administrative necessity. The US Supreme Court for example has held that the legislative right to object to 'war in any form'[116] does not provide for particular objections to war but only overall objections.[117] Furthermore, the Court did not find any constitutional violation due to the distinction between general military conscientious objectors and selective conscientious objectors. The Court found a neutral, secular, purpose for distinguishing them; namely to ensure

---

[112] See e.g. Resolution 1995/83 at paragraph 3.
[113] Defence Legislation Amendment Act 1992, Division 2-5.
[114] Siesby (1992) noting that some selective political objectors, such as refusing to serve under a capitalistic social order, would have a stricter burden of proof.
[115] Vermeulen (1992) noting objections to NATO, politically based - such as to capitalist systems, or nuclear weapons.
[116] Currently - 32 CFR section 75.3(a) (1991).
[117] Gillette v. US 401 US 437 (1971).

for a proper administration of the military and allow for a fair method of discerning sincere from insincere objectors.[118]

Even in Germany, where military conscientious objection is a constitutional right,[119] no right exists to claim selective conscientious objection.[120] The reasoning is based on the phrase 'active military service' in Article 4(1) of the Grundgesetz. The Federal Administrative Court has defined the phrase as exempting an objector opposed to killing another human being. Hence, the right is only for individuals wholly opposed to killing another and does not provide protection for individuals opposed to a particular war or form of warfare.[121] The only right to a limited selective conscientious objection derives from a particular legislative enactment providing for military conscientious objection based on an objection to nuclear war. Such an approach indicates an acceptance of a specific form of selective conscientious objection.

In states where conscription exists, military conscientious objection is a difficult enough right to provide, especially upon considering the reasons why a state maintains a draft. Conscription might exist as a response to a perceived security threat from its neighbour or due to an ongoing external or internal conflict that would make selective conscientious objection quite a difficult right to recognise. Selective conscientious objection raises the level of administrative concerns within the military and could wreak havoc on the overall preparedness of a military.

Despite the general indifference by international bodies and domestic states towards selective conscientious objection, the possibility of making such an assertion is not a dead letter. Following a discussion of the key underlying problems associated with selective conscientious objection and an attempt to address these issues, this chapter will focus on various international and domestic laws that seem to provide for the right to selective conscientious objection, particularly when considering that the right derives from the right to freedom of conscience.

---

[118] *Gillette v. US* 401 US 437 (1971); *See also* Greenawalt (1971).
[119] *See* discussion *supra*.
[120] Kuhlmann and Lippert (1990;98).
[121] Loschelder (1992;33) referring to BVerfGE 12, 45 and BVerwGE 60, 336. *See also* Germany's 1996 Report to the HRC, CCPR/C/84/Add.5, noting that its constitutional provision for military conscientious objection is to be narrowly interpreted.

Underlying Problems

Similar to the in-service objector, selective conscientious objection poses problems of administrative difficulty. Presumably, the selective conscientious objector can object at any time, especially when a particular action confronts the objector in the military theatre, thereby creating a burden to the operation of the military.[122] The possible loss of control or decrease in military morale is a problem as a result of having disagreement within its ranks and possible conflicts among the soldiers.[123]

Additionally, sincerity is a major factor for determining the validity of the objector's claim. Hence the problem of in-service objectors, where the burden of proof will weigh against the objector who has already consented to participating in the military but has developed his beliefs during service. An even greater burden confronts the selective conscientious objector. The selective conscientious objector not only has initially consented to participate in certain military actions, but also will continue to do so, pending the objection to certain military actions or use of particular weapons. From a practical standpoint, it is difficult to distinguish the sincere from insincere selective conscientious objector, especially when based on a secular belief. The asserted beliefs are not associated with any particular practice or doctrine and arguably can shift depending on the practice of the military.[124]

Another problem centres on the nature of the claim. The selective conscientious objector is generally objecting to the method of a state's warfare. As noted in the 1983 Report of the CHR's rapporteurs, states are not willing to acknowledge that their actions are morally incorrect or contrary to international law.[125] Furthermore, due to the focus on a particular form of action as the basis for the objection, a reviewing body will treat the claim as having a political bent rather than being a matter of manifesting a conscientious belief.[126] For example, the government might interpret an objection to a particular military action that violates international norms as a political reaction to the state's decision to enter a conflict rather then reliance on a conscientious belief.

---

[122] Fogarty (1983;655).
[123] Langan (1989;101-104). *See also* Kuby and Kunstler (1992;681-684) describing discriminatory treatment towards objectors to the Persian Gulf conflict.
[124] *See e.g. Gillette v. US* 401 US 437 (1971); Greenawalt (1971;56 and 64).
[125] Eide and Mubanga-Chipoya *Conscientious Objection to Military Service* E/CN.4/Sub.2/1983/30/Rev.1 at 29. *See also* Langan (1989) (outlining the specific problems of selective conscientious objection).
[126] Langan (1989;100).

Addressing the Problems

As noted from the discussion regarding the right to military conscientious objection, the human rights treaties that codify the right to freedom of conscience are beginning to emerge as the basis for the right to military conscientious objection in international law. The significance of such a development for the right to selective conscientious objection is that it highlights the selective conscientious objector's assertion of a belief and the underlying desire to adhere to a particular conscientious belief. In making a claim, the selective conscientious objector is in essence manifesting a belief, be it against a particular war or due to a particular method of warfare, such as using illegal weapons, or because an action will entail the violation of a conscientious belief. Moving away from the context of military conscientious objection and considering selective conscientious objection as any other conscientious assertion allows for an analogy to other *forum externum* beliefs of the right to conscience.

By contrast, a mere whim or desire also might be the basis for the selective conscientious objector's claim. In such an instance the selective conscientious objector is not asserting any particular belief. Rather the selective conscientious objector can be understood as a free expression claim, for example as making a political statement regarding a particular war. Hence the problem with many objectors to the Vietnam War whose assertions centred on their political opinions regarding the US action overseas. Basing the selective objection on political evaluations does not necessarily lead to the assertion of a conscientious belief.

Nonetheless, almost every form of military conscientious objection raises the possibility of political argument. For example, a government can equate a military conscientious objection against all forms of warfare with a political statement against the inefficient or overabundant allocation of resources towards the military. Attempting to distinguish military conscientious objection from selective conscientious objection appears futile when considering personal variances and particular circumstances that would alter the individual's stance, such as a pacifist's willingness to defend one's family if there is an armed invasion. As noted by Greenawalt when discussing the ramifications of the US Supreme Court's decision that nullified the right to selective conscientious objection:

> The difficulty of drawing an acceptable line between general and selective objection when convictions are clear and fixed and the further difficulty imposed by the uncertainties of an estimate of one's moral response to hypothetical situations are reasons for treating objection to participation in particular wars on the same level as objection to participation in all wars.[127]

The notion of coercing an individual to violate a belief, which is one of the key basis' for the military conscientious objection, similarly operates for the selective conscientious objector being forced to perform an act in violation of the conscience.[128] Indeed, once a state provides for the right to military conscientious objection there does not seem to be any qualitative difference between a general and selective assertion of a secular objection. Both forms of objection raise the same type of administrative and practical difficulties. The military is confronted with issues of sincerity in both instances that entail similar forms of evaluation. A selective conscientious objector can be asserting a belief, such as one desiring to adhere to the just war doctrine or a set of principles or standards mandated by the international legal system.

Although the US Supreme Court rejected such contentions, the claim of unjust war and general humanist and ethical grounds served as the basis for the selective conscientious objection in *Gillette v. US*.[129] An assertion based on internal beliefs also was the ground for Israeli soldiers objecting to the Lebanon War of the early 1980s.[130] Indeed, an *ex post* psychological study of the objectors to the Israeli-Lebanese War found that their objections were based on personal moral beliefs, such as objection to the improper bombing of civilian centres, rather than due to political opposition to the military operation.[131] Such instances relate to assertions of beliefs that merit protection on a scale equivalent to any other asserted conscientious or religious belief.[132]

Furthermore, selective conscientious objection is not merely a political objection, even if the objection might revolve around political

---

[127] Greenawalt (1971;67).
[128] Capizzi (1996).
[129] *Gillette v. US* 401 US 437 (1971).
[130] See e.g. H.C. 734/83 *Shein and others v. Minister of Defence* P.D. 48(3) 393 (1984).
[131] Linn (1989;129) (author conducted psychological study of selective conscientious objectors, finding that their reasoning generally centred on moral reasoning and a common moral consistency regarding their objection to the method of Israeli warfare in Lebanon).
[132] Greenawalt (1971;54-55).

debate.¹³³ Recognising the right to freedom of conscience as protecting a person's eating habits¹³⁴ or manner of employ¹³⁵ also should provide for the protection of a person's beliefs concerning the required method or form of warfare ordered to carry out. The selective conscientious objector desires to manifest a conscientious belief; preventing the selective conscientious objector's claim can result in a violation of the belief in a manner equivalent to a military conscientious objector¹³⁶ or to other assertion of a conscientious belief.

From a more practical approach, providing for the right to selective conscientious objection can improve the administrative efficiency of a military. The military would run smoother by avoiding a loss of morale within the troops serving with a selective conscientious objection. The selective conscientious objector forces a military to confront the selective conscientious objector's reasoning and possibly to alter the improper practice, while upholding its effectiveness by winnowing out individuals who cannot conscientiously act according to military directives.¹³⁷ In a military framework, the preference would seem to be for obedient individuals. The selective conscientious objector can serve the military in another capacity rather then be forced to violate a belief system.¹³⁸ This right is in a sense easier to uphold than the in-service objector since the selective conscientious objector desires to continue in the military service despite the disagreement with the military's actions or practices. Such willingness serves to indicate that the selective conscientious objector is not making a political statement regarding the military but is acting to adhere to a particular belief system.¹³⁹

A possible reason for overlooking the selective conscientious objector's claims as a means of asserting the right to freedom of conscience is due to the narrow approach taken to such claims. Not only have courts associated selective conscientious objection claims with political assertions,¹⁴⁰ but they have narrowly interpreted military conscientious objection laws as preventing the possibility of selective conscientious

---

[133] Capizzi (1996;339); Langan (1989).
[134] 18187/91 *H v. UK* 16 EHRR CD44 (1993).
[135] *Thomas v. Review Board* 450 US 707 (1980).
[136] Capizzi (1996); Fogarty (1983).
[137] Fogarty (1983); Capizzi (1996).
[138] Langan (1989).
[139] Langan (1989).
[140] See e.g. Capizzi (1996).

objection. For example the German Court's approach to 'active military service' as being limited solely to one who objects to the entire form of service or US law being only for a complete prohibition overlook the assertion being made and are rather narrow views of military conscientious objection. The Council of Europe and ECHR Resolutions also have adopted a similar narrow approach.

Hence, the notion of a selective conscientious objection might still seem a rather odd right, particularly due to the deleterious affect the right can have on the effective operation of the military. Yet, as demonstrated in the next section, selective conscientious objection is already recognised within certain contexts, such that providing for a selective conscientious objection claim is not as administratively impossible as first imagined. This would especially seem to be the case for states that provide a general right to military conscientious objection since the legal framework exists to incorporate the right to selective conscientious objectors as well.

Current Examples of Selective Conscientious Objection

Certain religions do not necessarily preach a wholly pacifist doctrine yet the state upholds their claims to military conscientious objection. Islam recognises the eventuality of a 'holy war' yet Muslims maintain the ability to assert a military conscientious objection claim. The religious doctrine of the Jehovah's Witnesses, the consummate example of a pacifist oriented religion, requires them to raise up arms in a theocratic war or use carnal weapons in the battle of Armageddon.[141] The underlying assertion of the Jehovah's Witness is not necessarily religious objection to all forms of warfare but the objection to participating in the state apparatus. Hence their military conscientious objection is both to the military and to alternative service.[142]

Similarly, the US military granted Islamic believers the status of military conscientious objection during the Persian Gulf War because Islam prohibits the killing of a fellow Muslim.[143] US case law also has upheld military conscientious objection claims for individuals who would

---

[141] See e.g. *Sicurella v. US* 348 US 385 (1955); *Kretchet v. US* 284 F.2d 561 (9th Cir 1960).

[142] 402/1990 *Brinkhof v. Netherlands* (1993).

[143] Larsen and Hess (1992;695). But see *Petition for Naturalisation of Kassas* 788 F.Supp. 993 (M.D.Tenn. 1992) (Naturalisation denied to Muslim refusing to take oath regarding bearing arms in case he would be confronted with the problem of killing a fellow Islamic believer. The Court compared the issue to military conscientious objection, noting that selective conscientious objection is not allowed).

raise up arms to defend their family or friends if there is a foreign invasion[144] or if the objection improves society by offering a pacifist viewpoint as a counterbalance to the military.[145]

The General Assembly, relying on UDHR Article 18, passed a resolution upholding the right of individuals to object to a military that condones apartheid.[146] The indication is that these individuals did not necessarily dismiss all forms of warfare but were military conscientious objectors due to a particular belief.

The following examples of selective conscientious objection provide some of the groundwork for recognising a selective conscientious objection right. The main contention is that restricting military conscientious objection to a total objection to all warfare or all use of arms is over-broad. Such a narrow treatment of the right does not adequately consider the variety of conscientious beliefs that the international system currently protects.

Right to Asylum for Military Conscientious Objectors

Granted that the right to asylum for selective conscientious objectors is somewhat different than recognising the right to selective conscientious objection within a state's military. Nonetheless, the policy issue regarding a state's acknowledgement of an illegal action by a foreign state is in a sense even harder to consider in asylum cases. The determination of the selective conscientious objector's claim invokes a judgement regarding the actions of

---

[144] *US v. Purvis* 403 F.2d 555 (1st Cir. 1968) (objector would agree to defend US against armed attack and use force to restrain an individual from committing a wrong act but objected to participating in military service); *Goldstein v. Middendorf* 535 F.2d 1339 (1st Cir. 1976) (use of force to restrain wrongdoing, but not to use in military); *Goodrich v Marsh* 659 F. Supp. 855 (W.D. Ky. 1987) (support of use of force in civilian law enforcement work). *Cf. Rosenfeld v. Rumble* 515 F.2d 498 (1st Cir 1975) (military conscientious objector status denied after applicant admitted he would take up arms to defend himself against an invading force intent on killing members of his religion).

[145] Greenawalt (1971;53). In *Welsh v. US* 398 US 333 (1970) for example, the US Supreme Court upheld an objection based on the objector's approach to international politics and the wastefulness of military expenditures.

[146] A/33/165 (1978). *See also* discussion *infra*.

a foreign state.[147] Furthermore, it demonstrates that the selective conscientious objector's assertion can function in an administrative sense by allowing external bodies to review the merits of a selective conscientious objector's assertion. The development of the right within the asylum context further allows for a clearer definition of the right to selective conscientious objection by providing a framework within which a reviewing body can operate.

The preamble to the Commission on Human Right's 1995 Resolution refers to UDHR Article 14 and mentions the notion of granting asylum to military conscientious objectors who have fled their native land.[148] The 1998 Resolution specifically 'encourages' states to consider granting asylum to individuals who are persecuted for military conscientious objection.[149] The Commission on Human Rights deemed it a relevant issue based on the General Assembly's resolution calling for the right to asylum for military conscientious objectors against a military used to support the policy of apartheid.[150] As early as 1978, the UN General Assembly passed a declaration entitled *Status of persons refusing service in military or police forces used to enforce apartheid*[151] that recognised the right to object to participation in a military used to enforce apartheid, and called upon all UN member states to grant such individuals asylum as refugees.[152]

Another important source demonstrating the association between refugee law and selective conscientious objection is the 1979 *United Nations High Commissioner on Refugees Handbook on Procedures and Criteria for Determining Refugee Status*. Following the establishment of the High Commissioner by the General Assembly in 1950,[153] one of the key duties of the High Commissioner was to interpret the Protocol Relating to

---

[147] See e.g. *MA v. INS* 899 F.2d 304 (4th Cir 1990) (court hinted that asylum issues involving selective conscientious objectors could be approached as a non-justiciable foreign policy issue).

[148] See e.g. Resolution 1995/83.

[149] E/CN.4/RES/1998/77 at paragraph 7. The Resolution can be understood as limiting the capacity to request asylum since it applies where there is 'no adequate provision' for conscientious objectors. This narrows the claim for objectors presumably to the standards provided for in the Resolution.

[150] Wolff (1982;79).

[151] A/33/165 (1978).

[152] A year later, UN General Assembly Resolution A/34/93 (1979) called on individuals to refrain from enlisting in the South African armed forces. The 1983 Commission on Human Rights Report also had discussed the right to asylum for military conscientious objectors, noting that although granting asylum is really a matter of domestic law, UDHR Article 14 requires the granting of asylum to military conscientious objectors forced to desert the military. CHR Reporters at 26.

[153] Doc/A/1252, UN General Assembly Resolution 319A.

the Status of Refugees.¹⁵⁴ The project emanated from the requests of UN member states desiring guidance for determining refugee status.¹⁵⁵ The Handbook therefore is one of the central products of the Office of the High Commissioner. It has served as a seminal means of clarifying the extents of the rights of refugees,¹⁵⁶ as recognised in domestic jurisdictions.¹⁵⁷

Concerning the right to asylum for military conscientious objectors, the Handbook notes that a 'well-founded fear of persecution', the key determinant for receiving asylum protection, does not arise for an individual who has evaded conscription or deserted the military.¹⁵⁸ Rather, what is essential is that one evading the military would suffer disproportionate punishment because of one's race, religion, nationality, membership in a group, or political opinion.¹⁵⁹ Such a disproportionate punishment would arise for the military conscientious objector who refuses military service based on a specific belief. The Handbook bases such beliefs on religious grounds¹⁶⁰ and the developing right for secular-based military conscientious objectors.¹⁶¹

It is possible that the secular-based military conscientious objection has a higher burden of proof as it is more difficult to prove one's secular beliefs in a foreign court. The religious military conscientious objection can more readily acquire proof from a local minister or fellow congregant. Yet domestic legal systems recognise a secular-based military conscientious objection, which possibly acquired greater acceptance since the drafting of the Handbook in 1979. This is particularly the case when

---

¹⁵⁴   606 UNTS 267 (1967) *see* in particular article II(1).
¹⁵⁵   See preamble to the Handbook at paragraph iv.
¹⁵⁶   *Cf.* Goodwin-Gill (1996;fn.91) noting inherent ambiguities in the Handbook.
¹⁵⁷   See e.g. *INS v. Cardoza-Fonseca* 480 US 421 (1987) noting, at fn. 22 the significance of the Handbook in interpreting the limits of the Protocol; *M.A v. INS* 899 F.2d 304 (4th Cir. 1990) (Department of Justice acknowledged that Handbook is key source and that Congress was aware of criteria stated therein when drafting the 1980 Refugee Act); *Canas-Segovia v. INS* 902 F.2d 717 (9th Cir. 1990) (Handbook as an authoritative source). *Cf. Budgaycay v. Sect. of State* (1987) 1 AllER 940 (refugee denied asylum following illegal entry to country, despite contrary statement in Handbook).
¹⁵⁸   Handbook at paragraphs 167-168.
¹⁵⁹   Handbook at paragraph 169.
¹⁶⁰   Paragraph 172.
¹⁶¹   Paragraph 173.

considering the various resolutions and recommendations discussed *supra* that were passed in the 1980s and 1990s.[162]

What is significant about the Handbook is the provision regarding selective conscientious objection. The Handbook grants asylum status to an individual required to participate in military actions contrary to one's political, religious, or moral beliefs, or for 'valid reasons of conscience'.[163] Courts have interpreted this provision as protecting military conscientious objectors who conscientiously object to particular actions of the military. Hence a country should grant asylum to a soldier facing a court martial due to a refusal to participate in the random killing of civilians.[164] The objection need not be to the military in its entirety, but to specific actions committed therein.

The Handbook further grants refugee status to a soldier who has a reasonable probability of being involved in military actions condemned by the international community.[165] This proviso provides a means of narrowing the right of selective conscientious objectors seeking asylum, specifically when the objection centres on a difference of political opinion.[166] It is different if a military is violating humanitarian norms or human rights principles. Then a military conscientious objector would seem to have the right to seek asylum.[167] Condemnation by the international community however invokes different forms of considerations. The prime example of this sort of objection would be soldiers refusing to participate in the South African military due to their potential involvement in upholding the apartheid state.[168] The key indication of condemnation by the international community in this regard is the 1978 General Assembly Resolution 33/165. As noted *supra*, the Resolution recognised the right to asylum for refusing to participate in military or police forces enforcing apartheid.[169]

Some states also reflect the approach adopted by the Handbook. Courts in the US for example have granted asylum protection for

---

[162] The right to military conscientious objection based on political opinion, which can raise unique evidentiary problems, might be limited to actions condemned by the international community. Handbook at paragraph 171; Musalo (1989).
[163] Handbook at paragraph 170. The approach presents an interesting contrast to the CHR's resolutions.
[164] *See e.g. Barraza Rivera v. INS* 913 F.2d 1443 (9th Cir 1990).
[165] Handbook at paragraph 171.
[166] Musalo (1989).
[167] Kuzas (1991).
[168] Kuzas (1991;469).
[169] Doc A/33/45 (1978).

individuals who experience persecution due to their beliefs,[170] such as refusing to commit illegal acts like shooting army deserters.[171] Australia also adheres to the standards of the Handbook in granting asylum for pacifists or religious believers.[172] In the UK, persecution of the asylum seeker must result from a military conscientious objection based on a belief rather then opinion.[173] Sweden maintains a vestigial law from the Vietnam War that grants resident permits to selective conscientious objectors. The permit holders are not granted asylum per se, but they are granted the right to reside in the country.

Direction for the Selective Conscientious Objector

The asylum claim provides an operative context for selective conscientious objection within a domestic system. An important development for the asylum seeker is that the objection encompassed conflicts associated with the policy of the military as well as the conduct of the military.[174] In determining the relevance of an asylum-seeker's selective conscientious objection claim, the key focus has been the reproach of the international community towards the military action, evidenced by development of international norms in both human rights and humanitarian laws,[175] specific condemnations by regional and international bodies,[176] and the willingness of the state in question to address the problematic issues.

Although the asylum seeker's objection is linked to specific international norms that serve as a basis for the objection, the asylum seeker demonstrates two important aspects regarding selective objection. The grounds for the selective conscientious objector's claims are determinable without necessarily making a judgement regarding a foreign state's particular actions. Similarly, a determination regarding a selective conscientious objector in the domestic context need not entail a judgement

---

[170] *Abedini v. INS* 971 F.2d 188 (9th Cir. 1992).
[171] *Ramos-Vasquez v. INS* 57 F.3rd 857 (9th Cir. 1995).
[172] *Refugee Review Tribunal* V94/01589, 6/3/95 [Lexis].
[173] See e.g. *Borrisov v. Secretary of State for the Home Department* Ct. of Appeals (Civ. Div.) 20/3/96.
[174] Kuzas (1991;fn.84) referring to a letter from Gilbert Jaeger, one of the authors of the Handbook stating that 'type' of military action included the underlying policy motivating the military, as well as the actual conduct of the military.
[175] Musalo (1989;fn.26).
[176] Kuzas (1991).

as to the merits of a state's policy or conduct. Furthermore, the focus for an asylum seeker is on an individual's understanding of the state's action and whether persecution will result due to an individual's beliefs.[177] The determination should focus on whether a violation of the individual's belief system occurs as a result of specific action. One may account for external standards within the context of the selective conscientious objector's assertion to buttress the claim and not as a judgement of the military's conduct. In a sense this determination could assist to separate politically oriented selective conscientious objectors, where the burden of proof concerning international condemnation is higher, from conscientiously based selective conscientious objectors, where the proof will centre on the individual's belief and other positive international norms.

Objection to Nuclear Weapons

A further example demonstrating the possibility of the right to selective conscientious objection is the objection to a military's reliance on nuclear weapons. In Germany, objection to the use of nuclear weapons is grounds for upholding a military conscientious objection claim. Similarly, Norway recognises an objection to the use of weapons of 'mass destruction'.[178] The US generally transfers such objectors from units dealing with nuclear weapons,[179] thereby avoiding any official acknowledgement of the claim. One also may infer such an ad-hoc approach from the Netherlands' treatment of selective conscientious objectors to any association with nuclear weapons. In the HRC opinion *Brinkhof v. Netherlands*,[180] the applicant based his military conscientious objection claim on his participation in preparing for the use of nuclear weapons. The Netherlands implicitly recognised such a form of objection since the case centred on whether Brinkhof has the right to object to alternative military service.

The underlying problem with the nuclear weapons objection is that the objection generally centres on the illegality of such weapons in the international framework[181] yet there is no final resolution regarding the

---

[177] Goodwin-Gill (1996;59) noting the importance attached to an individual's conscientious belief. *See e.g. Abedinni v. INS* 971 F.2d 188 (9th Cir. 1992) where the court notes that it is the subjective perception that counts.
[178] *See* Norway's 1992 Report to HRC CCPR/C/70/Add.2.
[179] McGrath (1985).
[180] 402/1990 *Brinkhof v. Netherlands* (1993).
[181] In 402/1990 *Brinkhof v. Netherlands* (1993) for example, he asserted that nuclear weapons are a crime against the peace and a form of genocide. *Cf.* 509/1992 *ARU v. Netherlands* CCPR/C/49/D/609/1992 where the Dutch court had directed the selective conscientious objector to nuclear weapons to apply for military conscientious

legality of nuclear weapons. The HRC's Second General Comment to ICCPR Article 6 refers to the dangers of nuclear weapons, as do various General Assembly Resolutions. Yet nuclear states, such as the US, recognise the possibility of a limited, defensive, use of nuclear weapons.[182] Even states contending that nuclear weapons are illegal note the possibility that some form of limited use for such weapons might develop.[183] The International Court of Justice also acknowledged the possible use of nuclear weapons if the survival of the state is at risk.[184]

The consequence of the 1996 International Court of Justice Advisory Opinion regarding nuclear weapons is that the ICJ did not find any operative law prohibiting nuclear weapons as such. The ICJ tended to treat human rights law[185] as a secondary source for developing an international law violation to the use of nuclear weapons. Furthermore, a human rights basis, while relevant, tended to focus on humanitarian law principles of *jus in bello*.[186] The ICJ's decision however centred on humanitarian law principles of *jus ad bellum* that might provide for the possibility of using nuclear weapons in certain instances, such as when the survival of the state is at risk.

The significance of the ICJ's decision for the selective conscientious objector is the possibility of asserting the right to object to a military that, on a policy level, relies on such weapons to carry out military directives. The International Court of Justice focused on recognising a limited use of nuclear weapons, and even that part of the decision was subject to strong dissent. Coupled with the acceptance of an objection to nuclear weapons as a basis for a military conscientious objection claim in a variety of states, it is possible that a form of selective conscientious objection can arise for individuals objecting to the use of nuclear weapons.

---

objection status. The HRC subsequently dismissed the claim for failing to substantiate an Article 18 violation considering complainant's ability to undergo alternative service.

[182] McGrath (1985) The policy is called Counterforce, where the weapons would be used in non-civilian areas using low levels of radiation.

[183] The memorials to the ICJ regarding the General Assembly's Advisory Opinion request referred to the possible use of nuclear micro weapons.

[184] *Advisory Opinion on the Legality of the Threat or Use of Nuclear Weapons*, July 8, 1996, in 35 ILM 809 (1996).

[185] As well as environmental law.

[186] Hence there was some significance to the ICJ's reference to human rights as upholding human rights in warfare. Akande (1998;173).

One may glean from the aforementioned examples of selective conscientious objection that the objection is possible to administrate. Nevertheless, the aforementioned instances of selective conscientious objection pertained to situations where the objector essentially relied on predetermined normative standards, such as violations of humanitarian norms or legislative provisions regarding the use of nuclear weapons. Hence while the ability for some form of selective conscientious objection is recognised, it is in a limited format and not based on the deference towards an individual's conscientious belief.

Upon considering the basis for military conscientious objection as recognised by international fora, the ability to rely on the right to freedom of conscience, and therefore manifest one's conscientious belief, should equally apply to the selective conscientious objector. An objector to involvement with nuclear weapons, or whose conscientious belief prevents the destruction of the environment, should maintain the ability to manifest such beliefs. Included in such a manifestation would be the selective conscientious objection to carry out actions that are contrary to a belief. The individual has made a determination regarding what is deemed important and central to one's existence, such as not being involved with nuclear weapons, that mandates the inability to conduct certain actions. The conscientious belief reflects an inherent qualitative discrimination for the individual objector such that even if the objection is not necessarily to the military or even to the use of arms, the action being called upon to perform would lead to a violation of a conscientious belief. Considering that the importance of a conscientious belief is not merely its existence but also its application to specific instances, the application also should entail instances of selective conscientious objection. Along with the reliance on the right to freedom of conscience as a basis for the military conscientious objector comes the entire package associated with the right to conscience. That would include not only beliefs that are wholly opposed to using firearms or force, but also other individual conscientious beliefs that prevent the individual from participating in various military actions. The evaluation should not solely be the effects of the objection on the military but rather that the demanded actions entail a violation of a conscientious belief. That is in essence the basis for the right to military conscientious objection and seems equally to apply to selective conscientious objection.

Conclusion

Considering the importance of a viable international legal system, one must be wary of indiscriminately labelling a norm as encompassing customary law. This proviso certainly applies to the human rights context. The instinctual reaction is to attempt to develop as many rights as possible within the customary law umbrella. The hesitation arises however to allow for an adequate foundation of rights in the long term by not attempting to weaken the legal framework of the system.[187]

As noted at the outset, many commentators have labelled the right to military conscientious objection as a customary international norm. In principle, they might be correct. The right generally exists in state practice and there certainly seems to be an understated intention by the states to develop and expand the right. *Opinio juris* is implied from the resolutions of international and regional bodies and, most importantly, the treaties upholding the right to freedom of conscience are beginning to serve as a basis for a military conscientious objection right.

On a practical level, universal acceptance appears for certain aspects of the right. These would include, pursuant to the CHR's Resolutions, the recognition of a conscientious along with religious basis for the objection, a right to alternative service, due process in examining the military conscientious objection claim and allowing for an appeal, and possibly in-service objections.

Other forms of the right, such as selective conscientious objection, clearly are not customary law. Yet, with the development of military conscientious objection as deriving from the right to freedom of conscience, it is possible to recognise the emergence of selective conscientious objection especially since some states recognise the right, and the objection applies in other contexts.

On a broader level, the evolution of military conscientious objection as a customary right provides further impetus to clarifying the right to freedom of conscience. According military conscientious objection the status of a right raises the prospect of deriving other analogous forms of conscientious objection from the principal treaties that codify manifestation of a conscientious belief. Resolutions of international bodies indicate this derivation as does the *travaux preparatoires* of the General

---

[187] *See e.g.* Weil (1983).

Comment to Article 18. Although the General Comment focused on military conscientious objection to entrench the right within Article 18, the HRC noted that manifestation is to include a host of beliefs.[188] The right to military conscientious objection is in essence an example of the manner in which such beliefs can manifest.

While the international human rights system has begun to codify the right to military conscientious objection, additional forms of manifestation of one's conscientious beliefs have not been developed. The implication is that the international human rights system is providing for protection of the manifestation of a variety of conscientious beliefs comparable to military conscientious objection that merit manifestation. The next chapter will consider an additional form of manifestation with an analysis of the right to conscientious objection to taxes.

---

[188] *See* CCPR/C/SR.1237 for why the HRC focused specifically on the right to military conscientious objection in paragraph 11 of the General Comment.

7 Conscientious Objection to Taxes

Introduction

One of the key problems associated with assertions of a conscientious belief is the prospect that the belief will eclipse state directives and the rule of law. Such a development of course raises the questions mentioned when discussing the *forum externum* aspect of the right to freedom of conscience,[1] namely what is the scope to the manifestation of a conscientious belief and how can it be provided for in a legal system? Does an individual maintain the right to assert any conscientious belief as grounds for disregarding a particular state law?

Similar to military conscientious objection, the common factor among other possible manifestations of a conscientious belief is that the state is requiring action from the objector that would entail violation of a particular conscientious belief. Although the breadth of objection will be considerably narrower than the more developed right to military conscientious objection, referring to other forms of conscientious objection can begin to provide a framework for understanding the implication and scope for the manifestation of a conscientious belief. One example of conscientious objection considered in this chapter is the right to object to the payment of certain taxes.

Tax Objection

Equating the payment of a tax with the manifestation of a conscientious belief might initially seem to stretch the understanding of 'manifestation'. This is particularly so upon considering judicial decisions that limit the

---

[1] *See* discussion *supra* at Chapter Five.

manifestation of a belief to the actual 'practice' demanded from a conscientious belief. Making a tax payment does not appear to violate any practice, save for a belief that precludes a person from actually making a tax payment,[2] a position that would not seem to warrant manifestation due to the treaty limitations imposed on the right. Fundamentally, the objection does not seem to be based on any particular conflict entailing the manifestation of a conscientious belief.

Comparing a tax objection to a military conscientious objection claim can clarify how the objection manifests from a conscientious belief. Individuals assert the right to conscientiously object to a variety of tax payments because the tax is supporting state activity that violates one's religious or conscientious beliefs. The fiscal support provided to the state for activity that violates one's conscientious belief is, for the conscientious objector, comparable to physically conducting the action.[3]

Such a contention has some merit concerning the payment of taxes. States instituted certain taxes to provide governmental services where the individual could not perform them due to the public nature of the task, the scale of work involved, or the difficulty in creating satisfactory boundaries between individuals. In certain instances, paying tax is akin to engaging in an agency agreement with the government to carry out the task in one's stead. Hence, an 'actual practice' mandated by the belief can possibly prevent a variety of tax payments that are made in support of actions conflicting with the belief. The participation for the tax objector is broadened to include any form of support that would lead to a violation of a belief. The proviso is that the tax payment is a clear infringement upon an individual's conscientious belief.

For example, the military tax objector is conscientiously opposed to supporting the military both in a physical sense, by participating in military operations, or by being required fiscally to support the military. In the

---

[2] Such forms of objections are routinely rejected as the court refers the objector to the legislature to make an internal change. *Crowe v. CIR* 396 F.2d 766 (8th Cir. 1968) (objection to paying federal, as opposed to state, taxes as well as objection to welfare taxes); Lyall (1992;Fn.27) referring to fundamental opposition to poll tax payments in Scotland.

[3] Note that in many instances, commentators tend to commingle conscientious objectors with other forms of objection that are not necessarily based on a conscientious belief but derive from a desire to alter the values of society. *See e.g.* Kornhauser (1999;944) (leaning towards a political objection by focusing on the motives of tax objectors, such as to include individuals desiring to improve the state through peaceful means by limiting military expenditures. The author does distinguish war tax objection from other forms of conscientious objection, at 1015, by noting that the basis for tax objection is that one's beliefs are infringed due to the payment of the tax).

words of one military tax objector, 'If I were to say to you - I will not kill my neighbour but I will pay for someone else to do it - would you not question my integrity?'[4] For the tax objector, the action of physical participation or fiscal support results in the individual acting contrary to a conscientious belief. By contrast making a payment that would in some manner limit an individual's fiscal ability to practise a belief is not necessarily an infringement of the right. Hence, mandating the payment of maintenance payments that in turn might prevent the payee from attending religious services due to a shortage of funds does not translate into an infringement of one's right to manifest a belief.[5] Rather, the two incidents are sufficiently separated such that the action of making the maintenance payment does not entail any violation of the belief,[6] unlike the military tax objector where the payment itself is equivalent to conducting an action that directly violates a conscientious belief.

Despite the possibility that manifestation of a belief can prevent the making of payments to support contrary activity, in practice it is quite a limited form of manifestation. States are understandably hesitant in recognising this form of manifestation. The basic arguments against tax objection are divided into an examination of the internal beliefs mandating a tax objection, and an understanding of the external ramifications of not paying taxes. Internally, the problem generally is that there is no nexus between the tax objector's beliefs and the tax being paid. An objector has a difficult time demonstrating a violation of a belief by conducting a neutral activity such as paying taxes into a state's general budget fund. The revenue will go to support a host of state action, especially since it is indeterminable whether the objector's taxes are used to support an activity that violates the objector's belief. According to this reasoning, there is no assertion of any right to conscience since there is no infringement occurring to one's practice of a conscientious belief.

On an external level, the key problems derive from the legislature's determination that taxes are an important administrative necessity, particularly because they go to the very core of the state's prosperity and

---

[4] DiSalvo (1982;507 fn.60) quoting a pacifist's characterisation of tax objection from Durland, W. (ed.) (1980), *People Pay for Peace*.
[5] 24875/94 *Logan v. UK* 1 EHRLR 83 (1997).
[6] Save for instances whereby one's religion precludes such payments. The limitations to the right would again play a role, principally on the grounds of public policy.

existence.⁷ Furthermore, objecting to taxes creates an undue administrative and fiscal burden on the functioning of the system that cannot be justified because it might burden an individual's belief. The 'slippery slope' problem also is raised since upholding one form of tax objection opens the door to additional objections against funding programmes contrary to one's belief. This apprehension compounds the administrative problems that the tax objector raises due to the threat to the viability of the tax system.⁸

Note however that the external reasons for limiting the tax objector's claim, while acknowledging the existence of a right to conscience, do not appear to fall within the limitation standards established by the treaties codifying the right to freedom of conscience. The right to conscience is subject to very specific and focused limitations that do not necessarily incorporate administrative burdens. It is one thing for the state to supersede a belief against paying a tax supporting a no-fault car insurance policy.⁹ The policy could relate to a 'public safety' interest in protecting third parties injured in an accident with the tax objector. However to limit an assertion because of administrative reasons that are not based on any specific treaty limitation, such as an undue fiscal burden on the system, appears to extend the limitation beyond the scope of the treaty. Limitations in the interest of the public safety, order, health or morals do not seem to limit the right to tax objection, nor does the administrative necessity of the tax system appear to be a recognised limitation under any treaty.

In general, domestic judicial decisions involving tax objection direct the objector to the legislature as the proper forum within which to raise the issue of objection. A possible reason for this is that legislatures condone certain forms of tax objection through specific legislative action, thereby removing the burden from the judiciary. A state might exempt a tax objector from paying a tax that is contrary to a particular belief. The significance of such legal exemptions is that they demonstrate the possibility for instituting some form of tax objection system. The methods relied upon by legislatures in granting an objection can clarify possibilities for addressing other forms of tax objections in a manner that will avoid the administrative and fiscal burdens imposed on the state.

---

[7] Kornhauser (1999;963) referring to *Swaggart v. Board of Equalisation* 493 US 378 (1990) and *Hernandez v. Commissioner* 490 US 680(1988).
[8] See e.g. *US v. Lee* 455 US 252 (1982) at 260.
[9] 2988/66 *X v. Netherlands* 10 Ybk. Eur. H.R. 472 (1967).

Church Tax

The Church Tax is a method of taxation that requires all individuals to pay a certain amount to support the state church. Non-believers or individuals objecting to the payment of the tax on conscientious grounds are exempt from paying that portion of the tax used to support the religious activities of the church. Where however a state uses some portion of the tax to subsidise a church's non-religious activities that benefit the public, such as keeping birth records or taking a population census, the objector must pay that particular percentage of taxes as determined by the state.

In Switzerland for example, the state subsidises official state churches and they retain the ability to raise taxes. Non-believers and individuals of other faiths are exempt from paying the taxes used to fund the worship activities of the official local church pursuant to Article 49(6) of the Constitution. Oddly enough however the deduction does not apply to the share of general tax allocated to a canton's principal church, even if the funds are being used to support worship within such a church.[10]

In Iceland, the national church[11] receives direct support from the state. Individuals who are not members of a particular religious organisation are exempt from paying the tax.[12] The state gives part of an objector's taxes to the University of Iceland rather then the state church.[13] Note however that the imposition of the tax might have changed following Iceland's move away from a theo-centric constitutional model to one that recognises individual personal convictions as well.[14]

By contrast, in Finland, an individual generally cannot object to the imposed church tax. The state's reasoning is that the tax does not support any worship or church religious practices. Rather, the state imposes the tax to subsidise the Church's task of updating the personal register.[15] Note however that the religious authorities also use the tax to maintain church buildings.[16]

---

[10] 1995 Switzerland report to the HRC, CCPR/C/81/Add.8.
[11] Evangelical Lutheran.
[12] 1993 Iceland report to the HRC, CCPR/C/46/Add.5.
[13] Why Iceland requires funds to the University rather then a complete exemption was not clarified following a request by the HRC. See A/38/40 (1983).
[14] 1996 State Report of Iceland to HRC, CCPR/C/94/Add.2.
[15] 1979 Finland state report to HRC A/34/40.
[16] Finland did not address this point in its state report to the HRC.

Additionally, a Finnish 1994 Supreme Administrative Court decision upheld the imposition of the church tax on corporations whose members objected to the tax on conscientious grounds. The decision applied even if the partners composing the corporation were not members of the state church.[17] This decision was challenged before the ECHR Commission who deemed the complaint inadmissible. The Commission held that the applicant company, which was a limited liability corporation established for commercial purposes, was responsible for the tax payment and not the individual members raising the challenge.[18]

The Indian Courts use similar reasoning by focusing on the purpose for which the taxes are collected. The Courts do not deem funds as a religious 'tax' where the funds are used for educational purposes[19] or to ensure for improved secular administration or governance of religious trusts.[20] For example, the state had created a Distress Relief Fund to rebuild Hindu and Muslim temples that had been destroyed following local disturbances. The challenge to the use of funds in this manner was rejected since the purpose was not to support the religion, but to restore and repair the temples.[21]

The laws of some states that uphold the refusal to pay a particular tax are significant. They demonstrate that the dismissal of a tax objector's claims because of administrative necessity need not be universally applicable. It is possible to institute adequate and efficient schemes that address the beliefs of the tax objector without hampering the collection process. The ECHR hinted at such an approach in a case where it upheld a tax objection. In *Darby v. Sweden*,[22] the applicant objected to paying a church tax since he was not a member of the church nor was he even a resident in the state. The Court held that because the state granted an exemption for resident non-believers of a certain percentage of the church tax, it was discriminatory to deny the same to a non-resident with similar beliefs. While the Court decided the case on ECHR Article 14 grounds regarding discrimination between residents and non-residents, the Court

---

[17] 1994 State Report of Finland to HRC, CCPR/C/95/Add.6. Cf. 17522/90 *Ortega v. Spain* 72 D&R 256 (1992) where the ECHR Commission rejected an application by the Protestant Church to be accorded equal treatment to the Catholic Church, specifically regarding its granted tax exemptions.

[18] 20471/92 *Sundstrom v. Finland* VII (7) H.R. Case Digest 636 (1996).

[19] See e.g. *Khatun v. State* AIR 1981 Cal. 302; *Ahmed v. State* AIR 1976 Cal. 142.

[20] *Jagamath v. State* AIR 1954 SC 400.

[21] *Raghunath v. State* (1974) A.Ker. 48. Note that the Court also distinguished between fees and taxes, as the latter cannot support a religious institution pursuant to Article 27 of the Constitution.

[22] 11581/85 *Darby v. Sweden* 13 EHRR 774.

did not refer to the administrative or fiscal burdens that such an objection can raise.

Public Support Schemes

Many minority religions or beliefs object to the notion of participating in any form of public support. Although a state might recognise some objections, states deny the majority of challenges due to administrative and fiscal reasons. For example, the ECHR Commission dismissed a challenge to a pension programme tax in the Netherlands[23] because it held that tax revenues are placed in a central fund and are then transferred to the relevant receiving agency. The tax objector's money does not necessarily flow to the public support schemes.

An additional ECHR case centred on a compulsory auto insurance scheme that provided for an alternative tax to those religiously and conscientiously opposed to the requirement.[24] The Commission rejected the challenge to the alternative tax due to the limitations stated in ECHR Article 9(2). The legislature did not impose an alternative tax to provide public insurance for the tax objector but to protect third parties who might be involved in an accident with such believers. The need to protect the 'public safety' therefore served as the basis for the tax scheme. While the reliance on public safety for a no-fault insurance scheme is somewhat tenuous, the decisions reflect the deference accorded to states in instituting specific tax regimes for collecting revenue.

Turning to the right to claim a tax exemption from public support schemes, states generally deny individual challenges when based on personal or political reasons, such as a personal distaste for welfare recipients.[25] Nevertheless, some states provide for certain forms of tax objection. For example, in the US, public insurance scheme taxes are not paid on any funds received for services performed on behalf of a religious order objecting to public insurance.[26] Furthermore, a self-employed individual whose religious order conscientiously opposes insurance schemes may obtain an exemption. The criteria are that the objection

---

[23] *Reformed Church of X v. Netherlands* 5 Ybk 286 (1962).
[24] 2988/66 *X v. Netherlands* 10 Ybk 472.
[25] *Crowe v. CIR* 396 F.2d 766 (8th Cir. 1968).
[26] 26 USC section 1402(e)(1).

emanates from established tenets or teachings of the belief and the belief system provides alternative provisions for its dependent members.[27]

The problem with these allowances is that they tend to be unduly limiting and subjective. In particular the law granting an exemption for self employment tax protects only certain religions. A narrow interpretation of the law has excluded belief systems opposed to insurance schemes who do not have any formally instituted programme of support for their dependent members due to their internal belief,[28] or individuals who conscientiously cannot contribute to public programmes such as social security.[29] The courts reason that the US Congress provided for specific, limited, objections to tax only in instances where other forms of support were available to replace public assistance like unemployment or social security. Note however that the US law only provides an exemption for the self employed. Hence a Church doctrinally opposed to public insurance must pay the tax for hired employees,[30] even when the employees are also members of the Church.[31]

The more general reasoning for disallowing public support scheme tax objectors is best summed up in a 1982 US Supreme Court case, *US v. Lee*.[32] In *Lee*, Amish employers objected to paying Social Security tax for their Amish employees. The Supreme Court held that the law did not provide for an objection, it was a minor interference with a religious belief outweighed by the administrative and fiscal necessity of upholding the tax system,[33] and objection would encourage other forms of tax objection. Significantly, the Court distinguished prior accommodation cases involving unemployment compensation for those individuals refusing employment on their Sabbath[34] since unemployment is a *receipt* of a necessary benefit.[35] The Court held that receipt of a benefit differed from making a payment to a general fund, especially since the objectors can refuse receipt of social security when they reach the eligible age limit. Unemployment insurance

---

[27] 26 USC section 1402(g)(1)(A)-(E).
[28] See e.g. *Henson v. CIR* 66 TC 835 (1976) (Sari Baba Society, who believe that God will provide all their needs).
[29] *Droz v. CIR* 48 F.3rd 1120 (9th Cir. 1995); *Jaggard v. CIR* 582 F.2d 1189 (1978); *Palmer v. CIR* 52 TC 310 (1969) (Seventh Day Adventist objected to social security tax, even though it was not part of formal church doctrine).
[30] *South Ridge Baptist Church v. Industrial Commission* 911 F.2d 1203 (6th Cir 1990).
[31] *Bethel Baptist Church v. US* 822 F.2d 1334 (3rd Cir. 1987).
[32] *US v. Lee* 455 US 252 (1982).
[33] This is the same reasoning used to find no violation of the Establishment Clause. See e.g. *Bethel Baptist Church v. US* 822 F.2d 1334 (3rd Cir. 1987).
[34] See e.g. *Sherbert v. Verner* 374 US 398 (1963).
[35] Stevens, concurrence, at fn.3, referring to *Thomas v. Review Board* 450 US 707 (1981).

however is a necessity that should not be denied to an individual compelled to adhere to the specific practices of a belief.

The fiscal and administrative viability of the tax system, and the prevention of additional tax objection claims, has served as the central reasoning in cases involving tax objectors not only in the US,[36] but in other domestic jurisdictions including Australia,[37] the UK,[38] Canada,[39] and India.[40] The key limiting factor is that if the legislature has not provided a specific exemption for the objector, the assertion of the belief will be denied.

Relying on legislative action for the right to tax objection demonstrates a rather narrow approach to the understanding of a conscientious belief. As noted by Dignan:

> Forcing a man to act in contradiction to his conscience does constitute a denial of equal concern and respect which is not assuaged by allowing him to protest about it freely.[41]

Furthermore, because the right to object is a legislative grant, there is no established right to rely on one's conscientious belief.[42] The problem is similar to that of military conscientious objection when it is deemed a legislative grace rather then a right deriving from the assertion of a belief[43] since the legislature essentially ignores the less-established or formalised beliefs.

Tax administration also is not an insurmountable predicament, particularly since the state provides for specific exemptions. Indeed, the

---

[36] See e.g. Ballinger v. CIR 728 F.2d 1287 (10th Cir. 1984).
[37] Burrowers v. Deputy Commissioner of Taxation 91 ATC 5021 (1991) (military tax objection).
[38] Oxley v. Raunham 54 Tax Cas. 779 (1983) (objection to paying income tax because conscientiously opposed to governmental policies).
[39] Prior v. Queen (1988) 2 C.F. 371 (military tax objection).
[40] Ananthakaishman v. Madra AIR 1952 Madras 395 (power to tax is absolute right such that administration fee for attorney, even if not beneficial to public, can supersede right to freedom of profession).
[41] Dignan (1983;25).
[42] See e.g. Muste v. CIR 35 TC 913 (1961) where the US tax court denied plaintiff's analogy between military tax objection and military conscientious objection, discussed infra. The Court held that military conscientious objection derives from a legislative grace and is not a matter of right.
[43] See discussion supra at Chapter Six.

argument of administrative efficiency was a key basis for the military's protest against the right to military conscientious objection at the turn of the century. However as demonstrated by the church tax objection, a legislature can uphold some measure of tax objections in an administratively efficient manner. A number of countries even have proposed the establishment of an alternative Peace Tax in place of military taxes such that conscientious objectors to the military tax can have their military taxes paid to a neutral fund that will be used for non-militaristic activity.[44]

While deriving a tax objection from the right to freedom of conscience will encompass all forms of objectors, the possible development of a plethora of other forms of tax objection is still a problem. One can refer to a conscientious 'belief' to refuse to pay a specific tax, thereby wreaking havoc on the tax system. Individuals faced with the choice would desire to uphold their conscientious beliefs by withholding tax payments that support various governmental programmes. A right to lifer might not desire to support tax payments for abortion centres, prisons that rely on the death penalty or schools that dispense contraceptives to its students. The danger is that the possibilities truly are endless such that even if the right to freedom of conscience served as the basis for the objection, the state would still be confronted with endless forms of objections.

States raised such a contention when considering the right to military conscientious objection and the possible effect it would have on recruitment. The concern centred on a similar issue - how to provide for the proper manifestation of conscientious beliefs? The next section shall address this 'slippery slope' problem when considering the possibility of a military tax objection.

Objection to Military Tax

Manifesting a military tax objection is rather similar to military conscientious objection; both harbour a belief regarding the military that imposes breaking off any link to the military. The stark reality regarding the taking of a life presented by service in the military is equally present for the military tax objector since each instance presents some form of participation or connection with the military that is contrary to their

---

[44] *See* US - 140 Cong. Rec. S4464, 103rd Cong, 2nd Sess., 11/4/94; 104 HR 1402, 104 Cong., 1st Sess., 5/4/95 and Kornhauser (1999); Italy - Larricia (1992;140) referring to a 1989 Bill; The Netherlands - Vermeulen (1992;268) regarding a 1988-89 Bill.

beliefs.⁴⁵ Providing support for the state to conduct an action that is contrary to a belief is comparable to paying a church tax to support another religion. The result is that in each instance, the objector is either being compelled to conduct an action, through the payment of taxes, that is contrary to a belief or is prevented from manifesting a belief due to the tax requirement that prevents or hinders the manifestation.

Assertions of military tax objection have been raised in a number of international and domestic judicial tribunals and generally are denied. In *JP v. Canada*,⁴⁶ a Quaker desired to place his percentage of military tax into a peace fund account. The HRC held that 'while the Covenant certainly protects the right to hold, express, and disseminate opinions and convictions, including conscientious objection to military activities and expenditures, the refusal to pay taxes on grounds of conscience' is outside the scope of the article. Similarly, in *JVK v. Netherlands*,⁴⁷ the HRC denied the right of a nuclear weapons protester to place his military taxes into a peace fund since conscientious objection to taxes is outside the scope of ICCPR Article 18.

The approach adopted by the HRC is arguable considering their 1993 General Comment to Article 18 and recent developments regarding military conscientious objection.⁴⁸ Furthermore, in discussing the inclusion of a specific paragraph on the right to military conscientious objection in the General Comment,⁴⁹ the HRC noted in the paragraph addressing limitations to the right that other forms of manifesting a belief should not be overlooked.⁵⁰ Additionally, if the right to manifest a belief includes some form of military tax objection, the possible limitations to the right might not apply, especially when the objector desires to pay the money into a neutral peace fund.⁵¹

Interpretation of the ECHR has met with somewhat more defined analysis that reflects the reasoning adopted by judicial bodies confronted with tax objection. In 1983, the Commission denied the claims of a pacifist

---

⁴⁵ Kornhauser (1999;1009) noting the unique position of the military tax objector.
⁴⁶ 446/1991 *JP v. Canada* (1992).
⁴⁷ 483/1991 *JVK v. Netherlands* (1992).
⁴⁸ *See* discussion *supra* at Chapter Six.
⁴⁹ Paragraph 11 of the General Comment.
⁵⁰ Paragraph 8 of the General Comment. But see 568/1993 *KV and CV v. Germany* CCPR/C/50/D/568/1993 where the HRC dismissed a complaint similar to the *JVK v. Netherlands* case, one of the reasons being that it had already decided the issue.
⁵¹ Kornhauser (1999).

who refused to pay taxes that were used to support the military.[52] The Commission held that one does not possess the right to manifest all aspects of a belief's practices, nor to manifest all underlying attitudes intimately linked to the belief.

In 1983, a Quaker relied on his pacifist beliefs as grounds for a military tax objection.[53] The applicant noted that he was willing to pay the tax and that his objection did not raise any of the limitations in Article 9(2). The Committee however decided that a manifested 'practice' of a belief does not include every aspect of a belief's practice. This is especially the case for tax objection since paying one's taxes into a general fund does not violate any form of conscientious belief or practice per se. Additionally, taxation of income is an accepted form for collecting funds, it is administratively impossible to identify the final destination of the funds, and the ECHR preserves a state's power to tax in Article 1, First Protocol of the ECHR.

Domestic courts invoke similar reasoning when confronted with a military tax objector. In Australia, the Courts held that the right to conscience does not provide an adequate ground for tax objection because the payment is a neutral act that does not violate the asserted conscientious beliefs. The tax objector was referred to the legislature to institute a change in the law since raising revenue for the state was their domain.[54]

In Canada, the Court distinguished tax objection from military conscientious objection. In the latter instance, one is physically participating in the action, whereas tax payment is a neutral activity involving money being paid into a public fund that supports a variety of state activity.[55] Additionally, the Court referred to the 'slippery slope' problem raised by other potential tax objectors and the necessity for turning to one's legislature. The English courts also referred a military tax objector to the Parliament if a change was desired in the manner in which taxes are to be paid.[56]

Similar reasoning has resulted in the denial of military tax objector's claims in the US. Even when asserted within the context of a belief and not

---

[52] 10295/82 X v. UK 6 EHRR 558 (1984).
[53] 10358/83 C v. UK 37 D&R 142 (1983).
[54] *Burrowers v. Deputy Commissioner of Taxation* 91 ATC 5021 (1991). Plaintiff's reliance on international law was dismissed for similar reasons.
[55] *Prior v. Queen* (1988) 2 C.F. 371.
[56] *Boughton v. Inland Revenue Ct. of Appeal* Civ. Div., 31/3/93; *Cheney v. Conn.* (1968) 1 All ER 779 (challenge to military tax used to support nuclear weapons based on the Geneva Convention. Court held that the Convention had not been incorporated into law, such that must adhere to legislative policy).

as a political objection to a particular war,[57] the US Courts have dismissed the right to military tax objection.[58] Hence courts have dismissed military tax objector claims due to fiscal and administrative reasons that are better suited for the legislature, and the possibility of future claims by other forms of tax objectors. Furthermore, courts reject the Free Exercise claim since taxation is a neutral activity designed to ensure for the support of the government; taxation does not limit one's ability to abide by conscientious beliefs.

Military Tax as a Unique Objection?

There is an attempt to distinguish military tax objection from other forms of tax objection as a means of avoiding the 'slippery slope' argument. The contention is that military tax objection centres on a particular, fundamental, belief that desires to avoid any participation with the taking of life[59] and that has historically been protected by the legislature in other situations.[60] This differs from a politically based objection, such as welfare tax objection. The latter is a qualitative determination that tends to affect the fiscal rights of others.[61] The military tax objection relates solely to the fiscal relationship between the government and the objector, particularly when the objector is willing to make a payment into an alternative fund that will assist the government in some other manner.[62]

While the aforementioned distinctions might apply to differences between military tax objection and other tax objections such as to a welfare tax, other possible forms of tax objection analogous to the military tax objection remain. In particular, it is difficult to distinguish military tax objection from an objection to paying taxes supporting abortion or the death penalty. Both abortion and death penalty tax objections desire to

---

[57] Notably, the Vietnam War that was generally challenged as violating the Nuremberg Code. *See Russell v. CIR* 60 TC 942 (1973); *Egnal v. CIR* 65 TC 255 (1975); *Anthony v. Commissioner* 66 USTCR 367 (1976); *Autenrieth v. Cullen* 418 F.2d 586 (9th Cir. 1969); *Kalish v. US* 411 F.2d 606 (9th Cir. 1969).
[58] *See Kennedy v. Rubin* 1995 US Dist. LEXIS 19834; 77 AFTR2d (P-H) 558; *Jenny v. US* 755 F.2d 1384 (9th Cir. 1985); *Lull v. CIR* 602 F.2d 1166 (4th Cir. 1979); *Mckee v. US* 781 F.2d 1043 (4th Cir. 1986); *First v. CIR* 547 F.2d 45 (7th Cir. 1976).
[59] Kornhauser (1999); Cook (1980); Gray (1979); DiSalvo (1982).
[60] Kornhauser (1999); Gray (1979); DiSalvo (1982).
[61] Dignan (1983).
[62] DiSalvo (1982).

avoid any form of support for practices that, like the military, involve the state in the taking of human life. Thus fiscal support to the state can be a direct contravention of the asserted belief. Additionally, states in which abortion is legal generally provide for conscience clauses that allow a nurse or doctor to forgo participating in the procedure.[63]

Some have attempted to address this problem by referring to the historical basis for objecting to military participation.[64] Furthermore, because governments maintain huge defence budgets, the military tax objector has stronger grounds to have the legislature create an alternative peace fund.[65]

These quantitative reasons however do not provide a proper distinction. The assertion being made by the tax objector centres on a particular belief. Distinguishing a belief because of its fiscal quantity or historical basis disregards the underlying assertion being made by both the military tax objector and other tax objectors.

Rather, a possible distinction between military tax objection and other forms of tax objections based on a viable belief can relate to what the state is requesting the objector to support. In the case of the military, the objector does not believe in supporting an action that the government is compelling its citizens to undergo.[66] In reasoning similar to the development of the military conscientious objection right, the underlying premise for upholding military tax objection is to allow for an individual to abide by her beliefs. The connection with military conscientious objection is particularly apt as technological-oriented methods of warfare continue to develop, thereby requiring greater financial support with lesser reliance on the foot-soldier.[67]

In the case of abortion and the death penalty, or similar forms of tax objection, the objection relates to activity conducted by the state as a result of another person's unilateral action.[68] While the state might offer assistance to conduct an abortion, it is the individual making the decision to undergo the procedure. Similarly, being subjected to the death penalty as a form of punishment resulted from an individual's conscious decision to commit a particular crime.[69] While the burden on the individual's belief

---

[63] See e.g. Durham, Wood, and Condie (1982).
[64] Kornhauser (1999); Cook (1980); DiSalvo (1982).
[65] DiSalvo (1982).
[66] Cook (1980;fn.125).
[67] Dignan (1983); DiSalvo (1982).
[68] See also Kornhauser (1999;1013) for a similar point.
[69] Hence one of the reasons for international law's prohibition of the death penalty to minors.

will remain, the derivation of the burden is from external factors that are suitable for legislative redress, such as campaigning for a change in the abortion law.

Of course, the individual believer is still being called upon to support actions contrary to her belief even if the control over the eventual action is in the hands of another. One similarly may contend that military tax objection also pertains to other individuals who will eventually conduct the action. Furthermore, other forms of tax objection deriving from particular beliefs can occur. For example, one might refuse to pay education taxes that are used to support the teaching of sex education or creationism in the schools. In such an instance the state is compelling particular behaviour contrary to one's beliefs that one is being forced to support.[70] A state then should provide an alternative form of education or conduct the education in a neutral manner that does not violate the objector's principles. It also is conceivable that an individual may request to have tax education funds establish alternative teaching sessions for those who object to the general course, such as alternative sex education courses within a religious context or teaching a host of evolutionary theories along with creationism.

Conclusion

When compared to the right to military conscientious objection, the right to tax objection is somewhat limited. International and domestic judicial bodies generally do not recognise tax objection as a manifestation of a conscientious belief. From an administrative standpoint, the objection appears to entail a great deal of complications and the danger remains of the state being confronted with a variety of tax objection claims.

Yet, upon considering the reasons for rejecting a right to a tax objection, the analogy with military conscientious objection should not be overlooked. The reasons of public policy, deference to the legislature,

---

Some objections are based on the problem of wrongful convictions or racist juries. These contentions however centre on difficulties with the criminal justice system and not necessarily a conflict with a belief.

[70] It is possible that public policy limitations apply to the manifestation of a belief against sex education or the like since a state must educate its youth on general moral matters by non-indoctrinating, general, information. 5095/71 *Kjeldsen, Buck and Pederson v. Denmark* 1 EHRR 711 (1980).

administrative difficulties, and the slippery slope were all reasons originally offered for denying the right to military conscientious objection. Furthermore, preventing the manifestation of a conscientious belief on the aforementioned grounds can lead to a violation of the right since these limitations are broader than those provided in the treaties. While it is tempting to defer to other human rights as a means of objecting to a tax payment,[71] occasions do arise where paying the tax will entail a violation of one's conscientious belief.[72] As discussed throughout this chapter, it seems possible to provide for a limited form of tax objection when considering the belief being asserted and the particular demands emanating therefrom.

On a practical level, states already recognise certain forms of conscientious tax objection. What such particular systems demonstrate however is the states' preferences for individual exemptions that are usually focused on particular beliefs. While this indicates some deference towards an individual's belief, it also demonstrates the understandable hesitation by states in recognising the right to manifest a belief by way of a tax objection.

---

[71] Free speech, for example, can serve as a context for various challenges to tax payments. *See e.g. Superintendent v. Lahia* 1960(2) SCR 821 (political objection to irrigation rates in Upper Pradesh).

[72] *See* discussion *supra* at Chapter Five.

8 Proposing a Group-Oriented Approach to the Right to Conscience

Introduction

While one may conceive the development and manifestation of a conscientious belief as an individual oriented process, the group notion of a religion or belief should not be discounted. Individuals associated with a particular belief system generally are disposed towards other individuals who maintain similar ideals. Although not a necessary development for individuals harbouring a belief, the banding together with other like-believers tends to alleviate feelings of alienation or isolation from society as well as assist the believer to achieve a common end in a more effective manner.[1] Certainly from a communitarian approach, where the social group is a categorical element in the individual's existence, and to a lesser extent in a pluralist framework, where voluntary and involuntary associations can serve as sources of value and identity for the individual,[2] one must consider the notion of a group orientation for the freedom of religion and belief. Indeed, there is a certain inherent element to many religious activities that mandate group activity, such that one should not reduce religious beliefs solely to an individual exercise, particularly when manifestation of a religion or belief involves social acts that affect individuals within and without the belief system.

On a more fundamental level, the notion of a group approach to the right to conscience is rather important for the international human rights system given the emergence of minority communities and other groups

---

[1] *See e.g.* Smith (1998;498).
[2] Evans, B. N. (1997; 229-231) (concluding that the goals of a pluralist society are to provide for the integration of various beliefs); Bader (1999;597).

within the state who assert the right to uphold their beliefs and way of life. Conflicts arise between the state and specific, belief-driven, groups, such as Scientologists in a number of European states or the Falun-Gong in China, which makes it difficult to distinguish and assess the interests and rights raised by religious assertions as compared to the needs of the state. Considering the role of a group oriented approach to the right to freedom of religion and conscience then could be of greater beneficence to the individual members of particular groups; a group approach begins to acknowledge the importance of communal activities as a form of manifesting one's individual beliefs.

The discussion in this chapter begins to address the potential conflicts that arise from the absolute nature of the *forum internum* right to freedom of conscience, both between groups and its individual members and among individuals within the group and outside the group. Activities of a group can mandate alterations to its members' internal belief system and create changes to the *forum internum* of individuals who are exposed to the group. Included in this evaluation is the *forum externum* aspect of a group belief given the inherent social conflicts that could arise between the group, the state, and other individuals as a result of a manifested belief.

Upon acknowledging the conception of a group right to conscience, one may consider the practical role of the right within a multi-cultural system. The significance of reflecting on the right to conscience from a group approach is that it provides for a sharper understanding of the relationship between culture and the other concomitant external influences upon the formation of a conscientious belief.[3] Cultural differences do not create absolute foundations for a belief, but rather are subject to a broader social process involving a wide swath of cross cutting cleavages resulting from internal and external influences both on individuals and the group.[4] Such influences are important for the right to freedom of conscience since they demonstrate the broad context for the right to conscience and provide the ability to consider the right as part of the social process rather than in conflict with it. Furthermore, the inherent conflicts presented by a group approach to the right are easier to address when considered part of the overall cultural environment and broader social development[5] rather than within the confined context of upholding a tolerable society.

---

[3] *See* discussion *supra* at Chapter Four.
[4] *See e.g.* Bauman (1999;92).
[5] *But see* Evans, B. N. (1997;228) (concluding that within the context of the US Constitution, the notion of a pluralist society prevents the advent of discordant groups).

More particularly, the group right to conscience is relevant for groups that engage in proselytising or if their belief system requires them to attempt to encourage other individuals to adopt the group's beliefs. Proselytising is a rather vexing problem in international law[6] because of the inherent conflict not only between the state and the group, but also between the rights of the group or the individual proselytiser and the rights of other individuals who might be the target of missionary activity.[7] Hence understanding the right to freedom of religion and conscience from the standpoint of a group can offer a broader perspective that incorporates a number of social elements including the group, its members, and individuals external to the group.

Placing the discussion within the international human rights context, one can account for the group notion of freedom of religion and conscience by considering the distinction between the human rights accorded to a minority group as compared to the rights of individuals. Particularly, Article 27 of the ICCPR, that codifies the rights of minorities, incorporates the right to freedom of religion for a minority group but without any stated limitations. It is not clear however how one is to ameliorate the broad system of minority rights with an individual's right to freedom *to*, and *from*, religion. May the minority group assert its right to practise a particular religious custom even if it infringes an individual's human right? Where does the group right of the minority end and the individual right begin, or vice-versa?

Recognising that the human rights of a minority group are not subject to any formal limitations or derogation,[8] the HRC limited the scope of Article 27 to operating in tandem with other rights to create practical limitations to the right.[9] As noted by the HRC in the General Comment to Article 27:

> The Committee observes that none of the rights protected under article 27 of the Covenant [ICCPR] may be legitimately exercised in a manner or to an extent inconsistent with the other provisions of the Covenant.[10]

---

[6] See e.g. Lerner (1998).
[7] Stahnke (1999;275-325) discussing the interests of the proselytiser, the target, and the state.
[8] *Compare* ICCPR Article 27 *with* Article 18(3).
[9] Gilbert (1997;133).
[10] General Comment to Article 27 at paragraph 8.

While the HRC's described relationship between minority rights and individual rights is understandable given the orientation of the HRC and the human rights system towards an individual based understanding of rights, conflicts still remain on a fundamental level. For example, one may interpret the actions of a minority group member either as an individual act of exercising one's right that possibly infringes another individual's rights, or as an act that emanates from the group's exercise of a minority right. The implication is that one must recognise some form of distinction between group versus individual action, particularly when dealing with acts such as proselytising that affect individuals within and outside the group as well as the group itself.

One manner of dealing with the group-individual rights conflict is to consider *how* the group notion of a conscientious or religious belief conforms to the normative structure proposed by the rights of minorities and the right to freedom of religion and conscience. The proposal suggested in this chapter centres on separating the elements of the right to freedom of conscience, such that one may derive the *forum internum* of the group from the individual right to freedom of religion and conscience, while the external manifestation of the group's beliefs, the *forum externum* of the group, derives from minority rights.[11] As will be discussed *infra*, such an approach recognises the variety of relevant interests that are raised by a group approach, while also providing a normative construct for the application of both an individual and a group aspect of the right.

Some General Points Regarding Group Beliefs

Introduction

Since the *forum internum* directs and shapes a conscientious belief, it is essential to acknowledge that elements forming the *forum internum* raise broader social concerns as well. As part of the conscientious evaluation discussed *supra*,[12] the individual's conscientious belief accounts for the underlying social impact of the belief. Hence, social influences also will serve to clarify and solidify a particular belief. Especially regarding a conscientious belief, where manifestation of the belief is a pivotal

---

[11] A similar problem exists for minority education rights given the tension between upholding the minorities belief system versus providing an equal opportunity of education to all children. *See* Cullen (1993) (leaning towards upholding the child's individual opportunity at the expense of pluralism in instances of conflict).

[12] *See* discussion *supra* at Chapter Four.

element,[13] the importance of adequately articulating the belief will affect the manner in which the conscience develops in the *forum internum*. While fundamental intuitive and rational reactions serve to underline a conscientious belief, social and cultural influences also assist in defining the boundaries of a conscientious belief, thereby requiring consideration of, and reference to, external sources as well.[14]

The relevant social considerations however can influence the *forum internum* in a variety of ways. This section will begin to consider the role of external social influences in the *forum internum* as part of the development towards understanding a group approach to the freedom of conscience. Particularly, a person may come across other individuals harbouring the same or similar belief. What is the significance of such contact for the *forum internum*, both for the individual who is shaping an internal conscientious belief and for a group of individuals who develop similar forms of beliefs?

The fundamental issue again relates to the boundaries to be imposed upon a belief. May a state serve as protector of its society's *forum internum* beliefs by limiting the influx of external influences? Will such policy goals of the state in turn lead to undue impositions on the *forum internum* of minority groups or other individuals? Although the state may impose limitations on the *forum externum*, the treaties prevent a state from imposing limitations upon the *forum internum*, such that the particular question of a group *forum internum* raises practical considerations given a belief that serves a constitutive role in shaping the group.

Referring to an example noted by Mill, society might uphold Sunday Closing Laws for non-religious reasons. Typically the reason might centre on the need for a general day of rest or time spent with family or friends. Nonetheless, such laws can infringe the *forum internum* beliefs of other minority groups whose religious day of rest is on another day of the week, such as Friday or Saturday.[15] The minority might not only suffer economic hardship because of the two days of rest, such as closing a business for religious reasons and subsequently for legal reasons, but they also are being forced to adhere to practices that impinge upon their internal belief process should Sunday not be designated as their day of rest.

Upon considering the possible tension between a state and a group, one is generally dealing with the relations between a specific minority

---

[13] See discussion *supra*.
[14] Taylor (1989;74).
[15] This issue was a major concern during the drafting of the post-World War One Polish Minorities Treaty, where the final article was watered down in its protection of the Jewish minority in Poland. *See* Evans, M. (1997; Chapter Three).

group and the state. A minority group desires to assert a belief that differs from the rest of society or that is contrary to the established beliefs of the state. As a result, the state focuses on the minority group to suppress it or remove the minority from the social milieu. Repression of religious beliefs generally results from claims that the minority group endangers the construct of the state.[16]

How then can the right to freedom of conscience conform to an approach that incorporates individual and communal interests? One need not pigeon hole the right to freedom of conscience in a vacuum as an individually based assertion of internal beliefs or solely as a conflict between the individual and society.[17] Rather, as one's conscience develops and manifests as a belief, the belief also can serve to contribute to the development of society and its communal values. One's conscience identifies with the community by influencing, and being influenced by, society. As noted *supra*,[18] conscience can be understood as an external, transgressive, notion. It need not solely be the domain of the atomistic individual but also assists in shaping and influencing the social community both in the sense of an individual and a group oriented approach. Hence there is an important significance to elaborating on the potentiality of a group conscientious belief given the effects the belief can have on society as well as the influence a group can have, or forcibly exert, on the beliefs of others. Noting therefore that a group approach to the *forum internum* can apply to society as a whole, it is important to sketch a boundary for the group *forum internum* by indicating possible applications and limitations for this form of the right.

Reference to the Treaties

In one sense, the terms of the treaties' such as the UDHR, ICCPR, ECHR, and AmCHR provide for at least an initial approach towards understanding a group notion of the right to conscience despite the individual oriented interpretation of human rights.[19] For example, the phrase 'either individually or in a community with others' noted in ICCPR Article 18(1) implies a protection that is focused on groups.[20] Similarly, the right to

---

[16] Bengoa (2000;15).
[17] *Contra* Boyle (1992;39).
[18] *See* discussion *supra* at Chapter Four.
[19] *See e.g.* General Comments of HRC to Article 27.
[20] GA Third Committee, Tenth Session, A/2929, Agenda Item 28 (1955) The Secretary General pointed out the lack of any specific protection for minority religious groups due to the potential conflict that could result with other religions.

educate according to one's belief in both the ICCPR[21] and the ICESCR[22] indicate a group context for application of the right.[23] Such an approach also is indicated from Article 18(2) of the ICCPR whereby the prohibition against coercion derived from the desire to emphasise the right to change one's belief through moral or intellectual persuasion,[24] while balancing such a right against undue coercion by external forces such as excessively zealous missionaries.[25] Likewise, the particular forms of manifestation, such as worship or teaching, indicate the recognition of the right being accorded to a group.[26] For example, teaching a belief implies some form of group context, even if it only involves one individual teaching another. Note that the UN General Assembly's 1992 *Declaration on the Rights of Persons Belonging to National or Ethnic, Religious and Linguistic Minorities*[27] has gone even further in providing for an individual and communal approach to the rights accorded to minorities,[28] including the right to uphold a belief.

The ICCPR, ECHR, and AmCHR also provide for the ability to educate one's children pursuant to one's belief, a fundamental and sensitive area of the *forum internum* with strong communal or group overtones. Education centres on developing the beliefs of individuals, generally within a group context, and can greatly influence a child's internal belief systems. While the motivation of education has recently focused on its economic function, a key goal of education also is to allow for personal growth and development of values.[29] Education therefore is one of the key methods for entrenching a group's or society's values.

This view of education is no more apparent than for minorities who desire to instil in their young the values and beliefs that they consider to be central to their existence. The importance to certain groups for developing their children's education demonstrates a more communal focus for the right to conscience. The <u>Minorities Declaration</u> indicates the important role of education to minority groups. The right to an education is a positive

---

[21] Article 18(4).
[22] Article 13(3).
[23] Hodgson (1996).
[24] E/CN.4/SR.319 (1955). *See* discussion *supra* at Chapter Three.
[25] GA Third Committee, Tenth Session, A/2929, Agenda Item 28 (1955) referring to the CHR's 5th Session.
[26] Frowein (1986;256).
[27] GA Resolution 47/135.
[28] <u>Minorities Declaration</u> at Article 3. Thornberry (1997;47) notes that the <u>Minorities Declaration</u> is providing for a broader form of right than ICCPR Article 27.
[29] Batelaan (1993;168-169) noting in particular the role of education in promoting democratic values; Hodgson (1996;238,257-258).

right in Article 4(4) of the Minorities Declaration, such that a state is, *inter alia*, to take measures to encourage the study of a minority's culture[30] and the minority is to ensure for a balanced education that also incorporates broader social values.[31] Similar considerations are apparent in the *Convention on the Rights of the Child*[32] and the *Migrant Workers Convention*.[33]

One may glean an additional indication of a group oriented approach for the right to conscience from HRC and ECHR cases. The HRC for example has acknowledged the role of the group in a number of cases, such as in *Lubicon Band v. Canada*,[34] where the HRC stated that a group of similarly affected individuals may collectively submit a complaint.[35] The ECHR Commission similarly has recognised that a group may raise an action on behalf of its members. The Church of Scientology for example was able to raise an Article 9 issue before the ECHR Commission on behalf of the entire sect[36] because the ECHR Commission considered its members linked by their collective beliefs.

The ECHR Court also has upheld the right of a community or group to challenge a state that was threatening certain social aspects of its spiritual life.[37] The state must consider a group's interests, even if conflicting with overall social ideals, so long as the group's interests do not violate the basic dignity of the person or preach views fundamentally contrary to the state.[38] For example, in *Serif v. Greece*,[39] the ECHR Court defined the terms of the treaty 'in community with others and in public, to manifest his religion in worship and teaching' as upholding a minister's ability to issue a public message to his congregants about the religious significance of an upcoming feast. Noting the importance of a pluralist society, the Court went on to hold that the Minister was a religious leader of a group that willingly followed him, despite the possibility of internal

---

[30] Thornberry (1997;49) notes that a minority is not only to educate its members about minority customs and the like, but also is to promote tolerance among its members by instructing and teaching about the society and culture surrounding the minority. See also Cullen (1993).
[31] Mehedi (1999;paragraphs 13-18).
[32] See e.g. *Convention on the Rights of the Child* at Article 30.
[33] The Convention essentially mirrors the language of ICCPR Article 18.
[34] 167/84 *Lubicon Band v. Canada* (1990).
[35] The HRC made this statement despite the interpretation of Article 27 as according an individual right.
[36] 7805/77 *Church of Scientology v. Sweden* 16 D&R 68 (1979).
[37] 11921/86 *Verein v. Austria* 57 D&R 81(1988).
[38] 7511/76 *Campbell and Cosans v. UK* 4 EHRR 293 (1982) (in context of public and private schools).
[39] 38178/97 *Serif v. Greece* decided 14/12/99.

divisions within the group, such that the state may not impose limitations on the minister's internal activities even pursuant to Article 9(2).[40]

The protection accorded to a minority group also will include an obligation to protect a belief that binds the group. The Permanent Court of International Justice recognised this protection in *Interpretation of the Greco-Bulgarian Agreement of December 9, 1927*,[41] and *Access to German Minority Schools in Upper Silesia*.[42] The Permanent Court of International Justice held that states must preserve ethnic, religious, and linguistic traditions of minorities and provide for a minority's peaceful coexistence among the population. Hence minorities merit protection for their religion, language, and ethnicity.[43] Indeed, the current protection accorded to minorities, as codified in ICCPR Article 27 and various GA declarations,[44] creates a positive obligation on the state to prevent not only discrimination, but also provide equal treatment to all that would presumably include protection for the group's beliefs. The 1992 Minorities Declaration provides for a similar obligation on the state.[45]

The international human rights system accords the beliefs of a minority group legal safeguards, hence the link between the protection of minorities and the right to freedom of religion and conscience. A minority can retain and develop a specific belief or ideology that serves as a binding or identifying force for the minority group. What distinguishes the minority from the majority, as well as from other groups, is that the minority embeds a particular practice into their way of life and identity in a similar manner to a group's adherence to a particular belief. Such an antecedent belief creates a group conception that differs from the majority[46] and merits specific protection. Intermingling the significance of an individual belief with a group conception of the idea serves to better explain the importance of a religion or belief for a minority group, especially given the ever-

---

[40] See also Gilbert (2000) noting at paragraph 3 that '...the *jurisprudence constante* of the Strasbourg organs has been to include within national minorities all those groups that would be termed minorities under the 1992 Declaration'.
[41] PCIJ Judgement No. 57, Advisory Opinion of 1932.
[42] PCIJ Judgement No. 52, Advisory Opinion of 1931.
[43] See e.g. Shaw (1992); Sohn (1981); Ermacora (1983); Capotorti (1991). All have defined protection for minorities based on notions of ethnicity, religion and language, and the inherent desire to uphold and preserve their unique community.
[44] See e.g. Alfredsson and deZayas (1993). A state's obligation towards minorities had previously been limited to non-interference, without any obligation to ensure for equality. See e.g. Sohn (1981).
[45] See e.g. Minorities Declaration at Article 2.
[46] See e.g. HRC General Comment to Article 27, at paragraph 5.1-5.2.

changing nature of a minority group's structure,[47] while assisting to uphold both the individual and the group right. One then can partially discern ICCPR Article 27 as giving practical effect to the communal sense of the right to freedom of religion and conscience.[48]

Owing to the link between minority rights and the right to freedom of religion and conscience, some commentators have attempted to distinguish these rights[49] by narrowing minority rights to specific group assertions regarding their existence as a unit. The focus is on a communal conception of the minority's existence,[50] such as physical enjoyment of the group's resources or manifestation of its cultural and ideological practices in society. For example, in *Lubicon Band v. Canada*,[51] the HRC centred its decision on the fact that Canada's restrictions imposed on the use of land was threatening the Band's way of life and culture.[52]

The treaties therefore recognise some form of group dimension to the human rights accorded to a minority group. Placing the context of minority protection within that of a group whose identity centres on a particular belief, *forum externum* applications then are possible, such as a group of pacifists collectively objecting to the testing of nuclear arms.[53] Can the protection for the *forum internum*, which is a more subtle right, be extended to groups as well? Indeed, is there any practical significance to the *forum internum* aspect? What is the implication, if any at all, of a 'community' freedom for an internal conscientious belief? The possible avenues for addressing this query shall be considered following a more focused understanding of the meaning and implications of a 'group' belief and its attendant rights.

---

[47] Bengoa (2000;8) outlining the difficulty in defining a minority in any realistic sense; Eide (1999;2-4) noting that defining a minority group will not necessarily create a normative standard given the various conceptions of the term 'minority' and the desire for a broad understanding of the term.
[48] Triggs (1988;145).
[49] *See e.g.* Dinstein (1992); Thornberry (1991).
[50] Thornberry (1991); Shaw (1992); Ermacora (1983).
[51] 167/84 *Lubicon Band v. Canada* (1990).
[52] Yet, the HRC has stated in the General Comment to Article 27 that the rights enshrined in the Article are individual rights. It is possible that the HRC desired to distinguish minority rights from the right of self determination, which is quite obviously a group or people's right. This might however be reading too much into the comments. *See also* Triggs (1988;154) noting that while the HRC will not deny a group conception to Article 27, it will lean toward an individual right approach.
[53] Frowein (1986;256) noting that while the right centres on freedom of association, it also 'must be seen as protected by Article 9 [freedom of conscience] already'.

Group Beliefs Defined

One proposed definition for the group phenomenon has been a spontaneous, yet permanent, joining of individuals for a specific purpose or due to particular qualities, depending on the individuals within the group and the greater community's view of the group as such.[54] Such a definition can readily apply to a group linked by a conscientious belief, especially when the belief serves as the antecedent foundation for the group's overall conception of itself as a group. For example, one can identify a group of pacifists engaging in public activism as a result of their common views regarding the military or nuclear weapons.

Yet this definition appears to relate more to the *forum externum* as it centres on external action in establishing the group context. Is it also possible to account for a group as such by considering the *forum internum* aspect of the group or is one to define a group *forum internum* by way of external actions, similar to the approach suggested by the individual *forum internum*? Further, is such an attempt to identify a group *forum internum* an anomaly in itself given the so called internal domain of the *forum internum*, implying an individual approach that would be difficult to place in an externalised group context?

The basic premise supporting a group oriented approach towards the *forum internum* right is that a conscientious belief, in a manner similar to religious beliefs,[55] creates a common identity among individuals within a group. The belief serves a social function by identifying the person with the external world through one's belief. The result is that a religious or conscientious belief is not necessarily representative of absolutes, but rather forms a part of the discursive processes. As part of one's ongoing existence and personal development, and in response to external social stimuli such as distributions of social authority or unique cultural peculiarities, changes occur to one's belief system.[56] The ensuing discourse that an individual believer might be engaged in tends to influence and shape the development of a belief such that it provides a contextual bearing for the individual's cultural and social position.

---

[54] Lerner (1991).

[55] See *e.g.* Berger (1969) (religion as a social function that creates an identification with the external human world by legitimating one's empirical reality of existence with an ultimate reality).

[56] Bauman (1999;22) noting the importance of recognising the discursive formations for religion rather than attempting to define it as an absolute idea that is non malleable and therefore the cause for internal social tension and minority unrest.

Upon a closer examination of the characteristics of an internal group belief, it is imperative to note the function of the belief as a constituting factor that differentiates a group belief from an individual belief. The key factors for identifying a group belief are rather similar to that of identifying a minority. The belief serves as an important element for the group's existence, the members of the group are consciously aware of the shared belief, and the belief regulates the actions of the members regarding the group.[57] A member of a 'group' might not be consciously aware of another individual with shared beliefs, but the belief would still serve to regulate an individual's actions. The importance in focusing on a group belief is that it broadens the application of the *forum internum* right to freedom of conscience by considering social factors that might be part of the conscientious process, while beginning to address the possible conflicts that can arise between individuals and group conscientious beliefs. This is an important aspect when considering that in certain instances one has to refer to external action to define the *forum internum*.

Examining the group belief from a *forum internum* standpoint also can assist in sharpening the rights of groups as they attain a greater level of protection in international law.[58] The 'formation' of a group with an identified conscientious belief need not be a formal occurrence. Rather, an individual might be aware of other individuals with similar beliefs because such beliefs regulate their external actions,[59] thereby creating a similar pattern of action for the group members. A pacifist group is a typical example since a belief in pacifism binds its members and regulates their actions in a common way, such as refusing military service.

The external actions of the group members can however differ as individuals resort to varied degrees of manifested action. Pacifists might retain a common belief against the use of nuclear weapons that constitutes them as a group, but their actions can range from massive protest demonstrations to underhanded tactics against nuclear armament plants. The group members might not agree with all of these manifested actions and yet still retain a sense of group structure resulting from the common foundational belief that formed the group. The underlying pacifist belief still serves a constitutive purpose for the group. As the belief becomes externalised, it will develop into a holistic notion among the group because the belief, and not the actions, will serve to define the essence of the group.

---

[57] Bar-Tal (1990;41 and chapter 4). See also Galanter (1989;5) for a narrower definition concerning the beliefs of cult members that will include consideration of behavioural norms and the charismatic power of the group.
[58] See e.g. Kingsbury (1992).
[59] As well as instil a measure of social cohesion. Galanter (1989).

Considering the significance of the underlying belief and its constitutive role for a group, the underlying belief developed in the *forum internum* is a constant factor that merits particular protection. The *forum internum* right to conscience can clarify other more externally driven rights such as minority rights,[60] by including consideration of the minority group's *forum internum* as well. The minority group's conceptions will not only exist, but also influence the development of culture and its necessary condition - society[61] - in structuring behaviour[62] and creating social changes. In this sense, the community is constitutive of the individual as well because it creates, and protects, an individual's rights.[63] Hence even within a liberal construct, the cognitive aspect of culture, whereby one generation transmits knowledge to another, will certainly influence, but also be influenced by, one's voluntary decisions regarding actions and values.[64]

Furthermore, because minority rights focus on external manifestations of a minority group's belief, the *forum internum* right of Article 18 can uphold the internal dimension of the right. This is particularly the case since a belief that formulates a minority group develops from an individual's antecedent experiences. The relationship then between minority rights and conscience can be the role that the right to conscience plays in preserving the group's *forum internum*, with the minority right protecting the group's external manifestations. Hence the <u>Minorities Declaration</u>, when declaring the right to freedom of religion, focuses on the profession and practice of the right, more externally driven manifestations, rather then the internal aspects regarding the development of a belief. In a similar vein, the terms 'profession and free practice' in the African Convention on Human Rights relate to the protection of groups such as the community or the tribe[65] given the Organisation of African Unity's focus on creating a more group oriented document. Acknowledging the importance of both the individual and group dimension to the rights of minorities also is somewhat more realistic since certain rights simply cannot but manifest in a communal, group setting, thereby providing a proper outlet for the individual's exercise of the right.

---

[60] Thornberry (1991) (noting overlap with article 18).
[61] Berger (1969;13).
[62] Geertz (1973;123-124).
[63] Taylor (1985); Bowring (1999;19-21).
[64] Merle (1998;264) (noting that the world is generally not a monocausal construct); Bauman (1999;86-88).
[65] *See* Nuituri (1995;376).

In a sense, this distinction between minority rights as relating to the *forum externum* and the right to conscience to the *forum internum* of a group belief results from the current construct of the human rights framework. Consider for example the ongoing, almost futile, attempt to identify the elements for a definitive definition of a 'minority'. Debate has raged between commentators[66] without anyone achieving an agreeable solution. One proposal that might begin to assist the proposed distinction offered here is classification pursuant to objective and subjective factors. The objective factors relate to external manifestations of the group that define it as a distinct entity, generally pertaining to language religion or ethnicity. The subjective factors however closely mirror the internal aspect of the group's construct by examining the will of the group and the drive to preserve its identity and distinct characteristics.[67] These latter elements relate more to the internal understanding of the individuals within the group and even of the individuals themselves on a singular basis, although the manifestation of the desire is of course what is eventually deemed pertinent.

It is possible therefore to delineate the extent of the *forum internum* protection for a group belief in an analogous manner to the form of protection accorded to the individual's *forum internum*. Similar to the lack of restrictions on an individual's *forum internum*, a state cannot impose restrictions on the internal beliefs of a group, with a view towards altering the group's constitutive beliefs. A violation occurs when using an external force to impose undue influence or coercion on a particular group by targeting their underlying belief. The coercion not only limits an external action of the group but also attempts to alter or eradicate the underlying group belief. The key consideration is not the external action taken by the state to limit the group, but the state's intentions towards the group's internal belief.[68]

One may classify the protection granted as the positive freedom *to* adhere to a belief (freedom *to*) or the negative resistance to external influences to either adopt or change a belief (freedom *from*). For instance, a typical example of freedom *to* is where the state engages in a

---

[66] *See e.g.* Packer (1999); Shaw (1992); Capotorti (1991); Sohn (1981); Simon (1997;512) (group conception based on an empirical assessment of past and present harms to the group); Alfredsson and deZayas (1993) (noting the lack of necessity for a definition). *See also Questions of definitions, attributes and categorisations of minorities*, E/CN.4/Sub.2/AC/1996/1 where the UN Working Group on Minorities began to address this issue.
[67] *See e.g.* Sohn (1981); Rehman (1998;620).
[68] Frowein (1986;257-259).

discriminatory policy that not only limits the practices of a belief but is so intolerant as to be viewed as a policy that intends to alter or undermine the belief itself. The ECHR Commission hinted at such a possibility when confronted with a challenge to the Swedish authorities' criticisms of the Church of Scientology.[69] The Commission intimated that a state's policy against a particular group belief could reach an intolerance level that would endanger the freedom of religion. The AfrCHR Commission noted a similar problem in *Les Temoins de Jehovah v. Zaire*[70] where the State's harassment of Jehovah's Witnesses amounted to a violation of AfrCHR Article 8. In each of these cases, the state policy focused on groups united by a particular belief, with an intention to alter or eradicate the belief.

Additional applications similarly will centre on occurrences involving a change to the internal constitutive belief of a group. Similar to discrimination against the individual, if the intention of a state's discriminatory policy is not only to suppress a group but also create a change in the group's internal belief system (freedom *from*) or alter one's view of the group's practices (freedom *to*), the *forum internum* also can be violated.[71]

Group and Individual Conflicts

The approach thus far in considering a group dimension to the right to freedom of conscience has focused on the relationship between the group and the surrounding social forces, particularly the state apparatus. Recognising the entitlement of a group to some form of *forum internum* protection under the right to freedom of religion and conscience, with the rights of minorities addressing the *forum externum*, creates an inherent conflict within the right between the individual and group *forum internum*. A group's belief can violate the individual's *forum internum* by coercing an individual to alter a previously held belief, as exemplified by the actions of a zealous missionary using underhanded tactics. On the other hand, a state based on fundamental principles of a particular religion might suppress a minority group that lacks any belief or maintains a different belief because the group is damaging to society. The freedom *from* aspect of the *forum internum* of a group or of an individual can be subject to attack and change as a result of coercive state actions.

---

[69] 8282/78 *Church of Scientology v. Sweden* 21 D&R 111 (1981).
[70] Communication No. 56/91 reported in 4(1) IHRR 89 (1997).
[71] Of course, there remains the broader problem relating to demonstrating the intent of the state. The actions of the state towards the group however will assist in that endeavour.

In a sense, the problems relating to group assertions of the right to freedom of religion and conscience present a rather ironic situation. Historically, the right to freedom of religion and conscience emerged from the protection sought by states for their missionaries located in foreign countries.[72] Yet as the right currently stands, when conscientious beliefs of a group require specific external action, such as proselytising, the required manifestation of the belief can heighten the conflict between the individual and the group. Either a state will act to protect individuals while suppressing the beliefs of the group, or the state will allow the group to practise its beliefs at the possible risk to the *forum internum* of other individuals. While the *forum externum* can be subject to the limitations stated in the treaties, a state seems caught between Scylla and Charybdis when attempting to uphold the *forum internum* for both the group and the individual since favouring one side will expose the other to possible undue change.

Various state reports to the HRC also refer to this conflict between individual and group *forum internum* rights. For example, Nigeria noted in its 1996 report that it will not tolerate any form of forceful public preaching, such as Islamic fanaticism.[73] The Ukraine also noted similar limitations of preaching sects on the grounds of upholding the public order.[74] Granted that these reports focused on the *forum externum* aspect of preaching. As noted, the external manifestation is subject to limitations and to the manner and scope in which the state might be applying the limits. For example, in *Kokkinakis v. Greece*[75] the ECHR Court referred to the scope of limitations available to a state in finding that Greece had disproportionately limited the rights of Jehovah Witnesses. Yet, one also must consider the relevant *forum internum* rights of minority beliefs that the state policy affects to determine the manner in which both the individual's and the group's *forum internum* is to take shape.

The drafters of the UDHR, ICCPR and the <u>Minorities Declaration</u> foresaw this problem when discussing missionary activity as an inherent corollary to the right to freedom of conscience and religion. For the UDHR and ICCPR drafters, protection for missionaries was a particularly sensitive issue since missionary work inevitably raised the problem of upholding the contested right to change one's religion or beliefs.[76] Countries opposed to

---

[72] *See e.g.* Evans, M. (1997;Chapter Two).
[73] ICCPR/C/92/Add. 1.
[74] CCPR/C/95/Add.2.
[75] 14307/88 *Kokkinakis v. Greece* 17 EHRR 397 (1993).
[76] *See* A/2929 (1955) and E/800.

the language 'to have or adopt' in Article 18[77] also opposed any protection to missionaries and the like. The <u>Minorities Declaration</u> further reflects this change. As a result, the ability to change one's religion has been, and remains, a rather delicate as well as undecided aspect of the freedom of religion and belief, with valid arguments remaining for both sides.[78]

Nonetheless, some religious movements view proselytising as an integral practice of their belief, with a goal no doubt of altering the *forum internum* belief structure of targeted individuals. Herein lies the crux of the issue since it is within a state's power to limit the activities of missionary groups, especially when using coercive tactics. Yet it is the individual's right to decide whether he or she desires to change a belief. Treatment towards proselytising belief movements therefore can provide a good example for elaborating on this inherent conflict between the *forum internum* of the individual and the group. The discussion also can further assist to refine our understanding of the *forum internum* and its form of protection since the empirical and sociological literature on proselytising sects, or New Religious Movements, provide a better understanding of the methodology of activity that is understood as the exemplary activity that violates the *forum internum*, namely brainwashing.[79]

Forum Internum *and New Religious Movements*

New Religious Movements do not universally derive from religious or theological origins. Rather, the goal of current-day New Religious Movements is to address the internal, personal, needs of its members and not to transform society, create a universal moral standard, or achieve the status of a formal religion.[80] New Religious Movements are therefore analogous to a group conscientious belief since an antecedent belief unifies the group and directs its members towards particular external action yet they are not linked to any specific universal standard.[81] Rather, a group

---

[77] *See* discussion *supra* at Chapter Three.
[78] *See e.g.* Boyle and Sheen (1997;8-9) noting the ongoing debate regarding the capacity to change one's religion, such that even though the HRC has noted in the General Comment to Article 18 that an individual maintains the right to change, many Islamic states do not, in practice, provide for that right.
[79] *See e.g.* Nowak (1993); Vermeulen (1993).
[80] Wilson (1990) referring to the Scientology movement; Robbins (1988;2-5) noting 1960s and 1970s development of counterculture movements as a form of cult development that did not have strict religious overtones.
[81] Evans, B.N. (1997;93) noting that NRMs should be accorded a standing equal to that of a religious belief to preclude a reviewing court from inquiring into the merits and status of the belief system.

forms a link by way of a common approach, similar to a group of pacifists uniting together for a specific purpose.

New Religious Movements also represent emerging belief systems of a minority group[82] that could become entrenched in the social consciousness. They maintain a similar position to religions that developed during the Reformation, such as Protestantism,[83] or the Salvation Army that was accused of using brainwashing tactics when initiating its operations in the late nineteenth century.

The Salvation Army provides an interesting contrast since the brainwashing charge is generally levelled against present day New Religious Movements.[84] The basis for this charge derives from the New Religious Movements' tenets that require their members to target new potential members as a basic practice of the belief.[85] The typical examples are the Jehovah's Witnesses[86] and members of the Moon sect whose members spend close to seventy per cent of their time on active recruitment duty.[87]

The basic attributes that sociologists have referred to in distinguishing acceptable New Religious Movements from coercive ones are whether the latter are rooted in ideological totalism characterised by those sects that use fear as a tactic, attempt to alter the social psychological abilities of the individual, and use a great deal of resources and time within which to coerce the individual. The key attributes of the *forum internum* that become the focus for coercion are the physiological and psychoanalytical abilities of the person. Sleep deprivation, ego destruction, over-stimulation of the nervous system, and weakening critical facilities by forced confessions alter these mental capacities.[88] In essence the identified improper tactics by New Religious Movements are analogous to the prohibition against mental torture; each action involves a desired change to the individual's *forum internum* by removing the individual's ability to exercise independent choice.

Thus brainwashing entails, among other things, a focus on the individual's belief, an intention to alter that belief, and the use of coercive

---

[82] *See* Wilson (1990;47) defining a sect as a religious minority that espouses a faith different from other religious bodies.
[83] Kamen (1967).
[84] Mayer (1993:58); Richardson (1991); Richardson (1996) (criticising reference to brainwashing claims given complexity of human mind and fact that group influences exist in all walks of life).
[85] Robbins (1988;63).
[86] *See e.g.* 14307/88 *Kokkinakis v. Greece* 17 EHRR 397 (1993).
[87] Beckford (1985).
[88] Robbins (1988;72) referring to a 1984 study by Snow and Machalek.

methods that effectively deprive the individual of the capacity to make a choice whether to adopt or forsake a belief. Such actions focus on one's internal thought processes and disallow any rational or reasonable method of assessment. The result is deprivation of individual autonomy and incapacity to form an independent volition.[89]

While brainwashing techniques would therefore violate an individual's *forum internum* such as to limit the coercive practices of a group, it does not mean that all proselytising groups engage in coercive behaviour. In analysing methodologies of New Religious Movements, sociologists have noted that the New Religious Movements' techniques, particularly deprivations of choice, have not been a typical method of indoctrination. Rather, recruitment, defined as a sudden action to join a group, has been the general means of acquiring new members following invitations to attend a meeting or learn a skill such as meditation. Actual conversion of those attending these meetings, defined as a more gradual and evolutionary process, rarely occurs.[90] One sociologist noted a 0.005 per cent success rate in indoctrination through public meetings and the like, with many of these individuals not committing themselves to the movement.[91] Of those who do remain with a New Religious Movement, many voluntarily depart within a short time.[92]

New Religious Movements then do not focus on the individual's cognitive beliefs to indoctrinate because they tend to rely on the affective and social responses of the person. The individuals who join New Religious Movements are seeking an internal change as they willingly adopt the sect's practices and beliefs.[93] Studies of Reverend Moon's movement have further found that the majority of individuals voluntarily leave the sect within one to two years and, somewhat meekly, return to their former lives without any significant lasting after-effects or mental scars.[94]

---

[89] Brown (1991). The author defines independent volition as a mental ability to desire to do something, and then transforming that desire to action.
[90] Robbins (1988;Chapter Three).
[91] Barker (1982;13).
[92] *See e.g.* Wilson (1990): Barker (1982); Beckford (1985). *Cf.* Robbins (1988;65-66) who contends that the reliance on voluntary departure is the result of a biased, *ex post*, reflection of apostates on their reasons for joining as well as an over reliance on the social dimension of the New Religious Movements, for example, as filling a gap for a socially dysfunctional youth, rather than giving any credence to the atomistic belief of the individual that might have actually been subject to a desired change.
[93] *See* Barker (1982): Wilson (1990).
[94] Beckford (1985).

Sociological studies of individuals within New Religious Movements further indicate that the brainwashing charge also might derive from the family's sense of loss because a family member has committed himself to the sect.[95] Indeed, attempts to deprogramme such individuals are generally a graver violation of the sect member's *forum internum* than any action taken by the sect.[96] The use of brainwashing by a New Religious Movement also derives from the public's view of a sect in a negative light, such as a sect whose leader has engaged in illegal practices.[97]

The result is that the so called radical attempts by fringe groups to alter one's *forum internum* does not appear to be a violation of the individual's right. While certain groups might engage in coercive practices, the factors indicating such coercion are not that the group demands its members to proselytise, but also derive from the context of action and particular instances, such as when a group member might have overstepped his bounds.

In particular, the result is that the *forum internum* can coexist as between the individual and the group member as long as no coercive tactics are used. In essence, the situation is analogous to the individual approach to the right to conscience. The important factor that indicates a *forum internum* violation is coercive practices that target the individual's belief system. The prohibition of such activity applies not only to a state, but also to a group. Even if the group is exercising its human right to freedom of religion and conscience by engaging in proselytising actiyities, limits on the manifestation of such beliefs apply when targeting the *forum internum* of other individuals. Yet without any coercive action, the group maintains the capacity to exercise its right to manifest a belief in the same manner as an individual, subject of course to the limitations noted in the treaties. When considering New Religious Movements, it seems that removing the capacity for the group right also could remove the capacity for individual action.

---

[95] Wilson (1990): Robbins (1988).
[96] Wilson (1990). Note that forced de-programming is on the wane due to legal deterrence (indicating that it can entail coercive action), the falling recruitment rates of NRMs in general, and the developing professionalism of anti-cult movements. Robbins (1988;96-97).
[97] Wilson (1990) distinguishing between internal factors, such as the New Religious Movement's organisation, and external factors, such as its depiction in the public or media, both of which can affect its status.

Conclusion

Given the proposed link between freedom of religion and conscience with minority rights, it seems that one of the aims of the international human rights system in protecting minority groups is not to 'preserve' the minority and its culture, a method that can be excessively paternalistic and even dominating, but to provide for continued development of the minority culture within society.[98] For example, one may straddle the fine line between state domination and group development by granting a minority group the ability to play an active part in the majority's social dialogue or educate its members both internally, regarding minority customs, and externally, regarding the customs of the majority. While the distinction between society and the group might be highlighted, the group members are still being exposed to social views without maintaining any necessary desire to adopt such views in place of their beliefs.

Upon considering the role of the right to conscience for a group, it seems beneficial to adopt a multicultural approach to provide the opportunity for a host of views to flourish and develop within society. A multicultural approach is an acknowledgement that there are a variety of ways in which to co-exist and assert a belief, such as to make for a broader, more varied, and pluralistic society. Indeed, a group might be reacting to the ideals of the society around it, and desire to reflect a change in its internal development and external customs. For example in considering the methods for addressing female circumcision in various tribal societies in Africa, some proposals focus on local custom and practices that will accord the woman a more developed social status, such as influence in making family decisions, and a broader role in modern society, such as engaging in commerce or a profession.[99] Similarly, external influences deriving from the human rights system can address the inherent conflict between the belief of the group as opposed to the individual's right against discrimination by focusing on a local, rather then a national, forum within which to educate and inform individuals.[100] Such an approach can allow for the natural development of change within society rather than force a group to adopt a particular belief system or stay rooted in a cultural context.[101]

---

[98] Eide (2000;6); Addis (1991).
[99] Mikell (1992).
[100] *See e.g.* Adjety (1995); Note (1993).
[101] This approach is reflected in the African Convention on Human Rights that is an attempt to combine the interests of the collective, such as the community or the tribe, with those of the individual, to provide the interpretative context for human rights in

The basis for the group approach therefore need not derive from a model of tolerance towards other ideas and beliefs, especially since toleration advances an internalised framework for a group existence that results in an external existence to the prevailing social framework. Such an internalised approach toward the right to freedom of religion and conscience does not meet the presumed demands of the human rights system to create some form of co-existence among society,[102] nor does it address the problems relating to conflicting forms of rights between the group and the state or between individuals. Rather, a tolerant based approach seems to cater towards isolating individual groups by constraining the ability of society to make corrections, or provide direction, to the manner of relations between individuals; any form of proposed change could be interpreted as adopting an intolerant approach.[103]

This chapter therefore suggested a possible approach to some of the issues regarding the significance of a group's belief by considering the relationship between the right to religion and conscience with minority rights. The international human rights system leans towards a multicultural understanding of society[104] such that reference to the manner in which minority rights and an individual's right to freedom of religion and conscience operate can assist with the application of the right to a group in a manner that conforms to the international human rights construct. The significance of referring to minority rights however is that the reference to culture prevents the state from imposing its own views of what is culturally significant by recognising the importance of minority views and the respect that is to be accorded to groups with different belief systems.[105]

The important aspect for the group is that the right to freedom of conscience provides the context for considering and assessing the actions of the group and of the members therein. The basis for a conscientious belief as incorporating social and cultural views, coupled with the importance of providing for some form of group existence and entrenchment of identity among like believers, points towards a group approach to the right to freedom of religion and conscience as a naturally imperative consideration.

---

      society. Nuituri (1995;376); Van Boven (1986); Ojo & Sesay(1986) (without desire to impose any superior status to one concept).
[102]   Eide (2000).
[103]   *See e.g.* Raz (1998;204).
[104]   Eide (2000;6-7).
[105]   Smith (1998;506) noting the importance for differentiating between cultural specificity that is embedded in diverse belief systems and a state's exploitation of culture. The author refers to Pollis (1996).

The dimensions of the individual and group *forum internum* develop along similar lines outlined in the human rights treaties. Social pressure or affective arousal of emotions for example need not be coercive such that groups as a unit may indeed continue to practise their beliefs as a group. What emerges is that a focus of the group right to freedom of religion and belief on the *forum internum*, with the rights of minorities incorporating the external dimension of the right, provides for a broad approach. Some form of coercive activity either by the state against the group or by the group against other individuals may discern a framework for upholding the right pursuant to the manner in which external forces, such as the state or an overbearing group, are operating.

9 Conclusion

As noted in the title, the aim of this book is to develop and facilitate the practical application of the international human right to freedom of conscience. The right to conscience has not merited a great deal of attention and yet every principal international human rights treaty has codified the right. Recognising the rather limited substantive development of the right to freedom of conscience in international law, this book begins to offer an initial approach for a broader application of the right to freedom of conscience.

In attempting to offer an understanding of the right to freedom of conscience, this book has been subject to some of the unavoidable pitfalls that trouble the international human rights system in general and the right to freedom of religion in particular. As noted at the outset, the key goal was to offer an alternative understanding to the right to freedom of religion that allowed for the consideration of so called alternative belief systems, referred to in this book as conscientious beliefs. By analysing the right to freedom of conscience, the idea was to offer a different approach to the right to freedom of religion and belief. A conscientious belief offers an informal belief system that is not necessarily analogous or equivalent in 'stature' to a formalised religious belief. Nonetheless, it is difficult not to attempt to offer descriptive interpretations of a conscientious belief or delve into the meaning or significance of a conscientious belief. For example, in analysing the phenomenon of conscience, and by analogy other forms of beliefs, one must consider the implications of a conscientious belief and the possible manner by which an individual adheres to such belief.

Hence, in one sense the book has referred to descriptive approaches towards a conscientious belief. Yet, what was attempted throughout the book, even when delving into the meaning and significance of a conscientious belief, was not necessarily to define a conscientious belief; rather it was to account for the implications of conscience and provide for the inclusion of new approaches towards the meaning and significance of a belief. The idea was to provide an understanding of a conscientious belief that would not prevent other forms of beliefs from manifesting, or at least from serving as some form of counter force to the bulwark of religious beliefs.

Particularly when comparing and contrasting a conscientious belief with a religious belief, the purpose was to demonstrate the similarities of difficulties inherent in the right. That is, upon discussing a conscientious belief and its importance for the individual making such an assertion, the goal was not to finalise any form of understanding or definition, but rather to demonstrate the similarity of issues and problems inherent in both the right to freedom of religion and freedom of belief. The contention that a conscientious belief is too nondescript while a religious belief provides a more readily identifiable normative or doctrinal framework is an unfair position. Such a claim can cause serious damage to the standing of the human right to freedom of religion by limiting the right to specific, state-mandated, belief systems.

The book therefore addressed the emergence of conscience as a viable belief system, and compared and contrasted the notion of a conscientious belief with the manner in which the human rights system has structured the protection accorded to religious beliefs. For example, the advent of a manifested conscientious belief as a singular right, separate from a religious framework, occurred at a later period along the historical continuum. While initial protection centred on the rights of minority religions, the League of Nations and certain Permanent Court of International Justice decisions began to allow for the development of a separate right to conscience. Certainly post World War Two, which experienced the beginning efforts to codify international human rights, the right to freedom of conscience achieved the status as a right meriting distinctive protection. The international and regional human rights treaty drafters' approach to the right to freedom of conscience belies the current interpretation of the term in international and domestic judicial fora given the broad application of a conscientious belief as a necessary consequence of the human right to freedom of conscience. The purpose of codifying the human right to the freedom of conscience was to provide for its application and manifestation, and not merely to serve as a weak corollary to the right to freedom of religion. Furthermore, the structure of the treaties is in a manner that distinguishes conscience and religion from other forms of conscious thought that might manifest through other human rights, such as freedom of expression.

Nonetheless, focusing solely on the *travaux preparatoires* of the treaties presents an excessively textual approach without offering any specific practical critique of the manner in which one is to apply the right. States may still adopt a narrow interpretation of the treaty terms and refer to religious principles at the expense of individual conscientious beliefs.

Furthermore, there were some contentious issues not fully resolved by the treaty drafters, as exemplified by the problem surrounding the ability to change one's belief.

Upon considering the structure of the right to freedom of religion and belief, the focus turns to the *forum internum* and *forum externum*. Attempting to outline the protection accorded to the *forum internum* proves quite a difficult task. The individual's internal understanding of a conscientious belief might not be so readily apparent considering the varied assertions that derive from a conscientious belief. On the other hand, broadly defining the *forum externum* can lead to conflicts between state directives and the belief or to clashes with other individuals harbouring a contrary belief. Furthermore, as intimated in the *travaux preparatoires*, defining a term such as 'conscience' might cause unduly narrow interpretations that do not account for evolving beliefs.

In examining the *forum internum* and *forum externum*, one may examine each forum as a reflection of the other. The approach has been to define the internal and external aspect of the right in a somewhat circular fashion. Referring to an external manifestation assists in identifying the internal belief, while considering the internal belief that is driving the individual to act allows for some insight into the *forum externum* such as to uphold manifestations of a conscientious belief.

More specifically, to promote an understanding of the internal protection accorded to a conscientious belief, one must discern the importance of a conscientious belief for an individual. The distinguishing characteristic of a conscientious belief from other forms of conscious thought is the specific adherence to, and application of, a conscientious belief. Thought focuses on psychological and other conscious ideas that an individual might possess without the necessity for external manifestation. Conscience however entails specific external action according to the conscientious belief. As indicated in the *travaux preparatoires*, removing the ability to manifest a conscientious belief tends to undermine the basis for the belief as well. Hence referring to the external application of a conscientious belief, the *forum externum*, can assist in understanding the internal belief that served as an antecedent basis for the external action.

Reference to the *forum internum* also was important as a means of discerning what the individual desired to manifest in the *forum externum*. The discussion therefore turned to the capacity for manifesting a belief as provided for in the treaties. The narrow approach towards the right to conscience overlooks the manifestation of a conscientious belief if it is beyond the religious sphere. In such circumstances, manifestation is limited to instances of freedom *from* other belief systems.

The main policy contention barring a broader approach to the right to conscience is that the asserted conscientious belief is practically indeterminable. This contention however equally applies to religious directives as well, as illustrated by the lack of any significant underlying definition of the freedom of religion and because inconsistencies in application of the right to freedom of religion routinely occur.

Other rights such as free expression or assembly also furnish an inadequate protection for a conscientious belief. For example, upholding the right to military conscientious objection as a form of free expression will not allow for a manifestation of the conscientious belief, even if one has the opportunity to express one's negative views of the military. The basis for the objection is to receive an exemption from military service, not influence the actions of others or improve the democratic nature of the state.

Further consideration was made of a broader approach to the right to manifest a conscientious belief. The basic premise of the broader approach to conscientious manifestation is that at times, one may manifest various motivations deriving from a conscientious belief. While this is not entirely apparent from the international system, there is support for adopting this broad approach. For example, the *travaux preparatoires* seem to adopt a broader understanding of the right to manifest a conscientious belief, as does the HRC in its General Comment to ICCPR Article 18. The point is that coupled with the inherent limitations to the right, it is conceivable to uphold the manifestation of a conscientious belief at least in a comparable manner to a religious belief.

Turning to the manifestation of a conscientious belief, military conscientious objection derives from a state ordering an individual to carry out an action contrary to the individual's conscientious belief. The conflict with the conscientious belief is apparent, although the range of state interference with the asserted conscientious belief depends on the requested state action. There is a difference between conducting military service as opposed to refusing to assist the military in an alternative, non-military, capacity. The focus on selective conscientious objection was meant to assuage such contentions by demonstrating that an assertion of any form of conscientious belief merits consideration in the same way as a general right to military conscientious objection.

The right to military conscientious objection could derive from the right to freedom of conscience, as demonstrated by the resolutions of various international bodies. This is quite a significant development since military conscientious objection can serve as an analogy for additional forms of manifestation. Furthermore, deriving military conscientious objection from the treaty right to conscience, as demonstrated by the activities of the HRC and a variety of international and regional bodies, serves to enhance the international customary status of the right to military conscientious objection. While concluding that military conscientious objection is a customary norm might be premature given the different applications of the right in various domestic legal systems, it certainly is an emerging norm.

The objection to making tax payments is different from military conscientious objection due to the manner in which the objection occurs. Although the objection is to what the government does with its tax revenue and not to the actual making of the tax payment, the objection still centres on a state request for the payment of funds that in turn support actions contrary to one's belief. The essential obstacle to this form of conscientious objection is the lack of connection between the manifested belief serving as the basis for the objection and the demanded state action. The payment of the tax to which the individual is objecting seems to be a neutral activity.

Nonetheless, states do allow non-believers to claim this form of conscientious objection to the payment of church taxes. One may employ alternatives whereby church tax funds support another, more neutral, institution. The contention is that a state may implement these alternative programmes in other instances where infringement of the individual's belief will result by making the tax payment. For example, one can uphold an objection to paying military tax should a state use the funds to support non-military state programmes. The problem is that a tax objection can lead to disarray of the tax system due to a possible plethora of other forms of tax objection claims, such as an individual asserting a belief against the welfare system. In such instances, and admittedly without fully addressing the problem that is being raised, it is important to consider the treaty limitations.

It also is critical to delineate a group-oriented approach towards the freedom of conscience as states begin to acknowledge the social vacuum created by the reliance on the position of the atomistic individual. States might attempt to create some form of general framework of principles to develop a model of social values, thereby diminishing the importance of a conscientious belief. Alternatively, it is not clear how a state is to address the inherent problems deriving from minority belief systems. The discussion of the group approach therefore considered the relationship between the right to freedom of conscience and the rights of a religious minority. The focus was on proselytising as a prime example of the intermingling between the rights of the believer, the state, and of other individuals.

Given the broad nature of the right to freedom of religion and belief and the unavoidable issues that a belief system raises for a state, it is apparent that further research is required. One area of focus is the external, social, issues that these forms of objection bring to the fore. For example, one conscientiously opposed to abortion also raises issues regarding privacy, the right to life, and additional ethical considerations. Tax objection raises issues of social duty that might very well override the assertion of a conscientious belief. The suggestion is that in furthering the development of the human rights system, we must incorporate social elements and ideas outside the sober normative framework given the influence of social factors and the role that they serve in shaping ourselves. It is important to remember that a conscientious belief is part of the social process and accounts for broader social considerations, as indicated by the functional analysis of the *forum internum*. Hence, further consideration of this individual-social dynamic is necessary to develop fully its significance for the international human rights system and the effect that it can have on a conscientious belief.

On a more philosophical level, additional research into the meaning and implication of a conscientious belief would enhance our understanding of the right to conscience. For example, some commentators on conscience adhere to the distinction between a legislative and judicial conscience, depending on the purpose served by the conscientious belief. The legislative conscience has been the focus of analysis here as that seems to be the understanding adopted in the *travaux preparatoires*. Nevertheless, the judicial conscience also serves a role especially when compared to a religious belief. The division can assist in understanding the different forms of asserting a belief, such as the freedom *from* and freedom *to*, and whether a distinction should be made between them.

Another important consideration that has only been alluded to thus far is the relative understanding of the conscience. In conducting further analysis, one must consider the integration between international human rights and domestic systems. Many implications arise from the freedom of conscience and there has not been any systematic analysis of the variety of interpretations accorded to the term. Cultural relativity is a factor for not only a society rooted in religious values, but also for a system that adopts a wholly different approach towards the meaning or importance of an individual's belief. The right needs to be integrated with other systems that have unique approaches to human rights or to the role of individual beliefs within society.

Recognising that a large part of the book was devoted to working with the interplay between religion and other forms of beliefs, and proposing a human right that accounts for a broader approach to incorporate all beliefs, apparently the already contentious right to freedom of religion will become even more problematic. That is, the book tended to address internal issues pertaining to the right, principally focusing on developing the right to freedom of conscience. Aside from further development of such ideas, one also is to account for the external effects of the development of the right to conscience on the international human rights system. Issues of beliefs and conflict with a state authority, or other individuals and their rights, tend to permeate all aspects of our existence. For example, the right to life is not only an issue for the military conscientious objector but also for one espousing a belief in euthanasia. The rights of the child or of women generally come to the fore when conflicting with a belief system that infringes upon their rights. The right of education has significant implications for a belief system, especially a minority belief system that is only beginning to emerge and assert its right. Upon deliberating the importance of social elements and the incorporation of same as part of one's subjective approach, one also recognises important factors external to the international human rights treaties that merit focus when considering the human right to freedom of religion and belief.

Bibliography

Abram, M. (1968), 'Freedom of Thought Conscience and Religion', *Journal of the International Commission Jurists*, vol. 8, p. 40

Addis, A. (1991), 'Individualism, Communitarianism and the Rights of Ethnic Minorities', *Notre Dame Law Review*, vol. 67, p. 615

Adjety, F. (1995), 'Reclaiming the African Women's Individuality: The Struggle Between Women's Reproductive Autonomy and African Society and Culture', *American University Law Review*, vol. 44, p. 1351

Akande, D. (1998), 'Nuclear Weapons, Unclear Law: Deciphering the Nuclear Weapons Advisory Opinion of the International Court', *British Yearbook of International Law*, vol. 68, p. 165

Alexy, R. (1993), 'Justification and Application of Norms', *Ratio Juris*, vol. 6, p. 157

Alfredsson, G. and deZayas, A. (1993), 'Minority Rights: Protection by the UN', *Human Rights Law Journal*, vol. 14, p. 1

Amnesty International (1991), *A Guide to the African Charter on Human and Peoples' Rights*, IOR 63/05/91, Amnesty International, England

Amor, R. (1998), 'The Mandate of the UN Special Rapporteur', *Emory International Law Review*, vol. 12, p. 10

Ankumah, E. (1996), *The African Commission on Human and People's Rights*, M. Nijhoff, The Netherlands

An-Naim (1994), 'State Responsibility Under International Human Rights Law to Change Religious and Customary Laws' in Cook (ed.), *Human Rights of Women: National and International Perspectives*, University Penn. Press, USA

Anstey, R. (1980), 'The Pattern of British Abolitionism in the Eighteenth and Nineteenth Century', in Bolt, C. and Drescher, S. (eds), *Anti-Slavery, Religion, and Reform*, W.M. Dawson & Sons Ltd., England

Arendt, H. (1971), 'Thinking and Moral Conscientiousness', *Social Research*, vol. 38, p. 417

Arjarvi, P. (1992), 'Article 26', in Eide, A., Alfredsson, G., Melander, G., Rehof, L. and Rosas, A. (eds), *The Universal Declaration of Human Rights: A Commentary*, Oxford University Press, Oxford

Bader, V. (1999), 'Religious Pluralism: Secularism or Priority for Democracy', *Political Theory*, vol. 27, p. 597

Bahm, A. (1964), 'Theories of Conscience', *Ethics*, vol. 75, p. 128

Baird, R. (1998), 'Traditional Values Governmental Values, and Religious Conflict in Contemporary India', *Brigham Young University Law Review*, vol. 1998, p. 337

Barendt, E. (1992), *Freedom of Speech*, Clarendon Press, Oxford

Barker, E. (1982), 'From Sect to Society: A Methodological Programme', in Barker, E. (ed.), *New Religious Movements: A Perspective for Understanding Society*, Edwin Meller Press, UK

Bar-Tal, D. (1990), *Group Beliefs*, Springer-Verlag, NY

Basu, D. (1988), *Shorter Constitution of India*, Prentice Hall, New Delhi

Batelaan, P. (1993), 'The school in a multi-religious society', in Council of Europe, *Freedom of Conscience*, Council of Europe, Strasbourg

Bates, M. (1945), *Religious Liberty: An Inquiry*, Harper and Brothers, NY

Bauman, G. (1999), *The Multicultural Riddle*, Routledge, NY

Beckford, J. (1985), *Cult Controversies: The Societal Response to New Religious Movements*, Tavistock, London

Beddard, R. (1993), *Human Rights and Europe*, Cambridge University Press, UK

Bengoa, J. (2000), 'Existence and Recognition of Minorities', E/CN.4/Sub.2/AC.5/2000/WP.2

Benito, O. (1989), *Elimination of all Forms of Racial Discrimination*, UN Press, NY

Bennett (1994), 'Locke's Philosophy of Mind', in Chappell, V. (ed.), *The Cambridge Companion to Locke*, Cambridge University Press, USA

Berger, P. (1969), *The Sacred Canopy*, Doubleday & Co., USA

Bernauer, J. and Mahon, M. (1994), 'The Ethics of Michel Foucault', in Gutting, G. (ed.), *The Cambridge Companion to Foucault*, Cambridge University Press, USA

Bevans, I. (ed.) (1974), *Treaties and Other International Agreements of the United States of America 1776-1949, Volume 8*, Department of State Publication, USA

Bharatiya, V. (1987), *Religion-State Relationships and Constitutional Rights in India*, Deep & Deep Publishing, New Delhi

Bhargava, R. (1994), 'Giving Secularism Its Due', *Economic and Political Weekly*, vol. 29, p. 784

Bharucha, R. (1994), 'In the Name of the Secular: Cultural Interactions and Interventions', *Economic and Political Weekly*, vol. 29, p. 2925

Bickenbach (1989), 'Law and Morality', *Law and Philosophy*, vol.8, p. 291

Bolt, C. and Drescher, S. (eds) (1980), *Anti Slavery, Religion, and Reform*, W.M. Dawson & Sons Ltd., England

Bourke, V. (1966), *Ethics: a textbook in moral philosophy*, Macmillan Company, NY

Bowring, B. (1999), 'Multicultural Citizenship: A More Viable Framework for Minority Rights?', in Fottrell, D. and Bowring, B. (eds), *Minority and Group Rights in the New Millennium*, M. Nijhoff, The Netherlands

Boyle, K. (1992), 'Commentary on the 1981 Declaration', *Conscience and Liberty*, vol. 4, p. 64

Boyle, K. (1993), 'Freedom of Conscience in International Law', in Council of Europe, *Freedom of Conscience*, Council of Europe Press, Strasbourg

Boyle, K. and Sheen, J. (eds) (1997), *Freedom of Religion and Belief: A World Report*, Routledge, London

Bracken, H. (1991), 'Toleration Theories: Bayle and Locke', in Graffier, E. and Paradis, M. (eds), *The Notion of Toleration and Human Rights*, Carlton University Press, Canada

Brandt and Kaplan (1996), 'The Tension Between Women's Rights and Religious Rights: Reservations to CEDAW by Egypt, Bangladesh and Tunisia', *J. Law and Religion*, vol. XII, p. 105

Broad, C. (1952), *Ethics*, M. Nijhoff, Dordrecht

Broad, C. (1969), 'Conscience and Conscientious Action', in Feinberg, J. (ed.), *Moral Concepts*, Oxford University Press, London

Brown, C. (1994), *Foundations of British Abolitionism*, Thesis on file with Oxford University

Brown, L. (1991), 'He Who Controls The Mind Controls The Body: False Imprisonment, Religious Cults, and the Destruction of Volitional Capacity', *Valparaiso University Law Review*, vol. 25, p. 407

Brown, F., Kohn, S. and Kohn, M. (1985-86), 'Conscientious Objection: A Constitutional Right', *New England Law Review*, vol. 21, p. 3

Buergenthaul, T. (1977), 'Implementing the UN Racial Convention', *Texas International Law Journal*, vol. 12, p. 187

Burgers, J. and Danelius, H. (1988), *The UN Convention against Torture: a Handbook on the Convention against Torture and Other Cruel Inhuman or Degrading Treatment or Punishment*, M. Nijhoff, London

Capizzi, J. (1996), 'Selective Conscientious Objection in the US', *Journal of Church and State*, vol. 38, p. 339

Capotorti, F. (1991), *Study on the Rights of Persons Belonging to Ethnic, Religious and Linguistic Minorities*, UN Publication, NY

Champion, J. (1999), 'Willing to Suffer: Law and Religious Conscience in Seventeenth-Century England', in McLaren, J. and Coward, H. (eds), *Religious Conscience, the State, and the Law: Historical Contexts and Contemporary Significance*, SUNY Press, NY

Chatterjee, P. (1994), 'Secularism and Toleration', *Economic and Political Weekly*, vol. 29, p. 1768

Childress, J. (1979), 'Appeals to Conscience', *Ethics*, vol. 89, p. 315

Childress, J. (1982), *Moral Responsibility in Conflicts*, Louisiana State University Press, Baton Rouge

Clark, R. (1978), 'The UN and Religious Freedom', *New York University Journal of International Law & Policy*, vol. 11, p. 197

Clarke, D. (1987), 'Acting According to Conscience', in Evans, J. (ed.), *Moral Philosophy and Contemporary Problems*, Cambridge University Press, UK

Coffman, E.D. (1997), 'Pielech v. Massasoit Greyhound Inc. (668 N.E.2d 1298 (Mass. 1996)): Can a "Sincerely Held Religious Belief" Have Meaning?', *New England Law Review*, vol. 32, p. 117

Cohen-Almogovar, R. (1994), *The Boundaries of Liberty and Tolerance: The Struggle Against Kahanism in Israel*, University Press of Florida, USA

Connelly, W. (1999), *Why I Am Not A Secularist*, University of Minnesota Press, USA

Constable, M. (1991), 'Foucault and Walzer: Sovereignty, Strategy, and the State', *Polity*, vol. 24, p. 269

Cook, D. (1980), 'War Tax Refusal under the Free Exercise Clause', *Wisconsin Law Review*, vol. 1980, p. 753

Cossman, B. and Kapur, R. (1997), 'Secularism's Last Sigh?: The Hindu Right, the Courts, and India's Struggle for Democracy', *Harvard International Law Journal*, vol. 38, p. 113

Council of Europe (1979), *Collected Edition of the "Travaux Preparatoires" of the European Convention on Human Rights*, M. Nijhoff, London

Cullen, H. (1993), 'Education Rights or Minority Rights?', *International Journal Law & Family*, vol. 7, p. 143

Cullen, H. (1996), 'Articles 9-11 ECHR in 1995: a "New Europe" Approach to Fundamental Freedoms', *European Law Review*, vol. 21, p. 29

Cullen, H. (1997), 'The Emerging Scope of Freedom of Conscience', *European Law Review*, vol. 22, p. 32

Cumper, P. (1995), 'Freedom of Thought Conscience and Religion', in Harris, D., and Joseph, S. (eds), *The ICCPR and UK Law*, Clarendon Press, Oxford

D'Arcy, E. (1961), *Conscience and its Right to Freedom*, Sheed and Ward, London

Daes, E. (1990), *Freedom of the Individual Under Law*, Centre for Human Rights, Geneva

Daget, S. (1980), 'A Model of the French Abolitionist Movement and its Variations', in Bolt, C. and Drescher, S. (eds), *Anti Slavery, Religion, and Reform*, W.M. Dawson & Sons Ltd., England

Davis, S. (1991), 'Constitutional Right or Legislative Grace? The Status of Conscientious Objection Exemptions', *Florida State University Law Review*, vol. 19, p. 191

Davis, S. (1995), 'Resolving Not to Resolve the Tension between the Establishment and Free Exercise Clauses', *Journal of Church & State*, vol. 37, p. 236

de Abranches, D. (1968), 'Comparative Study of UN Covenant on Civil and Political Rights and on Economic Social and Cultural Rights and of the Draft Inter-American Covenant on Human Rights', OEA/Ser.L/V/II.19 Doc. 18, in *(1973) Inter-American Yearbook of Human Rights 1968*, Inter-American Commission, Washington, DC

del Russo, L. (1971), *International Protection of Human Rights*, Lerner Law Books, USA

deZayas, A. and Bassiouni, M. (1994), *Protection of Human Rights in the Administration of Justice: A Compendium of United Nations Norms and Standards*, Transnational Publishers, NY

Dhavan, R. (1978), 'The Supreme Court and Hindu Religious Endowments 1950-1975', *Journal of the Institute for Indian Law*, vol. 20, p. 52

Dhavan, R. (1987), 'Religious Freedom in India', *American Journal of Comparative Law*, vol. 35, p. 209

Dickson, B. (1995), 'The United Nations and Freedom of Religion', *International and Comparative Law Quarterly*, vol. 44, p. 327

Dignan, J. (1983), 'A Right not to Render unto Caesar: Conscientious Objection for the Taxpayer', *Northern Ireland Law Quarterly*, vol. 34, p. 20

Dimitrijevic, V. (1991), 'Freedom of Expression in the Framework of the CSCE', in Bloed, A. and van Dijk, P. (eds), *The Human Dimension of the Helsinki Process: The Vienna Follow-up Meeting and its Aftermath*, M. Nijhoff, UK

Dinstein, Y. (1981), 'The Right to Life, Physical Integrity and Liberty', in Henkin, L. (ed.), *The International Bill of Rights*, Columbia University Press, NY

Dinstein, Y. (1992), 'Freedom of Religion and the Protection of Religious Minorities', in Dinstein, Y. and Tabory, M. (eds), *The Protection of Minorities and Human Rights*, M. Nijhoff, The Netherlands

DiSalvo, C. (1982), 'Saying "No" to War in the Technological Age- Conscientious Objection and the World Peace Tax Fund Act', *DePaul Law Review*, vol. 31, p. 471

Donnelly, J. (1985), *The Concept of Human Rights*, St. Martins Press, NY

Durham, W., Wood, M. and Condie, S. (1982), 'Accommodation of Conscientious Objection to Abortion: A Case Study of the Nursing Profession', *Brigham Young University Law Review*, vol. 1982, p. 253
Edge, P. (1996), 'Current Problems In Article 9 of The European Convention on Human Rights', *Juridical Review*, vol. 1996, p. 42
Edge, P. (1998), 'The European Court of Human Rights and Religious Rights', *International and Comparative Law Quarterly*, vol. 46, p. 680
Eide, A. (1999), 'Citizenship and the Minority Rights of Non-Citizens', E/CN.4/Sub.2/AC.5/1999/WP.3
Eide, A. (2000), 'Commentary to the Declaration on the Rights of Persons Belonging to National or Ethnic, Religious and Linguistic Minorities', E/CN.4/Sub.2/AC.5/2000/WP.1
Eide, A. and Chama, M. (1983), *Conscientious Objection to Military Service*, E/CN.4/Sub.2/30/Rev.1 and E/CN.4/Sub.2/1982/24
Eisgruber, C. and Sager, L. (1994), 'Mediating Institutions: Beyond the Public/Private Distinction', *University of Chicago Law Review*, vol. 61, p. 1245
Eleftheriadis (1996), 'The Analysis of Property Rights', *Oxford Journal of Legal Studies*, vol. 16, p. 31
Ermacora, F. (1983), 'Protection of Minorities Before the UN', *Recuil Des Cours - Collected Courses of the Hague Academy of International Law, Volume IV*, M. Nijhoff, The Netherlands
Escudero, G. (1967), 'Freedom of Expression Information and Investigation', in *1972 The Organization of American States and Human Rights 1960-1967*, OAS, Washington DC
Eurigenis (1979), 'Reflections on the National Dimension of the ECHR', in *Colloquy on ECHR in Relation to Other Human Rights Instruments*, COE, Strasbourg
Evans, B. N. (1997), *Interpreting the Free Exercise of Religion: The Constitution and American Pluralism*, University of North Carolina Press, North Carolina
Evans, M. (1997), *Religious Liberty and International Law in Europe*, Cambridge University Press, Cambridge
Fawcett, J. (1987), *The Application of the European Convention on Human Rights*, Clarendon Press, Oxford
Fish (1997), 'Mission Impossible: Settling the Just Bounds Between Church and State', *Columbia University Law Review*, vol. 97, p. 2255
Fitzpatrick, M. (1999), 'Enlightenment and Conscience', in McLaren, J. and Coward, H. (eds), *Religious Conscience, the State, and the Law: Historical Contexts and Contemporary Significance*, SUNY Press, NY
Fogarty, J. (1983) 'The Right not to Kill: A Critical Analysis of

Conscientious Objection and the Problem of Registration', *New England Law Review*, vol. 18, p. 655

Foucault, M. (1977), *Discipline and Punish: The Birth of the Prison*, Pantheon Books, NY

Foucault, M. (1980), *Power/Knowledge: Selected Interviews and Other Writings 1972-1977*, Harvester Press, Sussex

Foucault, M. (1989), *Foucault Live (Interviews, 1966-84)*, Lotringer, S. (ed.), Semiotext(e), NY

Fox, G. and Nolte, G. (1995), 'Intolerant Democracies', *Harvard International Law Journal*, vol. 36, p. 1

Franck, T. (1982), *Human Rights in Third World Perspective- Volume3*, Oceana Publishing Inc., USA

Frowein, J. (1986), 'Freedom of Religion in the Practice of the European Commission and Court of Human Rights', *Zeitschrift Fur Auslandisches Offentliches Recht Und Volkesrecht*, vol. 46, p. 249

Fuchs, J. (1987), 'The Phenomenon of Conscience: Subject-Orientation and Object-Orientation', in Zecha, G. and Weingartner, P. (eds), *Conscience: An Interdisciplinary View*, Reidel Publishing Co., Holland

Fuss, P. (1974), 'Conscience', *Ethics*, vol. 74, p. 111

Galanter, M. (1989), *Cults*, Oxford University Press, NY

Galanter, M. (1992), *Law and Society in Modern India*, Oxford University Press, India

Ganji, M. (1962), *International Protection of Human Rights*, Librarie E. droz, Geneva

Gardiner, R. (1997), 'Treaties and Treaty Materials: Role, Relevance and Accessibility', *International and Comparative Law Quarterly*, vol. 46, p. 643

Garnett (1965), 'Conscience and Conscientiousness', in Kolenda, K. (ed.), *Insight and Vision: Essays in Philosophy*, Rice University Press, Houston

Garvey, J. (1986), 'Free Exercise and the Value of Religious Liberty', *Connecticut Law Review*, vol. 18, p. 779

Gedicks, F. (1995), 'RFRA and the Possibility of Justice', *Montana Law Review*, vol. 56, p. 95

Geertz, C. (1973), *Interpretation of Culture*, Hutchinson & Co., London

Geoly and Gustaffson (1996), 'Religious Liberty and Fair Housing: Must a Landlord Rent Against his Conscience?', *John Marshall Law Review*, vol. 29, p. 455

Gewirth, A. (1982), *Human Rights: Essays on Justifications and Applications*, University of Chicago Press, Chicago

Gilbert, G. (1997), 'Religious Minorities and Their Rights: A Problem of

Approach', *International Journal of Minority Rights*, vol. 5, p. 97

Gilbert, G. (2000), 'Jurisprudence of the European Court and Commission of Human Rights in 1999 and Minority Groups', E/CN.4/Sub.2/AC.5/2000/CRP.1

Gittleman, R. (1982), 'The African Charter on Human and People's Rights: A Legal Analysis', *Virginia Journal of International Law*, vol. 22, p. 667

Goodwin-Gill, G. (1996), *The Refugee in International Law*, Clarendon Press, Oxford

Gray, C. (1979), 'The World Peace Tax Fund Act: Conscientious Objection for Taxpayers', *Northwestern University Law Review*, vol. 74, p. 76

Gray, J. (1983), *Mill On Liberty: A Defence*, Routledge & Kegan Paul, London

Greenawalt, K. (1971), 'All or nothing at all: The Defeat of Selective Conscientious Objection', *Supreme Court Review*, vol. 1971, p. 31

Greenawalt, K. (1988), *Religious Convictions and Political Choice*, Oxford University Press, NY

Grubb, A. (1988), 'Participating in Abortion and the Conscientious Objector', *Cambridge Law Journal*, vol. 1988, p. 162

Hamilton, M. (1993), 'The Belief-Conduct Paradigm in the Supreme Court's Free Exercise Jurisprudence', *Ohio State Law Journal*, vol. 54, p. 713

Hammer, L. (1999), 'Abortion Objection in the United Kingdom within the Framework of the ECHR', *European Human Rights Law Review*, vol. 6, p. 564

Harmer-Dionne, E. (1998), 'Once a Peculiar People: Cognitive Dissonance and the Suppression of Mormon Polygamy as a Case Study Negating the Belief Action Distinction', *Stanford Law Review*, vol. 50, p. 1295

Harris, D., O'Boyle, M., and Warbrick, C. (eds) (1995), *Law of the European Convention on Human Rights*, Butterworths, London

Hartman, J. (1981), 'Derogations from Human Rights Treaties in Public Emergencies', *Harvard International Law Journal*, vol. 22, p. 1

Harvey, E. (1970), 'Conscience and Law', *Dialog*, vol. 9, p. 284

Hauerwas and Baxter (1992), 'The Kingship of Christ: Why Freedom of "Belief" is Not Enough', *De Paul Law Review*, vol. 42, p. 107

Higgins, R. (1976-77), 'Derogations under Human Rights Treaties', *British Yearbook of International Law*, vol. 48, p. 281

Hodgson (1996), 'The International Human Right to Education and Education Concerning Human Rights', *International Journal of Children's Rights*, vol. 4, p. 237

Hourani, A. (1991), *A History of the Arab People*, Faber and Faber, London

Humphrey, J. (1985), 'Political and Related Rights', in Meron, T., (ed.), *Human Rights in International Law: Legal and Policy Issues*, Clarendon Press, Oxford

Humphrey, J. (1986), 'The International Bill of Rights - Part One', in UNESCO, *Philosophical Foundations of Human Rights*, UNESCO, Paris

Israel, F. (1967), *Major Peace Treaties of Modern History, 1648-1967*, Chelsea House Publishers, NY

Jain, M. (1987), *Indian Constitutional Law, 4th edition*, Tripathi, Bombay

Kamen, H. (1967), *The Rise of Toleration*, Arnoldo Mondodori, Verona

Kelly (1991), 'J. Locke: Authority Conscience and Religious Toleration', in Horton, J. and Mendus, S. (eds), *J. Locke; A Letter Concerning Toleration In Focus*, Routledge, London

Khawaya, J. (1992), 'Concept and Role of Tolerance in Indian Culture', in Balasubramanian, R. (ed.), *Tolerance in Indian Culture*, East-West Press, India

Kilcullen, J. (1985), 'Boyle on the Rights of Conscience', *Philosophical Research Archive*, vol. 11, p. 1

Killilea (1973), 'Standards for Expanding Freedom of Conscience', *University of Pittsburgh Law Review*, vol. 34, p. 531

Kingsbury, B. (1992), 'Claims by Non-State Groups in International Law', *Cornell International Law Journal*, vol. 25, p. 481

Kirk, K. (1948), *Conscience and its Problems*, Longman, Green & Co., London

Kiss, A. (1981), 'Permissible Limitations on Rights', in Henkin, L. (ed.), *The International Bill of Rights*, Columbia University Press, NY

Kohn, S. (1986), *Jailed for Peace: The History of American Draft Law Violators, 1658-1985*, Praeger, NY

Kordig, C. (1979), 'The Rights of Conscience', *New Scholasticism*, vol. 53, p. 375

Kornhauser, M. (1999), 'For God and Country: Taxing Conscience', *Wisconsin Law Review*, vol. 1999, p. 939

Krishnaswami, A. (1960), *Study of Discrimination in the Matter of Religious Rights and Practices*, UN, NY

Kuby, R. and Kunstler, W. (1992), 'Enduring the Storm: Conscientious Objectors in the Persian Gulf War', *St. Johns Law Review*, vol. 66, p. 655

Kuhlmann, J. and Lippert, E. (1993), 'The Federal Republic of Germany: Conscientious Objection as Social Welfare', in Moskos, C. and Chambers, J. (eds), *The New Conscientious Objection From Sacred to Secular Resistance*, Oxford University Press, NY

Kuzas, K. (1991), 'Asylum for Unrecognised Conscientious Objectors to Military Service: Is There a Right Not to Fight?', *Virginia Journal of International Law*, vol. 31, p. 447

Landskroen, P. (1991), 'Not the Smallest Grain of Incense: Free Exercise and Conscientious Objection to Draft Registration', *Valparaiso University Law Review*, vol. 25, p. 455

Langan (1989), 'The Good of Selective Conscientious Objection', in Noone, M. (ed.), *Selective Conscientious Objection: Accommodating Conscience and Security*, Westview Press, Colorado

Larsen, R. and Hess, T. (1992), 'Conscientious Objection in an All-volunteer Military', *St. Johns Law Review*, vol. 66, p. 687

Lauterpacht, H. (1945), *An International Bill of the Rights of Man*, Columbia University Press, NY

Leader, S. (1992), *Freedom of Association: A Study in Labour Law and Political Theory*, Yale University Press, New Haven

Lerner, N. (1980), *UN Convention on the Elimination of all Forms of Racial Discrimination*, Nijhoff & Noordhoff, The Netherlands

Lerner, N. (1991), *Group Rights and Discrimination in International Law*, M. Nijhoff, The Netherlands

Lerner, N. (1998), 'Proselytism, Change of Religion and International Human Rights', *Emory International Law Review*, vol. 12, p. 250

Levine, S. J. (1997), 'Rethinking the Supreme Court's Hands-Off Approach to Questions of Religious Practice and Belief', *Fordham University Law Journal*, vol. 25, p. 85

Linn, R. (1989), 'Moral Judgments of Israeli Soldiers in Lebanon', in Noone, M. (ed.), *Selective Conscientious Objection Accommodating Conscience and Security*, Westview Press, Colorado

Lippman, M. (1990), 'Civil Resistance: The Dictates of Conscience and International Law Versus the American Judiciary', *Florida Journal of International Law*, vol. 6, p. 5

Lorenzen, T. (1992), 'Freedom of Conscience as a Human Right', *Conscience and Liberty*, vol. 4, p. 91

Loschelder, W. (1992), 'The non-fulfillment of legally imposed obligations because of conflicting decisions of conscience - the legal situation in the Federal Republic of Germany', in European Consortium for Church-State Research, *Conscientious Objection in the EC Countries*, Dott. A. Giuffre' Editore, Milan

Luchterhandt, O. (1991), 'The CSCE Norms on Religious Freedom and Their Effects on the Reform of Soviet Legislation on Religion', in Bloed, A. and van Dyk, P. (eds), *The Human Dimension of the Helsinki Process: The Vienna Follow-up Meeting and its Aftermath*, M. Nijhoff, The Netherlands

Lyall, F. (1992), 'Conscience and the Law: UK National Report', in European Consortium for Church-State Research, *Conscientious Objection in the EC Countries*, Dott. A. Giuffre' Editore, Milan

Macartney, C. A. (1934), *National States and National Minorities*, Oxford University Press, London

Macciocchi (1982), *Status of the Right to Conscientious Objection to the Military*, EC Doc. 1-546/1982

Macdonald, R. (1989), 'International Prohibitions Against Torture and Other Forms of Similar Treatment or Punishment', in Dinstein, Y. and Tabory, M. (eds), *International Law at a Time of Perplexity: Essays in Honour of Shabtai Rosenne*, M. Nijhoff, The Netherlands

Machan, T. (1989), *Individuals and Their Rights*, Open Court, Illinois

MacIntyre, A. (1981), *After Virtue*, Duckworth, London

Mair, L. (1928), *The Protection of Minorities: the working and scope of the minorities treaties under the League of Nations*, Christophers, London

Major, M. (1992), 'Conscientious Objection and International Law: A Human Right?', *Case Western Reserve Journal of International Law*, vol. 24, p. 349

Malik, C. (1950), 'The Universal Declaration of Human Rights', *UN Bulletin*, vol. V(1)

Maneli, M. (1984), *Freedom and Tolerance*, Octagon Books, NY

Marcus, E. (1998), 'Conscientious Objection as an Emerging Human Right', *Virginia Journal of International Law*, vol. 38, p. 507

Marshall, W. (1983), 'Solving the Free Exercise Dilemma: Free Exercise as Expression', *Minnesota Law Review*, vol. 67, p. 545

Marshall, W. (1995), 'The RFRA: Establishment, Equal Protection, and Free Speech Concerns', *Montana Law Review*, vol. 56, p. 227

Martins and Nickel (1980), 'Recent Works on the Concept of Rights', *American Philosophical Quarterly*, vol. 17, p. 165

Mason, P. (1993), 'Pilgrimage to Religious Shrines: An Essential Element in the Human Right to Freedom of Thought, Conscience and Religion', *Case Western Reserve Journal of International Law*, vol. 25, p. 619

May, L. (1983), 'On Conscience', *American Philosophical Quarterly*, vol. 20, p. 57

Mayer, J. (1993), 'Sects', in Council of Europe, *Freedom of Conscience*, Council of Europe Press, Strasbourg

McConnell, M. (1998), 'Freedom From Persecution or Protection of the Rights of Conscience?: A Critique of Justice Scalia's Historical Arguments in City of Boerne v. Flores', *William and Mary Law Review*, vol. 39, p. 819

McDougal, M., Lasswell, H. and Chen, L. (1980), *Human Rights and World Public Order*, Yale University Press, USA

McDougal, M., Lasswell, H. and Miller, J. (1967), *The Interpretation of Agreements and World Public Order*, Yale University Press, USA

McGoldrick, D. (1991), *The Human Rights Committee: Its Role in the Development of the International Covenant on Civil and Political Rights*, Clarendon Press, Oxford

McGrath, E. (1985), 'Nuclear Weapons: The Crisis of Conscience', *Military Law Review*, vol. 107, p. 191

McGuire (1963), 'On Conscience', *Journal of Philosophy*, vol. 60, p. 253

Mehedi, M. (1999), 'Multicultural and Intercultural Education and Protection of Minorities', E/CN.4/Sub.2/AC.5/1999/WP.5

Merle, J. (1998), 'Cultural Minority Rights and the Rights of the Majority in the Liberal State', *Ratio Juris*, vol. 11, pp. 259-271

Meron, T. (1985), 'The Meaning and Reach of the International Covenant on the Elimination of all Forms of Racial Discrimination', *American Journal of International Law*, vol. 79, p. 283

Mikell, G. (1992), 'Culture, Law and Social Policy: Changing the Economic Status of Ghanaian Women', *Yale Journal of International Law*, vol. 17, p. 225

Mill, J. S. (1859), *On Liberty*, Hackett Publishing Co., USA, 1978

Miller, D. (1924), *My Diary at the Conference of Paris, with documents*, Appeal Printing Comp, NY

Milton, J. (1994), 'Locke's Life and Times', in Chappell, V. (ed.), *The Cambridge Companion to Locke*, Cambridge University Press, USA

Moens, G. (1989), 'The Action-Belief Dichotomy and Freedom of Religion', *Sydney Law Review*, vol. 12, p. 195

Moller, J. (1992), 'The Universal Declaration of Human Rights: How the Process Started', in Eide, A., Alfredsson, G., Melander, G., Rehof, L. and Rosas, A. (eds), *The Universal Declaration of Human Rights: A Commentary*, Oxford University Press, Oxford

Moskos, C. and Chambers, J. (eds) (1993), *The New Conscientious Objection: From Sacred to Secular Resistance*, Oxford University Press, NY

Musalo, R. (1989), 'Swords Into Plowshares: Why the United States Should Provide Refuge to Young Men Who Refuse to Bear Arms for Reason of Conscience', *San Diego Law Review*, vol. 26, p. 849

Neibuhr, R. (1945), 'Ego Alter Dialect and the Conscience', *Journal of Philosophy*, vol. 42, p. 352

New South Wales Law Reform Commission (1984), *Conscientious Objection to Jury Service*, Law Reform Commission, Australia

Niemi-Kiesilainen, J. (1992), 'Article 9', in Eide, A., Alfredsson, G., Melander, G., Rehof, L. and Rosas, A. (eds), *The Universal Declaration of Human Rights: A Commentary*, Oxford University Press, Oxford

Nino, C (1991), *The Ethics of Human Rights*, Clarendon Press, Oxford

Note (1993), 'What's Culture got to do with it? Excising the Harmful Tradition of Female Circumcision', *Harvard Law Review*, vol. 106, p. 1944

Nowak, M. (1993), *UN Covenant on Civil and Political Rights: Commentary*, NP Engel, Germany

Nowell-Smith, P. (1957), *Ethics*, Blackwell, Oxford

Nuituri, M. (1995), 'The Banjul Charter and African Cultural Fingerprints: An Evolution of the Language of Duties', *Virginia Journal of International Law*, vol. 35, p. 339

O'Brien, W. (1991), 'Butler and the Authority of Conscience', *History and Philosophy Quarterly*, vol. 8, p. 43

Ojo, O. and Sesay, A. (1986), 'The OAU and Human Rights: Prospects for the 1980s and Beyond', *Human Rights Quarterly*, vol. 8, p. 89

Oppenheim, L. (1955), *International Law: A Treatise, Volume 1 - Peace*, Longmans Green & Co., London

Opsahl, T. (1979), 'The Substantive Rights', in *Colloquy on ECHR in Relation to Other Human Rights Instruments*, COE, Strasbourg

Opsahl, T. (1992), 'Articles 29 and 30', in Eide, A., Alfredsson, G., Melander, G., Rehof, L. and Rosas, A. (eds), *The Universal Declaration of Human Rights: A Commentary*, Oxford University Press, Oxford

Oraa, J. (1992), *Human Rights in States of Emergency in International Law*, Oxford University Press, UK

Packer, J. (1999), 'Problems in Defining Minorities', in Fottrell and Bowring (eds), *Minority and Group Rights in the New Millennium*, M. Nijhoff, The Netherlands

Panichas (1985), 'The Structure of Basic Human Rights', *Law and Philosophy*, vol. 4, p. 343

Partsch, K. (1979), 'Elimination of Racial Discrimination in the Enjoyment of Civil and Political Rights', *Texas International Law Journal*, vol. 14, p. 191

Partsch, K. (1981), 'Freedom of Conscience and Expression and Political Freedoms', in Henkin, L. (ed.), *The International Bill of Rights*, Columbia University Press, NY

Perotti, A. (1993), 'Freedom of Conscience and Religion and Immigrants', in Council of Europe, *Freedom of Conscience*, Council of Europe Press, Strasbourg

Phillimore, W. (1917), *Three Centuries of Treaties of Peace*, John Murray, London

Pictet, J. (ed.) (1958), *Commentary to Geneva Conventions, Volume IV*, ICRC, Geneva

Pollis (1996), 'Cultural Relativism Revisited: Through a State Prism', *Human Rights Quarterly*, vol. 18, p. 316

Popper, K. (1945), *The Open Society and its Enemies, Volume II - Hegel and Marx*, Routledge, UK

Prebensen, S. (1998), 'The Margin of Appreciation and Articles 9, 10 and 11 of the Convention', *Human Rights Law Journal*, vol. 19, p. 13

Pritchard, J. (1990), 'Conduct and Belief in the Free Exercise Clause: Developments and Deviations in Lyng v. Northwest Indian Cemetery Protective Association (108 S.Ct. 1319)', *Cornell Law Review*, vol. 76, p. 268

Rawls, J (1972), *A Theory of Justice*, Harvard University Press, USA

Raz, J. (1989), 'Liberating Duties', *Law and Philosophy*, vol. 8, p. 3

Raz, J. (1998), 'Multiculturalism', *Ratio Juris*, vol. 11, p. 193

Rees, J. (1985), *J.S. Mill's On Liberty*, Clarendon Press, Oxford

Rehman (1998), 'Minority Rights in International Law: Raising the Conceptual Issues', *Australian Law Journal*, vol. 72, p. 615

Rembe, N. (1991), *The System of Protection of Human Rights under the African Charter on Human and People's Rights: Problems and Prospects*, Inst. of Southern African Studies, Maseru

Richards, D. (1986), *Toleration and the Constitution*, Oxford University Press, USA

Richards, D. (1993), *Conscience and the Constitution*, Princeton University Press, Princeton

Richards, D. (1994), 'Free Speech as Toleration', in Waluchow, W. (ed.), *Free Expression: Essays in Law and Philosophy*, Clarendon Press, Oxford

Richardson, J. (1991), 'Cult/Brainwashing Cases and Freedom of Religion', *Journal of Church & State*, vol. 33, p. 55

Richardson, J. (1996), '"Brainwashing" Claims and Minority Religions Outside the US: Cultural Diffusion of a Questionable Concept in the Legal Arena', *Brigham Young University Law Review*, vol. 1996, p. 873

Rimanque, K. (1993), 'Freedom of Conscience and Minority Groups', in Council of Europe, *Freedom of Conscience*, Council of Europe Press, Strasbourg

Robbins, T. (1988), *Cults Converts and Charisma*, Sage Publications, London

Robert, J. (1993), 'Freedom of Conscience, Pluralism, and Tolerance', in Council of Europe, *Freedom of Conscience*, Council of Europe Press, Strasbourg

Robinson, J. (1948), 'From Protection of Minorities to Promotion of Human Rights', *Jewish Yearbook of International Law*, vol. 1948, p. 115

Rodota (1993), *Report on the Right to Conscientious Objection to Military Service*, European Parliament Doc. 6752

Rorty, R. (1989), *Contingency Irony and Solidarity*, Cambridge University Press, USA

Rotenstreich, N. (1993), 'Conscience and Norm', *Journal of Value Inquiry*, vol. 27, p. 29

Rouse, J. (1994), 'Power/Knowledge', in Gutting, G. (ed.), *The Cambridge Companion to Foucault*, Cambridge University Press, USA

Russell, R. (1951-52), 'Development of Conscientious Recognition in the US', *George Washington Law Review*, vol. 20, p. 409

Ryle (1954), 'Conscience and Moral Convictions', in MacDonald, M. (ed.), *Philosophy and Analysis*, Blackwell, Oxford

Samnoy, A. (1993), *The Universal Declaration of Human Rights: Human Rights as International Consensus*, Berger Print, Norway

Sandifer, D. (1968), 'The Relationship between the Respect for Human Rights and the Effective Exercise of Representative Democracy', in *1972 The Organization of American States and Human Rights 1960-1967*, OAS, Washington, DC

Sandoz, Y. (ed.) (1987), *Commentary to the Additional Protocols of the Geneva Convention*, ICRC, Geneva

Scharr, J. (1967), 'Equality of Opportunity and Beyond', in *IX Nomos: Equality*, Atherton Press, NY

Scheinen, M. (1992), 'Article 18', in Eide, A., Alfredsson, G., Melander, G., Rehof, L. and Rosas, A. (eds), *The Universal Declaration of Human Rights: A Commentary*, Oxford University Press, Oxford

Schneewind (1994), 'Locke's Moral Philosophy', in Chappell, V. (ed.) *The Cambridge Companion to Locke*, Cambridge University Press, USA

Schwelb, E. (1966), 'The UN Convention on the Elimination of Racial Discrimination', *International and Comparative Law Quarterly*, vol. 15, p. 996

Schwelb, E. (1975), 'The UN, The Council of Europe, and Human Rights: Some Observations', in *VIII (3) revue de droit de l'homme*, A. Pedone, Paris

Searle, J. (1969), *Speech Acts*, Cambridge University Press, USA

Searle, J. (1991), 'How Performatives Work', *Tennessee Law Review*, vol. 58, p. 371

Shapiro, R. (1983), 'Of Robots and Persons and the Protection of Religious Beliefs', *Southern California Law Review*, vol. 56, p. 1277

Shaw, M. (1992), 'The Definition of Minorities in International Law', in Dinstein, Y. and Tabory, M. (eds), *The Protection of Minorities and Human Rights*, M. Nijhoff, The Netherlands

Shelton, D. (1986), 'Supervising Implementation of the Covenants: the first ten years of the Human Rights Committee', *American Society of International Law Proceedings*, vol. 80, p. 413

Shestack, J. (1983), 'The Jurisprudence of Human Rights', in Meron, T. (ed.), *Human Rights in International Law: Legal and Policy Issues*, Clarendon Press, Oxford

Sibley (1970), 'Conscience Law and Obligation to Obey', *Monist*, vol. 54, p. 556

Siesby, E. (1992), 'Conscientious Objection in Danish Law', in European Consortium for Church-State Research, *Conscientious Objection in the EC Countries*, Dott. A. Giuffre' Editore, Milan

Simon, T. (1997), 'Minorities in International Law', *Canadian Journal of Law and Jurisprudence*, vol. 10, p. 507

Simons, J. (1995), *Foucault and the Political*, Routledge, London

Sinclair, I. (1984), *The Vienna Convention on the Law of Treaties*, Manchester University Press, Manchester

Smith, R. (1993), 'Conscience Coercion and the Establishment of Religion: The Beginning of an End to the Wandering of a Wayward Judiciary', *Case Western Reserve Law Review*, vol. 43, p. 917

Smith, R. (1998), 'Responding to the Supreme Court's Effort to End the Conversation About Religious Exemptions and Welcoming Professor Sullivan into the Conversation', *Marquette Law Review*, vol. 81, p. 487

Snee, G. (1982), 'The Nuremberg Principle of Individual Responsibility as Applied in United States Courts', *St. Louis University Law Journal*, vol. 25, p. 891

Sohn, L. (1981), 'The Rights of Minorities', in Henkin, L. (ed.), *The International Bill of Rights*, Columbia University Press, NY

Sousa e Brito, J. (1999), 'Political Minorities and the Right to Tolerance The Development of a Right to Conscientious Objection in Constitutional Law', *Brigham Young University Law Review*, vol. 1999, p. 607

Stahnke (1999), 'Proselytism and the Freedom to Change Religion in International Human Rights Law', *Brigham Young University Law Review*, vol. 1999, p. 251

Stewart, D. (1993), 'US Ratification of the Covenant on Civil and Political

Rights: The Significance of the Reservations, Understandings and Declarations', *Human Rights Law Journal*, vol. 14, p. 77

Stolzenberg, N. (1993), '"He Drew a Circle That Shut Me Out": Assimilation, Indoctrination, and the Paradox of a Liberal Education', *Harvard Law Review*, vol. 106, p. 582

Stone, J. (1932), *International Guarantees of Minority Rights*, Oxford University Press, London

Stone, J. (1933), *Regional Guarantees of Minority Rights*, Macmillan and Co., NY

Sullivan, D. (1988), 'Advancing the Freedom of Religion or Belief Through the UN Declaration on the Elimination of Religious Intolerance and Discrimination', *American Journal International Law*, vol. 82, p. 487

Tahzib, B. (1991), 'Epilogue: The 1990 USSR Law on Freedom of Conscience and Religious Organisations', in Bloed, A. and Van Dijk, P. (eds), *The Human Dimension of the Helsinki Process: The Vienna Follow-up Meeting and its Aftermath*, M. Nijhoff, The Netherlands

Tahzib, B. (1996), *Freedom of Religion or Belief: Ensuring Effective International Legal Protection*, M. Nijhoff, The Netherlands

Taylor, C. (1985), *Philosophy and the Human Science: Philosophy Paper 2*, Cambridge University Press, UK

Taylor, C. (1989), *Sources of the Self: The Making of the Modern Identity*, Cambridge University Press, UK

Teale, A. (1952), *Kantian Ethics*, Oxford University Press, London

Ten, C. (1980), *Mill On Liberty*, Clarendon Press, Oxford

Thoreau, H. (1849), *Resistance to Civil Government*, Penguin Books, England, 1995

Thornberry, P. (1991), *International Law and the Rights of Minorities*, Clarendon Press, Oxford

Thornberry, P. (1997), 'The UN Declaration on the Rights of Persons Belonging to National or Ethnic, Religious and Linguistic Minorities: Background, Analysis, Observations, and an Update', in Phillips, A. and Rosas, A. (eds), *Universal Minority Rights*, Minority Rights Group, London

Toth, J. (1968), 'Human Dignity and Freedom of Conscience', *World Justice*, vol. 10, p. 202

Tretter, H. (1989), 'Human Rights in the Concluding Document of the Vienna Follow-up Meeting of the CSCE of January 15, 1989: An Introduction', *Human Rights Law Journal*, vol. 10, p. 257

Triggs, G. (1988), 'People's Rights and Individual Rights', in Crawford, J. (ed.), *The Rights of People*, Clarendon Press, Oxford

Tushnet, M. (1988), *Red White and Blue: A Critical Analysis of Constitutional Law*, Harvard University Press, USA

Umozurike, University (1983), 'The African Charter on Human and People's Rights', *American Journal of International Law*, vol. 77, p. 902

UN (1984), *Seminar Encouraging Understanding Tolerance and Respect in Matters Relating to Freedom of Religion and Belief*, ST/HR/SER.A/16

UN (1995), *The United Nations and Human Rights 1945-1995*, UN Department of Public Information, NY

UNESCO (1949), *Human Rights: Comments and Interpretations*, Allan Wingate, London

UNESCO (1950), *These Rights and Freedoms*, UN Department of Public Information, NY

Van Boven, T. (1986), 'The Relations Between Peoples Rights and Human Rights in the African Charter', *Human Rights Law Journal*, vol. 7, p. 183

Van Boven, T. (1989), *Elimination of All Forms of Intolerance and Discrimination Based on Religion or Belief*, E/CN.4/Sub.2/1989/32, Pt.1

Van Dijk, P. & Van Hoof, G. (1990), *Theory and Practice of the European Convention of Human Rights*, Kluwer, The Netherlands

Vattel, E. (1834 edition, translated from original French) *The Law of Nations*, Stevens & Sons, London

Verdoodt, A. (1963), *Naissance et signification de la declaration Universelle des droits de l'homme*, Lovan & Co., France

Vermeulen, B. (1992), 'Conscientious Objection in Dutch Law', in European Consortium for Church-State Research, *Conscientious Objection in the EC Countries*, Dott. A. Giuffre' Editore, Milan

Vermeulen, B. (1993), 'Scope and Limits of Conscientious Objection', in Council of Europe, *Freedom of Conscience*, Council of Europe Press, Strasbourg

Verzijl, J. (1958), *Human Rights in Historical Perspective*, M. Nijhoff, Dordrecht

Virt, G. (1987), 'Conscience in Conflict?', in Zecha, G. and Weingartner, P. (eds), *Conscience: An Interdisciplinary View*, Reidel Publishing Co., Holland

Walkate, J. (1983), 'The Right of Everyone to Change his Religion or Belief - Some Observations', *The Netherlands International Law Review*, vol. 30, p. 146

Walkate, J. (1989), 'The UN Declaration on Discrimination of Religion - Historical Overview', *Conscience and Liberty*, vol. 1, p. 30

Wallace, J. (1978), *Virtues and Vices*, Cornell University Press, NY

Walsh, B. (1990), 'Issues Which Arise in Relation to Freedom of

Conscience in National Constitutional Provisions', in Matscher, F. (ed.), *The Prohibition of Torture and Freedom of Religion and of Conscience: Comparative Aspects*, NP Engel, Austria

Walters, F. (1952), *A History of the League of Nations*, Oxford University Press, London

Wand (1961), 'The Content and Function of Conscience', *Ethics*, vol. 58, p. 765

Weil, P. (1983), 'Towards Relative Normativity in International Law', *American Journal of International Law*, vol. 77, p. 413

Weisbrodt, D. (1988), 'UN Commission on Human Rights and Conscientious Objection', *Netherlands International Law Journal*, vol. 35, p. 53

Wilson, B. (1990), *The Social Dimension of Sectarianism*, Oxford University Press, NY

Wilson (1928), *The Origins of the League Covenant*, Hogarth, London

Witte, J. & Van der Vyver, J. (eds) (1996), *Religious Human Rights in Global Perspective*, M. Nijhoff, The Netherlands

Wolff, R. (1982), 'Conscientious Objection: Time for Recognition as a Fundamental Human Right', *American Society of International Law International Law Journal*, vol. 6, p. 65

Yourow, C. (1996), *The Margin of Appreciation Doctrine in the Dynamics of the Europe Human Rights Jurisprudence*, Kluwer, The Netherlands

Name Index

Abram, M. 15
Akbar 11
Alfredsson, G. 256
Ankumah, E. 58–9
Anstey, R. 22
Aquinas, St. Thomas 10, 108

Bahm, A. 107
Barendt, E. 162, 165, 168, 170
Basu, D. 150
Bates, M. 9, 19
Bauman, G. 253
Bengoa, J. 252
Benito, O. 161, 173
Berger, P. 253
Bevans, I. 18
Bharatiya, V. 150–1
Bhargava, R. 149
Bharucha, R. 149
Bourke, V. 112–13
Boyle, K. 154, 173, 259
Bracken, H. 16
Brown, C. 22
Brown, F. 207
Brown, L. 261
Buergenthaul, T. 66

Capotorti, F. 13, 19, 26, 129, 251
Cecil, Lord 24
Champion, J. 17
Chatterjee, P. 149
Chen, L. 18, 25, 89
Clarke, D. 112
Clemenceau, Georges 23–4
Cohen-Almogovar, R. 161, 165, 169

Cossman, B. 149
Cullen, H. 142, 177, 246
Cumper, P. 42, 46, 182

Daes, E. 36–7, 48–50
Daget, S. 22, 143, 207
D'Arcy, E. 10
de Abranches, D. 55
del Russo, L. 19–20
deZayas, A. 256
Diderot, Denis 18
Dignan, J. 235
Dimitrijevic, V. 162, 164, 172, 174
Donnelly, J. 78, 83

Edge, P. 132
Eide, Asbjorn 197, 252
Eisgruber, C. 170
Erasmus 12
Ermacora, F. 251
Escudero, G. 56
Evans, B.N. 243–4, 259
Evans, M. 1, 9, 18, 20, 26, 29, 35, 42, 52, 54, 64, 184

Fawcett, J. 198
Fitzpatrick, M. 21
Foucault, Michel 100–2, 110
Fox, G. 97
Freud, Sigmund 107–8
Frowein, J. 252
Fuchs, J. 108

Galanter, M. 148–9, 254
Gardiner, R. 28
Garvey, J. 145

Gedicks, F. 145–6
Geertz, C. 100
Gewirth, A. 77, 82
Gilbert, G. 251
Gittleman, R. 59
Goodwin-Gill, G. 222
Greenawalt, K. 148, 160, 213–14
Grubb, A. 158

Hamilton, M. 146
Harmer-Dionne, E. 106, 144, 154
Hartman, J. 53
Hess, T. 76
Hourani, A. 20
Humphrey, J. 35, 53, 135, 137

Israel, F. 15

Kamen, H. 9, 12–13, 15, 17
Kant, Immanuel 108–9
Kapur, R. 149
Khawaya, J. 150
Kilcullen, J. 16
Kirk, K. 10
Kiss, A. 36, 47–9, 52
Kohn, S. and M. 207
Kordig, C. 9
Kornhauser, M. 228, 230, 237
Krishnaswami, A. 14, 23, 38, 89–90, 120, 132, 134–5, 157, 192
Kuby, R. 212
Kunstler, W. 212
Kuzas, K. 221

Lasswell, H. 18, 25, 28, 89
Lauterpacht, H. 9, 30
Lerner, N. 66
Linn, R. 214
Locke, John 16–18
Lorenzen, T. 153
Loschelder, W. 124–5, 182, 211
Luchterhandt, O. 68–9

Macartney, C.A. 9
McConnell, M. 144

McDougal, M. 18, 25, 28, 89
McGoldrick, D. 90, 132
Mair, L. 20
Maneli, M. 10, 16, 18, 21
Marcus, E. 139, 206
Marshall, W. 127
Mason, P. 167
May, L. 107
Merle, J. 255
Meron, T. 66
Mill, John Stuart 21, 73–4, 84–7, 95, 165
Miller, D. 24
Miller, J. 28
Mubanga-Chipoya, Chama 197

Neibuhr, R. 111
Nolte, G. 97
Nowak, M. 46, 48

Ojo, O. 264
Oppenheim, L. 14
Opsahl, T. 36-7, 133, 153

Partsch, K. 38, 66
Phillimore, W. 15, 20
Pictet, J. 65
Prebensen, S. 170

Rembe, N. 59
Richards, D. 15–18, 165, 167, 169
Richardson, J. 260
Rimanque, K. 133
Robbins, T. 259–61
Robert, J. 124
Roosevelt, Franklin D. 32
Rorty, R. 101
Rotenstreich, N. 113–14
Rouse, J. 101

Sager, L. 170
Samnoy, A. 31
Scheinen, M. 35, 161
Schwelb, E. 51, 66
Searle, J. 161

Sesay, A. 264
Shaw, M. 251
Sheen, J. 259
Siesby, E. 210
Simon, T. 256
Sinclair, I. 29
Smith, R. 144, 264
Smuts, Jan Christiaan 24
Sohn, L. 251
Spinoza, Baruch 10, 16
Stone, J. 23

Tahzib, B. 1, 28, 68
Taylor, C. 101, 108, 111–12, 157
Teale, A. 109
Thoreau, Henry 22–3
Thornberry, P. 250, 255

Toth, J. 9
Triggs, G. 252
Tushnet, M. 145

Van Dijk, P. 137, 161–2
Van Hoof, G. 137, 161–2
Van der Vyver, J. 1
Veniselos, M. 24
Verdoodt, A. 37, 48–9
Vermeulen, B. 133, 135, 210

Walkate, J. 173
Wilson, B. 259–60, 262
Wilson, Woodrow 23
Witte, J. 1

Yourow, C. 183

Subject Index

abortion 104–5, 117, 137, 158–9, 162, 174, 179–81, 196, 203, 236, 239–41, 271
abstract principles as basis for obligation 160
'actual practice' doctrine *see* practice of conscientious belief
administrative necessity 148, 229–30, 236, 238
African Charter on Human and People's Rights (AfrCHR) 57–60, 70, 91, 257
alternative belief systems *see* conscientious belief
American Convention on Human Rights (AmCHR) 54–7, 60, 70, 116, 161, 249
American Declaration on Human Rights (AmDHR) 55
American Law Institute 30
Amish religion 234
animal rights protestors 115
anthroposophy 140–1
apartheid 217, 220
apostasy 43–4, 135, 157
Argentina 41
armaments shipments, blocking of 179–81
Arrowsmith case 176
assembly, freedom of 139, 160–4, 168–71, 269
asylum seekers 217–22
atheism 33, 40–1, 62, 152, 173
Australia 155, 210, 221, 235, 238

Belgium 34

belief
 changes in 87–8, 91–4, 97–8, 118
 definition of 40–2, 63, 103, 121, 126, 130–4, 138, 172–3, 253–7
 internal development of 100–1
 shaping and forming of 105
 see also minorities, beliefs of
belief systems 2–5, 9–10, 110, 128, 130, 133, 145–6, 160, 233–4, 266–7
Berlin, Treaty of (1878) 20
Bowman case 162
Boy Scouts 146
brainwashing 89–90, 95, 259–62
Brazil 32, 41, 116
Brinkhof case 222
Buddhism 11–12
Bulgaria 63–4
Buscarini case 183

Canada 45, 67, 235, 238, 252
categorical imperative 107–8
Ceylon 40–1
child support 127–8, 141, 180–1
children's rights 58, 67–8, 72, 272
Chile 55
China 11, 244
Christianity 10
Church, the, power of 15–17, 22
Church of Marijuana 145
Church of Scientology 250, 257
church taxes 170, 231–3
circumcision, female 263
claims in relation to rights 76–84
clawback clauses 59

coercion 42-4, 50, 74, 87-92, 95-6, 118, 135, 249, 256-7, 260-2
co-existence within society 264
Commission on Human Rights (CHR) 31, 36, 38, 191-2, 197-201, 209-10, 218
common identity within groups 253
communal activities 243-4
Conference on Security and Cooperation in Europe 68
Confucianism 11
conscience
  and the community 248
  definition of 39-40, 70, 102, 107, 173, 268
  and *forum internum* 103-7
  historical development of notion 5, 12-13, 24-7
  internal and external right to 72, 75-6, 79-87
  and moral action 109-16
  open-ended nature of 158
  and religion 14-23, 140-51
  and self-identity 111-15, 118-19
  right to 103, 135, 154, 171-2, 175, 185
  social context of 112
conscience, freedom of 3-4, 70
  broader approach to 178
  cultural and social aspects of 6-8
  emergence of right to 9, 16, 21, 28-30, 35, 152, 266-7, 272
  in ICCPR 38-9
  as internal protection for a belief 64
  limitations on right to 35-7, 45-7, 52, 58-9, 112, 182-4
  and military conscientious objection 208
  in UDHR 31-7
conscientious belief 3-6
  based on norms 77
  as a counterbalance to religion 40, 267

effect on people's lives and actions 115-17
internal and external dimensions of 6, 19, 50, 64, 118
narrow approach to 134-40
as performative utterance 110-11
in relation to general thought 56, 105-7, 114-19
right to development of 74
subjective nature of 153-6
see also manifestation; practice
conscientious decisions 114
conscientious objection to military service 7, 28-9, 44, 76, 81-2, 121-9, 133-6, 139-42, 153, 167, 175, 186-226, 269
  declarations and resolutions on 195-206, 209-11, 218, 220, 223
  recognition in international fora 193-5
  selective 188-9, 203, 208-25, 270
  state practice with regard to 206-9, 217-24
  treaty provisions on 190-3
conscription 203, 211
Convention Against Torture and other Cruel, Inhuman or Degrading Treatment or Punishment 90
Convention to Eliminate Discrimination Against Women (CEDAW) 69
Convention Relating to the Status of Refugees (1950) 65
Convention Relating to the Status of Stateless Persons (1954) 65
Convention on the Rights of the Child 67-8, 250
'convictions' 45
Council of Europe 201-2, 209, 216
cultural influences 100, 244-7, 255, 264, 271
customary international law and

norms 186–9, 207, 225, 270
Cyprus 41
Czechoslovakia 32

Darby case 232
Declaration on the Elimination of all Forms of Intolerance and Discrimination Based on Religion or Belief 60–4, 70, 173–4
Declaration on Human Rights of Individuals who are not Nationals of the Country in which they Live 66
Declaration on the Rights of Persons Belonging to National or Ethnic, Religious and Linguistic Minorities *see* Minorities Declaration
Delgado case 97
democratic society 37, 47, 51–2, 166
Denmark 210
derogations 49–50, 53, 59, 169
deserters, treatment of 221
desires as distinct from beliefs 125–9, 138
dignity 85
discrimination against groups 256–7; *see also* religious intolerance and discrimination; women, discrimination against dissident groups 99, 103
duties of individuals 59; *see also* social duty
Establishment clause (of US Constitution) 19, 142–3, 145, 151, 157
ethics 17, 21, 200–1
European Convention for the Protection of Human Rights and Fundamental Freedoms (ECHR) (including ECHR Commission and Court) 29, 48–54, 73, 89, 93–4, 121, 125, 134–47, 161, 169, 175–7, 183, 190, 193–4, 202–5, 216, 232–3, 249–50, 257–8
European Parliament 204
euthanasia 272
expression, freedom of 55–6, 137–9, 160–71, 269

Finland 231–2
forced labour 191, 193, 199
forum externum and *forum internum* 72–4, 92, 100–20, 124–31, 136–7, 140, 146, 154, 171–2, 178–80, 183–7, 268
of groups as distinct from individuals 246–65
France 24–5, 33–5, 62, 191
Free Exercise clause (of US Constitution) 142–3, 145, 151, 157, 207, 239
free speech *see* expression, freedom of
freedom *to* and freedom *from* 96–102, 105, 122, 133–6, 140, 153, 156–8, 170, 184, 245, 256–7, 271

Geneva Convention regarding the Status and Treatment of Protected Persons (1949) 64–5
genocide 205
Germany 14, 63, 207, 211, 216, 222
Gillette case 214
Greece 45, 258
group rights 243–65, 270
treaty provisions on 248–57
Gulf War 216

Handbook on Procedures and Criteria for Determining Refugee Status 218–21
harassment 91, 98

'hate speech' 164
Helsinki Accords 68
human rights 74–5
  accorded to groups 245
  conceived as immunities 75–6, 80–1
  conscientious belief in relation to 6
  function of 80, 82
  inherent conflicts in 78, 83
  practical application of 75, 80
Human Rights Committee (HRC) 29, 98, 128, 132, 172–5, 194–205, 210, 222–3, 226–8, 245–6, 250, 252, 258, 269–70
humanism 12, 109

Iceland 231
ideals as distinct from beliefs 125
identity *see* common identity; self-identity
India 4, 11, 32, 89, 138, 140, 146–51, 159–67, 192, 232
indoctrination 261
inner domain of the individual 84–5, 88, 179
insurance schemes 233–4
Inter-American Court of Human Rights 167
International Convention on the Elimination of All Forms of Racial Discrimination 65–6
International Convention on the Protection of the Rights of All Migrant Workers 68–9
International Council of Jurists 55
International Court of Justice 223
International Covenant on Civil and Political Rights (ICCPR) 29, 38–50, 56, 87, 90, 93, 96, 98, 116, 121, 128, 131–2, 169, 173–5, 190–5, 199–201, 205, 223, 245–52 *passim*, 258
  influence on other treaties 64–8

International Covenant on Economic, Social and Cultural Rights (ICESCR) 45, 249
International Labour Organisation (ILO) 191
International Law Commission 30–1
IRA prisoners 129
Iraq 200
Islam 10–12, 14, 73, 95–6, 106, 115, 135, 216
Israel 192, 214
Italy 62

Jainism 149
Japan 11–12
Jehovah's Witnesses 91, 134–41 *passim*, 158–9, 163, 176, 193–4, 216, 257–60
Jews, tolerance of 13–14
journalists 167
judicial bodies, common tendencies of 73, 205
jury service 156
jus in bello and *jus ad bello* 223
jus cogens norms 205

Kjeldsen case 93
Kokkinakis case 176, 258

Larissis case 183–4
League of Nations 23–5, 267
Lebanon 32, 35, 191, 214
Lee case 234
legislative grants (as distinct from rights) 188, 206–9, 235
'lethal force' 175, 196, 203, 210
liberation theology 98
Liberia 40
liberty, concept of 15–18, 21, 74, 76, 78, 83
Lubicon Band case 250, 252

Maneka Ghandi case 162, 167
manifestation of conscientious belief

6–7, 26, 34–5, 39–42, 46, 50, 55, 58–64 *passim*, 70, 73–84, 88, 92, 95, 98, 102–7, 111, 114–18, 122–5, 130–1, 135, 137, 144,146, 151, 153, 160
  broader form of 177–84, 269
  definition of 126, 133–4, 139
  as distinct from actions linked to belief 186
  as distinct from manifestation of thought 166
  by a group 262
  limitations of 120–3, 140–2, 154, 171, 269
  see also forum externum
'margin of appreciation' doctrine 183
Migrant Workers Convention 250
minorities
  beliefs of 2–4, 9–10, 13, 19, 23, 254–6, 270
  definition of 256
Minorities Declaration 249–51, 255, 258–9
missionary activity 43–4, 50, 88–9, 96, 245, 249, 257–9
Moon sect 260–1
moral approval 108
morality 12–13, 16–17, 21–2
  and conscience 109–14
  individual and social 49, 114
  standards of 113
motivation 153, 177–80
  as distinct from manifestation 181
Mozambique 200
Mozert v. Hawkins 92
multiculturalism 263–4
Muslim religion *see* Islam

Netherlands, the 43–4, 210, 222, 233
New Religious Movements 259–62
New Zealand 33
Nigeria 258

norms 77, 82, 113, 205; *see also* customary international law and norms
Norway 222
nuclear weapons 211, 222–4
nuclearism 145
Nuremberg Principles 197–8

oath-taking 99, 102–3, 183
obligations in relation to rights 75, 80
opinio juris 205, 225
opinions as distinct from actions 85–7, 104
Organisation of African Unity 57, 255
Organisation of American States 55
Otto Preminger case 170

pacifism 122–42 *passim*, 152–3, 176–81, 216–17, 238, 253–4
Pakistan 41
pamphlets, distribution of 176–7
Panama 30, 32
peace funds 236–7
peaceful coexistence 23
Permanent Court of International Justice 26, 251, 267
personal identity *see* self-identity
personal views as distinct from beliefs 140–1
Philippines, the 41, 191–2
pluralism in society 23, 149, 263
Poland 23–5
political statements, conscientious objections as 212–13, 215, 222
polygamy 148, 151
pornography 95
practice of conscientious belief 124–5, 136–41, 145, 152, 159–60, 163, 184, 228, 238
  prevention of 106
preaching 258
proselytising 8, 35, 43, 55, 87–9,

166, 176, 183, 245–6, 258–61, 270
Prussia 18
'public morals' 112
'public order' 36, 47–8, 52–3, 258
'public safety' 48–9, 233
public support schemes 233–6

Reformation, the 13, 15, 22
refugee status 218–21
relativity within legal systems 78
religion
　change of 37, 39, 43–4, 61, 96, 258–9
　and conscience 140–56
religious belief
　definition of 3–4
　manifestation of 120
religious freedom 1–5, 13, 15, 20, 54–6, 143–50, 268, 272
religious intolerance and discrimination 10–11, 20–2, 25, 257
Renaissance, the 12
'right to life' 73, 187, 198–9, 205, 236, 271–2
rights
　categorisation of 75, 80
　entitlements as distinct from claims 78–9, 84
　see also children's rights; group rights; human rights; women, rights of
Romania 21, 63
Russia 41, 46, 62

saluting the flag 163
Salvation Army 260
Saudi Arabia 40, 43
Scientology 250, 257
secular states 4
self-fulfilment of individuals 169
self-identity 6, 111–15, 118, 178
Serif case 250

sex education 93–4, 241
Shirur Mutt case 149
sincerity of belief 154–6, 212, 214
slavery 21
social context 244–8, 271
social control 85
social duty 77, 80–2, 271
social interaction 101–2
'soft' law 54
South Africa 25
Spain 40, 63
state authority 16
Sunday trading 148, 247
Sunday work 144
superego, the 108
Sweden 221, 257
Switzerland 14, 231

taxation, conscientious objection to 7, 127, 135, 141, 180, 195, 203–4, 227–42, 270–1
　for military purposes 236–41
Teitegen Report (1949) 51–2
thought
　freedom of 34–5, 40–2, 55–6, 74, 94, 99, 161, 172–3
　nature of 103, 268
Togoland 24–5
tolerance of alternative beliefs 13–19, 23, 264
torture, mental or psychological 90–2, 260
transcendent factors in conscience and religion 159–60
Transylvania 14
travaux preparatoires 5, 28–30, 35, 46, 49–50, 61, 66–7, 70, 87–8, 116, 121, 130, 132, 173, 191, 225–6, 268–9
travel, right to 167
treaties
　and group rights 248–57
　historical 14–15, 18–29 *passim*
　and manifestation of belief 120–2, 131

and military conscientious
  objection 190–3
narrow interpretation of 268
and 'public morals' 112
regional 50–60, 70
and right to conscience 103, 185
truth
  search for 165–6
  social and individual
    understanding of 110
Turkey 32

Ukraine 258
United Kingdom 39–40, 221, 235
United Nations
  Charter 30
  Economic and Social Council
    (ECOSOC) 31
  General Assembly declarations
    and resolutions 218, 220, 223,
    249, 251
  High Commissioner on Refugees
    218
United States 4, 18–19, 92, 138,
  140, 144, 146, 151, 160–4, 206–
  7, 216, 220–3, 233–4, 238–9

Constitution 142–5, 151, 157
Supreme Court 143–8 *passim*,
  158, 210–11, 213–14, 234–5
Universal Declaration of Human
  Rights (UDHR) 31–7, 48, 51,
  199–200, 218, 258
Upper Silesia 26
Uruguay 55, 192
'use of arms' 203, 209

Valsamos case 163, 170
Venezuela 40
Vienna, Congress and Treaty of
  (1814–15) 19–20
Vienna Convention on the Law of
  Treaties 29
Vietnam War 213

war, law and rules of 198, 209
Westaphalia, Treaty of (1648) 14
Wingrove case 171
women
  discrimination against 69
  rights of 272

Zaire 91

9781138734227